MORMONISM UNVAILED

MORMONISM UNVAILED

Eber D. Howe

with critical comments by
DAN VOGEL

Signature Books | 2015 | Salt Lake City

jacket design by Jason Francis.

Printed on acid-free paper. Composed, printed,
and bound in the USA.

2020   2019   2018   2017   2016   2015   6   5   4   3   2   1

LIBRARY OF CONGRESS CATALOGING-IN-PUBLICATION DATA

Howe, E. D. (Eber D.), 1798-1885, author.
    Mormonism unvailed / by Eber D. Howe ; with critical comments by
Dan Vogel.
        pages cm
    Includes bibliographical references and index.
    ISBN 978-1-56085-231-5 (alk. paper)
1. Mormon Church—Controversial literature. 2. Church of Jesus Christ of
Latter-day Saints—Controversial literature. I. Vogel, Dan, 1955- writer of
added commentary. II. Title. III. Title: Mormonism unveiled.
    BX8645.5.H64 2015
    289.3—dc23
                            2014049995

CONTENTS

NOTE: Two of the chapters in the original printing were numbered 5, rendered 5a and 5b in this edition for the sake of clarity. Since only a few chapters had titles in the original publication, the first words of each chapter have been excerpted in place of the missing titles. The original book lacked a table of contents.

PREFACE

Described by Mormon leader Brigham H. Roberts as the "first Anti-Mormon book of any pretensions," E. D. Howe's 1834 *Mormonism Unvailed*[1] has become, in Roberts's words, the "chief source of 'information' for all Anti-Mormon publications which have followed it."[2] Its importance was largely achieved through the inclusion of fifteen affidavits that were gathered from Palmyra and Manchester, New York, dealing with the Smith family's reputation and seven others from Harmony, Pennsylvania, concerning Joseph Smith's activities in that area. Eight additional affidavits having to do with the so-called Spalding (or Spaulding) theory of Book of Mormon origins contributed to the notoriety surrounding Howe's book. My discussion will be limited to these affidavits and information the author and his research assistant reported, but not with the Spalding theory generally.

Eber D. Howe (1798–1884) was born at Clifton Park, New York, near Albany and Schenectady. He apprenticed with a series of small-town newspapers, including the *Buffalo Gazette*, at an early age. When he was twenty, he helped found the *Cleveland Herald*, then moved about thirty-five miles west

---

1. Howe reprinted his book in 1840 under the title *History of Mormonism* ... (Painesville, Ohio: E. D. Howe).

2. Roberts, *New Witnesses for God,* 3:360. For more on the influence of *Mormonism Unvailed* and other literature critical of the Mormons in the decades to follow, see Fluhman, *Peculiar People.*

to establish his own newspaper, the weekly *Painesville Telegraph*, distributing the first issue on July 16, 1822. The paper would later be described as "the oldest continuously published newspaper in the entire Western Reserve."[3] It covered local news and gave vent to Howe's opinion on subjects of national concern. His leanings were anti-Mason, anti-Jackson, and anti-slavery. He was also anti-Mormon. Prior to the release of *Mormonism Unvailed*, he published at least fifty articles and pamphlets on the new religion.

His interest began in September 1829 when the *Telegraph* reprinted an article, "Golden Bible," from the *Palmyra Freeman*.[4] He may have looked at this report with mild curiosity at first, but the topic gained more immediate importance in late October 1830 when missionaries arrived in Kirtland and converted a minister, Sidney Rigdon, and most of his congregation. With the arrival of Joseph Smith four months later, Kirtland and the surrounding communities, including Painesville ten miles from Kirtland, became the center of Mormon activity. Howe was undoubtedly displeased by the newcomers' support of Andrew Jackson, but he was even more alarmed when his wife, Sophia Hull Howe, and her sister, Harriet, converted sometime before 1834.[5]

At first Howe did not know what to make of the new sect, incorrectly associating it with the Masons. He seems to have

---

3. *Lake County Historical Society Quarterly* 14 (Aug. 1972): 2.

4. "Golden Bible," *Palmyra Freeman*, ca. Aug. 1829. The original article has not been located, but it was also picked up by the *Rochester Advertiser and Telegraph*, Aug. 31, 1829.

5. Jessee et al., *Joseph Smith Papers: Journals*, 1:415.

feared that people in the anti-Masonic counties would welcome the Mormons as political allies. The converts included
"zealous masons," he pointed out, as well as "republican jacks."
In fact, the "Mormon bible itself was printed and sent forth to
the world from a masonic printing office."[6] As Howe became
more familiar with the content of the Book of Mormon, he
reversed himself, observing that "the Nephites are represented
as being Anti-masons and Christians, which carries with it
some evidence that the writer foresaw the politics of New York
in 1828–29" (pp. 125–26 herein).

Meanwhile, Howe investigated the origins of the church
in New York by corresponding with Abner Cole, editor of the
Palmyra Reflector, and with William W. Phelps, editor of the
anti-Masonic *Ontario Phoenix* in Canandaigua. Obtaining
information from Mormons, however, proved difficult. The
advertisement prefacing Howe's book noted the "difficulty of
procuring, or arriving at the *whole truth,* in relation to a religious
imposition, which has been from its birth so studiously vailed
in secrecy, and generally under a belief that the judgments of
God would follow any disclosures of what its votaries had seen
or heard …" (iii). Indeed, Mormons were suspicious enough of
their enemies that they barred outsiders from their meetings.
Sidney Rigdon admitted in 1844 that the church had kept its
early meetings "secret." At a church conference, he said

we knew the whole world would laugh at us, so we concealed

---

6. *Painesville Telegraph,* Mar. 22, 1831. The term "jacks" is an abbreviation
for jackasses, applied to non-Masons who defended Masonry or supported Masonic candidates for office.

ourselves; and there was much excitement about our secret meetings, charging us with designs against the government, and with laying plans to get money, &c. which never existed in the heads of any one else, and if we had talked in public, we should have been ridiculed more than we were. ... So we were obliged to retire to our secret chambers, and commune ourselves with God. ... If we had told the people what our eyes behold this day, we should not be believed; but the rascals would have shed our blood, if we had only told them what we believed. ... There we sat in secret and beheld the glorious visions, and powers of the kingdom of heaven, pass and repass. ... The church never would have been here, if we had not done as we did in secret. ... There was no evil concocted when we first held secret meetings, and it is the same now.[7]

Jasper J. Moss, a Campbellite who taught school in Kirtland, described the Mormon practice of closed communion by saying "they partook of the Lords supper at night with darkened windows & excluded from the room all but their own till they got through & then they opened the doors & called [in] the outsiders."[8] Such practices undoubtedly aroused non-Mormon suspicion and frustrated Howe. Little wonder he initially associated Mormons with Masons.

Howe was stonewalled at every turn when he tried to investigate specifics of the new religion's claim to supernatural events. The three witnesses to the golden plates were specifically

---

7. "Conference Minutes," *Times and Seasons*, May 1, 1844, 522–24; rpt. in *The Prophet*, June 8, 1844.

8. J. J. Moss to J. T. Cobb, Dec. 17, 1878, in the A. T. Schroeder Collection, Wisconsin State Historical Society, Madison, Wisc.

told to say nothing beyond their published testimonies. A March 1829 revelation to Martin Harris told him to "say no more unto them concerning these things, except he shall say: I have seen them, and they have been shown unto me by the power of God" (D&C 5:26). This may explain the absence of detailed statements until years after Joseph Smith's death. The New York spiritualist Joel Tiffany was similarly frustrated when he interviewed Martin Harris in 1859. Harris declined to answer specific questions about his vision of the gold plates, stating that he was "forbidden to say anything how the Lord showed them to me, except that by the power of God I have seen them."[9]

During the early years, Joseph Smith was equally resistant to inquiry even when there were questions from family members. He responded before a conference of elders in October 1831, after his brother Hyrum had asked for more details about the discovery of the gold plates, that "it was not intended to tell the world all the particulars of the coming forth of the book of Mormon, & also said that it was not expedient for him to relate these things &c."[10] His evasiveness fueled curiosity and created more demand for further investigation, something Howe was happy to pursue.

This reluctance was overcome by apostates like Ezra Booth, who had been a Methodist minister before converting to Mormonism and became the first to write an exposé. He did so in a series of nine letters that were published in the *Ohio*

---

9. *Tiffany's Monthly*, Aug. 1859, 166.

10. Cannon and Cook, *Far West Record*, 23.

Star in late 1831. He not only supplied firsthand accounts of some major events, including the introduction of the high priesthood in June 1831 and the first church conference in Missouri, but he also provided the texts of some of Smith's unpublished revelations.

Joseph Smith's evasiveness was augmented by a hostile tone from Sidney Rigdon in 1831 when he "defied the world to refute the divine pretensions of the *Book of Mormon*" (*Painesville Telegraph,* Feb. 15). Thomas Campbell, the father of the man who founded the Disciples of Christ, said he was only too happy to accept the challenge, upon which Rigdon quickly withdrew his challenge, aware of his opponent's ability to debate. That did not mean that Rigdon tempered his bluster, however. He called Booth's letters "an unfair and false representation of the subjects on which they treat" and challenged its author to a debate.[11]

This tense atmosphere, combined with a lack of solid information, created a market for books on Mormonism. Into the vacuum came Doctor Philastus Hurlbut (1809–83), a convert in late 1832 who had been a Methodist class leader, exhorter, and lay minster in Jamestown, New York.[12] "Doctor" was his given name, not a title. Hurlbut traveled to Kirtland so he could see the prophet up close. Smith wrote that in March 1833 he "conversed with [Hurlbut] considerably about the book of Mormon. ... According to my best recollection, I heard him say, in the course of conversing with him, that if he

---

11. *Ohio Star,* Dec. 15, 1831.
12. Winchester, *Origin of the Spaulding Story*, 6; Reynolds, *Myth of the Manuscript Found,* 14.

ever became convinced that the book of Mormon was false, he would be the cause of my destruction."[13] If Hurlbut had reservations, he was sufficiently reassured by Smith to allow himself to be ordained an elder by Sidney Rigdon five days later. He also accepted a mission call to Pennsylvania.[14]

However, while Hurlbut was passing through Albion in the western part of the state, he came into contact with Lyman Jackson, a staunch Methodist and former acquaintance of the late Solomon Spalding (1761–1816). Jackson said the Book of Mormon may have been copied from an Indian romance his friend had written two decades earlier.[15] Diverted from his mission, Hurlbut decided to travel twenty-five miles south to Conneaut, where Solomon Spalding's younger brother, John, and wife Martha were still living. Interviewing them about the manuscript Solomon had read to them about 1811 (see pp. 391–92), and now faced with the possibility that the Book of Mormon was derivative, Hurlbut chose to abandon his mission and return to Ohio.

In Kirtland he learned that while he was interviewing the Spaldings, he had been excommunicated *in absentia* on June 3 by a bishop's court on the charge of "unchristian conduct with the female sex while on a mission to the east."[16] The suggestive wording was later clarified by Sidney Rigdon, who had officiated at the trial, when he wrote to the *Boston Journal* in

13. Jessee et al., *Joseph Smith Papers: Journals,* 1:27.

14. *History of the Church,* 1:334; Kirtland Council Minute Book, 14.

15. Winchester, *Origin of the Spaulding Story,* 6; Abner Jackson statement, in Gregg, *Prophet of Palmyra,* 444–50.

16. Kirtland Council Minute Book, 12; *History of the Church,* 1:352.

1839 that Hurlbut was cut off for "using obscene language to a young lady, a member of the said Church, who resented his insult with indignation."[17]

Hurlbut appealed to the Council of High Priests that "justice was not done me." On June 21 the council rescinded its decision "because of the liberal confession which [Hurlbut] made."[18] He later claimed he only pretended to seek reinstatement so he could gather more information about the church.[19]

Two days later a general council heard testimony from Solomon Gee and others that they had heard Hurlbut brag about having "deceived Joseph Smith's God, or the Spirit by which he is actuated."[20] In response, he was excommunicated once more, again in his absence. He responded by delivering an anti-Mormon lecture in Kirtland and then collecting donations from Orrin Clapp, Nathan Corning, Grandison Newell, and "many other leading citizens of Kirtland and Geauga Co[unty]" for a trip to New York to "obtain affidavits showing the bad character of the Mormon Smith family," as Howe later described it.[21]

He began by collecting written statements in support of the Spalding theory in Conneaut, Ohio. Three of the statements were written down in August and two in September. It was probably October by the time he visited Spalding's widow,

---

17. Rpt. in Mayhew, *History of the Mormons*, 33–36; cf. *History of the Church*, 1:355n.

18. Kirtland Council Minute Book, 21; cf. *History of the Church*, 1:354.

19. *Chardon Spectator*, Jan. 18, 1834.

20. Kirtland Council Minute Book, 22; cf. *History of the Church*, 1:355.

21. E. D. Howe affidavit, Apr. 8, 1885, Deming Collection.

Matilda Spalding Davidson, in Massachusetts,[22] only to learn that she had "no distinct knowledge" of the manuscript's contents.[23] She told him her husband's papers were stored at a cousin's house in Otsego County, New York, so Hurlbut tracked it down, only to find a negligible similarity to the Book of Mormon. He nevertheless took the manuscript with him to give it a closer inspection.[24]

Mormons speculated that Hurlbut suppressed the manuscript so it wouldn't be found to be irrelevant. For instance, Mormon writer George Reynolds suggested it was probably "burned so that it might never be brought up to confront those who claim that in it is to be found the origin of the Book of Mormon."[25] In fact, Hurlbut showed it to the residents of Conneaut and then left it with Howe for safe keeping. Howe finally discarded it as immaterial to the question of the Book of Mormon's origin.[26] Yet, Hurlbut held to what two witnesses said about Spalding having written several novels; the one Hurlbut found was not the one they had heard Spalding read to them, they said.[27] In this context, after the 1884 discovery of the lost manuscript in Honolulu among the papers of

22. Hurlbut and Matilda Spalding both said they met in early 1834, but an article in the *Wayne Sentinel* already on Dec. 20, 1833, stated that "the original manuscript of the Book was written some thirty years since, by a respectable clergyman [Spalding], now deceased, whose name we are not permitted to give. ... These particulars have been derived by Dr. Hurlbert from the widow of the author of the original manuscript."

23. See p. 403 herein.

24. Dickinson, *New Light on Mormonism*, 22.

25. Reynolds, *Myth of the Manuscript Found*, 18.

26. See p. 404 herein.

27. See pp. 403, 404 herein.

Lewis L. Rice, the announcement that the manuscript was not the source of the Book of Mormon only repeated a judgment Hurlbut had made a half century earlier in Pennsylvania.[28]

He next traveled to Palmyra and stayed over a month lecturing and collecting statements from the Smiths' onetime neighbors.[29] On December 6 the *Wayne Sentinel* took notice that "Doct. P. Hurlbert" was in town "in behalf of the people of Kirtland for the purpose of investigating the origin of the Mormon sect." Cornelius R. Stafford remembered that Hurlbut arrived at "our school house and took statements about the bad character of the Mormon Smith family, and saw them swear to them."[30] Through December 11, Hurlbut collected fourteen statements: twelve from individuals, one from eleven residents of Manchester combined, and one from fifty-one residents of Palmyra. Of the twelve individual affidavits, three of them pertained to Martin Harris and the remainder had to do with the Smith family.

That Hurlbut had a specific kind of testimony in mind is attested to by Benjamin Saunders, who said Hurlbut "came to me but he could not get out of me what he wanted; so [he] went to others."[31] Undoubtedly there were other people like Saunders who had good things to say about the Smiths, but

---

28. Spalding's manuscript was first published in 1885 by the Reorganized Church of Jesus Christ of Latter Day Saints in Lamoni, Iowa, then in Utah in 1886 (see Flake, *Mormon Bibliography*, 8309, 8310).

29. Hurlbut was perhaps inspired by the affidavit from ten Palmyra residents in the *Painesville Telegraph*, Mar. 12, 1831, regarding Smith's treasure-seeking activities.

30. *Naked Truths about Mormonism*, Apr. 1888, 3.

31. Saunders interview with Kelley, ca. Sept. 1884, 29.

perhaps nothing of relevance; on the other hand, Hurlbut had no trouble finding hostile witnesses.[32] A Mormon missionary, Elder John S. Carter, visited the Palmyra-Manchester area shortly before Hurlbut's visit and wrote in his diary that "the people [were] greatly opposed to the work of God. Talked with many of them, & found them unable to make out anything against Joseph Smith, altho they talked hard against him."[33] Likewise, following his own investigations in Palmyra, Henry Pratt informed his son Addison in May 1838 about how "they informed me at Palmyra that the character & conduct of Jo Smith & Martin Harris, did not correspond at all with the character & conduct of christians."[34] Unlike Hurlbut, neither Carter nor Pratt recorded the names of the individuals they spoke with.

If Hurlbut was guilty of choosing biased witnesses and ignoring favorable ones, Richard L. Anderson went too far to dismiss Hurlbut for having put words in the mouths of his witnesses.[35] Similarities in terminology can no doubt be credited to how Hurlbut phrased his questions. In any case, the affidavits were signed and many were notarized. Moreover, none of the witnesses ever recanted or corrected their statements.

---

32. Within a year following publication of the affidavits, Jonathan H. Hale visited Palmyra and recorded in his journal: "We went about in the Neighbourhood from house to house to inquire the Character of Joseph Smith jr previous to his receiving the Book of Mormon[.] The amount [conclusion] was that his Character was as good as young men in General" (cited in Bitton, *Guide to Mormon Diaries and Autobiographies*, 134).

33. Ibid., 62.

34. Henry Pratt to Addison Pratt, May 20, 1838, photocopy in LDS Church History Library.

35. Anderson, "Joseph Smith's New York Reputation Reappraised," 286–90.

Another researcher, Rodger I. Anderson (no relation), concluded for these reasons and others that the affidavits have to be considered, on balance, credible.[36]

Another fallacy, in my view, is the assumption that if Hurlbut was wrong about Spalding, he must have been wrong about everything. Citing Fawn Brodie's remark that Hurlbut probably did "a little judicious prompting," Richard Anderson concluded that the statements should be viewed as skeptically as the Spalding theory.[37] The reason this is ill-advised is because (1) the Spalding theory did not come from Hurlbut and (2) he went to such lengths to track down the manuscript, he clearly did not think he had extracted misleading testimony from his witnesses. To the contrary, the affidavits recorded firsthand observations about things that had occurred in the recent past, which distinguishes them from literary comparisons others made, based on fading memories of what Spalding had read to them twenty years earlier. Even Howe cautioned readers that the Spalding affidavits had their limitations.[38] My own view is that the individuals who heard Spalding read from his manuscript were probably sincere, just that they were wrong about its similarity to the Book of Mormon.

The neighbors had other things in mind in charging the Smith family with intemperance and money digging, as well as related criticisms about how much time they devoted to such ventures while neglecting their farm. The focus and tone of the

---

36. Anderson, *Joseph Smith's New York Reputation Reexamined*, 114.

37. Richard Lloyd Anderson, review of *Joseph Smith's New York Reputation Reexamined*, 3:59–62.

38. See p. 391 herein.

neighbors' testimonies are unbalanced, but this does not mean their observations were untrue. Under other circumstances, a confederate might testify to the same facts and put a positive spin on it; in fact, we find corroborating evidence in statements from friendly sources as well.[39]

Once he was back in Ohio, Hurlbut resumed his attack on Joseph Smith in public meetings, now armed with the affidavits which he read from. Howe mentioned that "Hurlbut returned to Ohio and lectured on the Origin of Mormonism and the Book of Mormon. I heard him Lecture in Painesville."[40] The presentations created a stir. In January 1834 Orson Hyde wrote that Hurlbut had "fired the minds of the people with much indignation against Joseph and the Church."[41]

The bitterness of Hurlbut's criticisms resulted in Joseph Smith complaining about them to the local justice of the peace, John C. Dowen, on December 21, 1833. Dowen recalled that "the Mormons urged me to issue a writ against [Hurlbut]. I did, as recorded in my docket, Dec. 27, 1833 on complaint of Joseph Smith, warrant returnable to [justice] William Holbrook, Esq., at Painesville, Ohio."[42] On January 4, 1834, Hurlbut appeared before Holbrook and requested a continuance, which was granted.

---

39. Each of these charges is treated in my notes on pp. 16–20, 346–48.

40. Howe affidavit, Apr. 8, 1885.

41. *History of the Church*, 1:475.

42. J. C. Dowen affidavit, Jan. 2, 1885, Deming Collection. For an overview of the case and legal issues between Joseph Smith and Doctor Philastus Hurlbut, see David W. Grua, "Joseph Smith and the 1834 D. P. Hurlbut Case," *BYU Studies* 41, no. 1 (2005): 33–54; Grua, "Winning against Hurlbut's Assault in 1834," in *Sustaining the Law*, eds. Madsen et al., 141–54.

Meanwhile, under the date January 11, 1834, a scribe recorded that the prophet and other leaders prayed "the Lord would grant that our brother Joseph might prevail over his enemy, even Doctor P. Hurlbut, who has threatened his life, whom brother Joseph has <caused to be> taken with a precept; that the Lord would fill the heart of the Court with a spirit to do justice, and cause that the law of the land may be magnified in bringing him to justice."[43]

The preliminary hearing was held over the space of three days, January 13–15. Dowen remembered "over 50 witnesses [who] were called" and that "Hurlbut said he would kill Jo Smith[,]" which Dowen thought "meant he would kill Mormonism."[44] Regardless, Hurlbut was bound over to appear at the next session of court in the town of Chardon, about twelve miles south of Painesville.

Smith and his associates arrived there the last day of March and spent the next day issuing subpoenas. "[M]y soul delighteth in the Law of the Lord," Smith recorded in his journal, "for he forgiveth my sins and <will> confound mine Enimies[.] the Lord shall destroy him who has lifted his heel against me even that wicked man Docter P. H[u]rlbut[.] he <will> deliver him to the fowls of heaven and his bones shall be cast to the blast of the wind <for> he lifted his <arm> against the Almity therefore the Lord shall destroy him."[45]

Smith's case was heard April 2–3, after which he returned home to await the court's decision. In a meeting on April 7,

---

43. Jessee et al., *Joseph Smith Papers: Journals,* 1:25–26.

44. Dowen affidavit, Jan. 2, 1885.

45. Jessee et al., *Joseph Smith Papers: Journals,* 1:37.

he prayed that "I may prevail against that wicked Hurlbut and that he be put to shame."[46] Two days later the Geauga County Court of Common Pleas found that "the said complainant had ground to fear that the said Doctor Ph[ilastus] Hurlbut would wound, beat or kill him, or destroy his property" and therefore set bail at $200 and charged Hurlbut to keep the peace.[47]

The legal entanglement must have dissuaded Hurlbut from publishing the affidavits on his own. Howe recalled that he "came to me to have the evidence he had published. I bargained to pay him in books."[48] The agreement was reached shortly after the pre-trial hearing in Painesville,[49] and for the next ten months Howe worked on preparing what would be the first book-length treatise on Mormonism. On February 4 he wrote to Joseph Smith's father-in-law, Isaac Hale, requesting a notarized statement confirming what Hale had written to Hurlbut.[50] According to W. R. Hine, when Hurlbut read Hale's initial letter at a public meeting, he was immediately challenged by Martin Harris. "Hale was old and blind and not capable of writing it," Harris insisted. Hine told the audience that, to the contrary, "Hale was called the greatest hunter on the Susquehanna, and two years before had killed a black deer

---

46. Ibid, 38.

47. "Ohio v. Dr. P. Hurlbut," Apr. 9, 1834, Book M, 193, Geauga County Courthouse, Chardon, OH. See also *Chardon Spectator and Gazette,* Apr. 12, 1834, 3.

48. Howe affidavit, Apr. 8, 1885.

49. This is determined by the date of Howe's letter to Isaac Hale, Feb. 4, 1834, wherein Howe stated that he had "taken all the letters and documents from Mr. Hurlbut, with a view to their publication" (*Susquehanna Register,* May 1, 1834).

50. *Susquehanna Register,* May 1, 1834.

and a white bear, which many hunters had tried to kill, also
that he was intelligent and knew the Scriptures."[51] In the wake
of this challenge, Howe must have thought it prudent to verify
Hale's statement and thereby head off lingering doubts about
the letter's authenticity.

On February 9, Howe penned a letter to Professor Charles
Anthon, who had seen an alleged specimen of writing from the
golden plates. Martin Harris, who had visited with Anthon,
said the professor had pronounced the transcript a genuine
sample of "reformed Egyptian hieroglyphics." In Anthon's response of February 17, he repudiated the claim and insisted
that the facsimile shown to him "contained any thing else but
'*Egyptian Hieroglyphics.*'" Despite this denial, Joseph Smith repeated that the famed linguist had pronounced the sample of
script to be "true characters" and the translation more correct
"than any he had before seen translated from the Egyptian."[52]

Howe's book was released in November 1834 under the
title *Mormonism Unvailed: or, A Faithful Account of That Singular Imposition and Delusion, from Its Rise to the Present Time.*[53] It
bore the marks of a hasty creation, although contrary to what
many people assume, *unvailed* was the preferred spelling at the
time. Otherwise, the book was mostly a collection of previously
published material. The opening chapter introduces the Smith
family by summarizing information from the affidavits, con-
cluding with an introduction to the three Book of Mormon

---

51. *Naked Truths about Mormonism*, Jan. 1888, 2.

52. *History of the Church*, 1:20.

53. The *Painesville Telegraph* announced that the book was available for
sale in its Nov. 28, 1834, edition.

witnesses, portions of which came from the *Painesville Tele-graph* and *Palmyra Reflector* (15–27). The account in chapter two of how the Book of Mormon came to be (35–44) draws heavily on the affidavits and ends with an expansion of Alexander Campbell's analysis of the Book of Mormon (47–148).[54] The description of church activities in Ohio and Missouri came largely from the *Telegraph* (149–253).[55]

The remaining chapters were more or less appendixes: the 1831 Ezra Booth letters, borrowed from the *Ohio Star* (255–312), two of Joseph Smith's revelations (LDS D&C 58, 89; pp. 313–23 herein), the affidavits from the Palmyra-Manchester area (326–68), and statements from the Hale family in Harmony (368–78). Howe also included letters from Charles Anthon (379–83), William W. Phelps prior to his conversion to Mormonism (384–85), an excerpt from Leman Copley's 1834 court statement against Joseph Smith (387–90), and claims by acquaintances of Solomon Spalding (391–412).

Smith loyalists denounced Howe's book as satanically inspired.[56] Word spread quickly of the behind-the-scenes involvement of Hurlbut, whom Smith called the book's "legitimate

---

54. Campbell published "The Mormonites" in the *Millennial Harbinger*, Feb. 1831, 86–97, and apparently later as a pamphlet (see *Painesville Telegraph*, Mar. 1, 1831). It was reprinted by Joshua V. Himes as *Delusions: An Analysis of the Book of Mormon, with an Examination of Its Internal and External Evidences, and a Refutation of Its Pretence to Divine Authority* (Boston: Benjamin H. Greene, 1832) and again in the *Telegraph* in two installments, Mar. 8, 15, 1831.

55. Due to an error in printing, there are two consecutive sets of pages numbered 175 and 176.

56. Oliver Cowdery said the book originated, more fundamentally, with "the father of lies." *Messenger and Advocate*, May 1836, 314.

author," implying a ghost-written work.[57] This was repeated so often that it was assumed to be true.[58] In fact, Hurlbut was only a researcher, not a writer, and of 290 pages, his research occupied only 40 pages. Oliver Cowdery concluded that the book required a comprehensive response, so he countered with an eight-part history of Joseph Smith and the church's founding, with input from Smith himself, for the *Messenger and Advocate*. They wanted "to convince the public of the incorrectness of those scurrilous reports which have *inundated* our land."[59]

Responding specifically to "accusers," Smith confessed that in his youth he "fell into many vices and follies," due to "a light and too often vain mind." He said he engaged in "foolish and trifling conversation," although not any "gross and outrageous violations of the peace and good order of the community."[60] Richard Anderson rightly interpreted this disclaimer as an allusion to treasure seeking even though the narrative avoided explicit details about treasure quests.[61] In October 1835 the serialized account elaborated on Smith's first attempt to take the gold plates from the hill and explained that he received a "shock … by an invisible power, which deprived him, in a measure of

---

57. *Messenger and Advocate*, Dec. 1835, 228; *History of the Church*, 2:269–70. Smith repeated this in the *Elders' Journal*, Aug. 1838, 59–60.

58. Orson Hyde claimed the book was "written by Mr. E. D. Howe, alias. Doct. P. Hurlbut" (*Messenger and Advocate*, Apr. 1836, 296). Francis W. Kirkham said it was "written mainly by Philastus Hurlbut" (*New Witness for Christ in America*, 1:18; 2:147). More recently James B. Allen and Leonard J. Arrington wrote that "although Howe took credit for the book, Hurlbut seems to have been the principal compiler" ("Mormon Origins in New York," 245–46).

59. *Messenger and Advocate*, Dec. 1834, 42.

60. Ibid., 40.

61. Anderson, "Mature Joseph Smith and Treasure Searching," 495.

his natural strength,"[62] which was nearly the same as what his neighbor, Willard Chase, had said about Smith being knocked down three times by a spirit guardian. Chase went on to say that, according to what he had been told, a toad-like creature at the location transformed itself into something that had the appearance of a man.[63] Continuing, Cowdery wrote that Joseph had "heard of the power of enchantment, and a thousand like stories, which held the hidden treasures of the earth, and [Smith] supposed that physical exertion and personal strength was only necessary to enable him to yet obtain the object of his wish."[64] In a subtle way, then, Smith gave his admission to having found the golden plates while hunting for hidden treasure, confirming what the neighbors had said.

In May 1838 Smith gave another response in the *Elders' Journal* to "a few questions which are daily and hourly asked by all classes of people whilst we are traveling,"[65] two of which must have arisen from Howe's book. To the question, "Was not Jo Smith a money digger[?]" he responded dismissively: "Yes, but it was never a very profitable job to him, as he only got fourteen dollars a month for it."[66]

In response to a second question, "Did not Jo Smith steal his wife[?]" evidently in answer to his father-in-law's discomfort that he "followed a business that I could not approve,"

---

62. *Messenger and Advocate*, Oct. 1835, 197.

63. See 340 herein.

64. *Messenger and Advocate*, Oct. 1835, 198.

65. *Elders' Journal*, Nov. 1837, 28.

66. Joseph Smith, "Answers to Questions," ibid., July 1838, 43; cf. Vogel, *Documents*, 1:53.

Joseph again relied on levity: "Ask her; she was of age; she can answer for herself."[67] In his 1838 history, Smith again minimized his money-digging activity by portraying himself as one of many hired hands who spent a month looking for a lost silver mine. "Finally," he reported, he had "prevailed with the old gentleman [Josiah Stowell] to cease digging after it." From that "arose the very prevalent story of my having been a money-digger."[68]

The account left unanswered how he came to be employed by Stowell, a well-to-do farmer, and why he was the one who would persuade his employer to discontinue the search. Joseph's mother recalled that the man had come to their home "on account of having heard that [Joseph] possessed certain keys, by which he could discern things invisible to the natural eye."[69] Stowell was allegedly amazed by the young man's ability to see distant places through his stone and hired him on the spot. They had a shared interest in the supernatural. That is why the young man had the influence over his benefactor that is hinted at in the 1838 history. Smith's statement to Justice Albert Neely in March 1826 was more forthcoming. According to the court record, Smith confessed that

> he [Smith] had a certain stone, which he had occasionally looked at to determine where hidden treasures ... were ... and had looked for Mr. Stowell several times[,] ... that at Palmyra ... he had frequently ascertained in that way where lost property

67. See pp. 369–70 herein.
68. *History of the Church*, 1:17.
69. Smith, *Biographical Sketches*, 91–92.

was … that he has occasionally been in the habit of looking through this stone to find lost property for three years.[70]

Perhaps the demands of leadership and pressure of potential converts prevented Smith from speaking more honestly and clearly about his past. However, in a roundabout way, his discomfort increased public curiosity and added to the value historians place on the interviews with Smith's neighbors. Within the affidavits are answers to questions that arise from passing references to various obscure topics. Only now, after the passage of time, are we able to weigh the testimonies in a reasonable way and ask which of them provide helpful information about otherwise unanswered historical questions and which of them are exaggerated or tainted by jealousy and self-justification on the neighbors' part. To help readers in their search for answers, I have included explanations, historical context, and references to other sources, followed by the first-ever index to Howe's book, all of which I hope will assist readers in at least getting a sense of the time and the issues surrounding these events.

—Dan Vogel, Westerville, Ohio
December 4, 2014

---

70. The original court record has evidently not survived, but it was excerpted in Charles Marshall, "The Original Prophet, by a Visitor to Salt Lake City," *Fraser's Magazine*, Feb. 1873, 225–35 (rpt. in *Eclectic Magazine*, Apr. 1873, 479–88); Daniel S. Tuttle, "Mormons," *A Religious Encyclopaedia*, ed. Philip Schaff (New York: Funk and Wagnalls, 1883), 2:1576; "A Document Discovered," *Utah Christian Advocate*, Jan. 1886.

P. 275-276. ... *"Let the sots combine, With pious care a Monkey to enshrine."* —DRYDEN.*

*Howe's description of the woodcut appears on pp. 387–90 of the current edition. The first panel shows "the finding of the plates" and the second depicts Joseph Knight's story about how the prophet encountered Moroni disguised as "an old man dressed in ordinary gray apparel." Dismissing the old man's offer to show him a monkey in a box for "five coppers," Joseph unwittingly missed an opportunity to see the gold plates. The quote is from John Dryden's translation of Roman poet Juvenal's *Satires*: "How Egypt, mad with superstition grown, / Makes gods of monsters, but too well is known: / ... Where these are mouldering, let the sots [drunkards] combine / With pious care a monkey to enshrine!"

MORMONISM UNVAILED:

or, a faithful account of that singular imposition and delusion, from its rise to the present time. With sketches of the characters of its propagators, and a full detail of the manner in which the famous golden bible was brought before the world. To which are added, inquiries into the probability that the historical part of the said bible was written by one Solomon Spalding, more than twenty years ago, and by him intended to have been published as a romance.

....
BY E. D. HOWE.
....

PAINESVILLE:
PRINTED AND PUBLISHED BY THE AUTHOR.
———
1834.

*The typography and layout have been standardized in this edition so that, for instance, the copyright notice is given on two lines instead of three and Howe's name, which was originally shown in all capital letters, is presented in normal roman type. A distinction is made throughout between real content and design flourishes. As another example, on the page to the right, the introduction began with a symbol called a manicule ☞ that has been removed. Readers may want to consult an online digital scan for typographical details.

The following work was undertaken with reluctance, at the earnest solicitation of a great number of friends, who had, with the author, long looked upon the subject of which it treats, with mingled feelings of abhorence and pity—the Impostors and their victims of delusion, were viewed through these two different media [abhorrence and pity]. The truth, and the whole truth, have been his constant aim: But the difficulty of procuring, or arriving at the *whole truth*, in relation to a religious imposition, which has from its birth been so studiously vailed in secrecy, and generally under a belief that the judgments of God would follow any disclosures of what its votaries had seen or heard— will be readily discovered. He fears, therefore, that the half is yet untold. He has, in all his enquiries, endeavored to pay the most rigid regard to all the ordinary methods of eliciting truth, from every source within his reach. If he shall have failed in his desires and exertions, in any important particular, it will be a matter of regret. That his statements should fully escape censure or contradiction, by a sect whose foundation was falsehood, and which has been built up of the same material, is more than he can expect. He is fully persuaded, nevertheless, that sufficient, and more than sufficient, has been developed by unimpeachable testimony, to satisfy every rational person, whose mind has not already been prostrated by the machinations of the Imposters, that the Supreme Being has had as little agency in the prosperity of Mormonism, as in the grossest works of Satan.

Painesville, (Ohio,) October, 1834. E. D. H.

INTRODUCTION.

Of all the impositions which "flesh is heir to,"[1] none ought to be more abhorred or dreaded, than those which come in the garb of sanctity and religion: But that none are more ardently seized upon and cherished, by a certain portion of mankind, all history goes to substantiate. Absurdities, like comets, move in orbits both eccentric and peculiar. At one time they are obscured and lost in distance; then again they are to be seen shining with a full face, frightening silly mortals from their sphere, and turning into chaos the majesty of mind. Astronomy has scarcely taught us to foretel the appearance of the one; but metaphysics will enable us to calculate the periodical return of the other, when it shall have enabled us to fathom the abysses of the human mind, and discover the srpings [springs] of human action.

There is nothing more curious than the connection between passion and credulity—and few things more humiliating and extraordinary, than the extent to which the latter may be carried, even in minds of no vulgar order, when under the immediate influence of any strong interest or excitement.[2] It is also true that we have frequently to encounter a perverse

---

1. Qtd. from Shakespeare's *Hamlet*.
2. He alludes to the spiritual hysteria that was displayed by some converts in Ohio, presented in more detail on pp. 155–58.

incredulity, and a callous insensibility to evidence, when we attempt to convince any one of what is contrary to his opinions, wishes or interests. But this is only another exemplification of the remarkable fact, that where any object, whether desirable, detestable, or dreadful, agitates the mind to a certain degree, our belief is very far from being regulated by the weight of testimony. In such a frame of mind, men are not in a situation to listen to the suggestions of sober reason; their attention is rivited to one particular view; they form their opinions with seeming deliberation, from circumstances which would be little regarded by minds of a sounder state, but which, seen through the medium of a distorted imagination, appear with an overpowering magnitude; and in fact, if a deep impression is made by any recital seriously delivered, or by any idea whose falsehood is not manifest, the strength of the impression is very apt to be mistaken for a sure proof of its reality. Even in cases where the greatest calmness and deliberation might be expected, and among those whose profession it is to investigate truth—the ambition of founding a sect, or displaying intellectual superiority—the veneration for great names, or long established opinions—and the anxiety to penetrate into the mysteries of nature—have sometimes produced, not modest querists and patient inquirers, but zealous preachers and zealous believers of the most fanciful creeds of philosophy; about the influence of the stars; the whirlpools that guide the planets in their course; about the concavity or internal regions of the earth; and about the formation of the skull as furnishing a sure index to the passions and propensities.

If such dreams are indulged in the calm investigation of

philosophy, what are we to expect when the mind is dazzled by supernatural objects, animated by supernatural hopes, and pressed upon the understanding by supernatural terrors? Our wonder therefore ceases, that mankind apparently delight in being misled by the grossest delusions; that the pure truths of Christianity are so strangely mingled with the wildest fancies that can be imagined by the lunatic, or invented by the designing knave.

"Every age of the world has produced impostors and delusions.[3] Jannes and Jambers withstood Moses, and were followed by Pharaoh, his court and clergy. To say nothing of the false prophets of the Jewish age, the diviners, soothsayers, the magicians, and all the ministry of idols among the Gentiles, by which the nations were so often deceived, the Impostors which have appeared since the Christian era, would fill volumes of the most lamentable details. The false Messiahs which have afflicted the Jews since their rejection of Jesus Christ, have more than verified the predictions of the "true and faithful witness." No less than twenty-four distinguished false Messiahs have disturbed the Jews. Many were deceived, and myriads lost their lives through their impostures. Some peculiar epochs were more distinguished for the number and impudence of those Impostors. If the Jews had fixed upon any year as likely to terminate their dispersion, and as the period of their return, that year rarely failed to produce a Messiah. Hence in the 12th century, no less than *ten* false Messiahs appeared. Numerous

---

3. The following two paragraphs are nearly verbatim from Alexander Campbell's 1831 "Delusions." The remainder of the introduction expands and paraphrases the same source (rpt. in *Millennial Harbinger*, Feb. 1831, 85–86).

have been the impostors among Christians, since the great apostacy began; especially since and at the time of the reformation. Munzer, Stubner and Stork[4] were conspicuous in the 16th century. These men taught that among Christians, who had the precepts of the Gospel to guide them, and the spirit of God to direct them, civil offices and laws were not only unnecessary, but an unlawful encroachment upon their spiritual liberty; that all Christians should put their possessions into common stock; and that polygamy was not incompatible with either the Old or New Testaments.[5] They related many visions and revelations which they had from above, but failing to propagate their doctrines by these means, they attempted to enforce them by arms. Many Catholics joined them, and in the various insurrections which they effected, one hundred thousand souls are said to have been sacrificed.

"Since the millennium became a subject of much speaking and writing, Impostors have been numerous. In the memory of the present generation, many delusions have been propogated and received, to a considerable extent. The Shakers, styling themselves the "Millennium Church," a sect instituted by Ann Lee,[6] in 1774, still maintain a respectable number. This "elect lady," as they sometimes styled her, was the head of the party,

---

4. Thomas Müntzer (ca.1489–1525) was a German theologian during the Reformation, a leader in the Peasant's War of 1524–25. Mark Thomas Stübner, the weaver Nicholas Storch, and Thomas Dreschel, the Zwickau Prophets, were precursors to the Anabaptist movement.

5. For polygamy among the Anabaptists, see Smith, *Nauvoo Polygamy*, 479–517.

6. Ann Lee (1736–84) led the United Society of Believers in Christ's Second Coming, informally known as Shakers. Born in Manchester, England,

and gave them a new bible. They asserted that she spoke seventy-two different tongues, and conversed with the dead. Through her all blessings flowed to her followers. She appointed the sacred dance and the fantastic song; and consecrated shivering, swooning, and falling down, acts of acceptable devotion. They hold all things in common, rank marriage among the works of the flesh, and forbid all sexual intercourse.

In 1792, Richard Brothers published a book of prophecies and visions, and an account of his daily intercourse with God, in London.[7] He too had his followers; and among them a member of the British Parliament, a profound scholar and one of the most learned men of his time. He even made a speech in the House of Commons, declaring his full belief in one of the craziest pieces of absurdity that was ever presented to a British populace.

Joanna Southcott,[8] the most disgusting old hag that ever pretended to 'set up for herself,' in the business of blasphemy and dupe-making, was countenanced and encouraged by respectable and wealthy individuals in England; who, not only

she emigrated after receiving a revelation in 1774 and settled with her followers near Albany.

7. Richard Brothers (1757–1824), born in Newfoundland and educated in England, was an adherent of so-called Anglo-Israelism, a movement that promoted the idea that Europeans, especially from Great Britain, were descended from the Lost Tribes of Israel. In 1794 Brothers published *A Revealed Knowledge of the Prophecies and Times, Book the First, Wrote under the Direction of the Lord God* (London, 1794).

8. Joanna Southcott (1750–1814) was a member of the Church of England from Devon who believed she was the woman prophesied in Rev. 12:1–6 and that at age sixty-four she would deliver a new messiah. It is estimated that by 1908 she had attracted over 100,000 followers.

believed in the divine origin of her ministration, but swallowed with most implicit faith, her *"Dialogue with the Devil,"* a farrago [mishmash] of filthy licentiousness that would suffuse [shadow] the face of a fisherwoman. By her arts of deception she succeeded in procuring the certificate of a respectable physician that she was pregnant of the Holy Ghost.

In Scotland a few years since, a Miss Campbell pretended to have come back from the dead, having the "gift of tongues," was believed in by many of the Clergy and Bar, and carried along with her a numerous train of lesser note. The pretensions of Jemima Wilkinson,[9] the Barkers, Jumpers and Mutterers, of our own time and country, are also well remembered.

But at these things we only intended to hint, in this place, in order to prepare the mind for a detailed account of the more recent, more absurd, and, perhaps more extensive, delusion of Mormonism. It will present in somewhat a new light, to the enquiring mind, the depths of folly, degradation and superstition, to which human nature can be carried. It will show that there is no turning a fanatic from his folly—that the distemper is more incurable than the leprosy—that the more glaring the absurdity, the more determined the tenacity of its dupes—and the more apparent you can render the imposture, the stronger become its advocates.

Our object, therefore, in the present undertaking, will not be so much to break the spell which has already seized and

---

9. Jemima Wilkinson (1752–1819), a Quaker from Rhode Island, recovered from a coma to announce a new identity as Publick Universal Friend, a new spirit occupying her body. As such, she began to teach sexual abstinence and founded the Society of Universal Friends.

taken possession of great numbers of people in our enlightened country, as to raise a warning voice, to those who are yet liable, through a want of correct knowledge of the imposition, to be enclosed within its fetters.

We make no pretensions to literary merit, and anticipate adding but little to the common stock of useful information. What is related, is in a plain, unvarnished style; such as we hope will be the more beneficial to those who are most usually obnoxious [susceptible][10] to religious impositions.

---

10. The preferred meaning of *obnoxious* in the 1828 dictionary was "subject to, answerable to."

MORMONISM.[1]

CHAPTER 1.

Containing a brief sketch of the characters of the modern prophet and his family, and some of the principal actors in the imposition.

With the exception of their natural and peculiar habits of life, there is nothing in the character of the Smith family worthy of being recorded, previous to the time of their plot to impose upon the world by a pretended discovery of a new Bible, in the bowels of the earth. They emigrated from the town of Royalton, in the State of Vermont, about the year 1820, when Joseph, Jun. was, it is supposed, about 16 years of age.[2] We

---

1. The word *Mormonism* appeared here in large bold type and thereafter throughout the book as the running head on every page. It was followed by CHAPTER I in all capital letters and roman numeral. Wherever Howe employed artistic flourishes, they have been eliminated here, although the exact wording, spelling, punctuation, and capitalization of initial letters are retained.

2. The Smiths emigrated from Norwich, Vermont, in 1816–17 when young Joseph was about ten or eleven. Howe probably follows the statements of several Manchester residents who told Hurlbut they first became acquainted with the Smiths in 1820 (pp. 333–34, 338, 351–53, 362). He can't be faulted for thinking they had lived in Royalton, however, because even Joseph's younger brother William thought so. Smith, "Notes," 34–35; Vogel, *Documents*, 1:489; cf. Smith, *Biographical Sketches*, 68; Vogel, *Documents*, 1:273–74.

find them in the town of Manchester, Ontario county, N.Y. which was the principal scene of their operations, till the year 1830. All who became intimate with them during this period, unite in representing the general character of old Joseph and wife, the parents of the pretended Prophet, as lazy, indolent,[3] ignorant and superstitious[4]—having a firm belief in ghosts and witches;[5] the telling of fortunes;[6] pretending to believe that the earth was filled with hidden treasures, buried there by

---

3. This is probably based partly on the Smiths' preoccupation with treasure seeking, which some people considered to be an idle pastime (see *Palmyra Reflector*, Feb. 1, 1831, 93; June 12, 1831, 36; July 7, 1831, 60), especially since final payment on the Smith property was due. Joseph Capron was aware that "while they were digging for money, they were daily harrassed by the demands of creditors, which they never were able to pay" (p. 364). For more, see addendum 1, "The Smiths in Manchester," at the end of this chapter.

4. Because of their belief in enchanted treasures and use of ceremonial magic, the Smiths, despite some education, were said to be ignorant and superstitious. It was in this context that the editor of the *Palmyra Reflector* called Joseph Smith an "ignoramous" (June 30, July 7, 1830) and wrote that the Smiths had "a propensity to superstition and a fondness for every thing *marvelous*" (Feb. 1, 1831, 92). Capron told Hurlbut they were "fond of the foolish and the marvelous" (p. 363).

5. Capron said the boy's seer stone "enabled him to see ... ghosts, infernal spirits, ... [and] invaluable treasures deposited in the earth" (p. 363), which Joshua Stafford corroborated (p. 362). Abner Cole associated seer stones with witchcraft (*Palmyra Reflector*, Feb. 1, 1831, 93; Vogel, *Documents*, 2:243).

6. Fortune-telling was mentioned by two neighbors (pp. 350, 353), and later Christopher Stafford said "Jo" claimed to be able to "tell fortunes. He told mine by looking in the palm of my hand and said ... I would not live to be very old" (Vogel, *Documents*, 2:195). Anna Ruth Eaton said mother Lucy Smith also "turned many a penny by tracing in the lines of the open palm the fortunes of the inquirer" (Eaton, *Origin of Mormonism*, 1; Vogel, *Documents*, 3:147; cf. Jesse Townsend to Phineas Stiles, 1833, 288; Philetus B. Spear, "Joseph Smith and Mormonism," 1923, 1).

Kid or the Spaniards.[7] Being miserably poor,[8] and not much disposed to obtain an honest livelihood by labor, the energies of their minds seemed to be mostly directed towards finding where these treasures were concealed, and the best mode of acquiring their possession. Joseph, Jun. in the mean time, had become very expert in the arts of necromancy,[9] jugling,[10] the use of the *divining rod*,[11] and looking into what they termed a

---

7. None of Hurlbut's Manchester witnesses specifically mentioned Spanish or pirate money. The claim was that there was bounty left in the area by "ancients," meaning Native Americans (pp. 328, 334, 361; cf. L. Saunders interview with William H. Kelley, 7; Vogel, *Documents,* 2:130). A different source mentioned the intent to find "where Captain Kidd had hidden money in Palmyra" ("Joseph Smith and Mormonism," 2; Vogel, *Documents,* 3:130), and Joseph Smith's father-in-law said they were looking for Spanish treasure (p. 369).

8. The claim that the family turned to money digging for financial rescue may contradict Howe's previous assertion that the Smiths were "pretending to believe that the earth was filled with hidden treasures."

9. The insinuation was that Joseph Smith communed with the spirits of the dead, which was different than seeing angels. Mormon theology would later conflate the two. For more, see addendum 2, "Treasure Spirits."

10. The word *juggler* had a wider connotation meaning a confidence peddler. The statute that allowed Joseph Smith to be tried in 1826 for being a "disorderly person" read: "All jugglers, and all persons pretending to have skill in physiognomy, palmistry, or like crafty science, or pretending to tell fortunes, or to discover where lost goods may be found ... shall be deemed and adjudged disorderly persons" (*Laws of the State of New York,* 1:114, sec. I; Vogel, *Documents,* 4:242–43; Quinn, *Early Mormonism,* 56–57). In 1830 Smith's legal counsel defended against "the crime of glass looking and juglin[g][,] fortune telling[,] and so on" (John S. Reed to Brigham Young, Dec. 6, 1861, 1; Vogel, *Documents,* 4:122). The *juggling* here was glass looking (*Palmyra Reflector,* Feb. 28, 1831, 109; Vogel, *Documents,* 2:246).

11. Peter Ingersoll mentioned that Joseph Sr. used a divining rod (p. 329). Years later another Palmyra resident remembered having seen Joseph Jr. use

"peep-stone,"[12] by which means he soon collected about him a gang of idle, credulous young men,[13] to perform the labor of digging into the hills and mountains, and other lonely places, in that vicinity, in search of gold. In process of time many pits[14] were dug in the neighborhood, which were afterwards pointed out as the place from whence the plates were excavated.[15] But we do not learn that the young impostor ever entered these excavations for the purpose of assisting his sturdy dupes in their labors. His business was to point out the locations of the treasures, which he did by looking at a stone placed in a hat.[16] Whenever the diggers became dissatisfied at not finding the object of their desires, his inventive and fertile genius would

one (Isaac Butts statement, 1885, 2; Vogel, *Documents*, 2:202; cf. Quinn, *Early Mormonism*, 33).

12. As early as 1831, Howe had learned of Smith's seer stone by corresponding with Abner Cole (see *Palmyra Reflector*, Feb. 28, 1831, 109; Vogel, *Documents*, 2:246–47) and from a March 12 letter from ten people who knew of the "peep stone" (*Painesville Telegraph*, Mar. 22, 1831; cf. Quinn, *Early Mormonism*, 39–65).

13. That Joseph Smith and his father were part of a larger group of diggers was reported by Howe in the *Painesville Telegraph* on Mar. 22, 1831. This was confirmed in interviews with David and William Stafford (pp. 327, 336–37, 350, 363).

14. In 1831 William W. Phelps wrote to Howe that "the places where they dug for the plates, in Manchester, are to be seen" (p. 384).

15. Lorenzo Saunders visited the hill days after Smith's claimed extraction of gold plates and found no disturbance of the earth except "a large hole" left by the "money diggers" about "a year or two before" (Saunders to Thomas Gregg, Jan. 28, 1885, 135; Saunders interview with Kelley, Nov. 12, 1884, 16–17; Vogel, *Documents*, 2:147). For more, see addendum 3, "The Hill Cumorah."

16. Isaac Hale said his son-in-law's "occupation was that of seeing, or pretending to see by means of a stone placed in his hat, and his hat closed over his face" (pp. 369, 372). See Van Wagoner and Walker, "Gift of Seeing," 48–68.

generally contrive a story to satisfy them. For instance, he would tell them that the treasure was removed by a spirit just before they came to it, or that it sunk down deeper into the earth.[17]

The extreme ignorance and apparent stupidity of this modern prophet, were, by his early followers, looked upon as his greatest merit,[18] and as furnishing the most incontestable proof of his divine mission. These have ever been the wardrobe of impostors. They were even thrown upon the shoulders of the great prince of deceivers, Mohammed, in order to carry in his train the host of ignorant and superstitious of his time; although he afterwards became a ruler of Nations.[19] That the common advantages of education were denied to our prophet, or that they were much neglected, we believe to be a fact.[20] His followers have told us, that he could not at the time he was "chosen of the Lord," even write his own name.[21] But it

---

17. William Stafford helped dig on the Smiths' property when "the evil spirit ... caused the money to sink" into the ground (p. 336; cf. "A Document Discovered"; Vogel, *Documents*, 4:248–56).

18. Howe was right to question this claim because Joseph Smith's letters, sermons, and revelations all show him to be good with words.

19. Smith was often compared to the prophet Muhammad, especially after it was learned that, like the Saudi revelator, the American seer practiced polygamy. In this instance Howe is referring to an epithet in the Quran referring to "the unlettered prophet" (7:157–58).

20. Smith complained in 1832 about his family's poverty, which "deprived [him] of the bennifit of an education" (Smith, History, 1832, 1; Vogel, *Documents*, 1:27).

21. His wife, Emma, said with some exaggeration that he could not write "a coherent and well-worded letter, let alone dictating a book like the Book of Mormon" (Smith, "Last Testimony," 290; Vogel, *Documents*, 1:542). By contrast, historian Dale Morgan found that Joseph's early correspondence showed a "flair for words [and] measure of eloquence" (Walker, *Dale Morgan*, 147; cf. Jessee,

is obvious that all those deficiencies are fully supplied by a natural genius, strong inventive powers of mind, a deep study, and an unusually correct estimate of human passions and feelings.[22] In short, he is now endowed with all the requisite traits of character to pursue most successfully the humbug[23] which he has introduced. His address is easy, rather facinating and winning, of a mild and sober deportment, when not irritated. But he frequently becomes boisterous by the impertinence or curiosity of the skeptical, and assumes the bravado, instead of adhering to the meekness which he professes.[24] His followers, of course, can discover in his very countenance all the certain indications of a divine mission.

For further illustrations of the character of the Smith family, the reader is referred to the numerous depositions and certificates attached to this work.

Martin Harris[25] is the next personage of note in the Golden Bible speculation. He is one of the *three witnesses* to the truth of the book, having been shown the plates through the agency

---

Personal Writings, 255–58, 263–68, 277–80). William Smith said his brother "wrote a plain intelegable hand" ("Notes," 27; Vogel, *Documents*, 1:486).

22. Lucy Smith described her son as "much less inclined to the perusal of books than any of the rest of our children, but far more given to meditation and deep study" (Smith, *Biographical Sketches*, 84; Vogel, *Documents*, 1:296).

23. The 1828 dictionary defines *humbug* as slang ("a low word") for "an imposition."

24. This was in harmony with a friend's comment that he "would allow no arrogance or undue liberties; and criticisms, even by his associates, were rarely acceptable; and contradictions would arouse in him the lion, at once" (Benjamin F. Johnson to George F. Gibbs, [1903], 4, qtd. in Hill, "Joseph Smith the Man," 183; cf. pp. 290–91).

25. See addendum 4, "The Three Witnesses."

of an Angel, instead of the Prophet Joseph, who always had them in possession. Before his acquaintance with the Smith family, he was considered an honest, industrious citizen, by his neighbors. His residence was in the town of Palmyra, where he had accumulated a handsome property. He was naturally of a very visionary turn of mind on the subject of religion,[26] holding one sentiment but a short time.[27] He engaged in the new Bible [Book of Mormon] business with a view of making a handsome sum of money from the sale of the books,[28] as he was frequently heard to say. The whole expense of publishing an edition of 5000 copies, was borne by Martin, to secure the payment of which, he mortgaged his farm for $3000. Having failed in his anticipations about the sale of the books, (the retail price of which they said was fixed by an Angel at $1.75, but afterwards reduced to $1.25,[29] and from that down to any

---

26. Pomeroy Tucker recalled that Harris had a "belief in dreams, ghosts, hobgoblins, 'special provinces,' terrestrial visits of angels, [and] the interposition of 'devils' to afflict sinful men" (Tucker, *Origin*, 50; Vogel, *Documents*, 3:113). For more, see addendum 4.

27. Harris was a Quaker by upbringing, who had attended services at the Episcopal and Methodist churches. This is not to say he had joined these churches, as George Stoddard insinuated (see p. 365; John A. Clark to Dear Brethren, Aug. 24, 1840, 94; Vogel, *Documents*, 2:262). Harris himself said he was "taught of the Spirit that I Should not Join Eny Church, although I Was anxiousley Sought for by meny of the Sectarians" ("Testimony of Martin Harris," 1; Vogel, *Documents*, 2:331).

28. This was the suspicion of Harris's estranged wife and sister-in-law (pp. 355–60), but an agreement with Joseph Smith Sr. limited Harris's interest in the sales revenue to paying off the debt to the printer (Smith, Agreement, Jan. 16, 1830; Vogel, *Documents*, 3:483–85; MacKay et al., *Joseph Smith Papers: Documents*, 1:104–08).

29. Initially they sold the book for fourteen shillings and then reduced the

price they could obtain) he adopted Smith as his Prophet, Priest and King. Since that time, the frequent demands upon Martin's purse have reduced it to a very low state. He seems to have been the soul and body of the whole imposition, and now carries the most incontestible proofs of a religious maniac. He frequently declares that he has conversed with Jesus Christ, Angels and the Devil. Christ he says is the handsomest man he ever saw;[30] and the Devil looks very much like a jack-ass, with very short, smooth hair, similar to that of a mouse.[31] He says he wrote a considerable part of the book,[32] as Smith dictated, and at one time the presence of the Lord was so great, that a screen was hung up between him and the Prophet;[33] at other times the Prophet would sit in a different

price to ten shillings (p. 354; John A. Clark to Dear Brethren, Aug. 31, 1840, 99; Vogel, *Documents*, 2:271), as directed by Smith ("You will not sell the books for less than 10 Shillings," Smith to Harris, Feb. 22, 1831, in MacKay et al., *Joseph Smith Papers: Documents*, 1:264). David Marks visited the Whitmer family in Fayette on Mar. 29, 1830, and learned that the retail price had been set by an angel (Marks, *Life of David Marks*, 341; Vogel, *Documents*, 5:304). The British shilling was still in circulation at the time (McMaster, *History of the People of the United States*, 1:189–90).

30. Howe recycled this from the *Painesville Gazette*'s paraphrase that Jesus, according to Harris, was "the handsomest man he ever did see" (rpt. in *Guernsey Times*, Apr. 16, 1831).

31. Ibid., quoting Harris calling the devil a "sleek haired fellow with four feet, and a head like that of a Jack-ass."

32. This is incorrect. After Harris lost the first 116 manuscript pages in June 1828, he no longer acted as scribe.

33. According to the *Palmyra Reflector*, "Smith and Harris gave out that no mortal save Jo could look upon [the plates] and live; and Harris declares, that when he acted as *amanuenses*, and wrote the translation, as Smith dictated, such was his fear of the Divine displeasure, that a screen (sheet) was suspended between the prophet and himself" (Mar. 19, 1831, 126; Vogel, *Documents*, 2:248;

room, or up stairs, while the Lord was communicating to him the contents of the plates. He does not pretend that he ever saw the wonderful plates but once, although he and Smith were engaged for months in deciphering their contents. He has left his wife to follow the fortunes of Smith. He has frequent fits of prophecying, although they are not held in very high repute among his brethren. A specimen of his prophetic powers we subjoin.[34] They were written for the special information of a friend of his who placed them upon the wall of his office, and are in these words:

Within four years from September 1832, there will not be one wicked person left in the United States; that the righteous will be gathered to Zion, and that there will be no President over these United States after that time.[35] MARTIN HARRIS.

---

cf. John A. Clark to Dear Brethren, Aug. 24, 1840, 94; Vogel, *Documents*, 2:268). Harris told Edward Stevenson that there was no screen and that Smith peered at his seer stone at the bottom of his hat (Stevenson, "Three Witnesses," 389; Vogel, *Documents*, 2:324).

34. John A. Clark said Harris often traveled back to Palmyra to "proselyte old acquaintances" and that one of them said "he would not consent to [Harris] uttering his predictions any more orally, but that he must write them down and subscribe his name to them." He consented and produced the statements quoted here by Howe. According to Clark, Harris said "Palmyra would be destroyed, and left utterly without inhabitant before the year 1836" and that "before 1838 the Mormon faith would so extensively prevail, that it would modify our national government, and there would at that period be no longer any occupant of the presidential chair of the United States." If these predictions failed, Harris said, his friends had his "permission to cut off his head and roll it around the streets as a football" (Clark, "Gleanings by the Way," *Episcopal Recorder*, Oct. 10, 1840, 114).

35. The typesetter for the Book of Mormon heard Harris prophesy that "Jackson would be the last president that we would have; and that all persons

I do hereby assert and declare that in four years from the date hereof, every sectarian and religious denomination in the United States, shall be broken down, and every Christian shall be gathered unto the Mormonites, and the rest of the human race shall perish. If these things do not take place, I will hereby consent to have my hand separated from my body.
MARTIN HARRIS.

Martin is an exceedingly fast talker.[36] He frequently gathers a crowd around him in bar-rooms[37] and in the streets.—Here he appears to be in his element, answering and explaining all manner of dark and abstruse theological questions, from Genesis to Revelations; declaring that every thing has been revealed to him by the "power of God." During these flights

---

who did not embrace Mormonism in two years would be stricken off the face of the earth" (John H. Gilbert, "Memorandum," 4; Vogel, *Documents* 2:547). In 1832 Harris saw that Jackson would be re-elected and therefore extended his prediction four years (Vogel, "Mormonism's 'Anti-Masonik Bible,'" 26). In 1834 Smith said "the appointed time for the redemption of Zion" would be September 11, 1836 (Jessee, *Personal Writings*, 349; cf. *History of the Church*, 2:145).

36. The *Painesville Telegraph*, Mar. 15, 1831, described Harris as "flippant, talking fast and loud." Ezra Booth agreed that he was a "great talker, an extravagant boaster; so much so, that he renders himself disagreeable to many of his society; ... he understands all prophecies, and knows every thing by the spirit, and he can silence almost any opposer by talking faster, and louder than he can" (p. 265).

37. The *Painesville Telegraph*, ibid., reported that Harris "arrived here last Saturday from ... New York. He immediately planted himself in the barroom of the hotel, where he soon commenced reading and explaining the Mormon hoax, and all the dark passages from Genesis to Revelations. He told all about the gold plates, Angels, Spirits, and Jo Smith.—He had seen and handled them all, by the power of God! Curiosity soon drew around thirty or forty spectators, and all who presumed to question his blasphemous pretentions, were pronounced infidels."

of fancy, he frequently prophecies the coming of Christ, the destruction of the world, and the damnation of certain individuals. At one time he declared that Christ would be on earth within fifteen years,[38] and all who did not believe in the book of Mormon would be destroyed.

He is the source of much trouble and perplexity to the honest portion of his brethren, and would undoubtedly long since have been cast off by Smith, were it not for his money, and the fact that he is one of the main pillars of the Mormon fabric. Martin is generally believed, by intelligent people, to be laboring under a partial derangement;[39] and that any respectable jury would receive his testimony, in any case, of ever so trifling a nature, we do not believe; yet, the subjects of the delusion think him a competent witness to establish miracles of the most unreasonable kind. But we leave him for the present.

Oliver Cowdery[40] comes next in the catalogue. He was also a chief scribe to the prophet, while transcribing, after Martin had lost 116 pages of the precious document, by interference of the Devil. An Angel also has shown him the plates, from which the book of Mormon proceeded, as he says. He is a blacksmith

---

38. Ibid. This was commonly believed by Mormons. Oliver Cowdery, quoted in the *Painesville Telegraph*, "proclaim[ed] destruction upon the world within a few years" (Nov. 16, 1830). Missionaries were said to have "predicted the end of the world in 15 years" (*Ohio Star*, Dec. 9, 1830). See also Norman, "How Long, O Lord?"

39. Lorenzo Saunders said "Martin was a good citizen ... a man that would do just as he agreed with you. But, he was a great man for seeing spooks" (Saunders interview with E. L. Kelley, Nov. 12, 1884, 4; Vogel, *Documents*, 2:149). See also addendum 4.

40. See addendum 4, "The Three Witnesses."

by trade,[41] and sustained a fair reputation until his intimacy commenced with the money-diggers. He was one of the many in the world who always find time to study out ways and means to live without work. He accordingly quit the blacksmithing business, and is now the *editor* of a small monthly publication[42] issued under the direction of the prophet, and principally filled with accounts of the spread of Mormonism, their persecutions, and the fabled visions and commands of Smith.

David Whitmar[43] is the third special witness who signed the certificate with Harris and Cowdery, testifying to having seen plates. He is one of five of the same name and family who have been used as witnesses to establish the imposition, and who are now head men and leaders in the Mormonite camp.[44] They were noted in their neighborhood for credulity and a general belief in witches,[45] and perhaps were fit subjects for the juggling arts of Smith. David relates that he was led by Smith into an open field, on his father's farm, where

41. Cowdery was a shop assistant and a salesman with a printing company. He taught school briefly but was not trained as an educator. No other source says Cowdery was a blacksmith.

42. Beginning in October 1834, Cowdery edited the *Latter Day Saints' Messenger and Advocate* in Kirtland.

43. The preferred spelling is Whitmer, derived from the German *witmen* (to dedicate) or *Witwer* (widower). His parents spoke with a heavy German accent. For more, see addendum 4, "The Three Witnesses."

44. David's brothers, John, Jacob, Christian, and Peter Jr., were among eight additional witnesses to the gold plates.

45. This is similar to the assessment of the Reverend Diedrich Willers, pastor of the German Reformed Church in Fayette, New York. In June 1830, he wrote that the Whitmers were "easily excitable people, also superstitious to the highest degree so that they believe in witches" (Willers to Reverent Brethren, June 18, 1830, 5, as translated in Vogel, *Documents*, 5:278).

they found the Book of plates lying upon the ground.[46] Smith took it up and requested him to examine it, which he did for the space of half an hour or more, when he returned it to Smith, who placed it in its former position, alledging that it was in the custody of an Angel. He describes the plates as being about eight inches square, the leaves being metal of a whitish yellow color, and of the thickness of tin plates. The back was secured with three small rings of the same metal, passing through each leaf in succession; that the leaves were divided equidistant between the back and the edge, by cutting the plates in two parts, and again united with solder, so that the front might be opened, while the back part remained stationary and immovable, and was consequently a sealed book, which would not be revealed for ages to come, and which Smith himself was not permitted to understand. On opening that part of the book which was not secured by seals, he discovered inscribed on the aforesaid plates, divers and wonderful characters, some large and some small, but beyond the wisdom of man to understand without supernatural aid; this account is sometimes partly contradicted by Harris.[47]

46. This detail, and even the wording, is borrowed from the *Palmyra Reflector*, March 19, 1831. It is contradicted by Whitmer's own statements about an angel having shown him the plates (Vogel, *Documents*, 5:9–227; Cook, *David Whitmer Interviews*).

47. Howe borrowed this from the *Palmyra Reflector*, Mar. 19, 1831, 126 (Vogel, *Documents*, 2:249–50). The paper quoted Whitmer further that the pages of the gold plates were separated down the middle, "as it were by a hinge." This appears to be garbled compared with Whitmer's later descriptions. According to M. J. Hubble, for instance, Whitmer said the leaves were "bound togather at the back by having 3 rings run through & when a page was translated it turned back on the ring" (Hubble, Account, 6–7; Vogel, *Documents*,

ADDENDA

1. The Smiths in Manchester

A senior curator at the LDS Museum of Church History and
Art in Salt Lake City suggests that the Smith neighbors gave
an unfair appraisal in light of the family's 1830 property assessment. Donald Enders's assumption that the family had made
impressive improvements to the land (Enders, "Joseph Smith
Sr. Family," 213–25) overlooks the fact that in July 1830 when
the assessment was made, the new tenant, Roswell Nichols, had
been running the farm for sixteen months. No one doubts how
industrious the Smiths were when they cleared sixty acres of
heavily wooded land early in the 1820s, building first a cabin
and then a frame house. It appears that their enthusiasm diminished when Lemuel Durfee assumed ownership of their
100-acre lot in December 1825. Over the next three and a half
years, Samuel Smith worked each year for Durfee for six months
and then hired out, along with his brothers, for the other six
months while Joseph Jr. accepted work in Colesville with Joseph
Knight. Lorenzo Saunders probably had it right in clarifying
that the Smiths were generally known to be good workers for
hire but that young Joseph was a "lazy dog," due no doubt to the
treasure seer's other priorities (Saunders interview with E. L.
Kelley, Nov. 12, 1884, 12; Vogel, *Documents*, 2:147).

2. Treasure Spirits

From early statements about Joseph Smith's treasure hunting, it

6:184; cf. interview with P. Wilhelm Poulson, *Deseret Evening News*, Aug. 16,
1878; Vogel, *Documents*, 6:38).

seems he did so by discerning the presence of treasure-guardian spirits and by communing with them. This is how Abner Cole described it in the *Palmyra Reflector*, July 7, 1830, 60, and in three issues of the paper in Feb.–Mar. 1831 (Vogel, *Documents*, 2:236–37, 245–50). Joseph Capron, Willard Chase, Abigail Harris, and Joshua and William Stafford all mention the same thing (pp. 340–41, 335–36, 355, 362–64). Isaac Hale said the reason his son-in-law said he failed to find treasure in Pennsylvania was because "the enchantment was so powerful" (p. 369). Hale's nephew Joseph Lewis said Smith was expelled from their Methodist class because members considered it "a disgrace to the church to have a practicing necromancer, a dealer in enchantments and bleeding ghosts, in it" (Lewis, "Review of Mormonism," 1; Vogel, *Documents*, 4:311). Even Oliver Cowdery acknowledged in 1835 the assumption people made about Smith performing "some art of nicromancy" (Cowdery to W. W. Phelps, Oct. 1835, 201; Vogel, *Documents*, 2:464).

3. The Hill Cumorah

The unnamed hill, later called the Hill Cumorah after the hill by that name in the Book of Mormon, was on Manchester lot 85 east of Canandaigua Road. It was owned by Randall Robinson at the time. A neighbor who called it "Golden Bible Hill" in his diary in 1831 observed that it had "a hole 30 or forty feet into the side—6 feet diameter" (James Gordon Bennett diary, Aug. 7, 1831; Arrington, "James Gordon Bennett's 1831 Report," 353–64; Vogel, *Documents*, 3:282). This was "yet partially visible" to Pomeroy Tucker in 1867 and to Edward Stevenson in 1871 (Tucker, *Origin*, 34; Stevenson, *Reminiscences*, 12–13;

Vogel, *Documents*, 3:104, 387). Some residents assumed the excavation on the northeastern side was where the Book of Mormon was found. Smith said as much to Samuel Lawrence. However, Smith later denied he had shown Lawrence "the right place" (p. 342). According to Oliver Cowdery, the plates were taken from "the west side of the hill, not far from the top" (Cowdery to W. W. Phelps, 196; Vogel, *Documents*, 2:455; Vogel, "Locations," 209–13).

4. The Three Witnesses

Martin Harris (1783–1875) was born in New York State in what is now a suburb of Saratoga Springs. His parents moved to Palmyra when he was nine. In 1808, after becoming a farmer, he married his first cousin, Lucy Harris. They eventually had three children together. Martin was already seeing visions and receiving revelations in his pre-Mormon days. For instance, in 1826 God told him he "had a work for me to do." The next year he learned from Joseph Smith that the young man had seen him in vision, which resonated with Harris (*Tiffany's Monthly*, Aug. 1859, 163, 169; Vogel, *Documents*, 2:302, 309). Harris gave Smith fifty dollars in December to help the seer move to Harmony, Pennsylvania. A few months later, Smith gave Harris a sheet of paper with examples of symbols copied from the golden plates. Harris took the paper to some east-coast scholars to study (pp. 379–83) and then returned in April 1828 to be Smith's scribe, fully convinced of the prophet's claims. Unfortunately, Harris soon lost the dictation manuscript; his wife probably destroyed it. Despite his negligence, he was honored by being visited by an angel holding the golden plates, Harris one of the three primary witnesses to this miracle. Two months later Harris mortgaged his farm to finance the Book of Mormon's printing. In 1836 he married a young Mormon who was Brigham Young's niece. A year later Harris was excommunicated, and Caroline, despite their religious differences, remained with her husband for twenty years before leaving him to remarry in Utah. Martin affiliated with various Mormon factions in Kirtland and served as the temple caretaker until he followed his former wife's lead and moved to Utah in 1870. He died in the Logan area a few years after being rebaptized (James, *The Man Who Knew*, 95–169; Cook, *Revelations*, 9; Anderson, *Investigating*, 95–105; Walker, "Martin Harris," 29–43).

Regarding his visionary tendency, John A. Clark said Harris "had always been a firm believer in dreams, and visions, and supernatural appearances, such as apparitions and ghosts." He told someone in Palmyra that he had "met the Lord Jesus Christ, who walked along by the side of him in the shape of a deer for two or three miles, talking with him as familiarly as one man talks with another" (Clark to Dear Brethren, *Episcopal Recorder*, Sept. 5, 12, 1840, 94, 99; Vogel, *Documents*, 2:262, 271). Others heard him say he had seen "the devil, in all his hideousness, on the road" (Albert Chandler to William Lynn, Dec. 22, 1898, 49; Vogel, *Documents*, 3:223), looking like "a greyhound as big as a horse, without any tail, walking upright on his hind legs" until it "walked up the hill and disappeared" (Stephen S. Harding to Thomas Gregg, Feb. 1890, 45; Vogel, *Documents*, 3:160).[48]

---

48. Jesse Townsend put it bluntly when he said Harris was a "visionary

Oliver Cowdery (1806–50) was born in Wells, Vermont, less than fifty miles northeast of where Harris was born. When Cowdery gained young adulthood, he found work peddling books in New York and Canada (*Cleveland Herald*, Nov. 25, 1830) and worked at a store owned by his brother Warren in Lyons, New York. In 1828 a teaching position opened in nearby Manchester. Cowdery took the job and roomed with the Smiths, where he learned about the Book of Mormon dictation underway in Pennsylvania. While there, Cowdery said he had a vision in which "the Lord appeared" to him to show him the gold plates. According to Mother Smith, he became "so completely absorbed in the subject of the [ancient] Record, that it seemed impossible for him to think or converse about anything else" (Smith, History, 1832, 6; Smith, *Biographical Sketches*, 129; Vogel, *Documents*, 1:31, 376). At the close of the school term, he accompanied Joseph Smith's brother Samuel to Pennsylvania to meet the prophet, ending up staying on to become Joseph's scribe. He soon saw the angel and the gold plates as one of the three special witnesses.

On April 6, 1830, Cowdery was recognized as the church's "second elder" (D&C 20:3). He was instrumental the next year in converting Kirtland's firebrand minister Sidney Rigdon. Cowdery became editor of the *Latter Day Saints' Messenger*

---

fanatic" (Tucker, *Origin*, 289; Vogel, *Documents*, 3:22). Even people who could only "speak well of him" confessed that when it came to "religious subjects [they] thought him slightly demented" (William Hyde, "Birth of Mormonism," 2; Vogel, *Documents*, 3:194–95). Several people signed a group statement in 1841 that they had "ever regarded Mr. Harris as an honest man … [of] irreproachable character" but "naturally of a superstitious turn of mind" (*Rochester Daily Democrat*, June 23, 1841, 2).

and Advocate newspaper and "assistant president" of the church in 1834, but was excommunicated four years later, in part for his criticism of Joseph Smith for his affair with the maid Fanny Alger. Cowdery began practicing law in Ohio, then in Wisconsin until he was re-baptized at the end of 1848 in Kanesville, Iowa, then fell ill and died in Richmond, Missouri (Cook, *Revelations*, 14; Anderson, *Investigating*, 37–65).

David Whitmer (1805–88) was born in Harrisburg, about 100 miles west of Philadelphia, and met Oliver Cowdery while on business in 1828. Cowdery later wrote about how he thought Joseph Smith could read his mind. A follow-up letter explained that after wearing out their welcome in Pennsylvania, Cowdery and Smith needed some place to finish the Book of Mormon dictation. Whitmer arranged with his parents in Fayette, New York, to put them up. In 1829 David was baptized. Soon thereafter he enjoyed the visionary experience that made him one of the Book of Mormon witnesses. In 1832 he was ordained as Smith's successor, and two years later he became president of the church in Missouri. He was excommunicated six years later for, among other things, criticizing Smith's handling of money in Kirtland. He moved to Richmond, Missouri, and stayed there the rest of his life running a livery stable. He also became mayor. For a short time, he led a church that included, among its members, the former LDS apostle William McLellin and Book of Mormon witness Hiram Page (Cook, *Revelations*, 24–25; Cook, *David Whitmer Interviews*, ix–xxvi).

CHAPTER 2.

THE GOLDEN BIBLE AND ITS CONTENTS.

The various verbal accounts, all contradictory, vague, and inconsistent, which were given out by the Smith family respecting
the finding of certain Gold or brazen plates,[1] will be hereafter
presented in numerous depositions which have been taken in
the neighborhood of the plot.—Since the publication of the
book they have been generally more uniform in their relations
respecting it. They say that some two years previous[2] to the
event taking place, Joseph, Jun. began his interviews with Angels, or spirits, who informed him of the wonderful plates, and
the manner and time of obtaining them. This was to be done
in the presence of his wife and first child,[3] which was to be a

---

1. Howe probably borrowed the idea of "brazen plates" from Alexander
Campbell's 1831 statement that the witnesses "handled as many of the brazen
or golden leaves as the said Smith translated" ("The Mormonites," *Millennial
Harbinger*, Feb. 1831, 87, 95). Campbell was interpreting the vague Testimony
of Eight Witnesses that presents the plates as having the "appearance of gold"
but were not necessarily actual gold.

2. Smith began talking with supernatural beings about the golden plates
four years prior to obtaining the plates in September 1827, according to his accounts. Howe probably misunderstood the reason for Smith needing to borrow
Willard Chase's seer stone in 1825 (pp. 338–39), which was for the Pennsylvania treasure hunt, not for the Book of Mormon translation.

3. Howe mixed up two details: Emma Smith accompanying her husband
to the hill and Joseph's prediction that his firstborn son would translate the
plates at two years of age (pp. 344–46). Others had heard the prophecy about

son. In the month of September, 1827, Joseph got possession
of the plates, after a considerable struggle with a spirit.[4] The
remarkable event was soon noised abroad, and the Smith family commenced making proselytes among the credulous, and
lovers of the marvellous, to the belief that Joseph had found a
record of the first settlers of America. Many profound calculations were made about the amount of their profits on the sale
of such a book. A religious speculation does not seem to have
seriously entered into their heads at that time. The plates in
the mean time were concealed from human view, the prophet
declaring that no man could look upon them and live. They at
the same time gave out that, along with the plates, was found
a huge pair of silver spectacles,[5] altogether too large for the
present race of men, but which were to be used, nevertheless,
in translating the plates.

The translation finally commenced. They were found to
contain a language not now known upon the earth, which they
termed "reformed Egyptian characters."[6] The plates, therefore,

Smith's unborn son translating the text as a child (pp. 371, 375–76, 378). The
baby died the same day it was born, on June 15, 1828; even so, the translation
had already commenced before its birth, so the claim may have had to do with
another ancient record or perhaps the sealed portion of the plates.

4. This is derived from Smith being knocked down twice by the spirit,
according to Chase (p. 340).

5. Smith used the term "spectacles" in his 1832 history. He subsequently
described them ambiguously as "two stones in silver bows" (Smith, History,
1832, 5; Vogel, *Documents*, 1:30, 64; *History of the Church*, 1:12; also p. 341,
herein). Charles Anthon was told Smith had obtained "an enormous pair of
'*gold spectacles*' [that were] ... altogether too large for the breadth of the human
face" (p. 360; *Palmyra Reflector*, June 12, July 7, 1830, 37, 60). Other sources in
Ohio must have clarified that the spectacles were silver-rimmed.

6. See Morm. 9:32.

which had been so much talked of, were found to be of no manner of use. After all, the Lord showed and communicated to him every word and letter of the Book. Instead of looking at the characters inscribed upon the plates, the prophet was obliged to resort to the old "peep stone," which he formerly used in money-digging. This he placed in a hat, or box, into which he also thrust his face. Through the stone he could then discover a single word at a time, which he repeated aloud to his amanuensis,[7] who committed it to paper, when another word would immediately appear, and thus the performance continued to the end of the book.

Another account they give of the transaction, is, that it was performed with the big spectacles before mentioned, and which were in fact, the identical *Urim and Thumim*[8] mentioned in Exodus 28–30, and were brought away from Jerusalem by the heroes of the book, handed down from one generation to another, and finally buried up in Ontario county, some fifteen centuries since, to enable Smith to translate the plates *without looking at them!*[9]

Before the work was completed, under the pretense that some persons were endeavoring to destroy the plates and the prophet, they relate that the Lord commanded them [Joseph

---

7. This description conforms to statements by Martin Harris, David Whitmer, Emma Smith, and others. See Van Wagoner and Walker, "Gift of Seeing," 48–68.

8. The word *spectacles* was gradually replaced by *Urim and Thummim*, removing the aura of magic and replacing it with a hint of biblical authority. See Lancaster, "Translation of the Book of Mormon," 97–112.

9. Isaac Hale said Smith put "the stone in his hat, and his hat over his face, while the Book of Plates were at the same time hid in the woods!" (p. 372).

and amanuensis] to depart into Pennsylvania, where they could proceed unmolested. Smith, accordingly, removed his family thither; but it appears that it was at the request of his father-in-law,[10] instead of the command of the Lord. A box, which he said contained the plates, was conveyed in a barrel of beans,[11] while on the journey. Soon after this, his father-in-law, Mr. Isaac Hale, on account of his daughter, agreed to sell Smith a part of his farm,[12] provided he would go to work and quit his impositions. He [Joseph] said he had given up his former occupation,[13] and concluded to labor for a living. But, in a few weeks Harris made his appearance[14] there, and soon after Cowdery, and Smith again commenced looking into the hat, and telling off his bible. In the mean time, Satan had made an assault upon Harris, and robbed him of one hundred and sixteen pages[15] of the bible, which had been translated. Cowdery

10. Peter Ingersoll, who helped Joseph and Emma move, said Emma's father offered to help them get established in Harmony if Joseph would discontinue treasure-seeking (p. 330).

11. Other sources corroborate the idea that the plates were transported in a barrel of beans (Pratt, *Interesting Account*, 13–14; Smith, *Biographical Sketches*, 113; Vogel, *Documents*, 1:158, 349; *Tiffany's Monthly*, Aug. 1859, 163–70).

12. On April 6, 1829, the day following Cowdery's arrival in Harmony, Isaac Hale transferred to Joseph and Emma the property they had been living on for more than a year, including a small house and thirteen acres of land (Agreement, Joseph Smith Collection, LDS Church History Library). On June 28, 1833, Smith sold the land to Joseph McKune Jr. for $300 (Susquehanna County deed books, Liber 9, 290).

13. Based on statements by Peter Ingersoll (p. 330) and Isaac Hale (p. 370).

14. Harris visited in February 1828, then acted as Smith's scribe from April 12 to about mid-June.

15. See the preface to the Book of Mormon, 1830 edition.

was the chosen scribe to complete the work;[16] after which the plates were again buried up by the command of the Lord, in a place unknown to the prophet or any other person.

The Golden Bible[17] was finally got ready for the press, and issued in the summer of 1830,[18] nearly three years from the time of its being dug up. It is a book of nearly six hundred pages, and is, unquestionably, one of the meanest in the English, or any other language. It is more devoid of interest than any we have ever seen. It must have been written by an atheist,[19] to make an experiment upon the human understanding and credulity. The author, although evidently a man of learning, studied barrenness of style and expression, without an equal. It carries condemnation on every page. The God of Heaven, that all-wise Being, could never have delivered such a farrago of nonsense to the world. But we must proceed to examine it more in detail. The title page says:—

> The Book of Mormon, an account written by the hand of Mormon, upon plates taken from the plates of Nephi;

16. Oliver Cowdery arrived on April 5, 1829, and commenced taking dictation two days later, helping Smith complete the manuscript by late June.

17. This term was used by several of Hurlbut's witnesses and by Abner Cole in the *Palmyra Reflector*, Sept. 2, 23, 1829, 2, 14.

18. The first bound volumes were ready for sale in late March 1830, the entire run of 5,000 not being finished until the following summer. See *Wayne Sentinel*, Mar. 26, 1830; Tucker, *Origin*, 53; and Vogel, *Documents*, 2:219, 3:114.

19. David Marks came to the same conclusion: "From all the circumstances, I thought it probably had been written originally by an infidel, to see how much he could impose on the credulity of men" (Marks, *Life of David Marks*, 341). More apparent is an agenda of trying to turn a tide of unbelief (Hullinger, *Joseph Smith's Response to Skepticism*).

wherefore it is an abridgment of the record of the people of Nephi; and also of the Lamanites, which are a remnant of the house of Israel, and also to Jew and Gentile; written by way of commandment, and also by the spirit of prophecy and of revelation: written, and sealed up, and hid up unto the Lord, that they might not be destroyed; to come forth by the gift and power of God, unto the interpretation thereof; sealed by the hand of Moroni, and hid up unto the Lord, to come forth in due time by the way of the Gentiles; the interpretation thereof, by the gift of God; an abridgment taken from the book of Ether.

Also, which is a record of the people of Jared, which were scattered at the time the Lord confounded the language of the people, when they were building a tower to get to Heaven, which is to show unto the remnant of the house of Israel, how great things the Lord has done for their fathers; and that they may know the covenants of the Lord, that they are not cast off forever; and also to the convincing of Jews and Gentiles, that Jesus is the Christ, the Eternal God, manifesting himself to all nations. And now if there be fault, it be the mistake of men; wherefore condemn not the things of God, that ye may be found spotless at the judgment seat of Christ. By Joseph Smith, Jun. Author and proprietor.[20]

It is necessary that the reader should constantly bear in mind, that the impostor is held out to be a very ignorant person, so much so, that he can write nothing except it be dictated to him, word by word, by the mouth of the Lord. Here then we have a specimen of a title page according to *infinite wisdom*; constituting Joseph Smith, Jun. "Author and proprietor,"

20. The final line establishing literary proprietorship was replaced beginning in 1837 with "Translated by Joseph Smith, Jun."

in order that he may have the sole *profit* of the work. Although the Mormon[s] may have a faculty of pointing out examples, and proving every thing by scripture, we think it will trouble them to find an instance where the Great Jehovah has ever sent a message to fallen man, and that in the most miraculous way; and constituted any individual its *retailer*, and sole sharer of its *profits!* But we are told that "the ways of God are past finding out," and he has therefore given to Joseph Smith a "copy right" to sell this last message, and that too from under the hand and seal of "R. R. Lansing, clerk of the Northern District of New York."[21]

But a saving clause is inserted in the title page, and several times repeated in the book. It seems that neither the Lord or Smith, were willing to avow themselves the authors of the whole fable: "and now if there be fault, it be in the mistake of men"!!! Here then we have an acknowledgment that there may be *faults*, a bundle of truths and falsehoods, sent forth to imperfect man, without a single rule being given to distinguish one from the other!!! Oh! the credulity of man!

The real author, notwithstanding his studied ignorance, was well acquainted with the classics. The names of most of his heroes have the Latin termination of *i*, such as Nephi, Lehi, and Moroni.[22] The word *Mormon*, the name given to his book, is the

---

21. Richard Ray Lansing (1789–1855) is listed in an 1817 city directory for Utica, New York, as an attorney with an office on Catherine Street and a house on Broadway.

22. A Latin name would more likely be Nephus or Nephia (without inflection). Howe was even less skilled in Old Testament Hebrew than he was in Latin, apparently being unaware that the word *nephilim* meant *giants* and *lehi*

English termination of the Greek word *"Mormoo,"*[23] which we find defined in an old, obsolete Dictionary, to mean *"bug-bear, hob-goblin, raw head, and bloody bones."* It seems, therefore, that the writer gave his book not only a very appropriate, but classical name. His experiment upon the human mind, he thought, would be more perfect, by giving it a name, in addition to its contents, which would carry upon its very face the nature of its true character—*a fiction of hob-goblins and bug-bears.*

Next comes the "Preface,"[24] signed "the Author," which shows that the Lord was willing to approve and adopt the most modern plan of making books, by inserting a title page, copy right, and a preface. The substance of the preface is, that the author had translated one hundred and sixteen pages from the plates of Lehi, written by the hand of Mormon,[25] which

---

meant *jawbone*, resulting in the biblical (and apocryphal) place names Lehi in Judges 15:9 and Nephi in 2 Maccabees 1:36.

23. The word *mormo* appears in dictionaries from the period with the definition "bugbear; false terror." Joseph Smith replied, tongue-in-cheek, that the word came from "the Egyptian, *mon*," meaning *good*, and combined with *mor* could only mean *more good* (*Times and Seasons*, May 15, 1843, 194; Joseph Smith, Journal, May 20, 1843). Walter F. Prince suggested that Mormon was a play on anti-Masonic martyr William Morgan's name (Prince, "Psychological Tests," 373–89), a conclusion similarly drawn by an anti-Mormon in 1843 when he told a missionary "he knew all about Mormonism and what it sprang from, it sprang from masonry or the death of Morgan, that Mormon was derived from the word Morgan" (Oliver B. Huntington diary, 1:12, Special Collections, Lee Library; see also *Painesville Telegraph*, Mar. 1, 1831).

24. The preface to the first edition of the Book of Mormon drew heavily on what is now LDS Doctrine and Covenants section 10, which was a May 1829 revelation regarding the loss of the translation manuscript. It was written down shortly before the typesetting began in August.

25. Evidently the lost manuscript was largely written in third-person, as

were stolen by some persons; "and being commanded by the Lord, that I should not translate the same over again, for Satan had put it into their hearts to tempt the Lord their God, by altering their words, that they did read contrary from that which I translated, and caused to be written; and if I should bring forth the same again, they would publish that which they had stolen, and Satan would stir up the hearts of this generation, that they might not receive this work; but behold the Lord said unto me, I will not suffer that Satan shall accomplish his evil design in this thing: therefore shalt thou translate from the plates of Nephi, until you come to that which ye have translated, which ye have retained, and behold ye shall publish it as the record of Nephi; and thus I will confound those who have altered my words."

The facts respecting the lost manuscript,[26] we have not been able to ascertain. They sometimes charged the wife of Harris with having burnt it;[27] but this is denied by her.[28] They were, however, taken from the possession of Harris, by a miracle wrought by Satan. The prophet has undertaken to inform the reader how the Lord got him out of this dilemma: "thou shalt translate from the plates of Nephi until thou come to that which ye have translated, which ye have retained, and behold ye shall publish it as the record of Nephi." Here the Lord, in

---

is the rest of the narrative from Mosiah to 4 Nephi, while the replacement text consisting of 1 Nephi to the Words of Mormon is in first-person.

26. For the incident involving the lost 116 pages, see *History of the Church*, 1:21; Smith, *Biographical Sketches*, 117–23; Vogel, *Documents*, 1: 71–73, 356–68.

27. For more on this, see addendum 1, "Fate of the Lost Manuscript."

28. Hurlbut interviewed her in November 1833; however, her formal affidavit failed to mention the lost manuscript.

order to counteract the works of the Devil, is represented by Smith as palming off upon the world an acknowledged false-hood,—the records of Lehi must be published as the records of Nephi. Again, how could Smith know when he came to that which he had translated, without looking at the plates, (which he could not read if he did,) for he does not pretend that there was any miracle in this operation. But who, except one fully endued with the folly and wickedness of "the author," can be-lieve for a moment, that the Lord would make known his will in such language. Again, an important record which had been made by a miracle, kept for ages by a miracle, dug from the ground by a miracle, and translated by a miracle, was *stolen* by some one, so that even a miracle could not restore it; and thus were the designs of the Lord counteracted by "Satan putting it into their hearts to tempt the Lord."

ADDENDUM

1. Fate of the Lost Manuscript

Lorenzo Saunders said that sometime before Lucy Har-ris's death in 1836, she told him she had, in fact, burned the manuscript (Saunders interview with Kelley, Nov. 12, 1884, 4). James H. Reeve wrote a short biographical sketch of Mar-tin Harris for the newspaper in 1872 and explained that the "farce became so obnoxious to the good wife, that finally she determined to end it, and, accordingly, one night when Mar-tin was dreaming that 'he dwelt in marble halls,' Aunt Dolly [Lucy] rose quietly and taking the roll of manuscript, went to the fire-place and laid it between the charred logs, and ere the morning came, it had ascended in smoke through the throat of the great chimney" (*Palmyra Courier*, May 31, 1872). At first Martin thought his wife had given the manuscript to individuals who would ridicule it (Clark to "Dear Brethren," *Episcopal Recorder*, Sept. 5, 1840, 94), but finally concluded that she had burned it (Pilkington, "Dying Testimony of Martin Harris"). Her interest was no doubt primarily in curtailing her husband's financial entanglement in the project.

CHAPTER 3.

THE SAME SUBJECT CONTINUED.

"The Book of Mormon," is divided into a number of books, each one purporting to have been written by different individuals upon plates of brass, so far as the history of Lehi, the founder of the vast settlements which were situated on the isthmus of Darien,[1] were concerned; and upon plates of gold, so far as it relates to one Jared and his posterity, who were not confounded at the destruction of Babel, but were miraculously navigated by the hand of the Lord across the ocean. The history of Lehi and his posterity, commences in the reign of Zedekiah, King of Judah, six hundred years before the Christian era, and ends about four hundred years afterwards, which concludes the history, or fiction. The whole work is written in a miserable attempt to imitate the style of king James the first, and the sameness is such, and the tautology of phrases from the beginning to the end of the work, that no one can be left in doubt in identifying the whole with one individual author.[2] We

---

1. Like Alexander Campbell, Howe assumed that the "narrow neck of land" mentioned in the Book of Mormon was the Isthmus of Darien, later renamed the Isthmus of Panama (*Millennial Harbinger*, Feb. 1831, 94).

2. In imitating Elizabethan style, the Book of Mormon was at times noticeably awkward, as in Mosiah 4: 24–25: "And again, I say unto the poor, ye that have not and yet hath sufficient, that ye remain from day to day; I mean all you that deny the beggar, because ye have not; I would that ye say in your

are not aware that the style of king James is better calculated to reveal the will of Heaven, than is the modern and more refined language; but is a strong evidence against the work now under our consideration. If God chose to reveal himself, it would be reasonable to expect that it would be done definitely, and in such language as could be clearly understood by all; and why this long circumlocution of history? it has nothing to do with salvation. Christ, nor the inspired writers of the new testament, furnish no such example; the bare facts of the plan of redemption is set before us, and a few self evident rules to govern our moral conduct.

The first book is entitled "the book of Nephi," and commences its narrative with the departure of Lehi from Jerusalem. He had four sons, Laman, Lemuel, Sam, and Nephi; the last of whom is the principal hero in the present book, and the historian. He is a scholar, an engraver, and a worker of metals; for he says: "Behold I make an abridgment of the record of my father, upon plates of brass,[3] which I have made with mine own hands; wherefore, after that I have abridged the record of my father, then will I make an account of mine own life." Lehi

hearts, that I give not because I have not; but if I had, I would give." Alexander Campbell detected what he called the "uniformity" of style and "Smithisms," showing the book was "evidently written by one set of fingers" (*Millennial Harbinger*, Feb. 1831, 93). Mormons responded that the failings were due to the human limitations of the translator. See, e.g., Roberts, *Defense of the Faith and the Saints*, 1:278, 307.

3. The identification of brass was Howe's interpolation. It was an honest one since only brass plates are mentioned in the Book of Mormon, outside of the artifact said to have been left by a lost civilization, the Jaredites. The only other references to gold in the Book of Mormon have to do with excessive wealth in the form of jewelry and money.

dreams marvelous dreams previous to his departure from Jerusalem, and sees wonderful visions. He goes about prophesying of the great calamities that await the Jews, and warns them to flee from the wrath to come. The people become vindictive at his clamor, and threaten his destruction.

To rescue Lehi, and to bring about wonderful events, God warns him to flee into the wilderness, and leave all his great possessions, his gold and his silver, and take nothing with him but his family, his tents, and provisions.[4] A miserable condition for the wilderness indeed; no clothing, no weapons, nor tools to make them with.

The command is obeyed, and he travels until he arrives on the borders of the Red sea. The three elder brothers become disaffected, probably from their adversity and privations, and accuse the father with being visionary, &c. Nephi represents himself as being a particular favorite with the Lord, (or his narrator does for him) for he says: "And it came to pass that I, Nephi, being exceeding young, nevertheless being large in stature, and also having great desires to know the mysteries of God," &c. God blesses him, and makes a covenant with him, and promises him a choice land, which is above all others.—*p.* 9.[5] Nephi is commanded by his father, together with his three brothers, to go back to Jerusalem, to the house of one Laban, who has in his possession a record of the Jews, engraven on plates of brass, as he is informed by the Lord in

---

4. Even though Lehi departs with "nothing … save it were his family, and provisions, and tents" (1 Ne. 2:4), he and his family did take weapons (16:18, 21).

5. The original Book of Mormon lacked versification. This citation would today (since 1879) be given as 1 Ne. 3:20.

a dream; and that it likewise contained the genealogy of his ancestors. Nephi is ready to obey, and by some little persuasion, the four brothers embark for the plates at Jerusalem. Laban, who has them in possession, refuses to give the plates to the embassadors. But Nephi was not to be foiled. Two unsuccessful attempts are made, and, the third time, Nephi finds Laban drunk within the walls of the city, and says: "And I, Nephi, beheld his sword, and I drew it forth from the sheath *thereof,* and the hilt *thereof* was of pure gold, and the workmanship *thereof* was exceeding fine; and I saw the blade *thereof* was of most precious steel." *p.* 12.

This is the earliest account of steel to be found in history. Alexander the Great, who lived about three hundred years after the period here spoken of, employed iron for points to his implements of war, as Josephus[6] tells us; and the same author says, that he complained that his weapons were so easily blunted; now, if steel had been in use, either at Rome, Jerusalem, or Damascus, at the time here spoken of, in Alexander's time it would have been common, and he would have used it for his weapons instead of iron. Damascus was once famous for manufacturing swords, but it was long after the Christian era. A coarse kind of steel, or iron carbonated, was used in the days of Julius Caesar, about one hundred years before Christ.

The covenant with Nephi gives him a choice land. And again he says that his father has obtained a promise from the Lord that he should have a choice land, *p.* 14. Whether these are separate lands, we are left to conjecture. If they are the

---

6. Josephus discussed the Jewish military leader Alexander Janneus, not Alexander the Great. See *Ant.* XIII, xii, 5.

same, one of the promises is gratuitous; because when the Lord covenanted with Abraham, he promised him the land of Canaan, which should be inherited by his posterity forever. It is true, the covenant was renewed with Isaac; but he was the rightful heir. If the Lord had have covenanted with Abraham, and with Isaac, for a land, we should naturally infer that they were different countries, especially if the covenant had been made with Isaac first. Nephi says the promise of the choice land, is to him, exclusively, as can be seen on page 9; consequently each have a seperate land. But the sequel of the fiction informs us, that they all embark into one ship,—land on this side of the Atlantic, and dwell together until Lehi dies.

Nephi says, he drew forth the sword of Laban, and cut his head off, which enabled him afterwards to obtain the plates by false pretences and deception. Thus we see the author would have us believe, that the Lord sometimes accomplishes his designs by murder and lying.

Lehi receives the plates from his sons,—examines them, and finds to his great satisfaction, that he is a descendant from Joseph, the son of Jacob. "And now, when my father saw all these things, he was filled with the spirit, and began to prophecy concerning his seed; that these plates of brass should go forth unto all nations, kindreds, tongues and people, which were of his seed. Wherefore, he said that these plates of brass should never perish, neither shall they be dimmed any more by time." *p*. 15.

The above plates have not been found; if they have, we have not been furnished with a translation.

Nephi, and his brethren, are again sent back to Jerusalem, to bring with them into the wilderness, a man by the name of

Ishmael, and his family, which consists of daughters and sons
enough, to furnish each family with husbands and wives. They
all arrive in the wilderness, and very soon a quarrel ensues between the different individuals of the families, which Nephi
settles in a most masterly manner; after which, the males of
both families take wives, with which the provident author has
kindly provided them.

The three next pages, to wit: 18, 19, and 20, are taken up
in relating a marvelous dream, or vision, in which Laman and
Lemuel are represented as being finally apostates, and would
be cut off.[7]

Nephi informs us, that he is at that time employed in en-
graving, or writing, on the plates, which he now names after
himself; and whether the plates of Laban are included, we are
not told, nor are we informed how they were disposed of. The
plates, hereafter, are called the plates of Nephi, *p.* 21.

A little further, on the same page, he says he has a commandment from the Lord, to make plates for the special
purpose of making a record of his own ministry, and of his
own people.

Here our hero introduces himself as a minister, and as having the charge of a people—he is in the wilderness destitute
of any thing, nothing but tents and provisions, every thing was
left behind, gold, silver, no metals or tools as a matter of course,
but the command to make his plates is obeyed. We shall be
compelled to institute a chapter of miracles in order to account

---

7. If Joseph Smith's mother remembered correctly, her husband had the
same dream years before Joseph Jr. dictated it as part of the Book of Mormon.
See 1 Ne. 8; Smith, *Biographical Sketches*, 58–59; Vogel, *Documents*, 1:256–59.

for the manner of making brass plates in the wilderness,[8] without tools or metals, and likewise to satisfy our readers upon many other points in our review. Miracles will account for any thing, however ridiculous, whenever our minds preponderate in favor of the subject to which the story may be attached. Any thing, however preposterous and false it may be, if believed to be of divine origin, needs no evidence, because nothing is impossible with Deity.

Lehi comes out with a marvelous prophecy, considering the period in which it is made; not so much on account of the prophecy as the language, in which he uses to express it. After the doctrine of the fall is explained, he speaks of the Messiah, and calls John by name, and quotes the words from Isaiah, or Matthew's gospel: "Prepare ye the way of the Lord: make his paths straight;" and continues, "for there standeth one among you, whom ye know not; and he is mightier than I, whose shoes' latchet I am not worthy to unloose."—John 1. 26–27.[9] Here is another miracle in choosing the exact language of King James' translation, more than two thousand years before it was arranged, and six hundred before the sentiment was uttered. The plan of redemption is explained at the same time, and the only way of salvation proclaimed; consequently the law was abrogated at that time, and the Nephites were christians. The prophets of the old testament, doubtless, had very clear views of the promised Messiah, and of the atonement

---

8. Despite Howe's objections, Nephi is said to have constructed a "bellows wherewith to blow fire" and smelt ore to make tools (1 Ne. 17:9, 11; 18:25).

9. Cf. 1 Ne. 10:8.

through his blood. But that they preached the law, and felt themselves bound by it, we never entertained a doubt. In the wise dispensations of God, man was not to avail himself of the redeeming doctrines of the gospel, until the time was fully come, when Christ was to appear to fulfill the law, and offer mercy through grace. Christ must appear on earth—die, and be raised from the dead, before all was fulfilled, as the sacred writers understood it, and taught the disciples, and the world of mankind. If it were possible for the plan of redemption to have been unfolded, without the actual appearance of Christ in the flesh, why did not the patriarchs with whom God made his covenants, and his promises, preach redemption through the atonement, instead of sacrifices and ceremonies? But we are informed by this same prophet Lehi, that "all mankind was in a lost, and in a fallen state; and ever would be, save they should rely on this Redeemer." *p.* 22. From the last paragraph, the author views the matter in the same light with us, that is, that the Christian religion was revealed and made known to the Nephites, six hundred years before the advent of Jesus Christ. Lehi speaks by the power of the Holy Ghost, which power he received by faith on the son of God. "And the son of God was the Messiah." Let us compare the above sentiments with the declarations and views of the inspired writers of the New Testament. "But when the comforter is come, whom I will send unto you from the father," &c. John 15.26. From this we should infer, that the Holy Ghost was yet in anticipation, because he is promised; and to confirm our view of this subject, we will cite a few other passages. "It is expedient for you that I go away; for if I go not away the comforter will not come unto you," John 14.7. "And when he is come, he will reprove the world of sin, and of righteousness, and of judgment." John 16.8. "But ye shall receive, after that the Holy Ghost has come upon you," Acts 1.8. In the second chapter of the Acts, we find all the above promises fulfilled.

Lehi continues his preaching, speaks of John and of the Virgin Mary, and calls her the "mother of God," and declares the way to salvation, by Jesus Christ, through faith and repentance, *p. 25*.[10] All the prophets of old, were far behind our Lehi, and they prophecied falsely too, if our book of Mormon is true, according to our apprehension of the doctrines which they taught. If any one can reconcile the contradictions and incongruities between the sacred writings and Lehi's prophecies, we should be gratified to hear it, and will be among the first to acknowledge our misconceptions and error. We are among the last who would be willing to villify, and ridicule, any thing that is counted sacred, without the best evidence of its falsehood and imposition. We consider, and believe, the prophecies and doctrines of the Bible of divine origin, and any thing which contravenes its precepts, or its revelations, will be regarded by us as false.

Our hero, Nephi, next presents himself in the drama, as a dreamer and a prophet, and is more explicit as to particular incidents than his father. In his vision, he is made acquainted with all the particulars of our Savior's birth and life, to his

---

10. This reference to the "mother of God" (now 1 Ne. 11:18) was changed in the 1837 edition to read "mother of the son of God," although the original language was in keeping with the book's overall modalistic theology. See Vogel, "Earliest Mormon Concept of God," in Bergera, *Line Upon Line*, 17–33.

baptism, which he witnesses, and sees the Holy Ghost descend in the form of a dove, and abide upon him. It is worthy of remark, that no circumstance is mentioned by Nephi, in relation to the life and ministry of our Savior, only what can be found in the New Testament. Very little is said by the evangelists of Jesus Christ, between the time of his birth and his entering upon the ministry. But we might expect some little incidents from such a revelation as the book of Mormon, which would throw some light upon that interesting subject, which is not to be found in the New Testament. It furnishes to us good evidence that the author was guided by the new Testament, when his low and licentious imagination conceived, and brought to light the "Book of Mormon." He could not, nor dared not, fabricate any thing, for fear of detection, which could not be found in the historical part of the sacred writings. But upon any thing which pertains to spiritual affairs, and is not susceptible of contradiction, only through the medium of reason, every license is taken by our author.

Nephi's vision gives us a poor account of the corruptions of the Roman church, showing that the author understood very little of church History.[11] The name of Jesus Christ is mentioned on page 28,[12] and of John, the apostle, page 35. Nephi's vision takes up about ten pages, from page 25, and gives, as his

---

11. Howe refers to Nephi's vision of the "great and abominable church" (1 Ne. 13–14), which itself draws on Revelation 17. The dislike of Catholics at the time supported an American view of the "great whore" of the Apocalypse as being the Roman church, as in the report of the *New York Telescope* on Mar. 12, 1825: "Our clergy call the church of Rome 'Mystery, Babylon the Great, the mother of harlots and abominations of the earth.'"

12. 1 Ne. 12:18. The appellation "Jesus Christ" was changed in the second

own views, a cursory account of the popular doctrines which have been agitated since the Reformation. To give credit to the pretence, that Nephi, living six hundred years before the christian era, could, or would, have had the name of Jesus and John revealed in preference to any other prophet, is repugnant to common sense, and in direct violence to the universal belief of those who have ever been distinguished for piety, and a critical knowledge of the holy Bible. Besides, we cannot reconcile a view of revealed truth, with a disquisition on Church schisms, such as we find in Nephi's vision. If the Book of Mormon is a revealed truth from God, we are compelled, irresistibly, to conclude, that Paul was mistaken when he said the twelve apostles of the Lamb, developed certain secrets which were hid from ages and generations, and were ordained before the world to their glory, that they should have the honor of announcing them. But our author pretends that Nephi, together with sundry other prophets which he has created, had the whole christian system developed to them, many centuries before the twelve apostles, of which Paul speaks, had the honor of announcing it, and preached it to a set of Jews, who had been miraculously landed on, or near the Isthmus of Darien. Not only this, if we are to take the brass plate revelation for sacred truth, we must infer that there has been a great deficiency in the record of our Savior's mission, or that he did not exhibit his truths while here, as fully, and as clearly as he did to these Nephites, through their prophets; and consequently left the

---

edition to "Messiah" to avoid contradicting Nephi's brother Jacob when he hears the name for the first time from an angel (2 Ne. 10:3).

world in darkness, to grope their way in superstition and ignorance, until the mineral-rod necromancy of Joseph Smith,
Jun. searching after Robert Kidd's money, which was buried
in Manchester, Ontario county, New York, found the plates of
Nephi, which had been buried there one thousand four hundred and twenty-eight years. How long he kept them, we are
not informed; but they were taken from him, and hid up again
by the Lord, so that no divination, nor legerdemain, will enable
him to find them.

"And it came to pass," says Nephi, "that the voice of the
Lord spake unto my father, and commanded him, that on the
morrow he should take his journey into the wilderness. And it
came to pass, that as my father arose in the morning, and went
forth to the tent door, to his great astonishment he beheld upon
the ground, a round ball of curious workmanship; and it was of
fine brass. And within the ball were two spindles, and the one
pointed the way whither we should go into the wilderness."
Which way the other pointed, we are not told, but probably
the way they should not go. If this ball was a compass,[13] as we
are hereafter told by the author, many improvements have been
made upon that instrument, except in the construction of the
negative spindle, since that time. But what is most ridiculous,
is, that it was a fine brass ball, and yet the spindles could be
seen to traverse in the inside of it. Perhaps Lehi had a stone
which favored his vision, and enabled him to look into opaque
bodies as well as into futurity.

The revealing stone, and the stone spectacles, will hereafter

---

13. It was not a compass in the normal sense because it operated by magic
(1 Ne. 16:9–10; 18:12).

be described, which will account for many wonderful things, without searching into the chapter of miracles.

From page 39 to 42,[14] is principally taken up in giving an account of eight year's travels, following the direction of one of the spindles through the wilderness. It traversed eastwardly and southeastwardly, bringing them all safely on the borders of the Red sea, with the exception of Ishmael, who dies in the mean time.

Nephi is now commanded by the Lord, to repair to the top of a mountain, where he sees a vision, in which he is informed that he must build a ship, and where he can find ore from which to manufacture tools. We are now presented with our hero in a new character,—that of a ship-builder. So that in his youth he is a scholar, a historian, a worker of metals, a ship-carpenter, a prophet and a priest. It now seems that ore and tools are necessary, in order to construct a ship; but to make plates of brass, neither ore, tools, nor metals were essential. Six pages are next occupied in giving an account of quarrels between Nephi and his brethren. But Nephi, in the mean time, builds a ship contrary to the opinions of his brothers, and the rational inference is, that he makes his own tools out of ore, and builds the ship without assistance from any one. It requires some little stretch of credulity, to believe that Nephi done all the above work, such as making iron from ore, and converting it into steel, and then making the tools necessary to build a ship, without tools with which to do it. The manner in which he built the ship, he accounts for in the following

---

14. 1 Ne. 16:11–17:5.

language:—"Now I, Nephi, did not work the timbers after the manner of men, &c. but I did build it after the manner which the Lord did teach me," *p*. 47.—How long he was in accomplishing this great work, we cannot learn; but if all was done by a miracle, as the author intimates, we can see no necessity for any interference on the part of Nephi, but give to him the glory who accomplished the work.

The patriarch Noah, had special directions for building the ark, the kind of wood, &c., and he built it after the model given him, and he had many years in which to accomplish it. And we have good reason to believe that the work was done in the same manner as other ships were built, and that he employed workmen to aid him in it. Nephi arrogates to himself a great preference with the Lord, over the patriarch Noah.

Lehi, and all his host, after the ship is completed by our hero, go on board, and immediately embark for the promised land. But the wicked dispositions of Laman and Lemuel would not allow the crew to remain in peace. A mutiny takes place on ship board, and our hero and admiral was taken, and bound so tight that he could not move. But the Lord is represented as being on Nephi's side, and a remedy was at hand at once. The famous brass ball-compass ceased to traverse! "and they knew not whither to steer the ship, insomuch, that there arose a great storm, yea, a great and terrible tempest." We will leave the reader to draw the inference, whether the terrible storm arose from the abuse of Nephi, or, because the compass would not traverse! *p*. 48.

If the bare statement of a succession of miracles, such as have been recorded thus far in the Book of Mormon, unaccompanied by any testimony, or carrying with it any plausible probability of truth, entitles the work to the credit of Divine authenticity, we have already failed in our attempt to prove it a fiction. But we apprehend our readers will not receive the ridiculous story of Nephi, although it be clothed in the mantle of sanctity, without first instituting a critical enquiry, and comparing the probabilities with the sacred truths of Holy Writ.

We might have mentioned, that Lehi had two sons born in the wilderness, after he departed from Jerusalem. The eldest was called Jacob, and the other Joseph; these two sons are somewhat important personages in the como-tragedy hereafter.

To return to our crew. Finding the compass would not traverse, they get frightened, and set Nephi at liberty; the magnet again operates—the seas become calm—and every thing quiet. Whether the ship had sails, or was propelled by oars, or by a current, or by the will, or by the power of the spindle, we cannot inform our readers, for it is not stated. But Nephi, or the author, says that they all landed safely on the promised land.

"And it came to pass, that we did find upon the land of promise, as we journeyed in the wilderness, that there were beasts in the forest of every kind, both the cow and the *ox*." *p.* 48. More miracles to substantiate the divine authenticity of the Book of Mormon. We had supposed that oxen were the result of a surgical operation upon bulls, changing their natures, in order to render them docile and useful to man; and nothing can be more ludicrous than to suppose the matchless power of the Almighty, had interfered with these animals in the wilderness, and caused the transformation of them as represented.[15]

---

15. Noah Webster defined buffalo as "a kind of wild ox or bull."

Nephi is again commanded to manufacture more plates to engrave upon, and in this land of promise materials are plenty.[16] The art of making them without materials is probably lost. Gold, silver and copper ores are found, and no others mentioned, but brass plates can be made, doubtless, by Nephi out of gold, silver, and copper ores, as well as out of nothing, as he must have done before he navigated the tribe across the ocean. *p.* 50.[17]

We are next presented with a recapitulation of the prophecies of Lehi, in relation to the coming of our Savior, together with a fictitious quotation from prophecies conceived by our author, and brought forth in his own miserable, barren style. "To be lifted up acccording to the words of Zenoch, and to be crucified, according to the words of Neum, and to be buried in a sepulchre, and according to the words of Zenos, which he spake concerning the three days of darkness." Here we are presented with three new prophets, which were known to our hero, prophecying of the most important events which have ever transpired, or ever will. The last of which uttered a falsehood, because he speaks of three days of darkness at the time of the crucifixion, *p.* 51. The evangelists in the New Testament, state, that there was a darkness over the land from the sixth to the ninth hour, varying from three hours to three days.[18]

---

16. Howe assumed wrongly that the first plates were made in the Old World, whereas the Book of Mormon has both sets manufactured in the New World (1 Ne. 19:1–6; 2 Ne. 5:29–33).

17. 1 Ne. 18:25. Even allowing for Howe's assumption that the plates were made of brass, Nephi states that the land of promise was blessed with "all manner of ore."

18. The contradiction Howe detects between Zenos's prediction of "three days" (1 Ne. 19:10) and the Gospel account of three hours (Matt. 27:45) may be

Profane history, likewise, corroborates the statement made by the evangelists. If such prophets as Zenoch, Neum, and Zenos, had ever existed, would not there have been some trace left, or allusion made, either in sacred or profane writing respecting them? The known characteristic of the Jews, from time immemorial, is conclusive evidence that these prophets are fictitious characters. The Jews have ever been distinguished for their tenacity to their traditions and religion. They have ever held their prophets in the highest veneration, particularly those who spake clearly of the coming Messiah.

We are now relieved by the author, from the coarse style in which the book is written, by the introduction of the 48th and 49th chapters of Isaiah, in the approved translation. To contrast the sublime style of the inspired writer, with the insipid and tasteless diction of the author of the Book of Mormon, requires more ability than we possess.

---

explained by the qualification that the prolonged sign was only for "those who should inhabit the isles of the sea." The Book of Mormon places Lehi's family, literally or poetically, on an "isle of the sea" (2 Ne. 10:20).

CHAPTER 4.

The marvelous always has something about it, to fascinate, however coarsely it may be clad; and fiction has its charms, and when combined and presented to the mind in the mantle of inspiration, it is not singular that the credulous and unsuspecting should be captivated. This propensity for the marvelous in the human mind, is constantly leading them into error and delusion, and to it the fabricators of the new revelation are indebted for their success.

Our moral faculties are always improved by embracing simple philosophical truths, and, in proportion as we reject them, we become depraved, and less capable of discriminating between falsehood and error. He who embraces falsehood and error, will sink deeper and deeper in the vortex of folly and madness; wild vagaries, apparitions, intercourse with the spirits of other worlds,[1] and ten thousand other follies, will dance through his imagination in shapeless confusion. Realities are no longer a subject worthy his attention, but he is guided by the whims of his imagination, which he believes to be the breathing of the Holy spirit, and an internal revelation, and thus we find him enveloped in the fatal cords of fanaticism.

---

1. This may be an allusion to eighteenth-century Swedish mystic Emanuel Swedenborg (1688–1772) who said he had spoken to spirits of people living on the moon and other planets.

Our object is to unvail the deceptions, and impositions, which are now practiced by the leaders of a sect which are called *Mormons*, or, as they have recently christened themselves, *"Latter day Saints;"*[2] and so place the Book, or Golden Bible, as it has been called, before the public, as to prevent any further deception. The subject of eternity is of infinite moment to all; and each individual has sufficient capacity to embrace truth instead of error, provided the due exercises of the faculties are instituted. Then, when any subject is presented to us in the garb of religion, we ought carefully to investigate it, and compare it with the standard which should be our rule of faith and practice. The divine authenticity of the Book of Mormon, is the question now before us. Is it presented to us, accompanied with such conclusive testimony as entitles it to our implicit credit, and such as we should be willing to risk our eternal all upon? If any doubts hang over the subject, it is reasonable that a scrupulous search, and a critical enquiry be instituted by us.

Permit us to examine in what way the two above named chapters of Isaiah, became introduced in the modern version. The translation of King James is the one used. We believe the translation to be a correct one, and that the translators were guided by truth as far as human frailty would permit; but, at the same time, they were governed by the then existing rules of the English language, which now vary considerably. The rules which governed at the time the translation was made, are so far lost, that we presume a new one made at this period under

---

2. The name was changed in May 1834 from the "Church of Christ" to the "Church of the Latter Day Saints." The current longer name was adopted another four years after that. *History of the Church*, 2:63; D&C 115:4.

our present rules, would vary the diction and phraseology very considerably, but not the true sense. We suppose that the object of the sacred writings, is to convey a definite meaning to the reader in his own language, without regard to words or phrases, and, consequently, if we were to receive a translation from the hand of the Lord at this time, we might rationally expect that it would appear in our own language, and not in that of King James' time, any more than in that of William the Conqueror. It is a remarkable coincidence that the author of our book should be able to give us an exact copy of those two chapters, reading them in a stone placed in a hat![3] We are truly inclined to accuse him of plagiarism, not only from the above circumstance, but because he attributes the authorship of the whole book to the Lord; and we cannot see why, if he [God] could dictate such grand and lofty sentiments to Isaiah, together with the unparalleled [other biblical] figures, he could not have maintained a style and diction through the rest of the Book of Mormon, that would have appeared decent, and been somewhat in the language of the present time. Again we remark, that the beginning of the quotation commences with the chapter, and closes with the next chapter, which is, of itself, evidence that it was copied, because the division of the prophecies into chapters is both modern and arbitrary—the

---

3. Howe is referring to 1 Ne. 20–21, which was an altered version of Isa. 48–49. Smith polished the wording in subsequent editions so that by 1840 he had Isaiah explicitly addressing baptism (20:1). Those who have studied such passages have not been able to detect improvements on the early Hebrew or Greek. See Walters, "Use of the Old Testament in the Book of Mormon," 50, 52; Wright, "'In Plain Terms That We May Understand.'"

original furnishes no such arrangement. Then it would have been natural for an ignorant plagiarist to have blundered into that method of copying. If the two chapters had have been inserted in the author's language, at the same time preserving the sense strictly, there would have been more plausibility, and the deception not so easily detected. But the ignorance of the author led him to suppose that the translation was the only one that could be made, and that the division into chapters was done by Isaiah himself.

Nephi is represented as a wonderful prophet. He could prophecy what would be said, in the precise sentences, six hundred years afterwards, and so arrange and punctuate it, that a translator, by means of a stone which was prepared for that purpose, could, two thousand four hundred and thirty years afterwards, copy sentences which had been arranged about two hundred and twenty years previously, by a set of learned divines, assembled under the authority of James the first, king of England. There are no prophecies in the old Testament which compares with this; we deem it beyond the marvelous. In our examination of the prophecies in the old Testament, (which we suppose is not tantamount authority to the Golden Bible with a "latter day saint,") we are unable to find even an attempt made by the inspired authors to prophecy of the doctrines of our Saviour, in the words in which he would utter them. Besides, the evangelists themselves, who heard the wonderful sayings as he spake them, choose their own manner of expressing it. Each had his own peculiar style, and penned the sentiments in their own way. Our Savior uttered many prophecies, but in all he said he never attempted to represent the diction and phraseology which would be used on a future occasion. But our hero, Nephi, is made by the author to far surpass the Savior.

We are next presented with something like a sermon, in which the prophecies of the old Testament, (which, we presume, the author had by him,) is the matter of discussion and explanation. The Arian doctrine is denied,[4] of which he, Nephi, has a prophetic knowledge, and instructs his readers after the popular doctrines of the present day. No particular denomination is sustained, but partakes of many, from which we suppose they had no articles of faith yet established; but in the sequel they become Anabaptists.[5] And thus ends the first "Book of Nephi."

The second Book of Nephi is introduced to the reader, by an attempt at a christian sermon, by Lehi, (Nephi having retired behind the curtain,) and in the course of his remarks, he makes several patriarchal promises to his sons; all conditioned upon a faithful and implicit obedience to the requirements and commands of Nephi. Lehi preaches repentance and remission of sins. He expounds the law as it relates to original sin, and

---

4. Arius was condemned by the Council of Constantinople for suggesting that Jesus was separate from and subordinate to the Father. In contrast, Nephi saw Jesus as the "condescension of God" and "the virgin" as "the mother of God, after the manner of the flesh" (1 Ne. 11:16, 18).

5. Anabaptists arose from the so-called Radical Reformation, contemporary with the Protestant Reformation, spawning the Amish, Hutterites, Mennonites, Quakers, and other groups in Europe and America. Howe's observation is that in repudiating infant baptism and predestination, the Nephites in the later part of the Book of Mormon paralleled the Anabaptists. It is said that Joseph Smith Sr. may have belonged to an independent Anabaptist group. See Williams, *Radical Reformation*; Vogel, *Documents*, 1:636–37.

settles many of the leading points which are subjects of dis-
putation between different denominations at the present day,
p. 72.[6] We will again, for the benefit of our readers, quote a
remarkable passage, which the bold blasphemer has presumed
to insert in his book, as matter revealed to him, and as having
been penned by Nephi, nearly six hundred years before it actually was!!! "And by the law no flesh is justified. Behold, he
offereth himself a sacrifice for sin." "Which layeth down his
life according to the flesh, and taketh it again by the power
of the spirit, that he may bring to pass the resurrection of the
dead, being the first that should rise." *p.* 63.[7]—

There are a variety of sermons in this discourse taken from
the new Testament, somewhat garbled and transposed, and so
varied as to suit the views of the writer, in his fictitious tenets.

Lehi next addresses his son Joseph, who was born in the
wilderness, and reminds him of the commandments of the
Holy one of Israel, and intimates that he is born for some great
purpose. "For behold thou art the fruit of my loins; and I am
a descendant of Joseph, which was carried captive into Egypt.
And great was the covenants of the Lord which he made unto
Joseph; wherefore Joseph truly saw our day. And he obtained
a promise of the Lord, that out of the fruit of his loin the
Lord God would raise up a righteous branch unto the house
of Israel. Not the Messiah," &c. He then goes on to explain
the covenant, by representing himself, and his posterity, as the
branch meant, to which the Messiah should be made manifest

6. Howe's reference is slightly off. Lehi's sermon concluded on page 69.
7. See Acts 13:39; Rom. 3:20; 1 Cor. 15:20; 2 Ne. 2:5, 7, 8.

in the latter days. We next have a question from the prophecies of Joseph. "Yea Joseph truly said, thus saith the Lord unto me: a choice seer will I raise up out of the fruit of thy loins. And unto him will I give a commandment," *p.* 66. "And thus prophecied Joseph, saying:—Behold that Seer will the Lord bless; and they that seek to destroy him shall be confounded. Behold I am sure of the fulfilling of this promise. *And his name shall be called after me, and it shall be after the name of his father. Yea, thus prophecied Joseph.*"—*p.* 67. Here is the prophecy which settles the matter as to Joseph Smith, Jun. He is, doubtless, from the lineage of Lehi, the father of the Nephites and the Lamanites, and a descendant of Joseph.[8]—The Lamanites were all cursed by the Lord, and all marked and transformed into Indians. A curse was pronounced upon all who should ever mix with them. The Nephites warred with each other until they exterminated the whole race except three, who were immortalized. Whether the object of their immortality was to perpetuate the notable branch of Joseph by crim[inal] con[version][9] we are left to conjecture.—We are not aware that [biblical] Joseph ever uttered the above remarkable sentences. He held the highest standing among his brethren, and if he had ever made them, we have no doubt full credit would have been given to his sayings, and they would have been preserved by the Jews, and handed down to the latest posterity among them, well authenticated. But, the fact is, the whole is a base forgery, and he who attempted to

---

8. Howe misreads 2 Ne. 3:7, which says that a modern Joseph would descend from the ancient one, not that the modern Joseph would descend from Lehi.

9. Criminal conversation (written here as "crim. con.") was a civil-law term for adultery.

palm it off as truth upon a credulous community, cannot but receive the frowns and punishments of a just God.

Again, on the same page, "And the Lord said unto me, also, I will raise up unto the fruit of thy loins; and I will make for him a spokesman. And the spokesman of thy loins shall declare it." This prophecy of Joseph is also fulfilled to the letter, in the person of Sydney Rigdon; he is also from this same illegitimate race.[10] It is true his name is not mentioned in the prophecy, but he fulfils the functions assigned him. Are not the circumstances mentioned in the prophecy, pointing out so plainly these two persons, Joseph Smith, Jun. and Sydney Rigdon, who are the founders,[11] and are still the leaders among the Mormon fanatics, good grounds to infer that they were, at least, advisers, if not the authors, of the present form of the Book of Mormon?

---

10. Sidney Rigdon (1793–1876) converted to the Mormon movement in 1830 and instantly rose to prominence as one of Smith's confidants. A former Baptist minister and one of the early leaders of the Disciples of Christ, Rigdon would have attracted Howe's attention, but the verse at 2 Ne. 3:18 more likely referred to Oliver Cowdery. It goes on to say that the individual would "write the writing of the fruit of thy loins." In addition to being an orator who delivered the first sermon in the new church, Cowdery was Smith's principal scribe during the dictation of the Book of Mormon (*History of the Church*, 1:81; Vogel, *Documents*, 1:99).

11. Rigdon's teachings were so similar to Smith's prior to December 1830, it was speculated that he may have secretly conspired to help write the Book of Mormon, an assumption that was later adopted into the Spalding theory. James Gordon Bennett at the *New York Enquirer* suggested this after he visited Palmyra in August 1831, writing that "Ringdon [was] a parson [and] in general—smart fellow," one who he thought might be "the author of the Bible" (Bennett diary, Aug. 7–8, 1831, New York Public Library; *Morning Courier and Enquirer*, Sept. 1, 1831; Vogel, *Documents*, 3:282, 289).

If they did not originally compose the book, they might easily, at the time of amending and copying, alter and insert the patent of their commissions, in order to give validity to their undertaking.

Joseph Smith, Jun. was well skilled in legerdemain, and the use of the divining-rods,[12] which afforded him great facilities in translating. He doubtless had become acquainted with mystifying every thing, and collected that class of people about him, who were willing dupes, and anxious devotees to the marvelous. To establish the truth of any pretension, however ridiculous and absurd it might be, required nothing but some little necromancy, and it would be received as of divine inspiration by them.

In the conclusion of the present chapter, Lehi bestows his last benediction. "And now, blessed art thou Joseph. Behold thou art *little*." We think the mind of this *little* Joseph must have been quite precocious, to have comprehended the whole rigmarole which has been addressed to him. Not only this; Nephi must have had a very tenacious memory, or have been a stenographer, in addition to his great literary attainments, in order to have engraved the oration of his father. The boy being *little*, perhaps might account for the circumlocution, and tautology, in the whole speech, if the whole book was not written in precisely the same words and phrases. The old and new

---

12. The authority of Howe's claim that Joseph Smith used a divining rod is unknown. In general, a forked divining rod was used to locate underground water and ore, as well as to ask questions of spirits. The spirits answered affirmatively by slightly nudging the rod downward and negatively by not moving the rod at all. See D. Michael Quinn, *Early Mormonism*, 34–35.

Testaments are written in an ancient and very perfect style, and there is no doubt that, at the time it was written, it was in all respects, the most finished, and complete production, into which our language was capable of being modeled.— But many improvements, and innovations have been made in our vocabulary, since that period, which now renders the style, measurably, obsolete. A translation from the original Greek, in our present improved language, would be desirable, and, if it could be accomplished, many scisms would be abandoned, and sectarianism would be greatly diminished. We mention this, as an argument against the divine authenticity of the Book of Mormon. A few years have only elapsed, since the pretended translation of that work took place, and instead of its being given us in a chaste and clear style, it is the most miserable and barren of any thing we ever saw, in the form of a book. Would it not be reasonable to conclude, that any book, whose author was the Holy Ghost, would be clear and perfect in all its parts; so plain that the wayfaring man need not err? particularly if the translation and style be chosen and dictated by himself, as it is pretended that the book of Mormon was. But we are forbidden this test, otherwise the book would fall to the ground at once.

Nephi is the next person on the stage, and commences his harangue. He recapitulates his father's prophecies, and those of their ancestor, Joseph, in nearly the same language which Lehi used, and reminds the whole family of the promises in the covenant. Lehi is now old, and after he finishes his valedictory, gives up the ghost, and is buried, *p.* 69. The scene is now changed wholly. Nephi is the *Major-domo.* Laman, Lemuel, and the sons of Ishmael, rebel against his authority; and Nephi is warned of the Lord to flee into the wilderness. A little previous, after the death of Lehi, Nephi is disconsolate, and a long soliloquy is penned, or engraved, upon the brass plates, which is principally patched up from detached sentences taken from Psalms and Jeremiah, badly arranged. *p.* 70.[13]—The rebellion and civil war is so great, that Nephi comes to the rare conclusion, after receiving his special command, to take another journey into the wilderness! The promised land is not yet obtained, according to page 49, where it says, "we did arrive at the promised land." Whether the land of both North and South America was in the charter, or not, we cannot say, but a part is surrendered forthwith, which is never restored again, therefore it was not the promised land, or the Lord had broken his covenant.[14]

"Wherefore it came to pass, that I, Nephi, did take my family, and also Zoram," (Zoram was a servant man of Laban's, whom Nephi and his brethren, decoyed from Jerusalem, at the time the renowned plates were obtained which contained the genealogy of Lehi,) "and Sam, and his elder brother, and his family, and Jacob, and Joseph, my younger brethren, and also my sisters, and all they which would go with me."

They journeyed through the wilderness, until they arrived at a place which they call Nephi, and their leader; those who were left behind, to wit: Laman and Lemuel, and their families, were afterwards called *Lamanites,* together with all their

---

13. Since the Book of Mormon doesn't mention what metal the Nephite record was inscribed on, Howe assumed it was brass. He was right about 2 Ne. 4:16–35 borrowing from Jer. 17 and Ps. 4, 9, 23, 31, 34, 40, 49, 52, 56, 89, 117, 143.

14. Contrary to Howe's criticism of 1 Ne. 18:23, the context of Nephi's vision of the promised land in 1 Ne. 13:12, 14 was that it was the entire western hemisphere.

descendants, without distinction. Nephi instructs his people to manufacture swords, after the manner of the sword of Laban, to defend themselves against the Lamanites. *p.* 72. Nothing can be more ridiculous, than to suppose it necessary to manufacture swords with which to defend themselves against the Lamanites, as there could not have been to exceed twenty adults, including both parties; for he says on the very next page, that thirty years only had passed away since they left Jerusalem, and five males constituted the whole at the onset. We will admit that five men were added; but Ishmael and Lehi are dead; and Jacob and Joseph are born, and but a short time since, Joseph is called *little*. But see what follows in immediate connexion with their removal, and previous to the time mentioned of thirty years having elapsed since the hegira of Lehi. "And I did teach my people that they should work in all manner of wood, and of iron, and of copper, and of brass, and of steel, and of gold, and of precious ores, which were in great abundance. And I, Nephi, did build a temple, and I did construct it after the manner of the temple of Solomon, save it were not built of so many precious things. But the manner of the construction, was like unto the temple of Soloman, and the workmanship thereof was exceeding fine."[15] All this was accomplished in the short time which remains after deducting eight or nine years previous to their embarking for the promised land, and the time they were located previous to Nephi's

---

15. Howe is probably right about the apparent contradiction. However, in fairness, the Book of Mormon distinguishes between the temple's construction and interior decoration, or more specifically between "precious ores" and "precious things" (2 Ne. 5:15, 16).

journey into the wilderness, where they now are with not more than twenty or thirty persons, including women and children. How much time remains from the thirty years which has not quite elapsed, we will leave for some Nephite, or Mormon, to determine. But this is not all—there is still another incongruity. Nephi has just told us, that gold, silver, *brass, steel,* iron, copper, and precious ores, in great abundance, were found; and in the next sentence he tells us, that he built a temple in all things like the temple of Soloman, "save it were not built of so many precious things, for they were not to be found upon the land." We know not the precious things that were in Solomon's temple, more than our book enumerates. Brass and steel are represented native. These were advantages which Solomon had not. He was compelled to mix and form his own brass,—steel he had none.[16] If any can reconcile all these incongruities, and unscientific mistakes, which have been exhibited thus far in the book of Mormon, with revealed truths from Heaven, we know not what inconsistencies, and fooleries, could be instituted under a pretence of divine authenticity, that would not have its enthusiastic devotees.

---

16. The Book of Mormon claims the Nephites began to *work* with brass and steel, not that they necessarily *found* them occurring naturally. However, the anachronism implied by *steel* is unavoidable.

CHAPTER 5a.[1]

If any man is curious to know the origin of the American Indian,[2] he has it here. "That inasmuch, as they will not hearken unto thy words they shall be cut off from the presence of the Lord." This is prophecy that Nephi pretends to repeat as coming from the Lord, against all those who would not hearken to him as their ruler. Nephi describes the Lamanites as being very white, fair, and delightsome, and very enticing to his people. "Therefore the Lord God did cause a skin of black to come upon them."—"And cursed shall be the seed of him that mixeth with their seed." *p.* 73 [2 Ne. 5]. The known habits and characteristics of the Indian, are briefly set forth, in order to satisfy the credulous inquirer. "And thirty years have passed away from the time we left Jerusalem." *p.* 73. Jacob and Joseph are now consecrated priests. It may not be improper to examine this subject of consecrating priests out of the families to which it belonged; and it will be recollected, that, according to the account given by the author, that neither Jacob, nor Joseph were yet thirty years old. God made a covenant with the Jews at Mount Sinai, and instituted three orders, *the high priests, priests, and Levites.* The high priesthood was made hereditary

---

1. Howe had two chapters numbered 5, labeled *a* and *b* here to avoid confusion. They were not so labeled in the original.

2. For a discussion of the theological difficulties surrounding discovery of Native Americans, see Vogel, *Indian Origins*, 35–52.

in the family of Aaron, and the first born of the eldest branch of that family, if he had no legal blemish, was the high priest. "Thou shalt appoint Aaron and his sons, and they shall wait on the priest's office, and the stranger that cometh nigh shall be put to death.—Numb. chap. III, 10.

The priesthood was conferred upon the tribe of Levi, and the covenant gave them the office, and it was irrevocable while the temple stood, or, until the Messiah came. "And the priests, the sons of Levi, shall come near, for them the Lord thy God hath chosen to minister unto him, and to bless in the name of the Lord, and by their word shall every controversy and every stroke be tried.—Deut. XXI, 5. Korah, Dathan, and Abiram, with two hundred and fifty men of renown, rebelled against the institution of the priesthood, and the Lord destroyed them in the presence of the whole congregation. This was to be a memorial that no stranger invade any part of the office of priesthood, Numbers XIV, 40. Fourteen thousand seven hundred of the people were destroyed by a plague, for murmuring against this memorial. Even Paul declared, that Christ, while on earth, could not be a priest, for he descended from a tribe concerning which Moses spake nothing of priesthood. So fixed was the covenant in regard to the priesthood in Levi, and of the high priesthood to Aaron, that even the Savior was excluded by the law!

Our author being ignorant on this subject, makes Lehi the offspring of Joseph, and represents him as "offering sacrifices and burnt offerings to the Lord," *p.* 15. And to cap the climax of absurdity, after preaching faith and repentance as the only way of salvation, from the very commencement of the campaign, Nephi tells us, "Notwithstanding we believe in Christ, we keep the law of Moses, and look with steadiness unto Christ until the law shall be fulfilled."!!! *p.* 105 [2 Ne. 25]. In answer, to the above difficulty, into which the author has plunged himself, the *priests* say that Lehi's priesthood was of the order of Melchisedic.[3]—In what way the laws of Moses could be kept under a new order of priesthood, we cannot determine. Paul says "For that after the similitude of Melchisedic, there ariseth another priest, who is made, not after the law of a carnal commandment, but after the power of an endless life." Heb. VII, 15–16. Here then the matter is set at rest, that a priest after the order of Melchisedec could not exist under the law, nor could such a priest offer sacrifices and burnt offerings, nor could the law of Moses, in any sense, be fulfilled without the three orders of priesthood. From what has been seen, the opinions of Paul, and the law of Moses, are at direct issue with the Book of Mormon.

Jacob and Joseph having been consecrated priests, they commence the duties of their holy office, with a few prefatory remarks, interlarded with quotations from the prophecies. *p.* 74.[4]

The 50th and 51st chapters of Isaiah, is inserted at full length for our relief. Whether the quotation was made as a

---

3. The Book of Mormon does not name Lehi's priesthood or mention the "order of Melchisedic." It says only that the high priesthood was of mystical origin, that the patriarch Melchisedec possessed it by the authority of Christ, who was "without beginning of days or end of years" (Al. 13). This reversed the meaning of Hebrews 7, that Christ assumed similar authority to that claimed by Melchisedec. See Wright, "In Plain Terms," in Metcalfe, *New Approaches*, 165–229.

4. In 2 Ne. 6, Jacob draws from Isaiah 11 and 49. Notice the different readings from similar passages in 2 Ne. 6:16–17; 1 Ne. 21:24–25.

matter of necessity by the young priest, or as being appropriate, we cannot determine from the connection in which it stands.

The choice in the quotation is certainly a good one, and is a great relief to the reader. The sublimity of sentiment and poetic style of Isaiah, is truly captivating, and in what manner it became inserted, according to the diction and phraseology of King James' translators, is, with us, a mystery—unless it was copied. Why not in the translation of J[ohn] Wickliffe, and J[ohn] de Travisa, of [William] Tindal[e], and [Myles] Coverdale, of [Martin] Luther, and of half a dozen others we might mention? Perhaps the author had not, while composing the Book of Mormon, any of the above copies; and he might not have known that any such translations were ever made.

After the accurate quotation from Isaiah, Joseph, who is now preaching, anticipates the apostle Paul in his own language, nearly, on the subject of the resurrection, baptism, and repentance, and many other leading points upon which he was so pre-eminent for his clearness of thought and doctrine. We should conclude from the manner in which the quotations are made, that it was done by the author from recollection, and that he had a tolerable knowledge of the gospel doctrines. The following are a few of the sentences quoted, or, as is pretended, that Joseph is the original author of, instead of the apostle, or the Savior.—"They which are filthy, are filthy still," "and they shall go away into everlasting fire," *p.* 80.[5] "And he commandeth all men that they must repent." "And where there is no law given, there is no

---

5. 2 Ne. 9:16. Cf. Rev. 22:11; Matt. 25:41.

punishment, and where there is no punishment there is no condemnation." *p.* 81.[6]

There are a variety of other sentences in this sermon which are taken promiscuously from the Old and New Testaments.[7] Who can be credulous enough to believe, that a preacher, five hundred and fifty years before the ministry of the Savior and his apostles, who taught the way of salvation, did preach and instruct not only the same principles, but the very words and phrases were used to convey the sentiments which are found in the evangelical writings?

Nephi next takes the stand, and testifies roundly to the truths which Joseph, his brother,[8] had been preaching, and adds that they both had seen the Savior, and he had declared that he would send his word forth to the people of Nephi. "Wherefore, by the words of three, God hath said I will establish my word." Who the three are, here referred to, we cannot say. It may be Oliver Cowdery, David Whitmer, and Martin Harris, who are appended to the Book of Mormon, to establish its divine authenticity; and they may be the immortal three, selected out of the three American apostles. The chapter of miracles will reconcile all this. Nephi says "his soul delights in the words of Isaiah" [2 Ne. 11:8], and he says he will write some of them for the benefit of his people, that they may "rejoice for all men,"

---

6. 2 Ne. 9:23, 25. Cf. Acts 17:30; Rom. 4:15.

7. The chapter borrows from Job 19; Isa. 55; Matt. 6, 7, 24, 25; Mark 16; Luke 6, 10; John 8, 15; Acts 17; Rom. 4, 8, 14; 1 Cor. 3, 15; 2 Cor. 11; 2 Thess. 2; Heb. 12; Rev. 2, 14, 20, 21, 22.

8. Howe is mistaken because Nephi follows his other brother, Jacob. See 2 Ne. 11:1.

p. 86.—Thirteen chapters of Isaiah are then copied,[9] commencing with the second chapter.

Nephi, after the quotation from Isaiah, comments upon it, and concludes by offering to prophecy a little plainer, so that all could understand him. The doctrines which are found in the new Testament, in relation to the coming Messiah, and his rejection by the Jews, is explained; a task not very difficult for any one in the nineteenth century. Nephi says it had been told him concerning the destruction which came upon those who remained in Jerusalem, immediately after his father had left it, and that they *then* were destroyed, and carried captive into Babylon [2 Ne. 25], *p.* 103.

We have been told by our author, a number of times, that Christ would make his appearance just six hundred years after Lehi left Jerusalem, and we have been told, likewise, that Lehi, and his family, travelled eight years about the borders of the Red sea, in the wilderness, after which time Nephi builds his ship. And between thirty and fifty five years, after the crusade commenced, he tells the people that Jerusalem is destroyed, and the Jews carried captive into Babylon. According to history, and according to Jeremiah, in the ninth year of the reign of Zedekiah, in the tenth month, Nebuchadnezzar, King of Babylon, besieged Jerusalem, which was six hundred and six years before the christian era.[10] Here we see the ignorant author has made

---

9. Isa. 2–14 (cf. 2 Ne. 12-24). Among other variant readings, the Sea of Galilee is misidentified in the Book of Mormon as the Red Sea (2 Ne. 19:1; cf. Isa. 9:1; Matt. 4:12–13)—one of several "geographical impossibilit[ies]," as one scholar put it (Walters, "Use of the Old Testament in the Book of Mormon," 66–67).

10. The authority upon which Howe based the date 606 BCE is unknown. Two of his contemporaries, Adam Clarke and Thomas Scott, dated

too great a mistake, for, according to the Bible, Jerusalem must have been besieged six years before the pretended departure of Lehi from Jerusalem, and the city destroyed, and the Jews carried captive into Babylon, four years and six months, for the siege lasted only eighteen months. So much for dates, which are given by Mormon inspiration.

We will give for the benefit of our readers, a specimen of Mormon inspired language. "And behold it shall come to pass, after the Messiah hath risen from the dead, and hath manifested himself unto his people, unto as many as will believe on his name, *behold Jerusalem shall be destroyed again*; for woe unto them that fight against God and the people of his church, *p.* 104.

In the valedictory of Nephi, we have the doctrines of salvation through Jesus Christ preached, and about twenty pages of the book are taken up. A great many of the incidents which transpired in the days of our Savior, is prophetically mentioned, together with the reasons why it was necessary to baptize Christ, *p.* 108.[11] We are likewise told, in the same discourse, that the plates, or book, would be sealed up, and should finally be found by an *unlearned* man, who should see them, and show them to three others, and then hide them again, for the use of the Lord. All this the Mormons believe that their prophet, Joseph Smith, Jr. translated, (and[12] as having been engraved by the hand of Nephi, on plates of brass, two thousand four

---

the fall of Jerusalem to 599 BCE. Today the consensus is for the earlier date of 597 BCE.

11. Nothing on the page Howe refers to is relevant; however, the chapters comprising 2 Ne. 25–33 are on pp. 102–22 of the 1830 book of Mormon.

12. The left parenthesis has been moved here from "when the plates were hid" to complete the parenthetical thought.

hundred years ago! when the plates were hid by Smith, but did not know where,) by means of a stone in a hat! Before Nephi concludes to die, he appoints a king over his people which they call second Nephi [Jac. 1], *p.* 124.

The ignorance of the author, has caused the sceptre to depart from Judah, hundreds of years before Shiloh came. It must be recollected, that all their people [tribe of Judah] were Jews, living under the law, to the fulfilling of it, and [the Book of Mormon has people] preaching the Gospel, baptism, and repentance, making priests out of those families, concerning which Moses spake nothing of priesthood, and kings, contrary to the blessings of Jacob, which he pronounced upon Judah.

Nephi prophecies that after the book of which he has spoken, shall be found, and written unto the Gentiles, and afterwards sealed up again unto the Lord, many would believe and carry the tidings to the remnant of their seed, which is the Lamanites, or the aborigines, and that they were of the Jewish parentage, and that they had had the Gospel preached to them six hundred years before there was a gospel.

"And it came to pass, that the Jews which are scattered also shall begin to believe in Christ; and they shall begin to gather in upon the face of the land, and as many as shall believe in Christ, shall also become a delightsome people." *p.* 117.

From the above prophecies, we may expect to see our Indians and the Jews flocking in, becoming Mormons, and the former laying aside their dark skins for white ones.

The prophecies continue, and inform us that at this time, the Lord will commence his work among all nations, kindred, tongues, and people, in order to restore them; and that great divisions will take place among the people, and terrible anathemas are pronounced against those who will not become Mormons, and [he] quotes Isaiah's poetic description of the commencement of the Millennium. *p.* 117.[13]

The sin against the Holy Ghost is defined as follows: after repentance, baptism by water, and by fire, and by the Holy Ghost, and [after one] can speak with a new tongue, and with the tongue of angels, and then deny the Savior, the unpardonable sin is committed [2 Ne. 31], *p.* 119. He tells the people he is not "mighty in writing like unto speaking" [2 Ne. 33], *p.* 121. For he says that he speaks by the power of the Holy Ghost.— We know not what kind of a speaker he was, but we have a sample of the author's composition, and we should readily concur with him that the inspiration of God had no agency in the composition. The Evangelists both spoke and wrote by inspiration, as we believe; at all events we find no apology made by them for not being able to convey their ideas, for want of language. Our author finally closes his sermon by making his hero possess the keys of the kingdom of heaven, and as having the power to seal on earth, &c. p. 122.

---

13. 2 Ne. 30:11–15; cf. Isa. 11:5–9.

CHAPTER 5b.[1]

We have thus far looked over the Book of Mormon, endeavoring to treat the sacred truths of the everlasting God, which have been profaned for one of the vilest of purposes, with the solemnity which it deserves; and to expose in a becoming manner, the falsehoods which have been interwoven for the purposes of fraud and deception. If the book had been presented to us, for our inspection, we should never have anticipated that a religious sect could ever have been established from its doctrines. We should have come to the conclusion that the author was a fearless infidel, and had attempted a ridicule upon the Holy Bible; and we still think that it is not improbable that the original design of the author was to bring down contempt upon the inspired writers, and the religion of Jesus Christ.

"THE BOOK OF JACOB THE BROTHER OF NEPHI."

Jacob commences his book fifty-five years after Lehi left Jerusalem, p. 123.[2] Jacob says, the word of the Lord came unto him, saying, "Jacob, get thou up into the temple, on the

---

1. The original edition of *Mormonism Unvailed* had two chapter 5s. The designation of *a* and *b* in the current presentation is for the sake of clarity.

2. As Howe indicates, page 123 of the Book of Mormon began with the heading, "The Book of Jacob the Brother of Nephi," indicating the third major division or "book" within the Book of Mormon. The quotations immediately following occurred on pp. 125–26, now Jacob 2:11–13.

morrow, and declare the word which I shall give thee, unto this people."

"And now behold, my brethren, this is the word which I declare unto you, that many of you have begun to search for gold, and for silver, and all manner of precious ores, in the which this land, which is a land of promise unto you, and to your seed, doth abound most plentifully. And the hand of Providence hath smiled upon you most pleasingly, that you have obtained many riches; and because that some of you have obtained more abundantly than that of your brethren, ye are lifted up in the pride of your hearts, and wear stiff necks and high heads, because of the costliness of your apparel, and persecute your brethren, because that ye suppose that ye are better than they." p. 126. Jacob received a special command from the Lord to get up into the temple and declare the above paragraph!!! There seems to be a prevailing passion in the writer to represent the Nephites as being great miners after the precious metals. They are often represented as diging and searching after gold and silver—which will perhaps be an apology for Joseph Smith's early habits in searching after hidden treasures, he being a remnant of the Nephites.[3] The love of gold among the Jews is proverbial; and it is a far more laudable method of obtaining it by diging after the deposits of pirates than by over reaching in commercial, or in other business transactions. There would seem but little prospect of obtaining pirate's money, either on the mountains, near the head waters of the Susquehannah, or in the town of Manchester, Ontario County, N. Y. But Don

---

3. Howe misread the Book of Mormon's claim that Joseph Smith was a descendant of Lehi (2 Ne. 3:7). See p. 71 herein.

Quixote told his squire Sancho, that great fortune was often very near when we least expected it; thus it was with Smith in diging after hidden treasures—the famous brass plates, the gold spectacles and the interpreting stone were found, perhaps, when he least expected it; and if the sword of Laban had been added,[4] instead of being found by "Guy of Warwick,"[5] in England, some centuries ago, we have no doubt but the mob in Missouri would have been quiet before this time, or Gen. J. Smith[6] would have slain the whole. A similar adventure will be noticed which can be found on page 272,[7] Book of Mormon.

In the third discourse, which Jacob favors us with, he informs us that only a small part of his doings can be engraved on plates; and in the close of the second discourse, he says that a hundredth part of the doings of these people could not be engraved on plates on the account of their having become so very numerous, p. 129, and all sprang from five or six females, in about forty years; and in the mean time they had had wars and contentions, and the reigns of kings, the history of which is written upon larger plates, which are called the plates of

---

4. It may be worth repeating that no one said otherwise when Howe called the record the "brass plates"; the Three Witnesses saw the artifact in vision and said it had a golden hue, not that it was gold. Howe vacillates on whether the spectacles were silver or gold where other sources said silver. The stone mentioned here is the divination stone the Chase family discovered when digging a well. Joseph Smith borrowed it and never returned it. For the sword of Laban, see 1 Ne. 4:9; 2 Ne. 5:14.

5. The hero of a popular English romance from about 1300 who was good with a sword.

6. The title is derived from Smith's para-military expedition in 1834 to rescue church members who had been evicted from their homes in Missouri.

7. In Alma 17 the missionary Ammon cuts off the arms of his attackers.

Jacob, p. 129. According to the most extravagant calculation, in point of increase among five or six females, the whole could not have amounted to more than about sixteen hundred, in the time mentioned, allowing no deaths to have occurred; besides, about one half of that number would be under ten years old. The story of wars and contentions, and of kings having passed away, is too ridiculous and inconsistent to be noticed and refuted in a serious manner.

Jacob reminds the people of a parable which the prophet Zenos spake, p. 131. In this parable, the author has no means of dissembling, there not being such a prophet nor such a parable, he is compelled to use his own phraseology, as he penned it.

The style of the Book of Mormon is *sui generis*,[8] and whoever peruses it, will not have a doubt but that the whole was framed and written by the same individual hand. The phrases, "And it came to pass," is at the beginning of every paragraph, with a few exceptions, throughout all the original part of the work. "Behold," "Beholdest," "exceeding," "Thereof," "also," "grieveth," are favorite phrases.

Let us compare a paragraph which the author pretends was spoken by the prophet Zenos, and repeated by Jacob, with one translated from the gold plates of Jared, about seven hundred years afterwards by the hand of Moroni.

The following are the words of the prophet Zenos:

"Ye shall clear away the branches which bring forth bitter fruit, according to the strength of the good and the size *thereof;* and ye shall not clear away the bad *thereof,* all at once, lest the

8. Literally "of its own kind," meaning in a category all of its own.

roots *thereof* should be too strong for the graft, and the graft *thereof* shall perish."

Seven hundred years afterwards, Moroni translated the following elegant description of the ships in which the Babelites navigated themselves across the ocean:

"And they were built after a manner that they were exceeding tight, even that they would hold water like unto a dish; and the bottom *thereof* was tight like unto a dish; and the sides *thereof* was tight like unto a dish; and the ends *thereof* were peaked; and the top *thereof* was tight like unto a dish; and the length *thereof* was the length of a tree; and the door *thereof*, when it was shut was tight like unto a dish," p. 542. We leave the intelligent reader to draw his own conclusions.[9]

The parable of Zenos occupies about nine pages, and is followed by Jacob with an explanation, and a short Christian exhortation to his people. The last chapter of the book of Jacob is principally taken up in relating an anecdote about a man by the name of Sherem, who came and preached to the people, denying Christ; Jacob finally confounds him by the power of the Lord, which struck Sherem to the earth, p. 141. Jacob is now grown old, and he gives the plates of Nephi to his son Enos, together with the commands which Nephi gave to him. Enos promises obedience, and Jacob bids farewell to the reader, p. 143.

"The Book of Enos."—Enos commences with giving his father a good name, as any dutiful son would do, and then tells us of a mighty wrestle he had with the Lord before that he

---

9. The intelligent reader may nevertheless have to study the two quotes from Jacob 5:65 and Ether 2:17 to detect that Howe wants us to see the overuse of the word *thereof.*

received a remission of his sins, he then exhorts the people to repentance and faith in Christ; he tells us he is a great prophet, but prophecies nothing. He says an hundred and seventy-nine years had passed away since Lehi left Jerusalem, p. 145.

"The Book of Jarom" is said to be written by Jarom the son of Enos, who is an engraver like all his predecessors in the priesthood; he tells us the plates are so small that he could engrave but little. About two pages in the Mormon translation is all, and delivers the plates to Omni, two hundred and thirty-eight years since the hegira of Lehi, p. 147.

"The Book of Omni."—Omni receives the plates from his father, who commands him to write a little to preserve the genealogy. Omni writes a couple of paragraphs, each commencing with, "And it came to pass," and confers the plates upon his son Amaron. Amaron writes a few sentences and delivers his plates to his brother Chemish. He follows the example in three or four sentences, and declares the plates genuine. Abinadom is the son of Chemish; he takes the plates by right, but declares he knows of no revelations, save what has been written, and says that is sufficient, p. 149. Amaleki is the son of Abinadom who takes the plates, and says he has something to say. A certain man, by the name of Mosiah was warned by the Lord to flee into the wilderness, with as many as would go with him. They all, with Mosiah for their leader, arrive at a place called Zarahemla, and bring with them the plates of brass, which pleased the people very much, because they contained the record of the Jews.

The people of Zarahemla, Mosiah discovered, came out from Jerusalem at the time of the Babylonish captivity, and

had become very numerous. Their language had become de-
generated so much that Mosiah could not understand them
at all; but Mosiah causes them all to learn the language of
the Nephites, and they make him king over the land, p. 149.
Mosiah discovered upon a stone which was brought him, with
hieroglyphics engraved upon it, [a story] which he interpreted
by the gift and power of God—and it gave an account of another people, which escaped the confounding of languages
at the tower of Babel, and of their destruction at the north.
They were called the people of Coriantumr. Amaleki says he
was born in the days of king Mosiah, and is acquainted with
Benjamin, who is his son, and succeeds his father in the regal
office, p. 150. Three or four more paragraphs, and the plates of
Nephi are full. The plates were transferred to king Benjamin by
Amaleki for safe keeping.

"The Words of Mormon."—The scene is now changed by
the author, and we are carried forward, "many hundred years
after the coming of Christ." But the inspired historian, who is
called Mormon, begins with his record at the precise period
when Amaleki delivers the plates to king Benjamin.[10] Mormon commences his history with a kind of preface, in which
he mentions that king Benjamin fought great battles with the
Lamanites, and says "he did fight with the strength of his own

---

10. If Mormon was editing the records of his predecessors, he would have
known where to insert a narrative bridge. The real mystery was how he knew
Martin Harris was going to lose the original dictation and would need a backup
copy, or rather an unedited replacement for everything up to the book of Mosiah. Mormon knew precisely where the seam would occur between the lost
dictation and the backup copy.

arm, with the sword of Laban," p. 152. We suppose the sword of Laban was probably a kind of keep-sake, and descended to their generals; and we are sorry to say that our Gen. Smith has not been favored with the possession of it. Such a specimen of antiquity, as a sword made 2400 years ago, which had slain so many in the hands of such renowned kings and prophets of God, would be a great curiosity.

Mormon is the author of the "Book of Mosiah."[11] King Benjamin is the father of three sons whose names are called Mosiah, Helorum and Helaman, who were taught in the language of their fathers, p. 154, which was the Egyptian;[12] thereby they were enabled to read the engravings upon the plates, p. 155. Lehi has been represented as a pious Jew, living in Jerusalem, and of the tribe of Joseph, who separated himself from the Jews, and departed into the wilderness, and never again associated with any community or nation of people, until king Mosiah found another settlement, who came off at the time of the Babylonish captivity, in the land of Zarahemla, who were likewise Jews. The sacred records of the Jews, and all their religious ceremonies in the temple, were in the Hebrew

---

11. Howe begins discussing the Book of Mosiah abruptly here. The previous four books, Enos through Words of Mormon, occupied only ten pages of the Book of Mormon and served as a kind of introduction to Mosiah, which took up sixty-eight pages.

12. "Our father Lehi could [not] have remembered all these things, to have taught them to his children, except it were for the help of these plates: for he having been taught in the language of the Egyptians, therefore he could read these engravings, and teach them to his children, that thereby they could teach them to their children, and so fulfilling the commandments of God, even down to this present time" (pp. 153–54; Mosiah 1:4).

language; and it is well established that no other language was in use among that nation in Jerusalem, until the temple was destroyed. It may be true that Jews who were born and lived in other countries, spoke other languages. But the known hostility of the Egyptians towards every other nation, and particularly towards the Hebrews, renders it improbable that the Egyptians had sufficient intercourse with the Jews, so as to have them adopt their language and literature.[13] The Jews have a religious veneration for the Hebrew tongue, which also furnishes a strong argument against the position that our pious Hebrews spake the Egyptian language, and recorded their holy religion in it upon plates of brass, to be handed down to posterity.

After king Benjamin had finished the education of his sons, he "waxed old"—and as it became necessary to confer the kingdom on some one, he caused Mosiah to come forth. He orders him to issue a proclamation that on the morrow he would preach in the temple, and proclaim Mosiah king, p. 154.

King Benjamin took care to give his son charge as to the affairs of the kingdom; and handed down the old legacy, consisting of the sword of Laban, the brass ball or compass, and the records on brass plates, p. 155.

The people assemble, according to the request of King Benjamin, in great multitudes—"And they took of the firstlings

---

13. More recent discoveries have shown a close connection between Palestine and Egypt. The Egyptians maintained fortifications in the region and the children of the Canaanite/Hebrew elite were sent to Egypt to be educated. It was due to the protection of Egyptian forces that Israelites were able to move out of walled cities into the hill country. See Redmoun, "Bitter Lives: Israel In and Out of Egypt," 96–119.

of their flocks, that they might offer sacrifice and burnt offerings, according to the law of Moses," p. 155.

In the sermon which king Benjamin is now preaching in the temple, where the people are offering sacrifice, we find the following sentences: "I am come unto you to declare the glad tidings of great joy," p. 160. "And he shall be called Jesus Christ, the Son of God, the Father of Heaven and Earth, the Creator of all things from the beginning, and his mother shall be called Mary, !! p. 160—for salvation cometh to none such, except it be through repentance and faith on the Lord Jesus Christ," p. 161.[14] We are at a loss, inasmuch as it is not defined, what kind of a dispensation it was, to preach salvation through Christ and offer burnt offerings at the same time, according to the law of Moses, which they could not do agreeably to the law, not having legal priests to officiate. "And moreover I say unto you, that there shall be no other name given, nor no other way nor means whereby salvation can come unto the children of men, only in and through the name of Christ, the Lord Omnipotent," p. 161. We cannot gather from any part of the sermon of Benjamin, any disapprobation of the ceremonial law, but infer that both the law of Moses and the gospel were binding upon them at one and the same time!!

The sermon is continued with many good doctrines extracted from the New Testament, with a pretense that it had been revealed to him by an angel.

The author doubtless had some knowledge of the revivals of religion, in the different churches; for he represents the

---

14. Mosiah 3:3, 12; cf. Luke 2:10.

whole congregation prostrated,[15] crying for mercy through the atoning blood of Christ—"For we believe in Jesus Christ the Son of God," p. 162. This would be judged *a priori* [before the facts], wonderful preaching, considering the period in which it took place, at least 300 years before the nativity of Christ.

Permit us to propound a few interrogatories to the reader, if he be a Mormon, or even has doubts in relation to the divine origin and authenticity of the new revelation: 1. When did God institute the ceremonial and moral laws? [2.] If upon Mount Sinai, when did it terminate, and in what? 3. For what purpose was those laws instituted? 4. If at the coming of the Savior, all the ceremonies of the law were done away, why were they in force among the Nephites as early as the gospel was made known to them, not relying upon the law and obedience to it, but upon the *Gospel*, six hundred years before the shepherds heard the glad tidings of great joy, which was unto all nations? except the Nephites, with whom the author pretends it was an old story.

Mosiah [II][16] is the next king, and is son to king Benjamin; he is consecrated a priest. The king's and priest's office seems to be inseparably connected at this time among our ancients.

Mosiah's reign commences four hundred and seventy-six years from the time Lehi left Jerusalem. He despatches sixteen of his strong men to reconnoitre and search after another settlement of the Nephites, which appears to be disconnected

---

15. For a brief discussion of the "falling power" exhibited in some revival meetings, see Vogel, *Religious Seekers*, 83–84, 89–90.

16. This Mosiah is said to be the grandson of the first Mosiah encountered in the Book of Mormon.

from the land of Zarahemla. They lose their way, not having been provided with the brass ball to direct them, and are taken prisoners by Limhi. After king Limhi ascertains that they are from the land of Zarahemla, he recounts to them his troubles, and represents himself as being under bondage to the Lamanites; and that one half of all their products were paid to them, annually, as a tribute. The prisoners are set at liberty; and plates containing their record, from the time they left the land of Zarahemla.—Ammon, who is represented as captain of the scouts, reads the record upon the plates. After which, king Limhi asks him if he could interpret languages—being answered in the negative, he [Limhi] commences a narrative of having sent out forty three of his men in search of the land of Zarahemla; and that they all got lost, and after many days they returned—having discovered a land that was covered with the bones of men and beasts! and was also covered with the ruins of buildings, having the appearance of being peopled as numerous as the hosts of Israel. As a testimony of the truth of their discovery, they brought home with them twenty-four plates of pure gold, containing a history of a people to which we have alluded, called the people of Jared, who were not confounded at the destruction of Babel. Ammon is again enquired of, whether he knows any one who can translate languages—he answers in the affirmative, and says "for that he hath wherewith to look, and translate all records that are of ancient date: and it is a gift from God; and the things are called interpreters; and no man can look in them, except he be commanded"—the king of Zarahemla is the man, p. 173. We will make no remark on the gold spectacles, but will leave the intelligent reader to infer whether the story and the manner in which it is told, comports with his views of divine revelation or not.

The Record of Zeniff.—Zeniff is the leader of a band of Nephites, who left the land of Zarahemla, and is the father of Noah, who is the father of Limhi the king, of whom we have been speaking.

Zeniff confers the kingdom upon his son Noah, whose people become wicked, and wars ensue between them and the Lamanites, and they are mostly all destroyed; hence they became tributary, as above alluded to. About this time, a prophet makes his appearance, by the name of Abinadi. He attempts to imitate Isaiah in his prophecies,[17] and quotes many passages from the Old Testament, which were pronounced against the Jews for their wickedness and rebellion, and foretelling the destruction of Jerusalem—pretending that he is the author of the sentiments,[18] and declares them against these Nephites, upbraiding them for [t]heir disobedience to the commands of Christ, and describes the awful calamities which shall follow, and concludes with the decalogue, p. 184.[19]

The decalogue here inserted, is in our approved translation, like every thing else which is taken from the Old and New Testament. It is true that the pronoun *which* is used twice or three times, instead of *that*, consequently, we should infer that the quotation was made from recollection. The fact that so

17. In Mosiah 14, Abinadi quotes and expounds on Isaiah 53, and in the next two chapters Mosiah comments on Isaiah 52.

18. Despite Howe's criticism, Abinadi introduces his comments with, "Doth not Isaiah say?" (Mosiah 14:1).

19. Mosiah 12:34–36; 13:12–24; cf. the ten commandments in Ex. 20:2–7.

great a proportion of the whole book being made from quotations from the Bible, a part of which was not written until six hundred years after the pretended period of our author, places the matter beyond controversy, and is conclusive testimony that the author was an infidel.

The prophet Abinadi was somewhat expert in the sacred scriptures, and measurably understood the views of modern theologians;—he says, "And now ye have said that salvation cometh by the law of Moses. I say unto you that it is expedient that ye keep the law of Moses as yet; but I say unto you, that the time shall come when it shall no more be expedient to keep the law of Moses," p. 185. The doctrines of salvation and the law, according to our prophet, were inseparably connected in their time, and both were indispensable to salvation. Whether the ceremonial and moral laws were both included by our prophet, we cannot determine; but to reconcile the idea that the ceremonial law which was typical of Christ, and was only obligatory until the gospel church was erected, with the literal obedience of it, by a community of people who had the gospel as fully revealed to them, as it was to the rest of mankind at any future period whatever, is a task beyond our abilities, so long as we view the writings of St. Paul as inspired of God. In immediate connection we are told that the Jews were a "stiff-necked people, quick to do iniquity"—"therefore, there was a law given them, yea, a law of performances and ordinances, a law which they were to observe strictly"—"But behold, I say unto you, that all these things were types of things to come," p. 185. We are next led into the doctrines of the New Testament; and are told of the coming of the Messiah, and of his doctrines and crucifixion, about as well as any tolerably well informed man, who made no pretensions to literature, would do at the present time, having the scripture before him.

In the following quotation, we have the views of our author on the resurrection—"And if Christ *had* not risen from the dead or have broken the bonds of death, that the grave should have no victory, and that death should have no sting, there could have been no resurrection," p. 189.[20] In this quotation the cloven foot is uncovered—the deformity brought into open day light. The prophet is represented by the author, as living some centuries before our Savior's nativity; but the slightest examination of the text quoted, will show the reader that the subject is spoken of in the imperfect tense, representing the event of the resurrection as past and finished, which was doubtless the truth, at the time it was written. The phrase, "if Christ had not risen" implies past time; again, in the same sentence, "there could have been no resurrection," implies past time; but if the author had said, if Christ does not rise, &c.— there will be no resurrection, we could have understood him, in reference to the time in which he represents his prophet speaking, to wit, some centuries before the great event of which he spake, took place, according to his own calender.

The sagacity of our imposter has not been sufficient in all instances, to avoid detection. His deliberations were insufficient to supply the place of erudition, and consequently, he plunged himself into a thousand absurdities, equaling the one just quoted. We are no less of the opinion, than heretofore, that

---

20. Mosiah 16:7; cf. Isa. 25:8; 1 Cor. 15:54–55.

divine inspiration would be an unerring guide in all things, as well in language as in the matter to be conveyed by it, which renders the book in question, good evidence against itself, that it is a miserable forgery and a libel upon the Christian religion. We will venture to predict that if the golden bible[21] should be rendered into intelligible English, there would not remain a single *honest* Mormon who should examine the book, (provided he possessed common capacity,) among *"the latter day saints."*

Alma is the next hero, who is represented as a descendant of Nephi, and having repented of his sins, commences preaching and repeating the prophecies of Abinadi, who had recently fallen a victim, by the hands of king Noah's priests. Our hero is more successful than his predecessor, as he succeeds in converting king Noah to the Christian faith, together with many of his subjects.

After their conversion, the ceremony of baptism is to be performed, and the manner in which it was accomplished, in the first exhibition, is somewhat unique. The priest with his disciple are represented as going down into the water, in the river Mormon, and at the same time the believer is buried in the water, he buries himself with him. We are not told whether it was accidental or intentional that they both were immersed at the same time, but we learn, in immediate connection, that the mode adopted at the present day by the anabaptists,[22] was followed and practiced afterwards.

The gospel doctrines, according to the views of our author

---

21. Note that Howe switches his reference from brass plates to the "golden bible," though without necessarily implying gold plates.

22. See Mosiah 18:12–16. Anabaptists believed in having an officiator

have, in his clumsy manner, been spread before us, beginning with the hegira of Lehi, pretending that the whole plan of redemption was exhibited by a special revelation to an apostate Jew, six hundred years before our Savior expressly declares the ceremonial law was abrogated and the gospel preached—"The law and the prophets were until John: since that time the kingdom of God is preached, and every man presseth into it," Luke 16. We will leave the controversy whether the book of Mormon is true, on the subject of this special revelation, or the words of Jesus Christ, as recorded by the evangelist, to be determined at the great BAR of Justice.

The Book of Mosiah is continued by narrating the most ludicrous events, of wars and church schisms, imaginable, under the pontificate of our first immersed king, and the last one in our notable history.

Alma being warned by the Lord to flee his country, he gathers a large concourse of people, and they all start into the wilderness, and travel eight days where they pitch their tents, and afterwards build buildings. The sojourners with Alma endeavor to make him accept the royal sceptre, but he piously declines, and establishes a pontificate and builds a church, p. 203. Alma consecrates divers priests, and they were all just men, and they built a city and called it Helam; but in the midst of their prosperity and devotions, an army of the Lamanites appeared upon their borders, and they all fled, and finally arrived at the land of Zarahemla, under king Mosiah. The king receives the pilgrims with great kindness, and Alma

---

immerse their adult initiates in water, although only the convert was immersed, not the officiator.

is continued his high priest. He is authorized by the king to establish churches and ordain priests over them. Seven churches are forthwith built and dedicated to the Christian religion, in which, faith, repentance and baptism is preached by king Mosiah's priests, in its primitive purity. Alma has a son who has at this time arrived at manhood, (we should infer from this that he was not a Catholic Pontiff,) who persecutes the Christians, to their great annoyance. But the Lord would not suffer his chosen Christian Jews to be persecuted; and therefore, in the full tide of his wicked career, he is converted, not very unlike that of Paul the Apostle,[23] according to our narator, p. 213. The miracle of young Alma's conversion is described in the following language. An angel appeared unto Alma and said, "Go thy way, and seek to destroy the church no more, that their prayers may be answered"—"And now Alma, and those that were with him, fell again to the earth, for great was their astonishment" &c.—"And it came to pass, after they had fasted and prayed for the space of two days and two nights, the limbs of Alma receive[d] their strength; and he stood up and began to speak," &c. and said, "I have repented of my sins, and have been redeemed of the Lord; behold I am born of the spirit."

Mosiah's sons are zealous Christians, all of them; they decline, severally, the regal honors, and choose the humble station of missionaries. They consequently all embark with a view of christianizing the heathen. Mosiah suggests the propriety of abolishing the office of king among them, because his sons had all refused, and that if any other should be crowned over

---

23. Mosiah 27:10–19; cf. Acts 9:1–18; 26:11–18.

them, the rightful heir might return and claim the crown as his legal patrimony, which would create contention, &c. among the people, p. 217.—King Mosiah's sons are represented as being extremely humble and devout, they are willing to abandon all for the cause of Christ—home, country, and their princely fortunes—and go missionating. But the eagle eye of the king looks upon his sons with suspicion, or the author of the Golden Bible is under the necessity of bringing up this kind of reasoning, in order to frame a pretence to change his government to one which will appear to the ignorant reader as much like the Jewish polity as possible. The reign of the Judges is next instituted, as answering the author best. Previously, however, we are presented with the following tirade of nonsense. Mosiah causes all records to be revised—"therefore, he took the records which were engraved upon the plates of brass, and also the plates of Nephi; and all the things which he had kept and preserved according to the commandments of God, and after having translated and caused to be written [the records which were][24] upon the plates of gold which had been found by the people of Limhi, which was delivered to him by the hand of Limhi: and this he done because of the great anxiety of the people, for they were desirous beyond measure to know concerning those people which had been destroyed. And now he translated them by the means of *two stones*, which was fastened into the two rims of a bow. Now, things were prepared from the beginning, and were handed down from generation

---

24. In transcribing this quote, Howe missed the words re-inserted here in brackets and made other smaller errors as well.

to generation, for the purpose of interpreting languages; and they have been kept and preserved by the hand of the Lord, that he should discover to every creature which should possess the land, the iniquities and the abominations of his people: and whosoever has these things, is called seer, after the manner of old times."[25]

We were told by Lehi that the plates should not perish, nor be dimmed by time; but our king has found it necessary, not only to revise, but to transcribe them; so much for Mormon promises.

Mosiah, after a long period, is enabled to translate the gold plates, by means of a pair of goggles, which he must have had in his possession from the time he was made king, because he says they had been kept with the plates from the beginning. It is certainly very remarkable that he should have kept in his possession a pile of gold plates, known to have been found by Limhi, for thirty years,[26] with every facility for reading them, and yet never bestowed one leisure moment to examine their contents.

After the gold plates were examined, and were found to contain a full and complete history of a people who came from Asia, and which God had preserved at the time of the destruction of the tower of Babel, and navigated in a miraculous manner to this continent at that time, but now, or at the pretended period of our history, were totally extinct; he expresses great satisfaction at arriving to such important information!! In connection, we

---

25. Mosiah 28:11–16, found on page 216 of the 1830 edition.

26. The Jaredite record apparently came into Mosiah's possession in about 122 BCE (Mosiah 22:14). For some reason, he is said to have waited until the end of his reign, about 91 BCE, to translate the record (Mosiah 29:44, 46).

are promised a detailed account of these Babelites, by giving a translation of the plates in full. In the Book of Ether, which is placed at the end of the Book of Mormon, we shall see the wonderful translation, and make our remarks.

Mosiah reigned thirty-three years being sixty-three years old, and he dies—making the whole time since Lehi's departure from Jerusalem, five hundred and nine years, p. 221. Thus endeth the reign of the Mormon kings. Alma, of renowned conversion to the doctrines of the New Testament about an hundred years before it was published, is constituted Judge over the people of Zarahemla, and is also high priest over the church of Christ. He was the exclusive law-giver and umpire[27] in all matters, both civil and ecclesiastical, and the most absolute monarch of which we have ever heard or read.

---

27. According to Webster's 1828 dictionary, umpires were "arbitrators" of legal controversies, not yet baseball referees.

CHAPTER 6.

A new era has now commenced; Judge Alma, the high priest, is an engraver, as a matter of course, and is represented as keeping his own record: he tells us that in the first year of his reign a man was brought before him who had been preaching and bearing down against the church, persuading the people that ministers ought to become popular, and that they ought not to labor, but ought to be supperted—"and he also testified unto the people that all mankind would be saved at the last day," p. 221.[1]

The name of our ancient Universalist[2] is called Nehor, and is represented as quite successful in gaining proselytes. Gideon, an orthodox Nephite priest, meets Nehor, and a warm debate on Christianity ensues between them—they are represented as able combatants—but the Universalist finally gets angry, and he draws his sword upon pious Gideon and kills him, which was the occasion of his being arraigned before his honor, Judge

---

1. This narrative occurs early in the next book in the Book of Mormon, the Book of Alma (1:4), which at 186 pages is the longest section in the Book of Mormon. It was not 204 pages, as Howe mistakenly reports in the next paragraph.

2. Universalists advocated salvation for everyone regardless of earthly performance. A Mormon pamphlet from 1835, *References to the Book of Mormon*, commented similarly on "Nehor the Universalian" (Underwood, "Earliest Reference Guides," 77). Alexander Campbell mentioned three years earlier that the Book of Mormon weighed in on modern-age controversies such as those surrounding "eternal punishment" (*Millennial Harbinger*, Feb. 1831, 93; see Vogel, "Anti-Universalist Rhetoric," in Metcalfe, *New Approaches*, 21–52).

Alma. The declaration includes two counts—one of being guilty of priestcraft, and the other for attempting to enforce it by the sword. The murder of good old Gideon, was not set forth in the declaration, and therefore we suppose it was no crime to commit homicide in that early day, although it be a priest who is the victim. Nehor is, however, sentenced to die, as an example to those who might be guilty of the high crime of priestcraft, thereafter. But the sequel informs us that the ignominious death of Nehor, served no purpose in preventing priestcraft, and from that period the Nephites were greatly annoyed by impostors and preachers of the *Devil*.

The Book of Alma contains 204 pages and reaches down to the sixty-ninth year of the Judges, and is principally taken up in giving accounts of mighty wars and great generals. The civil, the military, and the ecclesiastical authority, were usually vested in the same individual; representing them as conducting the government much after the Mosaic polity. The miserable manner in which the story is told, renders it extremely irksome to the reader; but the knight errantry of Don Quixote bears no parallel, nor does the story of the Peloponnesian wars speak of such generals, nor of such brave achievements, as the book of Alma.— Besides, in the sixty-nine years, many large cities were founded and built, fortifications were erected, military costumes of great splendor were manufactured and worn.—Their implements of war consisted of swords, spears, scimitars, javelins, bows and arrows, slings, &c. We can see no propriety in the omission by the author of the use of guns and amunition. We think it would have been as credible as most of the events of the narrative, and would have been matter for Mormon credulity and admiration.

A mint for coining money was probably in operation, for it is mentioned that they had an abundance of gold and silver, and they were used for money. The names of the gold coins[3] were senine, seon, shum, simnah, antion and shubloon, making in all, six varieties; their relative value is stated, but not within our comprehension. Let the reader fancy for a moment that all these things are true, will he not enquire whether any of the coin which was so abundant, has ever been found. It is a well known fact that gold is not subject to oxidation, and is therefore indestructible—and if such coin had ever existed, specimens would have been discovered among the ancient ruins of our country, which our present Mormons believe, on the authority of their high priest and the golden bible, were the remains of the settlements of the Nephites. Copper and silver have often been found, (but not in the form of coin,) in the mounds on the Ohio River, and other places. The copper is usually in flat corroded plates, and the silver in the form of a ferule.[4]

Next in order, comes the silver coin, which are called senum, amnor, ezrom and onti; their relative values are stated, but equally unintelligible with the former. Why has none of the silver coin been discovered? fifteen hundred or even two thousand years would not be sufficient to destroy a piece of

3. Daniel C. Peterson wrote in the BYU-sponsored *FARMS Review of Books* 8, no. 1 (1996): 97, "For the umpteenth time, the Book of Mormon never claims that there were coins in the ancient New World." Other apologists have similarly interpreted Alma 11:4 to imply weights of gold and silver, not minted coins, in reference to "the different pieces of their gold, and of their silver."

4. A ferule was a paddle or a "scepter [with] a long stem or shank, with a flat square head," according to the 1828 Webster dictionary.

silver of the size and value of a dollar, lying in the ground or out of it, p. 252.

The doctrine of personal identity and of the resurrection is explained by our chief judge and high priest, which, if John Locke or the Bishop of Worcester[5] had read, that great matter of controversy between them would have been avoided, and they would both have been satisfied of their error. Just hear him—"The spirit and the body shall be raised again, in its perfect form; both limb and joint shall be restored to its proper frame, even as we now are at this time; and we shall be brought before God, knowing even as we know now, and have a bright recollection of all our guilt—and be arraigned before the bar of Christ the Son of God the Father, and the Holy Spirit which is one Eternal God, to be judged according to their works whether they be good or whether they be evil." If the Bishop of Worcester had been in possession of the above paragraph, he would probably not have suffered such a disgraceful defeat as he did in the controversy with Dr. Locke; nor would the learned divines of Harvard University spread heresy any longer.[6]

The civil, military and ecclesiastical departments of the government being incorporated and concentrated in the supreme power of our hero and historian—no movement can be detailed, either of the one or of the other, without including

5. From 1697 to 1699 philosopher John Locke (1632–1704) engaged in an epistolary controversy with Edward Stillingfleet (1635–99), bishop of Worcester. Locke's rejection of a physical resurrection was one of the topics they discussed.

6. Beginning in 1804 the Unitarians who dominated Harvard's theology department denied the deity of Jesus, something that is clearly in opposition to the preceding passage and the Book of Mormon generally.

the whole. If a military campaign is the subject matter of any story in the book of Mormon, civil and ecclesiastical rites and ceremonies are inseparably connected, as best suits the author's views, to aid him out of difficulties. When any religious matter is interlarded, in a particular narrative of any event, which is usually the case throughout the whole book, they are the opinions of the author concerning the doctrines, together with garbled extracts from the New Testament.

We have been in the habit of viewing human nature in a state of moral depravity, but not wholly without some redeeming qualities—not such, indeed, as would justify any one before the all-searching scrutiny of an Omnipotent God, but such as constitute a social being. But the contents of the work before us presents the author, and consequently human nature, in an entirely new light. We could not have believed that any man would have attempted to have prostituted every moral virtue which wisdom and ages have established. If the Bible is a fabrication and a forgery, it is the foundation upon which our rights, our civil privileges, our personal safety, and in fine the whole of human happiness are based. If any one denies this position, let him examine those countries where they have not the Bible, or even communities where it is disregarded, and we will venture to predict that his opinion will be with ours. We have carefully examined the works of Hume, Gibbon, Voltaire and Volney,[7] and with all their sarcasm against the divine

---

7. Scottish philosopher David Hume (1711–76) was known to be a skeptic; English historian Edward Gibbon (1737–94) blamed the decline of the Roman empire on its conversion to Christianity; French philosopher François-Marie Arouet de Voltaire (1694–1778) rejected miracles; and

authority of the Bible, they have addressed themselves to the most noble and learned of the human family; they left the field covered with rubbish, it is true, but of such materials as soon evaporated to the four winds. But the work before us—which is doubtless, not only an attempt to institute a new religion, but to bring contempt and reproach upon Christianity—is fabricated upon the pretension of inspiration, and is placed at an era which denies all research. If a history or a doctrine be known to have been revealed from God, the subject matter is not to be questioned, however improbable it may appear; consequently, whenever the fact is established in the mind that the Book of Mormon is true, the victory is gained, and whatever fictions, absurdities, contradictions or doctrines it may contain, they will be received as unerring as Deity himself.

In our review, we are left without weapons to combat the crodulous[8] Mormon believer; but we trust that to any man who is not a Mormon maniac, who has not inhaled the malaria of the imposter, enough has been said to place the matter beyond the shadow of a doubt, that the Book of Mormon is a fabrication, and that the author has addressed the work to the lowest of our passions. No one but the vilest wretch on earth, disregarding all that is sacred, intrepid and fearless of eternity, would ever dared to have profaned the sacred oracles of truth to such base purposes.

---

historian Constantin-François de Chasseboeuf (1757–1820), known as the Comte de Volney, was a deist.

8. Either the typesetter mistook an "o" for an "e" (see the reverse in the first paragraph of this chapter where an "e" stands for an "o" in "supperted") or had a limited number of vowels to work with and had to make substitutions.

We have not yet done—the task, however loathsome, shall be honestly pursued, and placed before the reader.

Above, we have seen that the doctrine of Universalism was preached by Nehor, for which he was put to death.—The next sect was a kind of Episcopalians,[9] who were also heretics—who "gathered themselves together on one day of the week, which day they called the day of the Lord—and they had a place which was high and lifted up, which held but one man, who read prayers, the same prayers every week, and this high place was called Rameumptom, which being interpreted is the holy stand,["] p. 311. The Episcopalians and Universalists can claim, on Mormon authority, great antiquity for their orders, at least fifty years before the gospel dispensation.

To amuse the reader, we will narrate an event which is found on page 271. One Ammon, a gospel missionary, who had previously devoted himself to the missionary cause, went among the Lamanites to preach baptism, repentance, and the remission of sins, through Jesus Christ. The servants of king Lamoni of the Lamanites, took Ammon prisoner and brought him before the king, who being rather pleased with his [Ammon's] sober honest deportment took him into his service. The king's servants, together with Ammon, were sent to water the flocks at some distance. On their way they were met by another party of Lamanites, who sought a quarrel by scattering the king's flocks—a loss of any one of the cattle was punished

---

9. Howe follows Campbell's interpretation of the Zoramites of Alma 31:12–23 as "a sort of Episcopalians" (*Millennial Harbinger*, Feb. 1831, 88), probably for the similarity in high-church worship and doctrine of predestination.

by death. This circumstance presented a fine opportunity for
Ammon to distinguish his knight errantry; for he was a brave
knight, as well as a priest. The servants of the king were greatly
frightened, as they might well be, in consequence of the severe
penalty, in case any of the flock should be lost, which would
[mean they would] unavoidably be executed. But Ammon
seized upon this favorable opportunity, and said to the other
servants, "encircle the flocks round about, that they flee not;
and I go and contend with these men which do so scatter our
flocks—Ammon stood forth and began to cast stones at them
with his sling; yea, with mighty power he did sling stones
amongst them; and thus he slew a certain number of them,
insomuch that they began to be astonished at his power; nevertheless they were angry because of the slain of their brethren,
and they determined that he should fall; therefore, seeing that
they could not hit him with their stones, they came forth with
their clubs to slay him. But behold, every man that lifted his
club to smite Ammon, he smote off their arms with his sword,
insomuch that they began to be astonished, and began to flee
before him; yea, they were not a few in number; and he caused
them to flee by the strength of his arm. Now six of them had
fallen by the sling, but he slew none, save it were their leaders;
and he smote off as many of their arms as was lifted against
him, and they were not a few." In this Don Quixote adventure,
there are two important circumstances worthy of our consideration and investigation, to wit: that this horde of Lamanites
should be *astonished twice*, inasmuch as Ammon only killed
six and cut off the arms of, perhaps, not more than twenty!!
And the other is, that they got angry because Ammon slew

a few of them. Ammon certainly showed great forbearance, for he only killed their captains and leaders, and punished the rest by simply loping off a few of their arms. The result shows us that the battle was very unequal, much more so than the conflict between Sampson and the Philistines; for Sampson had no sword, but our hero [Ammon] not only had a sword, (which afterwards fell into the hands of [the mythological] Guy of Warwick,) but he doubtless understood the scientific use of it. Missionaries in those days [medieval period when the Warwick story is set] wore swords, and for aught we know the *chapeaux des bras*.[10] We are ready to give full credit to the whole account, provided it can be proven that those Lamanites got *angry* once and were astonished twice—those circumstances seem improbable on so slight an occasion.[11]

Chief Justice Alma has three sons, viz: Helaman, Shiblon and Corianton—towards the end of his career, three commandments, one for each son, were written, each in separate chapters. We should view them rather as patriarchal valedictories, if they were not headed commandments.

---

10. A Napoleon-style hat that can be folded flat and carried under the arm, sometimes three-cornered and pocket-sized.

11. What Howe is saying is that the hero's supernatural skills are lost on the unworthy opponent, the Lamanites staring dumbly and charging again, without strategy or emotion, as mere background characters to further the plot, as BYU Professor Douglas Thayer noticed about the Book of Mormon enemy never being "particularly well organized or led. They seem to simply swarm out of the wilderness painted with blood (or at least before they got armor), hoping to … overcome the opponent by the sheer weight of numbers," he wrote. "You would think the Lamanites would wise up after they were tricked the first time. … They are quite inept," Thayer added (Thayer, *Nephites at War,* xx–xxii).

To Helaman he commits the plates of Nephi, or the records, as he calls them, which he says shall be preserved by the
hand of the Lord, and shall go forth into every nation, kindred
and tongue, p. 326.

We are presented with another method of translating the
plates—possibly the spectacles may get lost, or they may not suit
the eyes of all. "And the Lord said, I will prepare unto my servant
Gazelam, a stone, which shall shine forth in darkness unto light,
that I may discover unto my people which serve me, that I may
discover unto them the works of their brethren; yea, their secret
works, their works of darkness and abominations," p. 328.

Now, whether the two methods for translating, one by a
pair of stone spectacles "set in the rims of a bow," and the other
by one stone, were provided against accident, we cannot determine—perhaps they were limited in their appropriate uses—at
all events the plan meets our approbation.

We are informed that Smith used a stone in a hat, for
the purpose of translating the plates. The spectacles and plates
were found together, but were taken from him[12] and hid up
again before he had translated one word, and he has never seen
them since—this is Smith's own story. Let us ask, what use
have the plates been or the spectacles, so long as they have
in no sense been used? or what does the testimony of Martin

---

12. After Martin Harris lost the dictation in mid-1828, the angel took
back the plates and spectacles, then returned them in September when Smith's
wife began acting as scribe (*History of the Church*, 1:21, 23; Smith, *Biographical
Sketches*, 124–25; Vogel, *Documents*, 1:73, 370). The scribes said the dictation
proceeded with Smith simply looking at a seer stone in his hat without any
plates or spectacles in the vicinity, as Howe reported.

Harris, Oliver Cowdery and David Whitmer amount to? They solemnly swear that they saw the plates, and that an angel showed them, and the engravings which were upon them. But if the plates were hid by the angel so that they have not been seen since, how do these witnesses know that when Smith translated out of a hat, with a peep-stone, that the contents of the plates were repeated and written down? Neither of the witnesses pretend that they could read the hieroglyphics with or without the stone; and, therefore, are not competent testimony—nor can we see any use, either in finding the plates or the spectacles, nor of the exhibition of them.

The notable ball [compass] is committed to the charge of Helaman, by the right of the law of primogeniture, with the following descriptive and pathetic remarks from his father—"And now my son, I have somewhat to say concerning the thing which our fathers call a ball or director, or our fathers called it Liahona, which is, being interpreted, a compass: and the Lord prepared it." The sons of Alma were all priests, and were called missionaries, because they devoted their time to traveling and preaching among the heathen, declaring unto them the glad tidings of great joy. Alma now prophecies of the destruction of the Nephites; he says, that four hundred years after the coming of Christ they will entirely lose their religion, p. 348.

The following extraordinary doctrines were preached in the days of the Judges; and believers were called Christians, and "baptism unto repentance" was declared the only door of salvation. "And it came to pass that they did appoint priests and teachers throughout all the land, over all the churches,["] p. 349. "And those who did belong to the church were faithful;

yea, all those who were true believers in Christ took upon them gladly the name of Christ or Christians, as they were called, because of their belief in Christ," p. 301.[13] "And it came to pass that there were many who died, firmly believing that their souls were redeemed by the Lord Jesus Christ: thus they went out of the world rejoicing," p. 353. The word was preached by Helaman, Shiblon, Corianton, Ammon, and his brethren, &c. "yea, and all those who had been ordained by the holy order of God, being baptised unto repentance," (John's baptism) "and sent forth to preach unto the people," p. 362. "And that great and last sacrifice will be the son of God; yea, infinite and eternal; and thus he shall bring salvation to all those who believe on his name; this being the intent of this last sacrifice, to bring about the bowels of mercy, which overpowereth justice and bringeth about means unto men that they may have faith and repentance,["] p. 320.

It will be remembered that the author pretends that the above doctrines were preached from about fifty to an hundred years before Christ's nativity. The clumsy manner in which the above quotations are written, cannot be attributed to the veil which hangs over the spirit of prophecy, for the doctrines are as distinctly explained as the same author can do it at this time, unless he has, since writing the Book of Mormon, undergone a classical drilling, which is far from probable.

Moroni is the next important personage in the drama; he is represented as master of all the modern military tactics, according to the record of Helaman, and [Helaman] is now the

---

13. Actually page 351 (Alma 46:15).

scribe of all the important matters that are passing; but not the author yet of a book.[14]

Moroni, who now commands all the forces of the Nephites against the Lamanites, is represented as conducting the war with great skill, and the number which was slain in the battles surpasses any other account in the annals of history. The prowess of Gen. Moroni is only equaled by Ammon in his battle with the Lamanites, where he killed *six* and cut off the arms of "*not a few.*"

In the thirty-sixth year of the reign of the Judges, Helaman dies, and delivers the old legacy over to Shiblon, which consisted of the brass plates, gold plates, the compass, the big sword, the stone spectacles and the peep-stone, all sacred relics!! In the thirty-sixth year, Moroni dies, after having in a pious manner killed hundreds of thousands of the heathen.

At about the conclusion of the Book of Alma, one Hagoth is ushered on the stage as an old ship carpenter—"And it came to pass, that Hagoth, he being an exceeding curious man, therefore he went forth and built him an exceeding large ship, on the borders of the land *Bountiful*, by the land *Desolation*, and launched it forth into the West Sea, by the narrow neck which led into the land northward.—Query—did John Bunyan, when writing his Pilgrim's Progress, pilfer terms from the Book of Mormon, or had the author of our new revelation

---

14. The hand-off to Helaman occurs in the last chapter of Alma (63:11) before Helaman begins his own record. The Book of Helaman follows and runs forty-four pages. The character named Moroni is a military leader and not to be confused with his namesake at the end of the Book of Mormon. The Book of Helaman will be discussed in chapter 7.

become familiar with the words Bountiful and Desolation by reading that eccentric but excellent production?[15]

The ship which Hagoth built, was large and commodious for passengers. Many are said to have embarked in this ship for other countries northward, and our ship carpenter built a great many more within the term of *two years!*—This furnishes the credulous Mormon with a plausible account of the first inhabitants upon the Islands in the Pacific Ocean,[16] and of those west of the Rocky mountains.

The sacred legacy, consisting of the plates and the peep stone, is next conferred upon Helaman, the son of Helaman, which ends the account of Alma, and his sons Shiblon and Helaman, p. 406.

---

15. Howe's memory is wrong because the word *bountiful* occurs only once in *Pilgrim's Progress* and does not lend itself to being the inspiration for a place name in the Book of Mormon. In fact, Bunyan has fun with the reader when he writes that one of his minor characters has "a sister named Bountiful." It would be even more far-fetched to think the jocular metaphor employed by the main character in saying, "I came from the town of Stupidity; it lieth about four degrees beyond the City of Destruction," could be the inspiration for the Land of Desolation, the word *destruction* being the closest thing to *desolation* in *Pilgrim's Progress*.

16. In agreement, see Shumway, "Polynesians," in *Encyclopedia of Mormonism*, 3:1110–12.

CHAPTER 7.

The Book of Helaman.—Helaman, the son of Helaman, is the next writer of a book, which commences with the fortieth year of the reign of the Judges and reaches down to the ninetieth, and is the year preceding the nativity of Jesus Christ.

In the commencement of this book, we are presented with the account of mighty wars and battles, with great slaughter—next, with multitudes of holy prophets, prophecying of the coming of the Messiah. Thousands were baptised unto repentance and for the remission of sins. "And the Holy Spirit of God did come down from heaven, and did enter into their hearts, and they were filled as with fire, and they could speak forth marvelous words," p. 421. Freemasonry is here introduced and is said to have originated with a band of highwaymen.[1] This institution is spoken of in very reproachful terms, in consequence of the members having bound themselves by secret oaths to protect each other in all things from the justice of the law. The Nephites are represented as being Anti-masons and Christians, which carries with it some evidence that the writer

---

1. Alexander Campbell quoted Hel. 5:45 to show the book's perspective that "Masonry was invented about this time; for men began to bind themselves in secret oaths to aid one another in all things, good and evil" (*Millennial Harbinger*, Feb. 1831, 88). Martin Harris agreed that the Book of Mormon was an "Anti-masonick Bible" (*Geauga Gazette,* Mar. 15, 1831).

foresaw the politics of New York in 1828-29, or that work was revised at or about that time.[2]

Nephi, who is the son of Helaman,[3] now receives the sacred charge of keeping the plates, &c. together with the power of loosing and sealing in Heaven, and the gift of working miracles. He invokes a famine, which follows, as a matter in course, in order to bring the people to the remembrance of their religion. The distress and suffering occasioned by the famine is beyond description, without the aid of Mormon inspiration.

The Nephites, notwithstanding all their wars and difficulties, were not idle—they made progress in the sciences; their arts were not confined to the building of temples, houses and large ships, &c., but they understood astronomy,[4] of which any one will be convinced after reading the following elegant extract: "If he saith unto the earth thou shalt go back that it lengthen out the day for many hours, and it is done; and thus

2. Thurlow Weed of Rochester and others countered Andrew Jackson's 1828 bid for office by spreading fear about his Masonic membership (see Vogel, "Mormonism's 'Anti-Masonick Bible,'" 17–30). Howe's parenthetical statement allowed for the possibility that Rigdon might have edited Spalding's manuscript. Later Howe will speculate that Spalding himself may have harbored a "strong antipathy to the Masonic Institution" (pp. 403–04).

3. There are several Nephis in the Book of Mormon. This one's son, the grandson of Helaman, will have the Book of Third Nephi named after him.

4. See Hel. 12:14–15; cf. Josh. 10:12–14; Isa. 38:7–8. Responding to critics of scriptural inspiration, Bible commentator Adam Clarke suggested that the phrase "the sun stood still" could be interpreted metaphorically or even as literally true but incomplete if God caused the earth and sun to both stop simultaneously (Clarke, *Holy Bible,* s.v., Gen. 2:48). In a similar way, the Book of Mormon tried to explain the miracle in a way that was "more acceptable" to modern science, according to Hullinger, *Joseph Smith's Response to Skepticism,* 156.

according to his word the earth goeth back, and it appeareth unto men that the sun standeth still; yea, and behold, this is so: for sure it is the earth that moveth, and not the sun." If the prophet Elijah[5] had taken the same precaution when he commanded the sun to stand still, and explained it in such a clear and astronomical manner as did our Nephite prophet, the infidel caviling of [David] Hume, [Edward] Gibbon, and others, would doubtless have been avoided upon the subject of that miracle. But we perceive that the prophets of the Old Testament were of the minor class or were only satellites, when compared to an inspired Nephite.

The events of our history are growing more and more important—the heathen or the Lamanites send forth a prophet, (in what way it is brought about after all their curses we cannot see, but such is the fact) among the Christians; his name is Samuel, and he foretells the coming of Christ, and says the night before he will be born, will be as light as day, but in order that the people may distinguish the two periods of time, they shall see the sun rise and set, but the light would not be extinguished but remain as bright as day all night, p. 445. The crucifixion and death of our Savior is also foretold and described in the following poetic style: "The sun shall be darkened and refuse to give light unto you; and also the moon and stars; and there shall be no light upon the face of this land, for the space of three days," and he adds that great earthquakes and convulsions, hills and mountains shall be leveled, and valleys shall become mountains; and divers atmospherical

---

5. He means Joshua (Josh. 10:12–14).

phenomena, such as thunder and lightning, tempests, &c. will take place, p. 446-7.

Samuel likewise prophecies of the restoration of the Lamanites, to the true religion of the Redeemer, and that they finally would be numbered among his sheep. Samuel is persecuted as usual among the Nephites, by the infidels, but he is represented as having so much of the spirit of God, that he was invulnerable to their missiles and other weapons.

"The Book of Nephi, the Son of Nephi, which was the son of Helaman," p. 452[6].—The great and notable year has at length arrived, "and it was six hundred years from the time that Lehi left Jerusalem." This is the year in which the Savior must be born, and the event is consequently brought about by our author, accordingly. During this year the infidels rallied all their forces, and towards the close they had rejoicings and festivities because they fancied that Samuel had prophecied falsely. They not only rejoiced, but sent forth threatenings against the Christians! But Nephi prayed to God for protection, who informed him that the time was at hand, that, that very night the sign should be given—and lo! the sun set, and the brightness of the day continued, to the discomfiture and confounding of the infidels. A star appeared, which every body saw even in the bright light of day. By what kind of vision it could be seen, we cannot conjecture, unless through the medium of those huge magic spectacles. The power of seeing stars in a *bright light* day was never heard of previous, nor since that time, unless

---

6. In the original edition, this subdivision was identified as quoted here and not yet as 3 Nephi.

through the medium of optical instruments; but whether the spectacles were used, or whether the star was as large and as bright as the sun, we cannot determine.

We have heretofore mentioned that free-masonry originated with a band of robbers, and at the present period of our history, that class of men are the most formidable foes of the Nephites. They inhabited the mountains and lurked in secret caverns of the rocks, and could not be ferreted out. The only safe-guard which the Nephites possessed, was, to appoint such men as were filled with the spirit of prophecy and revelation for their chief captains and generals; and by this means they could not be surprised and destroyed by the mountain robbers.

We do not object to this mode of making rulers over the people; but we cannot see why, when God appointed and anointed Joseph Smith his high priest on earth, and ruler over his people, he did not give him sufficient prophetic knowledge so that he might have avoided the disturbances in Missouri and his own *tom fool's* errand,[7] together with about three hundred deluded followers, to reinstate the disinherited from the "promised land"?

Mighty battles are fought between the Nephites and their mountain enemies, but the former are always successful, on account of their inspired rulers and generals. "And thus they did put an end to all those wicked, and secret, and abominable combinations, in the which there were so much wickedness, and so many murders committed," p. 463.

---

7. Howe alludes to Smith's failed attempt to redeem his Zion in Missouri from enemies in May–June 1834.

The writer says his name is Mormon, and is a "pure descendant of Lehi," p. 464.[8] He assures us that his record is true, but complains of the impoverished condition of their language, and that many things cannot be written in consequence of it. This is the first instance of any complaint that we have ever met with, where an inspired writer could not convey divine history, for want of language. In this case, the Almighty is represented as forestalling himself by undertaking to make a history of important events without language, through the medium of a brass plate engraver.—Preposterous!!

In the thirty-fourth year of the reign of the Judges, Samuel's prophecies are realized. A great and terrible tempest is described, which lasted three hours; thunder and lightning, such as were never before witnessed. The great city of Zarahemla took fire, and the city of Moroni sunk in the depths of the sea, cities which were in vallies were destroyed & their location became mountains, the rocks were split asunder and the face of the whole earth became *"deformed,"* p. 470-1.

After the terrible tempest, then came on darkness, which was so intense that it could be felt—candles, nor torches, nor fires, however dry the fuel, would not give the least scintillation of light—all was darkness; "the sun, nor the moon, nor the stars," were any more useful. In this terrible period, sixteen cities were destroyed, together with their inhabitants; some were burned, and others sunk into the depths of the sea!! p. 471-2.

8. In this section of Third Nephi, Mormon introduces himself to readers, writing that he is drawing on accounts left by Nephi and others to summarize what happened during this portion of the history (3 Ne. 5:9-12, 20; cf. W of M 1:3–5).

The troubles of the Nephites and the destruction at this time, is represented by our author as surpassing all other events, and if the description was truth, we should not differ with him in the least. But let us see how it compares with the words of our Savior, as recorded in St. Matthew's gospel [24:21]—"For there shall be great tribulation, such as was not, nor ever shall be." Here our blasphemer is at direct issue with the Son of God.

After the description of the great signs which were seen and heard during the three days of darkness and trouble, the people gather themselves in a great multitude about the temple, which was situate[d] in the land Bountiful, and were expressing their astonishment of the past events, and conversing about Jesus Christ, when they heard a voice from heaven, which "caused their hearts to burn"—they cast their eyes toward Heaven, and they saw a man descend, clothed in a white robe. Fear came upon all for they thought it was an angel. The whole multitude are called upon to thrust their hands into his side and examine the points of the nails, and they did so, one by one, which satisfied them that [th]is was the Son of God. After having authorized Nephi and a number of others to baptize, the Savior issues the following explicit command in relation to receiving members into the church: "Behold, ye shall go down and stand in the water, and in my name shall ye baptise them. And now behold, these are the words which ye shall say, calling them by name, saying—Having authority given me of Jesus Christ, I baptize you in the name of the Father, the Son, and of the Holy Ghost, Amen. And then shall ye immerse them in the water, and come forth again out of the water." It seems to us that the instructions here given are wholly gratuitous, for this mode, precisely, has already been practiced by the Nephites, for about four hundred years, or since King Noah was baptized, in the river Mormon.[9]

The number which were authorized to administer and preach, were *twelve*, which were afterwards called apostles.[10] After every thing is organized the beatitudes are repeated to them in a translation corresponding with that found in the 5th Chap. of St. Matthew's Gospel, together with the sermon on the mount,[11] somewhat transposed, but the variations are inconsiderable. The Savior is represented as continuing to address the multitude with almost precisely the same sentences which are recorded by the evangelists, somewhat picked up, and not very judiciously arranged.[12]

The preaching is finally finished, and Christ departs into Heaven, and we are then presented with apostolic writing, from which we extract the following beautiful, descriptive sentence: "And after this manner do they bear record; the eye hath never seen, neither hath the ear heard before, so great and marvelous things as we saw and heard Jesus speak unto the Father; and no tongue can speak, neither can the hearts of men conceive so great and marvelous things as we both saw and heard Jesus speak; and no one can conceive of the joy

---

9. It was Helam who was baptized, not King Noah. Nevertheless, the mode was the same. Cf. Mosiah 18:13; 3 Ne. 11:25.

10. The Nephite preachers were called "twelve disciples," not "twelve apostles."

11. Cf. 3 Ne. 12–14; Matt. 5–7.

12. The borrowings from the evangelists (3 Ne. 15–28) are from Matt. 7, 21 and John 5, 8, 10, with additional biblical material from Isa. 52, 54; Mic. 4, 5; Mal. 3–4; Acts 2–4; 1 Cor. 11, 15; 2 Cor. 12; and 2 Pet. 3.

which filled our souls at the time we heard him pray for us unto the Father." p. 489.

The only additional commandments which were given to the American apostles on this special visit of the Savior, were—"Pray in your families unto the Father, always in my name, that your wives and your children may be blessed"—"meet often, and forbid no man from coming unto you, when you shall meet together," p. 492.

Nephi, our present hero, was the archbishop—he baptized himself, and then baptized the eleven,[13] whose names were Timothy, Jonas, Mathoni, Mathonihah, Kumen, Kumenonhi, Jeremiah, Shemnon, Jonas, Zedekiah, and Isaiah—"They were baptized with fire and the Holy Ghost."—Many marvelous sayings are represented to have been uttered, but not one of them could either be spoken or written, although he [Christ] spoke for many days!!

The plates of Nephi were critically examined, and only one omission could be found which was, that no mention was made of the resurrection of the saints which were raised in America at the time of the great tempest, who were very numerous!!

"The Book of Nephi, the Son of Nephi."[14]—This book includes only four pages, and contains the whole history of three hundred and twenty years after Christ.—Events appear to be unimportant, or otherwise they are of that character which cannot be written nor spoken.

---

13. Even though the term *archbishop* is foreign to the Book of Mormon, it approximates Nephi's position in the church. The details of Nephi's baptism (23:7–13) are ambiguous; cf. 3 Ne. 19:11.

14. This is now called Fourth Nephi.

In the thirty-sixth year, all the inhabitants of the land were converted and baptized, and a perfect community of peace was the result. This condition of Millennial happiness, continued for one hundred and seventy years. Three of the apostles were immortalized and were seen four hundred years after their induction into the sacred office by the Savior. Where they are at this time, has not been revealed, but it is conjectured by some that the three witnesses appended to the Book of Mormon,[15] to establish the truth of the brass-plate revelation, are the identical immortal three.[16]

We cannot be dismissed by our author until we are told that sectarianism commenced among the Christians, which terminated in wars and bloodshed, and almost a total extinction of vital religion, which happened in the year, A.D. 320.

All the events, from the time when Amaleki delivered the plates to king Benjamin up to the present period of our history, have been written by Mormon, who is the recording angel of the whole matter.[17] And he now keeps the record under his own observation; and commences a book in the following

---

15. Oliver Cowdery, Martin Harris, and David Whitmer.

16. Since no other sources corroborate this conjecture, it is assumed to have been sarcasm.

17. Perhaps this should be taken poetically since Ether is also soon referred to as the "recording angel" (p. 138; see also the reference on p. 390 to Moroni). If Howe meant to identify Mormon as the angelic messenger in the Joseph Smith story, there was no consensus among Mormons about this; Oliver Cowdery was the first to identify the supernatural visitor as Moroni (*Messenger and Advocate,* Apr. 1835, 112). When Joseph Smith compiled his history in 1838, he said it was Nephi, and this was repeated in the *Times and Seasons,* Apr. 14, 1842, 753; the 1851 Pearl of Great Price, p. 41; and in the history written by Joseph's mother, *Biographical Sketches*, 79.

sublime language; "And now I, Mormon, make a record of the things which I have both seen and heard, and call it the Book of Mormon." We have never read of so great a general, nor so great a Christian as was our hero Mormon. He commanded in one engagement against the Lamanites, 42,000 men, all with splendid equipage, and under complete martial discipline. The terrible battle was fought, and Mormon came off victorious, as a matter of course, A.D. 330.

A definitive treaty was concluded, after the great battle between the two hostile powers; and the Lamanites took South America and the Nephites North America; there being only a small remnant left of either side. Mormon exhorts the people to obey the commands of Christ, and laments over the slain, and represents that thousands of females had fallen in the great battle, p. 530.[18]

Moroni is the next on the stage, and finishes what his father left undone, and continues the history down to A.D. 400. He complains that the plates are so small, (the art of manufacturing the sacred brass leaves we suppose is lost) he is obliged to make the record in "Reformed Egyptian," otherwise he would have written or engraved the whole matter in Hebrew. The whole record "being handed down and altered according to our manner of speech," p. 538.—He says that no one shall disbelieve his record, because of its imperfections! and declares that all who receive it, will not condemn it for that reason, and promises to those who believe, not doubting, [that they] shall know far greater things, p. 532. *He that condemneth it shall be in danger*

---

18. This is the 21-page section of the Book of Mormon bearing Mormon's own name. For the passage cited, see Morm. 6:11–22.

of hell fire." We are told by Moroni,[19] in a lamentable manner, that Free-masonry will be very prevalent[20] in the days that the *unlearned man* shall find the plates; and establishes the doctrine that miracles will never cease unless it be through unbelief.

Previous to baptism each applicant must relate his religious experience, as being a duty and satisfaction to the church, and be sure not to partake of the *sacrament unworthily*.

The "Book of Ether," which commences, "And now I, Moroni, proceed to give an account of the ancient inhabitants which were destroyed by the hand of the Lord, upon the face of this north country." The privilege of recording the great events of the people of Jared, has been reserved for our hero, Moroni. The people of Jared are those who were not confounded in their language at the destruction of Babel, but built ships, eight in number, and came to America, nearly 4000 years ago. The record is taken as we are told, from the gold plates which were found by the forty men whom king Limhi despatched to make discoveries.

One Ether is the reputed author of the engravings on the gold plates, and in the translation by Moroni, *alias* Smith, we are presented with a genealogy of the fathers down to Jared, who left the great Tower, together with sundry other families and embarked for America. The genealogy is somewhat amusing; he gives us twenty-nine generations down to the time of

---

19. Moroni takes over from his father and writes the last two chapters of the section called Mormon, prior to compiling his own book.

20. Howe borrowed wording from Campbell, who said Moroni "laments the [future] prevalency of free mansonry in the times when his Book should be dug up out of the earth" (*Millennial Harbinger*, Feb. 1831, 90).

Jared, and the time when the Lord confounded the languages. According to the writings of Moses, the Tower was built in the days of Shem, the son of the patriarch Noah, and agreeably to the evangelist Luke, there were only ten generations between Shem and Adam!![21] If we are not allowed the Bible to prove the Book of Mormon false, we must resort to the reasonableness of the story and positions taken.

To rescue Jared and his people, God marched before them in a cloud, and after reaching the sea he directed them to construct eight barges, in which to cross the seas. The whole eight are finally built, after the directions given by the Lord, and when finished they were air tight! The Lord directs them how to remedy the evil—they are commanded to make a hole in the top to admit air, and one in the bottom to admit water; in each hole was put a *molten stone*,[22] which, when touched by the finger of Jesus, becomes as transparent as any glass, and gave them light under the "mountain waves," as well as above the water. He that touched these stones appeared unto the brother Jared, and said, "Behold I am Jesus Christ, I am the Father and the Son." Two of these stones were sealed up with the plates, according to a prediction before Abraham was born. How, and in what manner they became set in the "two rims of a bow," and fell into the hands of the Nephites, has not been explained, nor what has become of the remaining fourteen molten stones, [which] is likewise hidden in mystery.

---

21. The genealogy pertains to Ether, not to Jared. Ether is said to have lived centuries later, so his list of ancestors is much longer.

22. The shining stones were placed at "each end" of the eight vessels (Eth. 6:2) rather than in the air holes (cf. 2:20).

Moroni says, in his Book of Ether, that he that should find the plates, should have the privilege of shewing them unto those who should assist him in publishing the book, "and unto *these* shall they be shewn by the power of God: wherefore they shall of a surety know that these things are true," p. 548.

Those barges or ships are literally described on page 57 [93] of this work as it is found on p. 542 [of the Book of Mormon].[23] The barges are represented air tight, and after diving and swimming three hundred and forty four days, they all safely arrive at the land of promise.

The people of Jared had the Gospel of Jesus Christ revealed and preached to them—and in the lapse of ages and generations, they became very numerous, and wars and contentions ensue. Two renowned generals take the command of the two hostile forces; one is named Coriantumr and the other Shiz. Shiz pursues Coriantumr to the sea shore, where a battle is fought with unparalleled slaughter, which lasted three days— three battles more are fought, and Coriantumr is represented successful in every rencountre [hostile encounter], but on the fifth attack, Shiz comes off conqueror.

Coriantumr now remembers the prophecies of Ether, and he counts his slain, and they amount to nearly two million!! How many Shiz lost, is not computed. However, the cessation of hostilities did not last long; the two generals commenced rallying together their troops, which occupied four years; and every person was enrolled that was in all the land—"men, women and children,"—on one side or the other, except Ether, who was then the recording angel and prophet. "And it came

---

23. Ether 2:17.

to pass that when they were all gathered together, every one to the army which he would, with their wives and children; both men, women and children, being armed with weapons of war, having shields, and breast-plates, and head-plates, and being clothed after the manner of war, they did march forth, one against another, to battle, p. 572.

They fought five successive days without conquering, and the slain could not be numbered; but the remains of Coriantumr's army were fifty-two, and those of Shiz, sixty-nine. The next day the forces met again, and the soldiers of Coriantumr were reduced to twenty-seven and those of Shiz to thirty-two; and on the next day they fought again—they were all killed except the two generals. Coriantumr took advantage of Shiz, and cut off his head, and then he "fell to the earth and became as if he had no life," p. 573. This story cannot be doubted, for Ether went forth and saw it, and finished his record; and adds, that he is uncertain whether he shall be translated or not, and concludes by saying that it is no matter if he can be saved in the kingdom of God. Thus ends the Book of Ether, giving an account of the people of Jared, who were of a different race from the lineage of Adam, because we have their genealogy, which embraces twenty-nine generations, and begins to count back from the days of Shem. Neither Noah nor any other of the antediluvian patriarchs are mentioned, consequently others must have been preserved from the flood than Noah and his family, if this history be true. Besides the inspiration of Moses is not only contradicted in this particular, but in the plain declaration that the Lord confounded the language of the whole human race, Gen. XI. 9.

"The Book of Moroni,"—Moroni is the *last* of the Nephites! He has survived his whole race, amidst wars and carnage, for the important purpose of *"abridging"* the records of the people of Jared and of sealing up the plates of Nephi, which is done, A. D. 420.

Contrary to his expectations, he lives, and concludes to write a book for the benefit of his brethren the Lamanites, which he hopes will ultimately convert them. To avoid discovery, by the Lamanites, he remains *incognito*;[24] he expresses great fear of assassination by them, if discovered, on account of his great belief in Christ, which he asserts, roundly, he will not renounce, p. 574.

The manner of ordaining priests and teachers, and of "administering the flesh and blood of Christ" is the first subject explained; after which, the particular qualifications for admission into Christ's visible church, is described, together with the ordinance of baptism, which must be done by immersing the candidate under water.

Moroni notices the manner in which the ancient Nephites worshiped, and says they met often to converse about the welfare of their souls, and met often to partake of the *bread and wine*, in remembrance of the Lord Jesus. It was customary to forgive their members for their transgressions, as often as they required it, and the confessions were made before the Elders of the church. Previous to the death of Mormon, he wrote a

24. Howe inserted an asterisked footnote here: "Moroni, however, has been seen by Smith, as he says, in Susquehannah Co., Pa., since the plates were translated. A more particular account of this interview will be found in a subsequent part of this work." See pp. 389–90.

few epistles to his son Moroni, which he inserts, and then concludes to write something which seems good to him. Spiritual gifts, he assures us, will never cease, only through unbelief and want of faith. And when the plates of Nephi should be dug up out of the earth, Moroni "exhorts you that ye should ask God, the Eternal Father, in the name of Christ, if these things are not true; and if ye shall ask with a sincere heart, with real intent, having faith in Christ, and he will manifest the truth of it unto you by the power of the Holy Ghost," p. 586. Here we are directed how we can all become Mormons, to wit: first believe all the fooleries, and forgeries, and lies of Jo Smith's translation of the brass plates; and then pray to be convinced of its divine authenticity, not doubting, and then, by the power of the Holy Ghost, it will all be made manifest!!

We now have gone through with the new revelation, or the Bible of the Mormonites, the analysis of which we present to our readers. The task has been a laborious one, and we acknowledge but little has been effected, and would cheerfully make an apology to our readers for the uninteresting results, if the forest through which we have traveled had furnished better materials for our review. We should have abandoned the task, were it not that so many of our worthy fellow citizens have been seduced by the witcheries and mysterious necromances of Smith and his colleagues, from the paths of wisdom and truth, into folly and madness. We anticipate the bitter vituperation and sneers of the Mormon leaders and their influence over their already numerous followers, and do not expect to accomplish a reformation amongst them; but if we shall serve to enlighten *any*, who are not already the slaves of Mormon madness, *alias* the Devil, we will feel richly compensated.

The next subject is the testimony of the "three witnesses," Oliver Cowdery, David Whitmer and Martin Harris, which is appended to the Book of Mormon, to establish its divine authenticity.[25] It is as follows:

The Testimony of Three Witnesses.

Be it known unto all nations, kindreds, tongues, and people, unto whom this work shall come, that we, through the grace of God the Father, and our Lord Jesus Christ, have seen the plates which contain this record, which is a record of the people of Nephi, and also of the Lamanites, his brethren, and also of the people of Jared, which came from the tower of which hath been spoken; and we also know that they have been translated by the gift and power of God, for his voice hath declared it unto us; wherefore we know of a surety, that the work is true. And we also testify that we have seen the engravings which are upon the plates; and they have been shewn unto us by the power of God, and not of man. And we declare with words of soberness, that an Angel of God came down from heaven, and he brought and laid before our eyes, that we beheld and saw the plates, and the engravings thereon; and we know that it is by the grace of God the Father, and our Lord Jesus Christ, that we beheld and bear record that these things

---

25. In June 1829 Cowdery, Whitmer, and Harris accompanied Joseph Smith to a field near the Peter Whitmer farm in Fayette, New York, to see the plates. After praying for some time without result, Harris withdrew, believing he was the cause of their failure. In Harris's absence the others were visited by an angel, according to their statements. Afterward, Smith joined Harris, who was praying some distance away, and together they experienced the same vision (*History of the Church*, 1:54–55; Vogel, *Documents*, 1:83-86).

are true; and it is marvelous in our eyes: Nevertheless, the voice of the Lord commanded us that we should bear record of it; wherefore, to be obedient unto the commandments of God, we bear testimony of these things. And we know that if we are faithful in Christ, we shall rid our garments of the blood of all men, and be found spotless before the judgment seat of Christ, and shall dwell with him eternally in the heavens. And the honor be to the Father, and to the Son, and to the Holy Ghost, which is one God.

Oliver Cowdery, David Whitmer, Martin Harris,

The solemnity of an oath has been regarded sacred in all ages of the world; both by the pagan and the Christian. In all civil communities, like ours, when an individual calls the searcher of all hearts to whom he expects and firmly believes he must render a final account in a future state of existence, to bear him witness to the solemn truth of his assertions, we are irresistibly led to give full credit to his testimony. But experience has taught us, that sometimes individuals have purjured themselves, however revolting it may seem at first view; yet suspicions as to the credibility of a witness ought to be well grounded.

There are many circumstances which go to destroy the credibility of a witness, and his competency. By the common law, no person can be a witness, who does not entertain a just sense of the obligation of an oath, and disbelieves in a God, and a future state of accountability. Nor can any person be a witness who is interested in the event of a suit, that is, when he may gain or lose by the verdict.

These rules are taken, and are well founded, together with many others equally well established.

It is unnecessary for us, in this place, to give the reasons for the above rules of the common law; but the long application of them in our municipal courts, and the justice which has uniformly resulted from their operations upon the rights of individuals and communities, are sufficient arguments in favor of their equitable claim for continuance in all our civil tribunals.

At the end of the Book of Mormon the names of Oliver Cowdery, David Whitmer and Martin Harris, are affixed under a most solemn oath, testifying to the divine exhibition of the plates to them, and of their having been translated by the power of God!!

Here are positive declarations, under the solemnities of an oath, with circumstances that will justify us in an examination, as to the credibility and competency of the witnesses.

In the first place, do each of these witnesses entertain a just sense of the obligation of an oath? do they believe in a future state of existence and accountability? We think the rational answers are in the negative; nor will any one disagree with us, when we shall have proven that the Book of Mormon was a joint speculation between the "author and proprietor" and the witnesses.

How stands the matter? Martin Harris was the scribe for Smith, for a considerable part of the work, and then mortgaged his farm to the publisher as collateral security for the payment of $3000, and after the book was completed he claimed the whole profits of the sale, until he should be reimbursed. These are facts which can be substantiated in a court of justice. Then, was he not a partner? would not the law consider him connected with Smith and make him jointly liable?

Oliver Cowdery was the principal amanuensis, probably better qualified for the task, than his predecessor Harris.— How, and in what way he was connected we can only infer from circumstances. His pecuniary situation was very low, and the labor of writing, if he charged common wages, would amount to no inconsiderable sum, and Smith was wholly irresponsible to pay him, nor can we learn that Harris had indemnified him in any manner whatever. Then, the rational inference is, that after having the plot disclosed to him, he was willing to risk his chance for a fortune. He is now associated with the leaders, and appears in easy circumstances.

David Whitmer is a very inconsiderable person, but is in high standing, as a leader, among the Mormons. We know but little about him, only that he has been known as a man of small capacity, an anxious dupe to the marvelous, and a firm believer in witches. Whether he was suborned or deceived by the impostor we are unable to determine.

So far as it relates to Smith, Cowdery and Harris, we have clearly shown that they were connected in the outset, as the result has proven; a failure of which, would have reduced Harris to beggary, and blasted the fond hopes of Smith and Cowdery, and brought down upon them everlasting contempt and disgrace.

In addition to the joint speculation, we may connect the attempt to institute a new religion, contrary to the revelations of Jesus Christ, as revealed in the Bible—which we claim to have clearly shown in our analysis of the Book of Mormon. And he who would be guilty of so gross a sacrilege, necessarily disbelieves in accountability to God, and therefore would perjure himself, with impunity.

We contend, therefore, that no credit ought to be given to those witnesses; nor are they competent, firstly, because they were under no conscientious restraint, and secondly, their worldly prospects depended upon the issue.

Above, we have copied the solemn testimony of "the three witnesses," accompanied with circumstances which renders it proper for us to critically examine and analyze it. They call God to witness, that they have seen the plates from which the Book of Mormon is translated; and that the translation was accomplished by the power of God, for his voice had declared it unto them!! At what time this special revelation was made, is not specified; but we infer that the voice of God declared the fact to them in relation to the translation, at one time, and that they saw the plates at another;[26] and they were severally chosen, and no others, to bear the testimony to the world. Nor could any others have seen and heard as they did, had they been present.

If an individual swears to a particular fact or facts, in order that the testimony may be believed—time, place and other circumstances must be mentioned, without which others might be prejudiced, by not giving them an opportunity to rebut. If the time and the place had been mentioned, when and where the plates were seen, it is not impossible but that testimony of

---

26. When Whitmer was interviewed by Edward Stevenson in 1877, he said that "a Light appeared & it Grew Brighter until an Angle Stood before us and on [what had] the appearance of A table Was laid the Plates[,] Urim & Thumin[,] Ball or Director[,] Sword of Laban &c & a voice Declared & Bore record of the truth of the Translation[,] [the angel] turning the Leaves over & thus the vision ended" (Stevenson journal, 14:10–18, LDS Church History Library; Cook, *David Whitmer Interviews,* 11; *History of the Church*, 1:54-55; Vogel, *Documents*, 1:83–86).

equal credibility might be produced, to show that there was no such place; and that the witnesses were hundreds of miles from the country in which they testified they saw them. Then the testimony is vague and uncertain,[27] and not entitled to credit upon that ground. If the subscribing witnesses saw the plates and heard the voice of God; they themselves must have been in some place or places when the communications were made; and it is not unreasonable to enquire into it.

But this is not all. Testimony must be of such a nature that others, if they were present, could have testified to the same facts. But in the testimony, the three would have us believe that they were specially chosen to testify to the truth of the Book of Mormon, and no others, according to the predictions of the Mormon prophets, made over two thousand years ago. Besides all the transactions which have been and will be shewn in the course of this work, in relation to the getting up of the Book of Mormon, the testimony carries strong suspicions upon the face of it; and were it disconnected from all other circumstances of fraud and deception, it would not be believed, however solemnly declared, in a court of justice.

We have, likewise, the testimony of eight other witnesses subjoined, consisting of four Whitmers, Hiram Page, Joseph Smith, Sen., (the father of the prophet,) and two of his brothers.[28]

---

27. In fact, it is only through the witnesses' subsequent statements that we learn how Harris saw the plates separately or that there were other objects lying on the table. Nor would we necessarily know that the witnesses never saw a physical artifact.

28. Smith's history dates the three witnesses' experience to June 1829. The eight witnesses had about the same experience "soon after" that (*History of the Church*, 1:57; Vogel, *Documents*, 1:86). Lucy Smith said it was a "few days"

They testify that Joseph Smith, Jun., showed them the plates, and that they looked like gold, and that they saw the engravings and *hefted* them.

Who are the witnesses? four Whitmers of the same family with the one who subscribed to the miraculous exhibition of them, and three Smiths, the father and two brothers of the prophet. And what is their testimony? Why, that Jo Smith showed them some plates, that were yellow and had engravings upon them, which they could not read nor understand; but Jo probably told them that he had translated a part of them, and intended to continue the work until he had finished them. So much for the eight witnesses.

---

later. It occurred in Manchester, after Joseph and others had traveled there to arrange for the Book of Mormon to be printed. The men "repaired to a little grove where it was customary for the family to offer up their secret prayers" and were met "by one of the ancient Nephites" who had brought the plates with him from Fayette (Smith history, 1844–1845, 102, 104; Vogel, *Documents*, 1:395–96). John Whitmer said he saw and handled the plates on that occasion (*Messenger and Advocate*, Mar. 1836, 286–87) but later elaborated to a Mormon associate that "they were shown to me by a supernatural power" (Turley, "Memorandums," 1845, LDS Church History Library; *History of the Church*, 3:307).

CHAPTER 8.

Before the publication of the book, Smith found many who believed its contents, from the ghost stories which he related concerning it. Soon after it was issued from the press, a person by the name of Parley P. Pratt *happened* to be passing on the canal through Palmyra,[1] and hearing of the wonders of the gold plates and huge spectacles, called on the prophet, and was soon converted. This Pratt then resided in Lorain County, Ohio; and had, some time previous, formed an intimacy with Sidney Rigdon, and became a convert to his doctrines. This Rigdon was a man of great eloquence, belonging to a denomination of Christians, who style themselves, "Disciples," or "Reformers," and who are also, by their opponents, in derision, called "Campbellites." He resided in the County of Geauga, and but a few miles from the place which has since been made the head quarters of Smith. He was a very popular preacher, and had large congregations in different parts of the country. If there was a man in the world that could successfully spread and

---

1. Parley P. Pratt (1807–57) was born in Burlington, New York, thirty miles south of Utica. A minister with a restive mind, he became interested while traveling in the vicinity of Palmyra in August 1830 in reports he was hearing about Mormonism. He stopped to investigate and a month later he was baptized. Soon he became involved in helping convert Rigdon. The italics in *happened* indicate Howe's belief that the chance encounter was contrived, that Rigdon had a hand in writing the Book of Mormon.

give a name to the vagaries of the Smiths, it was Rigdon. They soon became convinced of this, by the representations of Pratt. We may here stop to remark that an opinion has prevailed, to a considerable extent, that Rigdon has been the *Iago*,[2] the prime mover, of the whole conspiracy. Of this, however, we have no positive proof; but many circumstances have carried a *suspicious* appearance; and further developments may establish the fact.

Either before or soon after the arrival of Pratt at Manchester, among the Smiths, it appears that an expedition was fitted out for the Western Country, under command of Cowdery, in order to convert the Indians, or Lamanites, as they called them. As a preparatory step, a long revelation was furnished by Smith, to Cowdery, to serve as his credentials. This curious document will be found in the succeeding pages, from which it will be seen that the prophet, at the outset, feared a rivalship, and took effectual means to put it down. His brother Hiram, it appears, also undertook to write some mysteries from a *stone*, which was forthwith *vetoed*, and pronounced to be the work of Satan.[3]

As Cowdery had been a scribe to the prophet, it became necessary to supply his place. He [Joseph Smith] therefore

---

2. A villain in Shakespeare's *Othello*.

3. This incident involved Hiram Page, not Hyrum Smith. A physician and farmer, Page (1800–52) was born in Vermont and married into the Whitmer family (Catherine), which is how he became one of the eight witnesses. Soon after he received his Mormon teacher's license in June 1830, he began receiving revelations through a seer stone until the revelations were denounced as satanic by Joseph Smith (D&C 28). Page moved to Ohio in 1831, Missouri in 1832, and withdrew from the church in 1838 when several Whitmer family members were excommunicated.

very prudently and *affectionately*, had the following command for his wife [Emma]:

A commandment to Emma, my daughter in Zion, A. D., 1830.—A revelation I give unto you concerning my will. Behold, thy sins are forgiven thee, and thou art an Elect Lady, whom I have called. Murmur not because of the things which thou hast seen, for they are withheld from thee and from the world, which is wisdom in me in a time to come; and the office of thy calling shall be for a comfort unto my servant Joseph, thy husband, in his afflictions, with consoling words in the spirit of meekness; and thou shalt go with him at the time of his going, and be unto him a *scribe*, that I may send Oliver whithersoever I will: and thou shalt be ordained under his hand to expound the scripture, and to exhort the church according as it shall be given thee by my spirit, for he shall lay his hands upon thee and thou shalt receive the Holy Ghost; and thy time shall be given to writing and to learning much; and thou needst not fear, for thy husband shall support thee from the church, for unto them is his calling, that all things might be revealed unto them whatsoever I will according to their faith; and verily I say unto thee, that thou shalt lay aside the things of this world and seek for the things of a better; and it shall be given thee also to make a selection of sacred Hymns as it shall be given thee, which is pleasing unto me to be had in my church, for my soul delights in the song of the heart, yea the song of the righteous is a prayer unto me, and it shall be answered with a blessing upon their heads, wherefore lift up thy heart, and rejoice and cleave unto the covenant which thou hast made—continue in the spirit of meekness—let thy soul delight in thy husband and the glory which shall come upon him—keep my commandments continually, and a crown of righteousness thou shalt receive; and except thou do this, where I am ye cannot come, and verily I say unto you that this is my voice unto all—Amen.[4]

These were some of Smith's first attempts at making his followers believe that the Lord was to make known his will constantly through him; and the persons chosen were, it must be acknowledged, the best of which the nature of the case would admit—his wife and Cowdery. In this operation, he abandoned his spectacles, or "peep-stone,"[5] and merely delivered it with his eyes shut. In this manner he governs his followers, by asking the Lord, as he says, from day to day. Every difficult question or dispute is thus decided—from it there is no appeal. He has taught them, that to doubt their divine authority, is to endanger their salvation. We shall have occasion, in the progress of this work, to give many curious specimens of his art of governing.

The expedition to the "Lamanites"[6] was finally fitted out

---

4. D&C 25, dictated July 1830 and published in the 1833 Book of Commandments. Variations point to a handwritten copy in Ezra Booth's possession (see pp. 262–63).

5. David Whitmer said "Joseph gave the stone to Oliver Cowdery" in early 1830 and told Whitmer "that he was through with it, and he did not use the stone any more … [but] would enquire of the Lord, pray and ask concerning a matter, and speak out the revelation" unaided (Whitmer, *Address*, 32; Vogel, *Documents*, 5:199–200). Cowdery kept Smith's brown seer stone to his death in 1850 when it was taken to Salt Lake City by Phineas Young and given to the First Presidency. There is evidence that Smith afterward occasionally used another seer stone (Quinn, *Early Mormonism*, 242–47).

6. The Shawnee and Delaware tribes had been relocated to the region west of the Missouri River in what is now Kansas. Since the Book of Mormon addressed the origin of American Indians, the indigenous people were thought to be good proselyting prospects.

by Smith, and was composed of Cowdery, Pratt, Peterson and Whitmer.[7] In the latter part of October, 1830, under the guidance of Pratt, they arrived at the residence of Rigdon, in Mentor, Ohio, well supplied with the new bibles.—They professed to rejoice at finding a people walking according to the scriptures, and pretended to acknowledge no other guide. They professed to have no commands for *them*; nevertheless, they called upon them to receive the book as from Heaven, which they said mostly concerned the western Indians, as being an account of their origin, and a prophecy of their final conversion to Christianity, and [to] make them a "*white* and delightsome people," and be reinstated in their lands, of which they have been despoiled by the whites.[8] When called upon for testimony, they appealed (like Mahomet) to the internal evidences of their book.—The book was read by Rigdon, and pronounced a "silly fabrication." When farther pressed upon the subject, they required the people to humble themselves before God, and pray for a sign from Heaven. Near the residence of Rigdon, in Kirtland, there had been, for some time previous, a few families belonging to his congregation, who had formed themselves into a common stock society,[9] and had become considerably fanatical, and were daily looking for some wonderful event to

7. Richard Ziba Peterson would leave the church in 1833, move to California in 1848, and die in the gold fields in 1849. Peter Whitmer Jr. (1809–36), another Book of Mormon witness and native of Fayette, would die of tuberculosis a few days short of his twenty-seventh birthday.

8. This account of the missionaries' exchange with Rigdon comes from Howe's previous article in the *Painesville Telegraph*, Feb. 15, 1831.

9. The group known as "the family" lived together communally on Isaac Morley's farm northeast of Kirtland, not unlike the Shakers in nearby North Union.

take place in the world. Their minds had become fully prepared to embrace Mormonism,[10] or any other mysterious *ism*
that should first present itself. Seventeen in number of these
persons, readily believed the whole story of Cowdery, about
the finding of the golden plates and the spectacles. They were
all re-immersed,[11] in one night, by Cowdery. At this, Rigdon
seemed much displeased,[12] and when they came next day to
his house, he told them that what they had done was entirely
without precedent or authority, from the scriptures—for they
had immersed those persons that they might work miracles,[13]
as well as come under their new covenant—showed them that
the Apostles baptized for the remission of sins, instead of miraculous gifts. But when pressed upon the point, they said it
was done merely at the solicitation of those persons. Rigdon
again called upon them for proofs of the truth of their book
and mission; they then related the manner in which they obtained faith, which was by praying for a sign, and an Angel was
showed unto them. Rigdon here showed them from scripture
the possibility of their being deceived: 'For Satan himself is
transformed into an angel of light.' But said Cowdery, "do you
think if I should go to my heavenly Father, with all sincerity,
and pray to him in the name of Jesus Christ, that he would not

---

10. Rigdon's congregation had separated from Campbell's movement and
was looking for a stricter restoration of primitive Christianity. See Vogel, *Religious Seekers*, 36–41.

11. They had already been immersed in water once as "reformed Baptists."

12. Howe italicized *seemed* to indicate his feeling that this was a ruse
intended to conceal Rigdon's prior involvement.

13. According to the converts, spiritual manifestations confirmed the
missionaries' authority. See Vogel, *Religious Seekers*, 38–39.

show me an Angel; that he would suffer Satan to deceive me?"
Rigdon replied, "if the heavenly Father has ever promised to
show you an Angel, to confirm any thing, he would not suffer
you to be deceived, for says John, 'this is the confidence we
have with him, if we ask things according to his will, he hear-
kens to us.'" But he continued, "if you should ask the heavenly
Father to show you an Angel, when he has never promised you
such a thing, if the Devil never had an opportunity of deceiving you before, you give him one now."

However, about two days after this, Rigdon was persuaded
to tempt God by asking [for] this sign, which he knew to be
contrary to his revealed will; he of course received a sign, and
was convinced that Mormonism was true and divine.—According to his own reasoning, therefore, the Devil appeared to him
as an angel of light; but he now imputed his former reasoning
to pride, incredulity, and the influence of the Evil One.

On the conversion of Rigdon, a most successful starting
point [for the new church] was thought to have been obtained.
Cowdery and his associates then began to develope the pe-
culiarities of the new imposition. Scenes of the most wild,
frantic and horrible fanaticism ensued.[14] They pretended that
the power of miracles was about to be given to all those who

---

14. This paragraph comes from the *Painesville Telegraph,* Feb. 15, 1831.
Mormon chronicler John Whitmer described the over-enthusiasm like this:
"Some had visions and could not tell what they saw. Some would fancy to
themselves that they had the sword of Laban, and would wield it as expert
as a light dragoon, some would act like an Indian in the act of scalping, some
would slide or scoot on the floor, with the rapidity of a serpent, which the[y]
termed sailing in the boat to the Lamanites, preaching the gospel. And many
other vain and foolish manoeuvers, that are unseeming, and unprofitable to

embraced the new faith, and commenced communicating the Holy Spirit, by laying their hands upon the heads of the converts, which operation, at first, produced an instantaneous prostration of body and mind. Many would fall upon the floor, where they would lie for a long time, apparently lifeless. They thus continued these enthusiastic exhibitions for several weeks. The fits usually came on, during or after their prayer-meetings, which were held nearly every evening.—The *young* men and women were more particularly subject to this delirium. They would exhibit all the apish actions imaginable, making the most ridiculous grimaces, creeping upon their hands and feet, rolling upon the frozen ground, [and] go through with all the Indian modes of warfare, such as knocking down, scalping, ripping open and tearing out the bowels. At other times, they would run through the fields, get upon stumps, preach to imaginary congregations, enter the water and perform all the ceremony of baptizing, &c. Many would have fits of speaking all the different Indian dialects, which none could understand. Again, at the dead hour of night, the young men might be seen running over the fields and hills in pursuit, as they said, of the balls of fire, lights, &c., which they saw moving through the atmosphere.

Before these scenes fully commenced, however, Cowdery had departed for the country inhabited by the Indians, with the expectation of converting them to Christianity, by means of his new bible, and miracles which he was to perform among them. These pretensions appeared to have taken possession of the minds of the young men in their aspirations. Three of them

mention" (Westergren, *From Historian to Dissident*, 57; Davidson et al., *Joseph Smith Papers: Histories*, 2:38).

pretended to have received commissions to preach, from the skies, after having jumped into the air as high as they could. All these transactions were believed to be the *Spirit of God*, by the whole congregation, which now numbered more than one hundred.—That they were honestly impelled by the same causes which have, in all ages of the world, contributed so much to debase human nature, we have no doubt. One of the young men referred to, freely acknowledged, some months afterwards, that he knew not what he did, for two or three weeks.—Such is the mind of man, when his reason is dethroned by physical causes. One of these aerial commissions,[15] which they all supposed was signed and sealed by Christ himself, we here subjoin, verbatim:

> Oh my servant, there is a great work for you and the other two of your brethren. I send a messenger to tell you where to go and find a piece of parchment that shall contain these words:—You shall teach repentance and remission of sins to all who shall come in the sound of your voice—I command you that you do these things in sincerity and in truth; and if you do, you shall be blessed.—The time is shortly acoming and is not far distant

---

15. Its publication in the *Painesville Telegraph*, Apr. 12, 1831, was accompanied by this: "Three young men, while in the spirit, had received commissions direct from Heaven, on parchment, which they caught in their hands in the air, and had only time to copy them, before the parchment disappeared. ... It was found in the pocket of young [Warner] Doty, who recently died among them." John Whitmer elaborated that Satan "took a notion to blind the minds of some of the weaker ones, and made them think that an angel of God appeared to them, and showed them writings on the outside cover of the Bible, and on parchment, which flew through the air, and on the back of their hands, and many such foolish and vain things" (Westergren, *From Historian to Dissident*, 13–14; Davidson et al., *Joseph Smith Papers: Histories*, 2:22).

when you shall be bound together for life—the names of your brethren are these: Burr Riggs[16] and Edson Fuller,[17] and if they are not faithful I will choose another in their stead—my work must be done. My servants, you shall go forth from place to place, and if you are true to your trust, they shall hear. Remember that I am the Lord your God—serve me above all others, and I will bless you, in the end, Amen.

That [which][18] you had a messenger tell you to go and get the other night, you must not show to any son of Adam.— Obey this and I will stand by you in all cases—my servants, obey my commandments in all cases, and I will provide.

Be ye always ready, Be ye always ready, Be ye always ready, whenever I shall call. My Seal[19]

There shall be something of greater importance revealed when I shall call you to go—my servants, be faithful over a few things, and I will make you a ruler over many.—Amen, Amen, Amen.

These commissions, they said, came on parchment, and they had only time to copy them before they vanished from their sight. With such papers in their pockets they actually went through the country, preaching, and made many converts. Two of the three afterwards obtained their reason, and left the

16. Burr Riggs (1811–60), physician, was born at New Haven, Connecticut. He was baptized and ordained an elder sometime before June 1831 and excommunicated in 1833 and 1839.

17. Edson Fuller (b. 1809), a carpenter from New York, was baptized and ordained an elder before June 1831, but his priesthood license was revoked in September.

18. Howe wrote, "That that you had …"

19. Howe placed a small illustration of the seal here: a line drawing of what looks like the sun coming over the horizon with "1+" written on the sun.

concern. All these things were afterwards pronounced by Smith to be the work of the Devil,[20] although more than one hundred had been converted to Mormonism, by merely witnessing the exhibitions. They professed, at all times, their inability to work miracles, but were secretly trying to perform them, and frequently proclaimed their success.[21] At a distance from the scene of action, many notable miracles were circulated.

During these performances, it would be remembered, that Rigdon was not present. In about three weeks after his conversion, he repaired to the *bible quarry*, in the state of New York, in order to have a personal interview with the prophet. Smith was prepared to receive him, of course; and a *commandment* was soon fitted out for him, every way calculated to suit his case and vanity. This being an important link in the chain of our history, we here transcribe it:

A Commandment to Joseph and Sidney,[22] Dec. 7. 1830: Saying, listen to the voice of the Lord your God; I am Alpha and Omega, the beginning and the end, whose course is one

20. Joseph Smith's revelation of May 1831 threatened to excommunicate anyone who did not denounce such "false spirits" (D&C 50). He said "the spirit was rebuked, and put down, and those who would not submit to rule and good order, were disfellowshipped" (*Times and Seasons*, Apr. 1, 1842, 747).

21. The *Western Courier*, May 26, 1831, reported that Mormons expected to "work divers miracles" at an upcoming conference, and afterward the *Geauga Gazette* found the Mormons "persist[ing] in their power to work miracles. They say they have often seen them done—the sick are healed—the lame walk" (June 21, 1831).

22. D&C 35 was published in the *Ohio Star*, Jan. 5, 1832, and the *Painesville Telegraph,* Jan. 17, after it was apparently obtained from Simonds Ryder (MacKay et al., *Joseph Smith Papers: Documents*, 1:219).

eternal round; the same to-day as yesterday and forever. I am Jesus Christ, [who] was crucified for the sins of the world, even as many as will believe on my name, that they may become the sons of God, even on me as I am in the father, as the father is in me, that we may become one. Behold, verily, verily I say unto my servant Sidney, I have looked upon thee and thy works; I have heard thy prayers, and prepared thee for a greater work—thou art blessed, for thou shalt do great things. Behold, thou wast sent forth even as John, to prepare the way before me and Elijah which should come, and thou knewest it not—thou didst baptize by water unto repentance, but they secured not the Holy Ghost; but now I give unto you a commandment, that thou shalt baptize by water and give the Holy Ghost by laying on of hands, even as the Apostles of old. And it shall come to pass that there shall be a great work in the land, even among the Gentiles, for their folly and their abominations shall be made manifest in the eyes of all nations; for I am God, and mine arm is not shortened, and I will shew miracles, signs and wonders, unto all those who believe on my name; and whosoever shall ask in my name, in faith, shall cast out Devils, they shall heal the sick, they shall cause the blind to receive their sight, and the deaf to hear, and the dumb to speak, and the lame to walk; and the time speedily cometh that great things are to come and be shown forth unto the children of men; but without shall nothing be shown forth except desolation and destruction upon Babylon, the same which hath made all nations drink of the wine of their fornication, and there are none that doeth good except them that are trying to receive the fulness of my Gospel, which I have sent forth to this generation.—Wherefore, I have called upon the weak things, that they are unlearned and despised, to thresh the nations by the

power of my spirit, and their arm shall be my arm, and I will
be their shield and their buckler; I will gird up their loins and
they shall fight manfully for me, and their enemies shall be put
under their feet; and I will let fall the sword in their behalf,
and by the fire of mine indignation will I preserve them, and
the poor and the meek shall have the gospel preached to them,
and they shall be looking forth to the time of my coming, for
it is nigh at hand, and they shall learn the parable of the fig-
tree, for even now already, summer is nigh at hand, and I have
sent forth the fullness of my gospel by the hand of my servant
Joseph, and in meekness have I blessed him, and I have given
unto him the keys of the mysteries of those things which have
been sealed, even things which have been from the foundation of the world, and the things which shall come from this
time till the time of my coming, if he abide in me, and if not,
another will I plant in his stead; wherefore, watch over him
that his faith fail not; as it shall be given by the comforter, the
Holy Ghost, which knoweth all things. And a commandment I
give unto you, that thou shalt write for him, and the scriptures
shall he [be] given, even as they are in mine own bosom, to the
salvation of mine own elect, for they will hear my voice, and
shall see me, and shall not be asleep, and shall abide the day of
my coming, for they [shall] be prepared, even as I am prepared,
and now, I say unto you, tarry with him and he shall journey
with thee—forsake him not, and surely these things shall be
fulfilled; and inasmuch as ye do not write, behold it shall be
given unto him to prophecy, and thou shalt preach my gospel
and call on the Holy Prophets to prove his words as they shall
be given him. Keep all the commandments and covenants by
which ye are bound and I will cause the Heavens to shake for
your good, and Satan shall tremble and Zion shall rejoice upon

the hills and flourish, and Israel shall be saved in mine own due time, and by the keys which I have given shall [he] be led and no more be confounded. Lift up your hearts and be glad, for your redemption is nigh. Fear not, little flock, the kingdom is yours until I come. Behold I come quickly, even so. Amen.

We, before, had Moses and Aaron in the persons of Smith and Cowdery, and we now have John the Baptist, in the person of Sidney Rigdon.[23] Their plans of deception appear to have been more fully matured and developed after the meeting of Smith and Rigdon. The latter being found very intimate with the scriptures, a close reasoner, and as fully competent to make white appear black, and black white, as any other man; and at all times prepared to establish, to the satisfaction of great numbers of people, the negative or affirmative, of any and every question, *from scripture*, he was forthwith appointed to promulgate all the absurdities and ridiculous pretensions of Mormonism, "and call on the Holy Prophets to prove" all the words of Smith. But the miraculous powers conferred upon him, we do not learn have yet been put in requisition. It seems that the spirit had not, before the arrival of Rigdon, told Smith any thing about the "promised land," or his removal to Ohio. It is, therefore, very questionable, "what manner of spirit" it was which dictated most of the after movements of the Prophet. The spirit of Rigdon, it must be presumed, however, generally held sway; for a revelation was soon had, that Kirtland, the

---

23. Howe interpreted the Moses and Aaron metaphor in 2 Ne. 3:18 as a reference to Smith and Rigdon (p. 72). The John the Baptist parallel is in D&C 35:4.

residence of Rigdon and his brethren, was to be the eastern border of the "promised land," "and from thence to the Pacific Ocean."[24] On this land the "New Jerusalem, the city of Refuge," was to be built. Upon it, all true Mormons were to assemble, to escape the destruction of the world, which was so soon to take place. The *width* of this Mormon farm, we have not heard described. The *revelation* concerning the promised land, we have not been able to obtain a copy of;[25] it is explained, however, in the following letter from Rigdon, written to his brethren in Ohio, soon after he became acquainted with the movements and designs of the prophet.

I send you this letter by John Whitmer.[26] Receive him, for

---

24. Howe took these words from the Feb. 1, 1831, *Palmyra Reflector*'s printing of a letter dated Jan. 26, 1831, from a resident of Waterloo, New York. The correspondent added that Rigdon "delivered a discourse at the Court House immediately preceding his departure. ... After denouncing [pronouncing] dreadful vengeance on the whole state of New-York, and this village in particular, and recommending to all such as wished to flee from 'the wrath to come,' to follow him beyond the 'western waters,' he took his leave. ... Their first place of destination is understood to be a few miles west of Painesville, Ohio, (the present place of the Elder's residence) which is just within the east bounds of this new land of promise, which extends from thence to the Pacific Ocean."

25. Howe is unaware that the revelation mentioning the "land of promise" given in January 1831 was published in *The Evening and the Morning Star* in 1833 and was included in the abortive printing of the Book of Commandments, now LDS D&C 38. Rigdon's belief that the revelation pointed to Kirtland as the blessed site was undercut three months later when it was revealed that Missouri was the intended "land of promise, and the place for the city Zion" (D&C 57:1–2).

26. John Whitmer (1802–78) was born in Pennsylvania and probably baptized with brothers David and Peter in June 1829. He was one of the eight witnesses; he served as one of Joseph Smith's scribes during the dictation of

he is a brother greatly beloved, and an Apostle of this church.[27] With him we send all the revelations which we have received; for the Lord has declared unto us that you pray unto him that Joseph Smith and myself go speedily unto you; but at present it is not expedient for him to send us. He has required of us, therefore, to send unto you our beloved brother John, and with him the revelations which he has given unto us, by which you will see the reason why we cannot come at this time.[28] The Lord has made known unto us, some of his great things which he has laid up for them that love him, among which the fact (a glory of wonders it is) that you are living on the land of promise, and that *there* is the place of gathering, and from that place to the Pacific Ocean, God has dedicated to himself, not only in time, but through eternity, and he has given it to us and our children, not only while time lasts, but we shall have it again in eternity, as you will see by one of the commandments,

---

the Book of Mormon, then for the Bible revision and copies of the revelations. He wrote that in January 1831 "the Lord manifested himself to Joseph the Revelator and gave commandment for me to go to the Ohio, and carry the commandments and revelations, with me, to comfort and strengthen my brethren in that land" (Westergren, *From Historian to Dissident*, 13). The *Painesville Telegraph*, Jan. 18, 1831, announced his arrival: "A young man by the name of Whitmer arrived here last week from Manchester, New York, the seat of wonders, with a new batch of revelations from God."

27. The words *elder* and *apostle* were used interchangeably at the time. There was not yet a quorum of twelve apostles. See the Articles and Covenants of the Church of Christ (especially D&C 20:38); Vogel, *Religious Seekers*, 145–46; Quinn, *Mormon Hierarchy: Origins*, 10–14; Prince, *Power from on High*, 13–15.

28. A revelation dictated in December 1830 stated: "Ye shall not go [to Ohio] until ye have preached my gospel in those parts [New York Finger Lakes], and have strengthened up the church whithersoever it is found, and more especially in Colesville; for, behold, they pray unto me in much faith" (D&C 37:2).

received day before yesterday.[29] Therefore, be it known to you, brethren, that you are dwelling on your eternal inheritance; for which, cease not to give ceaseless glory, praise and thanksgiving to the God of Heaven.—Yes, lift up your heads with joy, for the kingdom is ours till the Savior comes, even so, Amen— therefore, prepare your hearts to receive salvation which God has sent unto you, knowing that they [the revelations] have come from God; and know assuredly if you receive them, you shall receive greater things, yes, things unspeakable and full of glory—"such as eye hath not seen, nor ear heard, neither hath it entered into the heart of man to conceive," for our God hath in visions shown it unto me.[30] Therefore, I write with the greatest certainty of these things which he hath prepared for us—yes, even us, forever, who receive the revelations of the last days, [and] are the very people of whom the prophets spoke, and the very saints who shall rejoice with Jesus!!!

This communication caused a great rejoicing in the congregation. They were then residing upon their "eternal inheritance"!!! Rigdon tarried with Smith about two months, receiving revelations, preaching in that vicinity, and proving by the prophets that Mormonism was true, as he imagined. He then returned to Kirtland, Ohio, being followed in a few days after by the prophet and his connections.[31] This being the

---

29. The revelation (D&C 38) was received during a conference in Fayette on January 2, 1831, dating Rigdon's letter to January 4.

30. Ezra Booth reported that Rigdon was "favored with many extraordinary visions." The idea of Kirtland as a millennial city was an "expectation [that] was grounded upon Rigdon's visions, while he was in the state of N.Y." (Howe, p. 308).

31. Smith said he arrived at Kirtland in company with his wife, Rigdon, and Edward Partridge "about the first of February" 1831 (*History of the Church*,

"promised land," in it their long cherished hopes and anticipations of "living without work" were to be realized. Thus, from almost a state of beggary, the Smiths were immediately well furnished with the "fat of the land" by their fanatical followers, many of whom were wealthy.

1:145; Vogel, *Documents*, 1:140). The *Palmyra Reflector*, Feb. 1, 1831, and *Painesville Telegraph*, Feb. 15, 1831, reported that Rigdon traveled ahead and the rest of the party arrived mid-February (Howe, pp. 167–69).

CHAPTER 9.

On the return of Rigdon, many of his old friends called upon him to enquire about his new faith. The particulars of one of these interviews, we have on record by an eye-witness, which we shall give in his own words, with his remarks thereon:—

Feb. 1, 1831.[1]—Mr. Rigdon just returned from the state of New York. His irascible temper only left him for a little season. Two friends went from Mentor to see him[2]—required of him a reason for his present hope, and for his belief in the Book of Mormon. He declined; saying he was weary, having just come off his journey, had lost much sleep, and the like. After a number of words had passed, by way of solicitation on one side, and refusal on the other, one of the friends from Mentor said he thought there was no more evidence to confirm the Book of Mormon, than the Koran of Mahomet. At this, Mr. R. seemed very angry, rose up and said, "Sir, you have insulted me in my own house—I command silence—if people come to see us and cannot treat us with civility, they may walk out of the door

1. The report was probably written by Matthew S. Clapp, reprinted here from the *Painesville Telegraph*, Feb. 15, 1831, where the author is identified as M.S.C. Clapp. Matthew was the brother of Julia Clapp Murdock, who with her husband, John Murdock, had converted to Mormonism a few months earlier.

2. One of them was Matthew Clapp. His father, Judge Orris Clapp, had converted to the Disciples of Christ in about 1827 and was staunchly opposed to Mormonism. For more on this, see Morton, "Forgotten Daughter," 37.

as soon as they please." The person then made some apology.
Mr. R. said he had borne every thing; he had been insulted
and trampled upon, by old and young, and he would hear it
no longer. The two friends then departed. Two days after, I
accompanied several friends to Mr. R.'s residence, and found
him in conversation with a Methodist elder. That being soon
broken off, one of my friends modestly approached Mr. R. and
solicited him to give some reason for his present faith. Mr. R.,
with a great show of good nature, commenced a lang detail of
his researches after the character of Joseph Smith, he declared
that even his enemies had nothing to say against his character;
he had brought a transcript from the dockets of two magistrates, where Smith had been tried as a disturber of the peace,
which testified that he was honorably acquitted.[3] But this was
no evidence to us that the Book of Mormon was divine. He
then spoke of the supernatural gifts with which he said Smith
was endowed; he said he could translate the scriptures from
any language in which they were now extant, and could lay his
finger upon every interpolation in the sacred writings,[4] adding that he had proven him in all these things. But my friend
knowing that Mr. Rigdon had no knowledge of any language
but his own vernacular tongue, asked him how he knew these
things, to which Mr. R. made no direct reply.[5]

---

3. There were three justices involved in the trial in Colesville, Joel K. Noble
being one of them. For Smith's account, see *History of the Church*, 1:88–96; Vogel,
Documents, 1:114–26; and for Noble's account, see Vogel, *Documents*, 4:106–11.

4. This testimony regarding how familiar Smith was with the contents of
the Bible is supported by his non-canonical writings such as his letter to the
Colesville church from August 1830 (see Vogel, *Documents*, 1:13, 14).

5. The *Pittsburgh Telegraph,* Aug. 24, 1876, carried a report from someone
who remembered having seen Rigdon challenged on his Greek and said it was
"a stumper which closed up poor Sydney, who, after looking all around him,

Mr. Smith arrived at Kirtland the next day,[6] and being examined concerning his supernatural gifts, by a scholar, who was capable of testing his knowledge, he confessed he knew nothing of any language, save the king's English.[7]

Mr. R. asserted that *our* revelation came to us upon testimony—this we denied, and gave him reasons, which he himself formerly urged against *deists*. He then said the *old* revelations were confirmed by miracles, but the Book of Mormon would not be; it was not designed to be thus confirmed. (And Mahomet said, nearly twelve centuries ago, "Moses and Jesus were empowered to work miracles, yet the people did not receive them, wherefore, God had sent him without that attestation, to be the last and greatest prophet.") But in this Mr. R. contradicted his book, for that declares it is to be thus established.

We then asked Mr. R. what object we could have, in receiving the Book of Mormon—whether it enjoyed a single virtue that the Bible did not, or whether it mentioned or prohibited a single additional vice, or whether it exhibited a new attribute of Deity? He said it did not. "The Book of Mormon, (said he) is to form and govern the Millennial Church; the *old* revelation was never calculated for that, nor would it accomplish that

declared us to be such a set of unbelievers that he wouldn't open his mouth to us again that day" (Vogel, *Documents*, 1:50).

6. Clapp's recollection that Joseph Smith first arrived in Kirtland on February 4, 1831, is more specific than from any other source. Joseph never provided an exact date and wrote only that in "the latter part of January, in company with Brothers Sidney Rigdon and Edward Partridge, I started with my wife for Kirtland, Ohio, where we arrived about the first of February" (*History of the Church,* 1:45; Vogel, *Documents*, 1:140).

7. This "scholar" was certainly Matthew Clapp. Amos Hayden said he was "respectable" in Greek and "a good Latinist." In the 1840s Clapp studied Hebrew under Joshua Sexias, the same man who in 1836 taught classes to Joseph Smith's School of the Prophets. See Hayden, *Early History*, 198–200.

object; and without receiving the Book of Mormon there is no salvation for any one into whose hands it shall come." He said faith in the Book of Mormon was only to be obtained by asking the Lord concerning it. To this, scriptural objections were made. He then said, if we have not familiarity enough with our Creator to ask of him a sign, we were no Christians; and that, if God would not condescend to his creatures, in this way, *he was no better than Jugernaut!!!*[8]

Thus I have given a simple statement of facts. They proclaim the ancient gospel, putting their own appendages to it. When they think it will best suit their purposes, they say nothing about the Book of Mormon, and at other times make it their chief topic. Mr. R. said it was no part of his religion to defend the Book of Mormon, he merely wished the people to give heed to the *old* revelation. Again, there is no salvation without believing the Book of Mormon.—Mr. R. blames Cowdery for *attempting* to work miracles, and said it was not intended to be confirmed in that way. How then are we to obtain faith? Does the book offer any internal evidence of its divinity: It contains nothing but what might have been, and evidently was, borrowed from the sacred writings and from the history of the world. Was it so with the revelation that was from the beginning? Far otherwise. Respecting Smith and his followers, do they give any proof of their honesty? They can give none but their own ass[e]rtions. They have no sacrifice to make—no loss of fortune or reputation to sustain. They are in a land of liberty—very different were the circumstances of those who first promulgated the faith "once delivered to the saints." They had to forsake their friends and relations—leave their

---

8. A juggernaut was an oversized wagon carrying a large Hindu statue. The wagon crushed anyone in its path, according to reports circulated by westerners.

possessions, and forfeit their reputation. Twelve apostles sealed their testimony with their blood. So, whether their religion was true or false, they proved their honesty. But Mormonism is to be proved, from beginning to end, by assertions, and this we have in whole numbers. But we know that they cannot more roundly and positively assert, than hundreds of impostures who have gone before them.

From this point in the history of this delusion, it began to spread with considerable rapidity. Nearly all of their male converts, however ignorant and worthless, were forthwith transformed into "Elders," and sent forth to proclaim, with all their wild enthusiasm, the wonders and mysteries of Mormonism. All those having a taste for the marvelous, and delighting in novelties, flocked to hear them.—Many traveled fifty and an hundred miles to the throne of the prophet, in Kirtland, to hear from his own mouth the certainty of his excavating a bible and spectacles.—Many, even in the New England States, after hearing the frantic story of some of these "elders," would forthwith place their *all* into a waggon, and wend their way to the "promised land," in order, as they supposed, to escape the judgements of Heaven, which were soon to be poured out upon the land. The State of New York, they were *privately* told, would most *probably* be sunk,[9] unless the people thereof believed in the pretensions of Smith.

On the arrival of Smith in Kirtland, he appeared astonished

---

9. Missionaries were encouraged to visit the "great and notable cities and villages" to warn the inhabitants about the coming "desolation of abomination." Newel K. Whitney in particular was sent to Albany, Boston, and Manhattan to prophesy to the imminent "desolation and utter abolishment" (D&C 84:114,

at the wild enthusiasm and scalping performances, of his proselytes there, as heretofore related. He told them that he had
enquired of the Lord concerning the matter, and had been informed that it was all the work of the Devil. The disturbances,
therefore, ceased. Thus we see that the devil, for the time being,
held full sway in making converts to Mormonism. We must
here stop to introduce another document, which belongs to this
history. Soon after the return of Rigdon to Kirtland, in some of
his eloquent harangues on the subject of his new faith, he gave
a challenge to the world to disprove the new Bible, and the
pretensions of its authors. Elder Thomas Campbell, of Va. being
in the neighborhood, addressed him the following Letter:[10]—

Mentor, February 4, 1831.

Mr. Sidney Rigdon:

Dear Sir—It may seem strange, that instead of a confidential and friendly visit, after so long an absence, I should
thus address, by letter, one of whom, for many years, I have
considered not only as a courteous and benevolent friend, but
as a beloved brother and fellow laborer in the gospel—but
alas! how changed, how fallen! Nevertheless, I should now

---

117). The *Lyons Gazette*, Aug. 9, 1854, quoted Martin Harris prophesying that an
angel would visit Palmyra and "put one foot upon the sinful village and sink it."

10. Thomas Campbell (b. 1763) was a controversial Scotch-Irish minister
who immigrated to western Pennsylvania in 1807 to oversee a Presbyterian
congregation. He helped form the Christian Association, and his affinity for
baptism by immersion brought him into fellowship with Baptists. By 1830 his
son Alexander had followed his father so far from the mainstream that he could
break away from the Presbyterians altogether and form the Disciples of Christ.
The letter from Thomas Campbell was published in the *Painesville Telegraph*,
Feb. 15, 1831. See addendum, "Thomas Campbell's Introduction to His Own
Letter in the Newspaper."

have visited you as formerly, could I conceive that my so doing would answer the important purpose both to ourselves, and to the public, to which we both stand pledged, from the conspicuous and important stations we occupy:—you, as a professed disciple and public teacher of the infernal book of Mormon; and I, as a professed disciple and public teacher of the supernal book of the Old and New Testaments of our Lord and Savior Jesus Christ—which you now say is superceded by the book of Mormon—[saying also that the Bible] is become a dead letter—*so dead*, that the belief and obedience of [it], without the reception of the latter, is no longer available to salvation; to the disproof of this assertion, I understand you defy the world. I here use the epithets infernal and supernal in their primary and literal meaning, the former signifying from beneath, the latter from above, both of which are truly applied, if the respective authors may be accredited; of the latter of which, however, I have no doubt. But, my dear sir, supposing you as sincere in your present, as in your former profession, (of the truth and sufficiency of which you have frequently boasted with equal confidence,) neither yourself, your friends, nor the world, are therefore bound to consider you as more infallible in your latter than in your former confidence, any further than you can render good and intelligible reasons for your present certainty. This, I understand from your declaration on last Lord's day, you are abundantly prepared and ready to do. I, therefore, as in duty bound, accept the challenge, and shall hold myself in readiness, if the Lord permit, to meet you publicly, in any place, either in Mentor or Kirtland, or in any of the adjoining towns, that may appear most eligible for the accommodation of the public.

The sooner the investigation takes place the better for all concerned; therefore, it is hoped you will not protract the time beyond what may justly be deemed necessary for giving sufficient publicity to the proposed discussion—say one week after your reception of this proposal to accept the challenge you have publicly given, for the vindication and eviction of the divine authorship of Mormonism, which, if your assertion be true, that there is no salvation for any that do not embrace it; and not only so, but I am credibly informed you have asserted, that even those who have lived and died in the faith and obedience of the old book, in the triumphant assurance of a glorious resurrection and a blissful immortality, may be in hell for aught you know; therefore, I say again, the sooner this matter is publicly settled, the better. For my part, I do cordially assure you, sir, that if I were in the possession of a nostrum, upon the knowledge and belief of which, the salvation of every soul of man depended, I should consider myself responsible to the whole world for the speedy and effectual confirmation and publication of it; and if it be at all a revelation from God for the salvation of man, he must be wonderfully changed since he gave the former revelation of his will, for that important purpose, if he do not require you so to do, for he was then willing that all men should come to a knowledge of his will and truth and be saved; and therefore, he not only charged all to whom he made it known, by special revelation, to go into all the world and declare it to every creature, but also furnished them with such potent and evincive arguments, both prophetic and miraculous, as no candid inquirer could mistake, without abandoning both his senses and his reason. If then, the Book of Mormon, which you assume to vindicate as a divine revelation, upon the belief and obedience of which the salvation of all men stands suspended, be such, then surely the unchanged and unchangeable author, who, it seems, has communicated it to you and others, by special revelations, has, doubtless, furnished you with such special, intelligible, and convincing arguments, as are abundantly sufficient to convince every candid inquirer, as he did the heralds of the former dispensations.—Therefore, woe is unto you if you preach not your gospel. But why should I seem to doubt the philanthropy of my former friend and brother, more than I do my own, or that of the apostle Paul, that I should thus appear to urge his performance of a challenge, which, no doubt, the purest and most benevolent motives excited him to propose, for the purpose of promoting, as fast as possible, the benign intentions of his mission? Taking this for granted, I shall further add, in relation to the manner of conducting this all-important investigation, that, seeing it is purely for the discovery and confirmation of the truth, upon the belief and obedience of which, depends the salvation of the world, the parties realizing the deep and awful responsibility of the undertaking, and having no private and personal interest at stake, separate from the rest of mankind, will not only afford each other every facility of investigating and exhibiting the truth by all manner of fairness, both of argument and concession, but also by the mutual allowance of any assistance that can be contributed by the friends on each side, either suggesting matter to the speakers, or by correcting any mistakes that may occur in quotations, references, &c, in an amicable and an obliging manner, without giving or taking offence on these accounts; that for these purposes, each party shall be at liberty to select as many of his intelligent friends as he pleases to assist him as prompters; and if any difficulty occur, respecting time, order, &c, it shall be refered to a competent board of moderators, equally chosen by the parties, that the whole investigation may be conducted without the least shadow of disorder or partiality.

According to the spirit and tenor of the above proposals on my part, for the speedy and effectual determination of the momentous question at issue, I shall candidly inform you of the course I intend to take, for the confirmation and defence of my side of the question, that you may be the better prepared to meet my arguments with a solid and unanswerable refutation, if possible; as I can have no wish, nor can any man in his common senses, where the salvation of the soul is at stake, but to know and embrace the saving truth. The proposition that I have assumed, and which I mean to assume and defend against Mormonism and every other *ism* that has been assumed since the Christian era, is—The all-sufficiency and the alone-sufficiency of the holy scriptures of the Old and New Testaments, vulgarly called the Bible, to make every intelligent believer wise to salvation, thoroughly furnished for any good work. This proposition, clearly and fully established, as I believe it most certainly can be, we [will] have no more need for Quakerism, Shakerism, Wilkinsonianism, Buchanism, Mormonism, or any other ism, than we have for three eyes, three ears, three hands, or three feet, in order to see, hear, work, or walk. This proposition, I will illustrate and confirm by showing—

1st, That the declarations, invitations, and promises of the gospel, go to confer upon the obedient believer the greatest possible privileges, both here and hereafter, that our nature is capable of enjoying.

2nd, That there is not a virtue which can happify[11] or adorn the human character, nor a vice that can abase or dishappify, which human heart can conceive, or human language can express, that is not most clearly commanded or forbidden in the holy scriptures.

3rd, That there are no greater motives, that can possibly

---

11. The *Oxford English Dictionary* traces the verb *happify* to the early seventeenth century, after which it flourished for a while in America.

be expressed or conceived, to enforce obedience or discourage and prevent disobedience, than the scriptures most clearly and unequivocally exhibit.

These propositions being proved, every thing is proved that can affect our happiness, either here or hereafter.

We shall, however, if deemed necessary, next proceed to expose the blasphemous pretensions of Mormonism, by examining both its external and internal evidences.

1st. By examining the character of its author and his accomplices, as far as documents for that purpose may have come to hand.

2d. Their feigned pretensions to miraculous gifts, the gift of tongues, &c.; a specimen of the latter we shall afford them an opportunity of exhibiting in three or four foreign languages.

3d. We shall next proceed to expose the anti-scriptural assertions, that there has been none duly authorized to administer baptism, for the space of fourteen hundred years up to the present time, by showing that the church or the kingdom of Christ, must have been totally extinct during that period, provided its visible administration had actually ceased during that time, [and that this] is an express contradiction of the testimony of Jesus, Mat. xvi. 18.

4th. We are prepared to show that the pretended duty of common property among Christians is anti-scriptural, being subversive of the law of Christ, and inimical to the just rights of society.

5th. We shall next proceed to show, that re-baptizing believers is making void the law of Christ; and that the imposition of hands for communicating the Holy Spirit, is an unscriptural intrusion upon the exclusive prerogative of the primary apostles.

6th. We shall also show that the pretensions of Mormonism,

as far as it has yet been developed, are in no wise superior to the pretensions of the first Quakers, of the French Prophets, of the Shakers, of Jemima Wilkinson, &c. That all these pretended to as high degrees of inspiration, to propho[s]eyings, to visions, to as great humility, self-denial, devotion to God, moral purity, and spiritual perfection; declaimed as much against sin, denounced as heavy judgments against their neighbors, and against the professing world at large, for their corruptions of Christianity, &c. &c. as the Mormonites have done or can do; the two latter have also insisted as much upon the supposed duty of common property, and have spoken as certainly of the near approach of the millenium, and of their relation to that happy state, as any of the Mormonite Prophets, especially the Shakers, who pretend to be living subjects of that happy period, and[12] who have also given us an attested record of their miraculous operations.

The obvious conclusion of this sixth argument is evident, that if the Mormonite prophets and teachers can show no better authority for their pretended mission and revelations than these impostors have done, we have no better authority to believe them than we have to believe their predecessors in imposition. But the dilemma is, we can't believe all, for each was exclusively right in his day, and those of them that remain, are still exclusively right to this day; and if the Shakers be right, the whole world, the Mormonites themselves not excepted, are in the gall of bitterness and bonds of iniquity—quite as far from salvation as you yourself have pronounced all the sectarians on earth to be, namely, in a state of absolute damnation.

In the last place, we shall examine the internal evidence of the Book of Mormon itself, pointing out its evident contradictions,

---

12. The conjunction *and* was repeated twice here.

foolish absurdities, shameless pretensions to antiquity, restore it to the rightful claimant, as a production beneath contempt, and utterly unworthy the reception of a schoolboy.

Thus, my dear sir, I have given you a fair and full statement of my intended method of defence and attack, of the principal topics of argument *pro* and *con*, which I shall use, provided you stand to your proposed challenge. I have also used great plainness of speech, and spoken of things just as I believe they deserve, as you yourself are in the habit of doing; and who can do otherwise upon a subject of such vast importance, if he duly realize them? Nevertheless, I would not have you think, although I consider things just as I have spoken, that I suppose myself more infallible than you do yourself; but I should blush to fall short of any one, of any sect whatever, in my expressions of confident certainty of the truth of my profession, which has stood the test of most rigorous investigation for nearly eighteen hundred years, and which I have scrupulously examined, for upwards of forty, especially when the investigation is with sectarians of little more than three months standing.

But though I have spoken as positively as you have done, and we have both spoken positive enough, I will yet venture to assure you that you will find me, as changeable as yourself, provided you afford me evidence paramount to the evidence which I have proposed to produce for the ground which I at present occupy, for it has ever been with me a fixed principle, that the less should give way to the greater. But in case I should fail to convince you, or that you should fail to convince me, others may be benefitted; and we shall have the consolation of having discharged our duty, both to each other and the public, for no man liveth to himself.

In the mean time I wait for your reply, which you will please to forward per bearer. I hope you will be as candid and plain with me as I have been with you. My best respects to Mrs. Rigdon, and sincerest wish for the happiness of your family.

I remain, with grateful remembrances of the past, and best wishes for the future, your sincere friend and humble servant,

Thomas Campbell.

It is only necessary to say, that after Rigdon had read a few lines of the above, he hastily committed it to the flames.

ADDENDUM

Thomas Campbell's Introduction to His Own Letter in the Newspaper

The following letter[13] was elicited by a public challenge, given by Sidney Rigdon on the 30th ulto,[14] in a public meeting held in Kirtland, at which persons from different states were present, in which he defied the world to refute the divine pretensions of the *Book of Mormon.* The said letter was respectfully presented on the 6th inst. by Nathan P. Goodell, accompanied by Isaac Moore, Esq. both respectable citizens of Kirtland, who inform me, that when he had read about half a dozen lines, till he came to the epithet "*infernal*," which he found applied to his beloved book, he committed it to the flames, as Jehoiakim, the pious, meek and lowly king of

---

13. The letter appears on pp. 172–80. Howe reproduced the letter in its entirety as it appeared in the newspaper but not the introduction to it explaining that it was a response to the challenge made by Sidney Rigdon. What follows here is verbatim from the *Painesville Telegraph.*

14. The abbreviation *ulto*, for *ultimo*, signified the previous month, while *inst.*, for *instant* (see the next sentence) implied the current month.

Judah did Jeremiah's roll—(Jeremiah 36, 23). Had Mr. R's boasted humility, meekness and patience not been so quickly exhausted, he would have been duly informed that the writer meant neither to insult him, nor yet to depreciate his beloved author, more than Christ did the cavillous, Jews, when he said to them, "yet are from beneath."—(Jno. 8, 23) not meaning that they were from hell, as he after explains himself, in the following words, "ye are of this world." Had Mr. R. exercised as much patience as did those proud infidel Jews, he would have learned from my explanation in the very next sentence, that I applied the word *infernal* to the Book of Mormon, in a just and appropriate sense, according to the claims of the book itself, as being dug up out of the bowels of the earth, or from beneath the bottom of a hill; and, therefore, justly styled infernal, taken i[n] its primary literal sense, as I have explained and applied it in my letter. This, however, Mr. R. knows to be the easiest way to get rid of the matter, having no intention to verify his challenge, as he declared to the above named persons before my letter was presented. It also afforded him an opportunity of gratifying his proud resentment by a consequential highblood act of indignant retaliation, the most severe that was in his power to inflict; and which, in the meantime, I accept as a just expression of that spirit, which the Book of Mormon is calculated to inspire, and which has been so abundantly expressed in its murderous, scalping inspirations (excerpt from the *Painesville Telegraph*, Feb. 15, 1831).

CHAPTER 10.

About this time an opinion was propagated among them, that they should never *taste death*,[1] if they had sufficient faith. They were commanded to have little or no connexion with those who had not embraced their faith, and every thing must be done within themselves.[2] Even the wine which they used at their communion, they were ordered to make from cider and other materials.[3] All diseases and sickness among them were to be cured by the Elders, and by the use of *herbs*—denouncing

---

1. John Whitmer reported the belief among early converts "that those who obeyed the covenant in the last days, would never die: but by experience, they have learned to the contrary" (Westergren, *From Historian to Dissident*, 42; Davidson et al., *Joseph Smith Papers: Histories*, 2:33).

2. A revelation in February 1831 answered the question, "Shall the church come together into one place or remain as they are in separate bodies?" The answer explained that "every church shall be organized in as close bodies as they can be [because of the enemy]," the bracketed words coming from the manuscript version, LDS Church History Library. "How far is it the will of the Lord that we should have dealings with the world & how we should conduct our dealings with them?" the revelation continued. The answer: "Thou shalt contract no debts with the world, except thou art commanded" (Book of Commandments 44:55–57). These questions and answers were omitted from section 42 of the Doctrine and Covenants. See Cook, *Revelations*, 59–61; MacKay et al., *Joseph Smith Papers: Documents*, 1:246–49.

3. They were warned by revelation not to purchase "wine neither strong drink of your enemies" and to "partake of none except it is made new among you" (D&C 27:3, 4). The same revelation explained that "it mattereth not what ye shall eat or what ye shall drink when ye partake of the sacrament" (v. 2).

the Physicians *of the world*, and their medicines, as enemies to the human race.

They had one or two *root doctors* among them,[4] for whose benefit it is presumed the Lord made known his will, if at all. Notwithstanding, the prophet himself was the first one to break over the rules he had received from the Lord. Being much alarmed for the fate of his "elect lady," in an obstetrical case,[5] he *applied to the world*, (after all the Mormon remedies had failed,) for an eminent physician. This gave dissatisfaction to some of his followers, but like every thing else, was easily smoothed over.

About the last of March, a young man about 20 years of age, by the name of *Dota*,[6] became suddenly ill and died. He was duly commissioned, after their manner, to preach, was very active and zealous in the cause, and so fully did he believe in the divine mission and miraculous powers of Smith, that he had a firm expectation of living in the world a thousand years. This he made known to a near relation of his, about four weeks before his decease. Five days before he expired, he was suddenly attacked with an inflammation in the bowels. He was

---

4. This line is prefaced by a manicule (typographical index finger). The term "root doctors" referred to herbal practitioners such as Frederick G. Williams whose approach was endorsed by revelatory mention of "herbs and mild food" to treat disorders (D&C 42:43–44; Divett, "Medicine and the Mormons"; Smith, "Herbal Remedies").

5. On April 30, 1831, Emma gave birth to twins who died the same day. Little is known of what medical care she received.

6. This is undoubtedly Warner Doty, who received a written commission from heaven at the end of March 1831, previously mentioned. The story came from the *Painesville Telegraph,* Apr. 5, 1831. Assuming it was about Doty, his name was changed to Dota.

immediately removed to the residence of his parents, living in the neighborhood, who had no faith in the Mormon remedies for the cure of diseases. No persuasion, however, could induce the young man to have a physician called, so strongly was he impressed with the supernatural powers of Smith. Several of the Elders assembled around the sick man, where they continued to encourage him to persevere, and ministering to his delusion, by telling him that he was getting better, and would soon be well, till they saw he was about to expire, when they left him to his fate. Smith was sent for soon after he was taken sick, and proceeded towards the house of Dota, to heal him, but soon returned back, saying that he had received a commandment not to "cast pearl before swine." He, however, visited the sick man a day or two after, and protested against calling a physician, saying that he would get well. A physician was finally called, a few hours before he expired, who told him he had fallen a victim to his delusions. When the young man discovered that death was nigh, his faith in Smith's pretensions seemed to forsake him. He said, "what a wonderful mistake I have made." Addressing himself to an old man of the Mormon faith, he said, "you are a friend to every body—I must shake hands with you—this is a lesson which I have learnt by actual experience, by which you ought to profit, but with me it is too late."

The Mormons soon began to assemble in considerable numbers at and about Kirtland, the supposed "eternal inheritance," and those who were able, bought land; but the greater part of their dupes had thus far been the poor and needy, and came there with a view of enjoying all things "in common," as such doctrine had gone forth. Many, however, found out their mistake after their arrival; and the revelation appeared to be only that the prophet and some of his relations should be supported by the church.[7]— In consequence of their inability to purchase lands adjoining head-quarters, they were scattered about in several townships, much exposed to "wild beasts," and subject to have their faith shaken by the influence of reason. Several renounced it. They were daily running to the prophet with queries and doubts which were constantly arising upon their minds. He generally satisfied them by *explaining*; nevertheless, they annoyed him much, and the necessity of withdrawing them from the influences which surrounded them, became apparent: hence, their removal to Missouri, where they could, in time, purchase all the land which they should need at a low rate, and become a "distinct people."

As before noticed, Cowdery and his companions, proceeded on to the west, with the avowed intention of converting the Indians, under a command of the Lord. On their way they tried their skill on several tribes, but made no proselytes, although their deluded brethren at home could daily see them, in visions, baptizing whole tribes. They finally arrived at the western line of the State of Missouri, late in the fall of 1830, with the intention of proceeding into the Indian country, but were stopped by the agents of the general government,[8] under an act of Congress,

---

7. A February 1831 revelation read: "If ye desire the mysteries of the kingdom, provide for him [Joseph Smith] food and raiment, and whatsoever thing he needeth to accomplish the work wherewith I have commanded him" (D&C 43:13; also 41:7).

8. The missionaries were warned away by federal agent Richard W. Cummins. After a second warning, he threatened to arrest them (see Pratt, *Autobiography*, 53–57).

to prevent the white people from trading or settling among them. They then took up their winter quarters in the village of Independence, about 12 miles from the State line.[9] Here they obtained employment during the winter. In the following spring, one of them returned to Kirtland, with a flattering account of the country about Independence. About the 1st of June,[10] the prophet assembled all his followers, for the purpose of a great meeting, at which time it was given out that marvelous events were to take place. Here many new attempts were made by Smith to perform miracles and otherwise to deceive his followers. Previous to this time, it should be remarked, nearly all the Mormonites had arrived from the State of New York, under a revelation, of course, to take possession of the "promised land." There were, in all, about fifty families. At the above mentioned meeting a long revelation was manufactured, commanding all the leading men and Elders to depart forthwith for the western part of Missouri, naming each one separately, informing them that only two should go together, and that every two should take separate roads, preaching by the way.[11] Only about two weeks were allowed them to make preparations for the journey, and most of them left what business they had to be closed by others.

---

9. Independence is about ten miles east of Kansas City. As the name implies, Kansas City straddles the Missouri River and state line so that it is partly in Kansas and partly in Missouri. The region west of the river was Indian Territory.

10. At a priesthood meeting convened in Kirtland on June 3, 1831, Joseph Smith and twenty-two others were ordained to the high priesthood. See Ezra Booth's account on pp. 271–76.

11. This is now D&C 52, summed up in verse 42: "Assemble yourselves together to rejoice upon the land of Missouri, which is the land of your inheritance, which is now the land of your enemies." For context, see MacKay et al., *Joseph Smith Papers: Documents*, 1:327.

Some left large families, with their crops upon the ground, &c. &c., and embarked for a distant land, from which they have not yet returned. For further particulars of this expedition, its objects and return, we shall refer the reader to the statements of an eye-witness, who was one of the party, which are given at length hereafter, (see Booth's Letters.)[12]

On arriving at the village of Independence, they proceeded to purchase a lot of land, upon which the prophet directed Rigdon and Cowdery to perform the mock ceremony of laying the corner stone of a city,[13] which he called *Zion*. Of the future prosperity and magnificence of this city, many marvelous revelations[14] were had by the prophet and many more marvelous conjectures formed by his dupes. Among others, it was said that it would in a few years exceed in splendor every thing known in ancient times. Its streets were to be paved with gold; all that escaped the general destruction which was soon to take place, would there assemble with all their wealth; the ten lost tribes of Israel had been discovered in their retreat, in the vicinity of the North Pole, where they had for ages been secluded by immense barriers of ice, and became vastly rich; the ice in a few years was to be melted away, when those tribes, with St. John and some

12. See pp. 276–97.

13. On August 2, Joseph Smith helped "lay the first log, for a house, as a foundation of Zion in Kaw township, twelve miles west of Independence" (*History of the Church*, 1:196; Westergren, *From Historian to Dissident*, 85–87; Davidson et al., *Joseph Smith Papers: Histories*, 2:43–46).

14. Joseph Smith received several revelations in Missouri pertaining to the purchase of "every tract bordering by the prairies ... for an everlasting inheritance" (D&C 57:5), with a promise to one day enjoy "a feast of fat things, of wine on the lees [barrel-aged wine] well refined, that the earth may know that the mouths of the prophets shall not fail" (58:8).

of the Nephites, which the Book of Mormon had immortalized, would be seen making their appearance in the new city,
loaded with immense quantities of gold and silver.[15] Whether
the prophet himself ever declared that these things had been
revealed to him, or that he had seen them th[r]ough his magic
stone, or silver spectacles, we will not say; but that such stories
and hundreds of others equally absurd, were told by those who
were in daily intercourse with him, as being events which would
probably take place, are susceptible of proof.

The prophet and his *life-guard* of Elders, stayed in their
city about two weeks.[16] Revelations were had for a part of them
to return to Ohio, a part to stay and take charge of the city,
and a part to commence preaching "in the region round about"
[D&C 58:46]. Much dissatisfaction was manifested by some
of the dupes, as to the selection of the site, and the general
appearance of the country. Smith, Rigdon and Cowdery returned to the old head-quarters in Kirtland.—Their followers
immediately commenced selling their lands, mostly at a great
sacrifice, and made preparations for emigrating up the Missouri. All were now anxious to sell, instead of buying more land
in Ohio. A special command was given to seventeen families,
who had settled in one township, some three months previous,
to depart forthwith to the promised land, who obeyed orders,
leaving their crops to those who owned the land. Besides a
great variety of special revelations relating to individuals, and

---

15. Smith elaborated on the Book of Mormon's assumption that the lost
ten tribes would return (Morm. 5:12), saying it would be "from the north country" (*History of the Church*, 1:315).

16. Mid-July to August 9, according to *History of the Church*, 1:188, 202.

other matters, a general one was given to the proselytes to sell their lands and other property and repair to Missouri as fast as possible, but not in haste.[17] Accordingly, many went during the year, making sacrifices of property, (those few of them who had any,) in proportion to their faith and their anxiety to be upon their "eternal inheritance." In the mean time, thirty or forty "Elders" were sent off in various directions in pursuit of proselytes. This year passed off with a gradual increase, and considerable wealth was drawn in, so that they began to boast of a capital stock of ten or fifteen thousand dollars.

Their common stock principles appear to be somewhat similar to those of the Shakers. Each one, however, is allowed to "manage his own affairs in his own way," until he arrives in Missouri.[18] There the Bishop resides;[19] he has supreme

---

17. The congregation from Colesville, New York, immigrated *en masse* to Thompson, Ohio, outside Kirtland, and settled on property owned by Leman Copley, a recent convert from the Shakers. When Copley changed his mind about Mormonism, the immigrants were directed by revelation to pull up stakes once more and move to Missouri (D&C 54:8; 58:56).

18. John Whitmer criticized how people "would take each others clothes and other property and use it without leave: which brought on confusion and disappointments" (Westergren, *From Historian to Dissident*, 27; Davidson et al., *Joseph Smith Papers: Histories*, 2:22–23). Smith dictated a revelation in Feb. 1831 ending that experiment: "Thou shalt not take thy brother's garment; thou shalt pay for that which thou shalt receive of thy brother" (D&C 42:54). The new system was to allow individuals management of the property they had conse-crated, using it as a "stewardship." All they had to do was give their surplus to the common storehouse (vv. 30–39, 55; see also Arrington, "Early Mormon Communitarianism," 342–43; Cook, *Joseph Smith and the Law of Consecration*, 8).

19. Kirtland hatter Edward Partridge (1793–1840) traveled with Rigdon in December 1830 to Fayette to meet Joseph Smith. The following February Par-tridge was appointed bishop over Missouri. He later became a bishop in Illinois (Jenson, *Biographical Encyclopedia*, 1:218–22; Cook, *Revelations*, 53–54).

command in all pecuniary matters, according to the revelations given by the prophet. The one [revelation] relating to this branch of business reads in these words:

> If thou lovest me, thou shalt serve me and keep my commandments; and behold thou shalt consecrate all thy properties, that which thou hast, unto me, with a covenant and a deed which cannot be broken; and they shall be laid before the Bishop of my church, and two of the Elders, such as he shall appoint and set apart for that purpose. And it shall come to pass that the Bishop of my Church, after that he has received the properties of my Church, that it *cannot be taken from the Church*, he shall appoint every man a steward over his own property, or that which he has received, inasmuch as shall be sufficient for himself and family; and the residue shall be kept to administer to him who has not, that every man may receive according as he stands in need; and the residue shall be kept in my store-house, to administer to the poor and needy, as shall be appointed by the Elders of the Church and Bishop, and for the purpose of purchasing land, and the building up of the New Jerusalem, which is hereafter to be revealed; that my covenant people may be gathered in one, in the day that I shall come to my temple; and this I do for the salvation of my people. And it shall come to pass, that he that sinneth and repenteth not, shall be cast out, and *shall not receive again that which he has consecrated unto me:* For it shall come to pass, that which I spoke by the mouths of my prophets shall be fulfilled, for I will consecrate the riches of the Gentiles unto my people, which are of the House of Israel.[20]

---

20. This revelation was leaked to the Ohio *Western Courier* by Symonds Rider, a Mormon defector, and published on Sept. 1, 1831. It was picked up by the *Painesville Telegraph* twelve days later (MacKay et al., *Joseph Smith Papers:*

The next year commenced with something like a change of operations. Instead of selling their possessions in Ohio, they again began to buy up improved land, mills and water privileges. It would seem that the Missouri country began to look rather dreary to the prophet and his head men, supposing that they could not enjoy their power there as well as in Ohio. They could not think of undergoing the hardships and privations incident to a new country. Besides, the people there were not much disposed to encourage the emigration of such an army of fanatics—and their "Lamanite" brethren, under Gen. Black Hawk,[21] were about that time commencing a war upon the whites.

They, therefore, continued to extend their impositions by sending abroad every thing that could walk, no matter how ignorant, if they had learnt the tales and vagaries of their leaders. All that were so sent, were dubbed *Elders* or *High Priests*, and furnished with a commission, purporting to have been dictated by the Lord to the Prophet.[22] These requisites being added to their credulity, they were of course inspired with all necessary self-sufficiency, zeal and impudence. They were thus prepared to declare that every thing which they stated or imagined, was

---

Documents, 1:245n34) and then officially published in *The Evening and the Morning Star* in July 1832 and Book of Commandments (section 44) in July 1833. When it became section 42 of the Doctrine and Covenants in 1835, it was heavily emended.

21. A few hundred displaced Sauk and Fox Indians crossed the Mississippi from Iowa into Illinois in early 1832 under Chief Black Hawk. After attacking several frontier settlements, they were massacred while retreating back into Iowa.

22. This probably refers to D&C 52 instructing fourteen pair of missionaries to settle and preach in Missouri.

absolutely true—for the *Spirit* had so informed them. Many of them actually carried their power of discerning spirits, and their enthusiasm, so far, that they frequently declared, that if Smith and all his witnesses were now to come forward and say that his pretensions were a wicked deception, they would not believe a word of it—because the *Spirit* had shown that it was true. Here again, the intelligent mind will readily discover one of the principal sources of all error and delusion. Here is the sure refuge, the fast hold, of every impostor. This something, which is the *Spirit*, or the *Holy Spirit*, has been the standing, unequivocal, incontrovertible and true witness for at least 24 false Messiahs, for Mahomet, who is considered the prince of impostors, and for nearly fifty others who have come with pretended commissions from Heaven. They all had, or may still have, numerous followers, whose faith was wrought and confirmed by what they suppose to be the *Spirit*.

During the year 1832, considerable progress was made in writing out, and revising the Old and New Testaments,[23] which the prophet pretended to do by inspiration, or by the guidance of the Spirit. In this business, most of his leisure hours were occupied, Rigdon acting as scribe. They say that the Scriptures, in their present form, retain but little of their original purity and beauty, having been so often copied and translated by unskilful

---

23. Smith began trying to "restore" the original wording of the Bible in June 1830. By March 1831 he had reached Genesis 17 but was instructed by revelation to switch to the New Testament (D&C 45:60–61). He completed the New Testament midway into the next year (Jessee, *Personal Writings*, 274) and the Old Testament in mid-1833 (Matthews, *Plainer Translation*). Except for a few extracts, none of it was published during Smith's lifetime.

hands. The whole of the old Bible is now said to be ready for the press, in its amended form, and will be forthcoming, as soon as the state of their finances will permit. The curious, perhaps, may be anxious to learn what alterations the prophet has made in the numerous verses and chapters which he has copied into his book of Mormon, almost verbatim, and especially the thirteen chapters of Isaiah.[24]

Revelations and commandments still continue to be received. Visions were frequently had, and extraordinary prophecies given out verbally by Smith, to his followers, to strengthen and prolong their faith. Although he has assumed the name and title of prophet, he is very cautious how he commits himself. His predictions are always found far off, equivocal, and ambiguous, and always relate to some events which every one supposes to be quite probable, and delivered in such a way, that their failure is susceptible of an easy explanation, but if he happens to *guess right*, in any case, it is immediately placed to his credit as a true prophecy. We will give but a single specimen of this branch of his business: After the Cholera[25] had ceased its ravages in New York, in 1832, Smith prophecied it would return the ensuing year, with much greater severity and violence, and nearly depopulate the city. From the known character of that disease, its return was apprehended by most people, and with more fatal effects. This was thought by our modern prophet, to be too

24. For the most part, Smith carried over the altered biblical texts from the Book of Mormon into his revision.

25. Cholera is a deadly infection of the small intestine. *The Evening and the Morning Star* considered it evidence of a divine judgment on the world.

good an opportunity to pass unimproved, for establishing his reputation as a true prophet of God. But the prediction wholly failed.[26]

---

26. Joseph Smith noted the severity of the "cholera" epidemic in New York in July 1832 and predictably called it God's "judgment upon all the face of the earth" (Jessee, *Personal Writings*, 274). He was therefore surprised to learn, when he and Newel K. Whitney visited Manhattan three months later, that "there is but few Cases of the cholra in this City now and if you should see the people you would not that know that they people had ever heard of the <cholra>" (Jessee, *Personal Writings*, 279). The epidemic had abated during the cooler months. Smith thought it was still his duty "to lift up my voice in this City and leave the Event with God who holdeth all things in his hands," apparently stopping short of specifically predicting that the disease would return.

CHAPTER II.

On the opening of the year 1833, the "gift of tongues"[1] again made its appearance at head-quarters, and from thence extended to all their branches in different parts. Whether the languages now introduced, differed materially from those practiced two or three years previous, (and pronounced to be of the Devil,) we have not been informed. It appears that this last device, was all that was then lacking to make the system perfect. They had long before professed to be fully endowed with the power of healing all manner of diseases, discerning spirits, and casting out devils. But a succession of failures had rendered them rather stale, and given distrust to many of the faithful. A new expedient was therefore indispensably necessary, in order to revive the drooping spirits of the deluded, and at the same time, insure a new crop of converts. The scheme proved eminently successful. Hundreds were soon convinced of the truth of the whole, by hearing of and seeing the manner in which the "tongues" were performed, although the trick would seem more susceptible of discovery than any previous one. This gift was not confined to the Elders and high priests,

---

1. Upon meeting Joseph Smith in November 1832, Brigham Young spoke in tongues and Smith pronounced it a genuine gift (Young, History, 439; cf. *History of the Church*, 1:296–97). Young, a convert from New York, encouraged people in Pennsylvania to cultivate the same practice (see Vogel and Dunn, "Tongue of Angels").

who, in other respects, were supposed to have a superabundant share of "the spirit"; but nearly all the proselytes, both old and young, could show their faith by speaking with "tongues." And it would appear, from all the facts which we have been able to gather upon this subject, that if this gift were not supernaturally bestowed, it required but a few moments instruction from a priest, to render his pupil expert in various dead languages, which could never be understood by man or beast, except a supernatural power was at the instant given to some one present to interpret it.—They sometimes professed to believe that these "tongues" were the same which were "confounded" at the building of Babel.

Some curious particulars are related respecting these blasphemous practices, by a Mr. Higby,[2] who was eight months an Elder in the Mormon church, and which he published in a small pamphlet.[3] He says that shortly after he joined them, a Mormon Elder said to him, "you must go to work in the vineyard of the Lord as a preacher of the Gospel. I have viewed your heart by the spirit of discernment; I see what is in your heart, and what the will of the Lord is, concerning you all." Mr. Higby says that he was soon after ordained an Elder in the said church, and commissioned to preach and baptize, ordain Elders, confirm the churches, heal the sick, in short, that he was ordained to all the gifts of the church, which were the same as given to the apostles of old. He continues—"about the 10th of

---

2. This was most likely James Higby (Higbee), who was excommunicated on June 23, 1833, "for circulating false and slanderous reports, and not observing the order of the gospel" (*History of the Church*, 1:355–56).

3. This publication has not been located.

April following, R. Cahoon and D. Patton[4] came again to the place—a meeting was called, and previous to the meeting, they said that some one would speak with tongues before they left the place. Accordingly he [Patton] set himself to work at that meeting to verify his prophecy. During the meeting he said, 'Father H. if you will rise in the name of Jesus Christ, you can speak in Tongues.' He arose immediately, hesitated, and said, 'my faith fails me—I have not faith enough.'—Said Patton, 'you have—speak in the name of Jesus Christ—make some sound as you list, without further thought, and God will make it a language.' The old gentleman, after considerable urging, spoke and made some sounds, which were pronounced to be a correct tongue. Several others spoke in a similar manner, and among them was myself. I spoke as I listed, not knowing what I said, yet it was declared to be a tongue. The sound of the words used by some, in speaking in tongues, was a medium between talking and singing—and all, as I am now convinced, a mere gibberish, spoken at random and without thought.

"We had another meeting shortly after, at which there were present several others, besides those of the church.— Cahoon spoke in unknown tongues, as he pretended, going on at considerable length, which Patton interpreted nearly as follows: that the judgment of God should follow the men

4. Reynolds Cahoon (1790–1861) and David W. Patten (1799–1838). Cahoon was a tanner from upstate New York who was baptized by Parley P. Pratt and ordained by Sidney Rigdon. In 1832 Joseph Smith made him a counselor to Bishop Newel K. Whitney. Born in Vermont, Patten was farming in Indiana when he converted in 1832. He became one of the twelve apostles three years later. He was mortally wounded during the Missouri Mormon War in 1838.

of this generation; that their tongues should be stayed that they should not utter; and their flesh should fall from off their bones; their eyes pine away in their sockets; and it shall come to pass that the beasts of the forest and the fowls of the air shall devour them, nearly as it is written in the prophets. He then asked me to speak, which I did, and he interpreted as he thought proper.

"The next time those men came among us, they gave us a rule for speaking in unknown tongues, and also for interpreting what was spoken by others. This rule, they said, was perfect—that as long as we followed it we could not err. And so I believe; it was a perfect rule to lead men astray. The rule, as given by Cahoon, is this: rise upon your feet and look and lean on Christ; speak or make some sound; continue to make sounds of some kind, and the Lord will make a correct tongue or language of it. The interpretation was to be given in the same way."

Upon this, Mr. H. justly remarks:—"Men of sense may smile at this recital; and those who scoff at all religion and know nothing of those feelings of the human heart which the devotional man enjoys, in converse with his Maker, will doubtless ridicule what they consider the weakness of folly; but the man of religious feeling will know how to pity, rather than upbraid, that zeal without knowledge, which leads a man to fancy that he has found the ladder of Jacob, and that he sees the angel of the Lord ascending and descending before his eyes; while the Christian philosopher, who has read the history of mankind, will find abundant apology for that man, who, by a constant and over anxious exercise of mind, is led at length to fancy himself on the banks of the Ulai with Daniel, or on the Isle of Patmos with St. John."

They would frequently sing in this gibberish, forming a tune as they proceeded. The same songs, they said, would be sung when the lost tribes appeared in Zion, in Missouri.

Another seceder from this delusion, relates that he was present on a certain occasion, in an upper room in Kirtland, where were assembled from fifteen to twenty Elders and High Priests.[5] After sundry exhortation by the priests, the prophet himself arose, and with much earnestness, warned his followers to be zealous and faithful in their duties, saying, "It is our privilege to see God face to face—yes, (says he) I will prophecy unto you in the name of the Lord, that the day will come when no man will be permitted to preach unless he has seen the Lord—people will ask each teacher, 'have you seen the face of the Lord,' and if he say nay, they will say, away with this fellow, for we have a man to teach us that has seen the face of the Lord.'" After a short pause, he added, "the Lord is willing we should see his glory to-day, and all that will exercise faith, shall see the Lord of Glory." They then concluded to spend the day in fasting and prayer. Each one kept his seat with his eyes closed, and his body inclined forward. Soon after Joseph says, "Sidney (Rigdon,) have you seen the Lord?" He answered, "I saw the image of a man pass before my face, whose locks were white, and whose countenance was exceedingly fair, even surpassing all beauty that I ever beheld." Then Joseph replied, "I knew you had seen a vision but [you]

---

5. This is probably a meeting of the so-called School of the Prophets, convened during the winter of 1832–33 to train missionaries (see *History of the Church*, 1:322–33; D&C 88:68; 93:1).

would have seen more were it not for unbelief." Sidney confessed his faith was weak that morning. Hiram Smith[6] said he
had seen nearly the same as Sidney, which was pronounced by
Joseph to be the Redeemer of the world. Upon this, R. Cahoon
fell upon his knees, holding his hands in an erect position. In
fifteen or twenty minutes he arose and declared he had seen the
temple of Zion, filled with disciples, while the top was covered
with the glory of the Lord, in the form of a cloud. Another one
then placed himself in the same position, but saw no vision, his
faith being weak. Joseph next arose, and passing round the room
laying his hand upon each one, and spoke as follows, as near as
the narrator can recollect:—

"Ak man oh son oh man ah ne commene en holle goste en
haben en glai hosanne hosanne en holle goste en esac milkea
jeremiah, ezekiel, Nephi, Lehi, St. John," &c. &c. After administering the sacrament, several of the brethren were called
upon to arise and speak in tongues. Several of them performed with considerable applause. Our informant says he
was at length called upon to speak or sing, "in tongues," at his
own option—prefering the latter mode, he sung, to the tune
of Bruce's Address,[7] a combination of sounds, which astonished all present.

---

6. Hyrum Smith (1800–44) was the older brother of Joseph Smith,
trained as a cooper and farmer, one of the eight witnesses to the Book of Mormon and a member of the First Presidency from 1837. In 1844 he and his
brother were murdered in Carthage, Illinois (see Cook, *Revelations*, 19–20;
Jenson, *Biographical Encyclopedia*, 1:52).

7. This is a traditional Scottish song, "Scots Wha Hae," that was popular
in America as "Bruce's Address to His Army," with lyrics by Robert Burns composed in 1793 to celebrate Robert the Bruce's victory over the English in 1314.

This gibberish for several months was practised almost daily, while they were about their common avocations, as well as when they assembled for worship. But we will not dwell upon this part of our history. A particular recital of such scenes of fanaticism, gives too much pain to the intelligent mind, and excites a contempt for our species.

We would here, barely ask the subjects of this delusion, and all others who may become so, whether it be possible, that the great and intelligent Ruler of the Universe, can be thus miraculously engaged in bestowing all sorts of language upon a few people *merely for their own amusement?*—languages that can neither benefit themselves, or any one else, because no one can understand them. For the full introduction of the Gospel, the gift of tongues was wisely confered upon the Apostles & some others who were engaged in its first promulgation. But for what purpose? was it a mere pastime to them, by means of which they could divert each other, while assembled in their private rooms, without knowing the import of any thing they said? If such were the facts, then these modern tongues may be genuine—But no—they were for a wiser and more noble purpose—a purpose every way worthy of that exalted Being. The gospel was to be proclaimed and published to "every creature," to perhaps a hundred different nations, all speaking a distinct tongue—and to be preached, too, by a small number of men, who had been taught only a single language. Whenever they spoke in a language not their own, it was most clearly understood, by themselves and others, who had assembled from various nations, without the intervention of soothsayers, or one pretending to have the "spirit of interpretation." Will any one presume to compare the wisdom of God in those manifestations, with what has been related by Smith and his followers? Yes—a distorted imagination can discover infinitely more power and glory in the unintelligible jargon of Mormonism.

If what has been exhibited here, are truly languages, they must be such as are spoken and understood by human beings somewhere: otherwise the names of "tongues" or languages will not attach to them. But they are a mere gibberish. If these people had the "gift of tongues," as they impudently assert, how much more consistent with rationality, and worthy of the Deity, would it appear for them to show it forth and test its true character, before an audience of French or Spanish, or some of the numerous Indian tribes in our country, all speaking different tongues, and to whom they profess to be more especially sent? No—such an attempt would explode the whole system of folly and delusion. It would seem that they would much rather be talking their nonsense to each other, and declaring it to the world as an extraordinary manifestation of the power of God.

CHAPTER I2.[1]

The difficulties which had been for some time accumulating between the inhabitants of Missouri and the followers of Smith, began now to assume a more serious aspect. About a year previous, a small newspaper had been started at Independence, in which were published, monthly, the orders and decrees of the prophet, which were called revelations, together with all the other wild and fanatical dogmas of the sect. Like pilgrims to the tomb of Mahomet, they continued to wend their way from different parts, to the "promised land." To accomplish this journey was the height of their ambition. They really supposed their prophet had at that place opened the very gates of Heaven to them, and nothing else was necessary to insure all temporal and spiritual blessings, but their arrival there. Those of them who did not choose to sacrifice their property, however, stayed behind, leaving the poor, and those not encumbered with property, to be the pioneers. Their numbers, men, women and children, were now about 1200 in Jackson county. Besides the printing aparatus, they had also a mercantile establishment, (denominated the "Lord's Store House,") and some mechanic shops in Independence. This village was made their head quarters, although their converts had effected

---

1. Howe had a typographical error in the chapter heading so that it read "Chmpter XII."

small settlements in different parts of the county. Smith had appointed as his Bishop, one Edward Partridge, a very honest and industrious hatter, of Painesville, Ohio, who had, withal, a comfortable stock of the good things of the world. He was stationed at Independence, and had the sole control of all the temporal and spiritual affairs of the colony, always obedient, however, to the revelations promulgated by Smith, who still sat perched upon his throne, in Kirtland, with Rigdon, and most of his family connexions.

Under these circumstances, the people of Jackson Co. became somewhat excited and alarmed for their civil rights. Enmity had been for some time increasing, till finally an open rupture ensued. On the 20th July, 1833, a meeting was held of 400 or 500 persons, at Independence. They avowed their object to be, to take some effectual means to rid themselves of their fanatical neighbors. Col. Richard Simpson was appointed Chairman, and Col. J. D. Lucas and J. H. Flournoy, Postmaster, Secretaries. A Committee was then appointed to report [through] an address to the public, in relation to the object of the meeting. This Committee soon after submitted an address, which was unanimously adopted.[2] The address represented that the Mormonites in that county numbered about 1200 souls,—that each successive spring and autumn poured forth its swarms among them, with a gradual falling off of their characters, until they had nearly reached the low condition of the black population—that the citizens were daily told that

---

2. The report, dated July 20, is available in full in the *History of the Church*, 1:395–99. Howe's chronology is wrong since the committee was appointed prior to the courthouse gathering where its report was considered (1:374–76).

they were to be cut off, and their lands appropriated to the Mormons for inheritances—that they sometimes said this was to be accomplished either by the destroying angel, or by their own power, under the direction of God.[3] The said Committee expressed their fears, that, should this population continue to increase they would soon have all the offices in the county in their hands; and that the lives and property of the other citizens would be insecure, under the administration of men who are so ignorant and superstitious as to believe that they have been the subjects of miraculous and supernatural cures, professing to hold converse with God and Angels,—possessing and exercising the gift of divination and unknown tongues, and are withal so poor, as to be unable to procure bread and meat. The Committee further state, that "one of the means resorted to by them, in order to drive us to emigrate, is an indirect invitation to the free brethren of color in Illinois, to come like the rest, to the land of Zion." In conclusion, the Committee say, "of their pretended revelations from Heaven, their personal intercourse with God and his angels—the maladies they pretend to heal, by the laying on of hands, and the contemptible gibberish with which they habitually profane the Sabbath, and which they dignify by the appellation of "unknown tongues," we have nothing to say. Vengeance belongs to God alone. But as to the

---

3. Missouri was a slave state. In July, *The Evening and the Morning Star* had published an article by W. W. Phelps, "Free People of Color," which according to the committee's view invited "free negroes and mulattoes from other states to become 'Mormons,' and remove and settle among us," by which the Mormons intended to "corrupt our blacks [slaves], and instigate them" to insurrection (see D&C 87:4).

other matters set forth in this paper, we feel called upon by every consideration of self-preservation, good society, public morals, and the fair prospect, if not blasted in the germ, that awaits this young and beautiful country, at once to declare:—

1st. That no Mormon shall in future move and settle in this county.

2d. That those now here, who shall give a definite pledge of their intention, within a reasonable time, to remove out of the county, shall be allowed to remain unmolested until they shall have sufficient time to sell their property, and close their business without any sacrifice.

3d. That the editor of the "Star," be required forthwith to close his office, and discontinue the business of printing in this county: and as to all other stores and shops belonging to the sect, their owners must in every case comply with the terms strictly, agreeably to the 2d article of this declaration: and upon failure, prompt and efficient measures will be taken to close the same.

4th. That the Mormon leaders here, are required to use their influence in preventing any further emigration of their distant brethren to this county, and counsel and advise their brethren to comply with the above requisitions.

5th. That those who fail to comply with the above requisitions, be referred to those of their brethren who have the gift of tongues, to inform them of the lot that awaits them.[4]

After the propositions of the Committee had been considered and adopted, it was

---

4. The report appeared as "Mormonism," *Western Monitor*, Aug. 2, 1833 (original not located; cf. *History of the Church*, 1:389–99), and partially in the *Missouri Intelligencer and Boon's Lick Advertiser*, Aug. 10, 1833; available in Mulder and Mortensen, *Among the Mormons*, 77–80.

Resolved, That a committee of twelve be appointed forthwith to wait on the Mormon leaders, and see that the foregoing requisitions be strictly complied with by them; and upon their refusal, that the said Committee do as the organ of the county, inform them that it is our unwavering determination and fixed purpose, after the fullest consideration of all the consequences and responsibilities under which we act, to use such means as shall insure their complete and full adoption; and that said Committee, so far as may be in their power, report to this present meeting.

The Committee of twelve were appointed, composed of the most prominent men in the county, both civil and military. After an adjournment of two hours, the meeting again convened, and the Committee reported that they had called upon the Editor, the Bishop, and the "keeper of the Lord's Store House," and others, "who declined giving any direct answer, to the requisitions made of them, and wished an unreasonable time for consultation, not only with their brethren here, but the prophet in Ohio." Whereupon, it was unanimously resolved by the meeting, that the printing office should be razed to the ground, and the type and press secured. This is said, by the [citizens in attendance at the] meeting, to have been accomplished with but little noise or disturbance, or any personal injury. The Mormon account, however, is, that there was a great tumult, books and printed sheets destroyed, the Bishop and one other person tarred and feathered, and that the keeper of the Store was compelled to pack up his goods and close his door.[5]

---

5. See *The Evening and the Morning Star*, Dec. 1833, 114, 118, which continued publication from Kirtland under a new editorship.

The meeting was then adjourned for three days, when a
much larger assemblage took place. Another Committee of seventeen was then appointed to wait upon the Mormon leaders,
who had intimated a wish to have a conference.—In two hours
this committee reported to the meeting, that they had entered
into an *amicable* agreement with them, in writing, and that they
had assured the editor of the *Star* that whenever he was ready
to remove, the amount of all his losses should be paid to him by
the citizens. The contract was in the following words:

Memorandum of an agreement between the undersigned
of the Mormon society, in Jackson County, Missouri, and a
Committee appointed by a public meeting of the citizens of
said County, made the 23d day of July, 1833:

It is understood that the undersigned members of the
society do give their solemn pledges each for himself, as follows, to wit:

That Oliver Cowdery, W. W. Phelps, Wm. McClelland,
Edward Partridge, Lyman Wight, Simeon Carter, Peter and
John Whitmer, and Harvey Whitlock, shall remove with their
families out of this county, on or before the 1st day of January
next; and that they, as well as the two hereinafter mentioned,
use all their influence to induce all the brethren now here, to
remove as soon as possible—one half, say, by the 1st of January next, and all by the 1st of April next; to advise and try
all means in their power to stop any more of their sect from
moving to this county; and as to those now on the road, they
will use their influence to prevent them settling permanently in
this co[u]nty,[6] but that they shall only make arrangements for

---

6. Howe had "connty."

their temporary shelter, till a new location is agreed on for the Society. John Carol and Algernon Gilbert are allowed to remain as general agents to wind up the business of the Society, so long as necessity shall require:—and said Gilbert may sell out his merchandize now on hand, but is to make no new importations.

The Star is not again to be published—nor a press set up by any of the Society in this county.

If the said Edward Partridge, and W. W. Phelps move their families by the 1st of January, as aforesaid, that they themselves will be allowed to go and come in order to transact and wind up their business.

The Committee pledge themselves to use all their influence to prevent any violence being used, so long as a compliance with the foregoing terms are observed by the parties concerned, to which agreement is subscribed the names of the above named Committee, as also those of the Mormon brethren named in the Report as having been present.[7]

Tranquility was thus measurably restored for a time.—The Mormons made no preparations for removing, but applied to the Governor for relief.[8] He informed them that he could furnish them no aid in the business, until they had resorted to the laws, and ascertained that they could not be enforced. They, therefore, commenced civil suits for the loss of property.[9] From

---

7. See Davidson et al., *Joseph Smith Papers: Histories*, 2:55–56; Westergren, *From Historian to Dissident*, 107–8.

8. This petition to Missouri Governor Daniel Dunklin, dated Sept. 28, 1833, and his reply of Oct. 19, are in *History of the Church*, 1:410–15, 423–24.

9. On October 30 church leaders retained the legal firm of Doniphan, Atchison, Rees, and Wood to defend their property rights (ibid., 424–25; Firmage and Mangrum, *Zion in the Courts*, 65).

this proceeding the citizens began to conclude that the Mormons did not intend to perform any part of their stipulation, and about the last of October, the people of the county again commenced depredations.[10] Forty or fifty made an attack upon a small portion, about ten miles from head-quarters, unroofed several houses, whipped some of the men, and frightened some of the women and children. The next night attacks were made upon another branch, and upon the "Lord's Store House," and the dwelling of its keeper, in Independence. For two or three days following, several parties met each other with fire arms, in which two of the citizens and one of the Mormons were *killed*.[11] The Mormons were finally compelled to cross the Missouri river into Clay county.

These proceedings, on the part of the people of Jackson county, were in total disregard of all law, and must be condemned by all. They were wholly at war with every principle of right, and the genius of our institutions. Outrages can never be justified upon any ground, although the *reasons* which induced them, ought to be stated. Among the Mormon fanatics, as among every other combination, there are the prudent and the imprudent—some who are very civil agreeable citizens, and some who are extremely intolerant, unmannerly, bigoted

---

10. Notice that where Howe previously insisted that everything the county did was carried out in a professional and kindly way, here he concedes that the "county again commenced depredations" against the Mormons. In the next paragraph he writes that what the older settlers did was "in total disregard of all law, and must be condemned by all."

11. Andrew Barber and non-Mormons Hugh Brazeale and Thomas Linville were all killed in the skirmish on November 4 (*History of the Church*, 1:429–31; *The Evening and the Morning Star*, Jan. 1834, 125).

and supercillious—priding themselves greatly upon their being supposed the peculiar favorites of Heaven, and their possession of greater light than all the world besides. These latter it is who deal out the anathemas, disclose the secret plottings, and expose the fanatical notions [a]nd[12] opinions which have been conceived by the leaders of this sect. The Mormons have endeavored to inculcate the belief, as extensively as possible, that their difficulties with the people of Jackson county, have arisen solely on account of their religion—because they were more pure and holy than any of their neighbors, and for that reason alone they have been *persecuted* as were the Apostles of old. This we are not disposed to believe. Their first salutations to every community that does not believe their book and pretensions, are, that destruction awaits them for their unbelief—that there has been no Christian church upon earth for 1400 years—no one has had any authority to administer ordinances till Smith dug out his golden bible—that he is the appointed one of God, to re-establish a church, and all that do not come to him for power and instructions will be damned. Add to this, some among them frequently boast of their increasing strength, and that consequently they will soon be enabled to possess themselves of all the secular power of the country, as they already have of the spiritual. This they calculate to accomplish by concentrating their forces in particular neighborhoods. We have been credibly informed that Rigdon has given it as his opinion that the Mormons will be able to elect a member of Congress in five years, and that in three years they would take the

---

12. Howe had *end* instead of *and*.

offices in the town of Kirtland. They say that when they get the
secular power into their hands, every thing will be performed
by immediate revelations from God. We shall then have Pope
Joseph *the First*, and his hierarchy.

Such things have been thrown out, and have, no doubt, had
a strong agency in bringing about the outrages i[n]¹³ Missouri.

Again, one of their leading articles of faith is, that the Indians of North America, in a very few years, will be converted
to Mormonism, and through rivers of blood will again take
possession of their ancient "inheritance."¹⁴ As their bible pretends to be a record of the aborigines, every effort will be made
to inculcate a belief in it among them. To facilitate this project, was one strong ground for their establishing themselves in
Missouri, knowing that the general government was taking active measures to remove all the Indians west of the Mississippi.
Were it possible, therefore, for Mormonism to be inculcated
among the tribes of the west, a religious spirit would be easily
excited.—One of the imaginary prophets in the Book of Mormon, says that such events will take place. He says, "Therefore, I
write unto you, Gentiles, (the whites,) and also unto you, house
of Israel, (the Indians,) when the work shall commence (Mormonism) that ye shall be about to return to the land of your
inheritance" [Morm. 3:17]. Again, in speaking to the Indians,
"Know ye that ye are of the House of Israel. Know ye that you
must lay down your weapons of war, and delight no more in
the shedding of blood, and take them not again, *save it be that*

---

13. Another typographical error has *is* where it should have been *in*.
14. See 3 Ne. 20:15–19; 21:12, 14.

God shall command you" [7:2–4] (through the mouth of Smith.)
He also prophesyed that they should be "driven and scattered
by the Gentiles," and after that the Lord would remember his
covenant with Abraham.—And then, "O ye Gentiles, how can
ye stand before the power of God—therefore, repent ye, lest a
remnant of the seed of Jacob (meaning the Indians) shall go
forth among you as a lion, and tear you in pieces, and there is
none to deliver" [Morm. 5:20, 24].

CHAPTER 13

After the conflict had subsided in Jackson Co., two or three High Priests[1] repaired with all possible speed to the prophet in Kirtland, magnifying greatly the events that had taken place. These new, unexpected and extraordinary circumstances, must be met in an extraordinary manner.—They were trying times, requiring the combined wisdom of the prophet and his head men, in bringing out a revelation upon the subject, which would astonish his dupes and strengthen their faith in the imposition, which had been so far shaken in many, that they proposed selling their new "eternal inheritance," in Jackson County, for a "mess of pottage." But the prophet more readily discovered the new advantages that would ultimately accrue to his cause, by a little perseverance. He well knew that the laws could not continue to be violated in our country for any length of time, and that he and his followers would, in the end, be the greatest gainers, by the cry of persecution which they could raise, and by showing to the world, in their ultimate triumph, that the Lord was on their side and directed all their movements in

---

1. Oliver Cowdery was dispatched to Ohio in July 1833 to inform Joseph Smith of the trouble in Missouri (*History of the Church*, 1:407). Following the expulsion of the Mormons from Jackson County in November, Parley P. Pratt and Lyman Wight were sent to give the prophet an update (ibid., 2:1).

putting their enemies to flight. The following was accordingly issued from their press in Kirtland, in the form of a handbill:[2]

Verily, I say unto you, concerning your brethren who have been afflicted and persecuted, and cast out from the land of their inheritance: I the Lord hath suffered the affliction to come upon them, wherewith they have been afflicted in consequence of their transgressions; yet, I will own them, and they shall be mine in that day when I shall come to make up my jewels.

Therefore, they must be chastened, and tried, even as Abraham, who was commanded to offer up his only son; for all those who will not endure chastening, but deny me, cannot be sanctified.

Behold, I say unto you, there were jarrings, and contentions, and envyings, and strifes, and lustful and covetous desires among them; therefore, by these things they polluted their inheritances. They were slow to hearken unto the voice of the Lord their God; therefore, the Lord their God is slow to hearken unto their prayers, to answer them in the day of their trouble. In the day of their peace they esteemed lightly my counsel; but in the day of their trouble, of necessity they feel after me.

Verily, I say unto you, notwithstanding their sins[,] my bowels are filled with compassion towards them: I will not utterly cast them off; and in the day of wrath I will remember mercy. I have sworn, and the decree hath gone forth by a former commandment which I have given unto you, that I would let fall the sword of mine indignation in the behalf of my

2. Some revelations were issued as handbills prior to their publication in the 1835 Doctrine and Covenants. A handbill for the following revelation, now D&C 101, is located at the Harold B. Lee Library, Brigham Young University (see Flake, *Mormon Bibliography*, 2920a). Howe reprinted it in the Jan. 24, 1834, issue of the *Painesville Telegraph*.

people; and even as I have said[,] it shall come to pass. Mine indignation is soon to be poured out without measure upon all nations, and this will I do when the cup of their iniquity is full.

And in that day, all who are found upon the watch tower, or in other words, all mine Israel shall be saved. And they that have been scattered shall be gathered; and all they who have mourned shall be comforted; and all they who have given their lives for my name shall be crowned.

Therefore, let your hearts be comforted concerning Zion, for all flesh [is] in mine hands: be still, and know that I am God. Zion shall not be moved out of her place, notwithstanding her children are scattered, they that remain and are pure in heart shall return and come to their inheritances, they and their children, with songs of everlasting joy; to build up the waste places of Zion. And all these things, that the prophets might be fulfilled.

And behold, there is none other place appointed; neither shall there be any other place appointed than that which I have appointed for the work of gathering my saints, until the day cometh when there is found no more room for them; and then I have other places which I will appoint unto them, and they shall be called stakes, for the curtains, or the strength of Zion.

Behold, it is my will, that all who call on my name, and worship me according to mine everlasting gospel, should gather together and stand in holy places, and prepare for the revelation which is to come when the veil for the covering of my temple, in my tabernacle, which hideth the earth, shall be taken off, and all flesh shall see me together. And every corruptible thing, both of man, or the beasts of the field, or of the fowls of heaven or of the fish of the sea, that dwell upon the face of the earth, shall be consumed; and also, that of [mineral] element shall melt with fervent heat; and all things shall become new, that my glory may dwell upon all the earth.

And in that day the enmity of man, and the enmity of beasts; yea, the enmity of all flesh shall cease from before my face. And in that day whatsoever any man shall ask it shall be given unto him. And in that day satan shall not have power to tempt any man. And there shall be no sorrow because there is no death. In that day an infant shall not die until he is old, and his life shall be as the age of a tree, and when he dies he shall not sleep, (that is to say in the earth,) he shall be changed in the twinkling of an eye, and shall be caught up, and his rest shall be glorious.

Yea, verily I say unto you, in that day when the Lord shall come he shall reveal all things; things which have passed, and hidden things which no man knew; things of the earth by which it was made, and the purpose and the end thereof; things most precious; things that are above and things that are beneath; things that are in the earth, and upon the earth, and in heaven. And all they who suffer persecution for my name, and endure in faith, though they are called to lay down their lives for my sake, yet shall they partake of all this glory.

Therefore, fear not even unto death; for in this world your joy is not full, but in me your joy is full. Therefore, care not for the body, neither for the life of the body; but care for the soul, and for the life of the soul: and seek the face of the Lord always, that in patience ye may possess your souls, and ye shall have eternal life.

When men are called unto mine everlasting gospel, and covenant with an everlasting covenant, they are accounted as the salt of the earth, and the savor of men. Therefore, if that salt of the earth lose its savor, behold it is thenceforth good for nothing, only to be cast out and trodden under the feet of men. Behold, hear wisdom concerning the children of Zion; even many, but not all: they were found transgressors, therefore, they must needs be chastened. He that exalteth himself shall be abased, and he that abaseth himself shall be exalted.

And now, I will show unto you a parable that you may know my will concerning the redemption of Zion: A certain nobleman had a spot of land, very choice; and he said unto his servants, go ye unto my vineyard; even upon this very choice piece of land, and plant twelve olive trees; and set watchmen round about them and build a tower, that one may overlook the land round about, to be a watchman upon the tower; that mine olive trees may not be broken down, when the enemy shall come to spoil, and take unto themselves the fruit of my vineyard.

Now these servants of the nobleman went and did as their lord commanded them; and planted the olive trees, and built a hedge round about, and set watchmen, and began to build the tower. And while they were yet laying the foundation thereof, they began to say among themselves, and what need hath my lord of this tower? And consulted for a long time, saying among themselves, What need hath my lord of this tower? seeing this is a time of peace!—Might not this money be given to the exchangers? for there is no need of these things!

And while they were at variance one with another, they became very slothful, and they hearkened not unto the commandments of their lord: and the enemy came by night, and broke down the hedge, and the servants of the nobleman arose, and were affrighted, and fled: and the enemy destroyed their works, and broke down the olive trees.

Now behold the nobleman, the lord of the vineyard, called upon his servants, and said unto them, Why! what is the cause of this gaeat [great] evil? Ought ye not to have done even as I commanded you? And after ye had planted the vineyard, and built the hedge round about, and set watchmen upon the walls thereof, built the tower also, and set a watchmen upon the tower? and watched for my vineyard, and not have fallen asleep, lest the enemy should come upon you, and behold, the watchman upon the tower would have seen the enemy while he was yet afar off: and then ye could have made ready and kept the enemy from breaking down the hedge thereof, and saved my vineyard from the hands of the destroyer.

And the lord of the vineyard said unto one of his servants, Go and gather together the residue of my servants; and take all the strength of mine house, which are my warriors, my young men, and they that are of middle age also, among all my servants, who are the strength of mine house, save those only whom I have appointed to tarry; and go ye straightway unto the land of my vineyard, and redeem my vineyard, for it is mine, I have bought it with money.—Therefore get ye straightway unto my land;[3] break down the walls of mine enemies; throw down their tower, and scatter their watchmen; and inasmuch as they gather together against you, avenge me of mine enemies; that by and by, I may come with the residue of mine house and possess the land.

---

3. Responding to this command to march on Missouri, some 200 armed Mormon men trekked over 800 miles from Ohio in an attempt to retake Jackson County. Five paragraphs later God reminds Joseph Smith of the American Revolutionary War and says, "I ... redeemed the land by the shedding of blood," then adds in a subsequent revelation, now D&C 103, that the militia was to "avenge me [God] of mine enemies" (v. 25) and not be "afraid to lay down your life for my sake" (v. 27), which according to the LDS *Doctrine and Covenants Student Manual* under the heading "Section 103: The Redemption of Zion by Power" "sounds like a call to arms." Since the mission was a failure, however, God must have had something else in mind, according to the manual. See the *Doctrine and Covenants Student Manual* for Religion 324 and 325 (Salt Lake City: LDS Church, 2001), 248–49, online at "2015 Lesson Manuals: Institute," www.lds.org/manual.

And the servant said unto his lord, when shall these things be? And he said unto his servant, when I will: go ye straightway, do all things whatsoever I have commanded you; and this shall be my seal and blessing upon you: A faithful and wise steward in the midst of mine house:—A ruler over my kingdom.

And his servant went straightway, and done all things whatsoever his lord commanded him, and after many days all things were fulfilled.

Again, verily I say unto you I will show unto you wisdom in me concerning all the churches, inasmuch as they are willing to be guided in a right and proper way for their salvation, that the work of the gathering together of my saints may continue, that I may build them up unto my name upon holy places; for the time of harvest is come, and my word must needs be fulfilled. Therefore, I must gather together my people according to the parable of the wheat and the tares, that the wheat may be secured in the garners to possess eternal life, and be crowned with celestial glory when I shall come in the kingdom of my father, to reward every man according as his work shall be, while the tares shall be bound in bundles, and their bands made strong, that they may be burned with unquenchable fire.

Therefore, a commandment I give unto all the churches, that they shall continue to gather together unto all the places which I have appointed: nevertheless, as I have said unto you in a former commandment, let not your gathering be in haste, nor by flight; but let all things be prepared before you, and in order that all things be prepared before you, observe the commandments which I have given concerning these things, which saith, or teacheth, to purchase all the lands by money, which can be purchased for money, in the region round about the land which I have appointed to be the land of Zion, for the beginning of the gathering of my saints; all the land which can be purchased in Jackson county, and the counties round about, and leave the residue in mine hand.

Now verily I say unto you, let all the churches gather together all their moneys; let these things be done in their time, be not in haste; and observe to have all things prepared before you. And let honorable men be appointed, even wise men, and send them to purchase these lands; and every church in the eastern countries when they are built up, if they will hearken unto this counsel, they may buy lands and gather together upon them, in this way they may establish Zion. There is even now already in store a sufficient; yea, even abundance to redeem Zion, and establish her waste places no more to be thrown down, were the churches who call themselves after my name willing to hearken to my voice. And, again I say unto you, those who have been scattered by their enemies, it is my will that they should continue to importune for redress, and redemption, by the hands of those who are placed as rulers, and are in authority over you according to the laws and the constitution of the people which I have suffered to be established, and should be maintained for the rights and protection of all flesh, according to just and holy principles, that every man may act in doctrine, and principle pertaining to futurity, according to the moral agency which I have given unto them that every man may be accountable for his own sins in the day of judgment. Therefore it is not right that any man should be in bondage one to another. And for this purpose have I established the Constitution of this land, by the hands of wise men whom I raised up unto this very purpose, and redeemed the land by the shedding of blood.

Now, unto what shall I liken the children of Zion? I will liken them unto the parable of the woman and the unjust judge, (for men ought always to pray and not faint,) which saith, There was in the city a judge which feared not God, neither regarded man. And there was a widow in that city, and she came unto him, saying, avenge me of mine adversary. And he would not for a while, but afterward he said within himself, though I fear not God, nor regard man, yet because this widow troubleth me I will avenge her, lest by her continual coming she weary me.—Thus will I liken the children of Zion.

Let them importune at the feet of the judge; and if he heed them not, let them importune at the feet of the governor; and if the governor heed them not, let them importune at the feet of the president; and if the president heed them not, then will the Lord arise and come forth out of his hiding place, and in his fury vex the nation, and in his hot displeasure, and in his fierce anger, in his time, cut off these wicked, unfaithful and unjust stewards, and appoint them their portion umong [among] hypocrites and unbelievers; even in outer darkness, where there is weeping, and wailing and gnashing of teeth. Pray ye therefore, that their ears may be opened unto your cries, that I may be merciful unto them, that these things may not come upon them.

What I have said unto you, must needs be that all men may be left without excuse; and that wise men and rulers may hear and know that which they have never considered; that I may proceed to bring to pass my act, my strange act, and perform my work. That men may discern between the righteous and the wicked, saith your God.

And, again I say unto you, it is contrary to my commandment, and my will, that my servant Sidney G. [Gilbert] should sell my store house, which I have appointed unto my people, into the hands of mine enemies. Let not that which I have appointed, be polluted by mine enemies, by the consent of those who call themselves after my name; for this is a very sore and grievous sin against me, and against my people, in consequence of those things which I have decreed, and are soon to befall the nations.

Therefore, it is my will that my people should claim and hold claim, upon that which I have appointed unto them, though they should not be permitted to dwell thereon; nevertheless, I do not say they shall not dwell thereon; for inasmuch as they bring forth fruit and works meet for my kingdom, they shall dwell thereon; they shall build, and another shall not inherit it: they shall plant vineyards, and they shall eat the fruit thereof; even so: Amen."

On the publication of this proclamation, it was taken up by all their priests and carried to all their congregations, some of which were actually sold for one dollar per copy. Preparations immediately began to be made for a crusade to *their* Holy Land, to drive out the *infidels*. As it was hinted in the revelation, "All the strength of mine house, which are my warriors, my young men, and they that are of middle age also, among all my servants, who are the strength of mine house," began to make ready for battle.—Old muskets, rifles, pistols, rusty swords and butcher knives, were soon put in a state of repair and scoured up. Some were borrowed, and some were bought, on a credit, if possible, and others were manufactured by their own mechanics. The 1st of May following being finally fixed upon, as the time of setting out on the crusade, "my warriors," which were scattered in most of the Eastern and Northern States, previous to that time, began to assemble at the quarters of the Prophet, in Kirtland, preparatory to marching. Several places farther west, were also selected for rendezvous, to those living in that direction. All the faithful pressed forward; but the services of some were refused by the prophet, in consequence of their not being able, from their own resources, to furnish some instrument of death and five dollars in cash. Old men, invalids, and females, not of the "strength of mine house," who could not endure the toils and hardships of a pedestrian excursion of 1000 miles, felt it to be a great privilege to contribute liberally, in the way of funds, and the *materiel* of war. Poor fanatical females, who could save no more than a shilling per day, by their exertions, threw in all they could raise, for the purpose of helping on with the expedition, and, as they supposed, thereby securing the smiles and blessings of the Lord.

About the first of May[4] the grand army of fanatics, commenced its march, in small detachments, from the different places of concentration. On the 3d,[5] the Prophet, with a life guard, of about 80 men, the *elite* of his army, left his quarters in Kirtland, with a few baggage wagons, containing their arms, amunitions, stores, &c.

The day before his departure, being Sunday, the Prophet had a general meeting of his troops and all the brethren in the neighborhood, on which occasion he and his vicegerant, Rigdon, harangued them to deeds of valor, to perseverance, and to a renewal of their faith in his commandments—dwelling largely, of course, on ancient persecutions of the Christians— their own persecution, and the beauties of martyrdom, as sure

---

4. An advance group of "more than twenty of the brethren left Kirtland for Missouri" on this date, "accompanied by four baggage wagons. They traveled to New Portage, and there tarried … until the remainder of the Kirtland company … arrived" (*History of the Church*, 2:61).

5. Actually the 5th.

passports to glory—assuring them that they should all return, safe and sound, if they followed his instructions.[6] On the morning of their departure, a meeting was assembled, and proceeded to business, after the "manner of the world," by appointing the Prophet *Chairman*, and Cowdery *Secretary*. Whereupon, Rigdon moved that they hereafter assume the title and name of the "Church of the Latter Day Saints,"[7] discarding the name of *Mormonite*, which they began to consider rather a reproach. This was carried unanimously, of course. What their particular object was in the movement, at that particular crisis, we have not been able to understand, unless for the purpose of denying, in the most positive terms, as they passed through the country, that they belonged to the sect known as Mormonites, thereby deceiving the people as to their true character, objects and intentions. But why was not this question settled, as all others are, by a revelation. The Lord had before given them directions not to chew tobacco,[8] nor feed corn to their horses; but in the important matter of giving them a *name*, by which they were ever after to be known, he had wholly refused to interfere, or they had not time to ask him.

6. Rigdon was full of bluster on that day, as he often was, but as George A. Smith recorded, Joseph Smith spoke about the "necessity of being humble, exercising faith, patience and living in obedience to the commands of the Almighty, and not murmur at the dispensation of Providence" ("History of George A. Smith," 14, LDS Church History Library, as cited in Launius, *Zion's Camp*, 54).

7. The name was changed on the 3rd at a church conference from the Church of Christ to Church of the Latter Day Saints (*History of the Church*, 2:62; *The Evening and the Morning Star*, May 1834, 160).

8. The reference here is to a revelation called the Word of Wisdom, LDS D&C 89, which was dictated on Feb. 27, 1833.

During the progress of these preparations, the brethren in Missouri waited patiently the coming of the "liberating army," or some new revelations, not daring to take any steps which their circumstances or necessities might seem to require. In the month of February, several of the Elders, at their request, were escorted back to Independence, by a company of the militia from another county, by the order of the Governor of the State, for the purpose of testifying before the court then sitting for Jackson county, against those who had been concerned in the former outrages and riots.[9] After staying one night under the protection of the guards, they were, in the morning informed, by the public prosecutor, that no indictments would be had, for the reason that the members of the Grand Jury were more or less implicated. Neither could any private suits be instituted for the loss of property, for similar reasons. The Elders were then marched back, it is said, to the tune of "Yankee Doodle," and set across the Missouri.

In the mean time, the people of Jackson county were not inattentive to the premediated attack of Gen. Smith, the Prophet.

---

9. This meeting between Mormon leaders and Jackson County officials was mentioned by W. W. Phelps in a letter dated Feb. 27, 1834. The Phelps letter may be the source of Howe's account (*The Evening and the Morning Star*, Mar. 1834, 139; *History of the Church*, 1:481–83).

CHAPTER 14

But to return to the grand army. On the second day of their march,[1] they arrived at New Portage, about 40 miles distant; where about 100 more fell into the ranks. Here the whole were organized into bands of fourteen men, each band having a captain,[2] baggage wagon, tents, &c. Just before leaving this place, Smith proposed to his army, that they should appoint a treasurer to take posession of the funds of each individual, for the purpose of paying it out as he should think their necessities required. The measure was carried, without a dissenting voice, of course. The Prophet was nominated and voted in, as Treasurer,[3] no one, of course, doubting his right. After pocketing the cash of his dupes, the line of march was resumed, and a white flag raised, bearing upon it, the inscription of "PEACE," written in red.[4]

Somewhere on their route a large black snake was discovered near the road, over five feet in length. This offered a fair

---

1. This was May 6, 1834, "they" being the main group that would soon catch up to the vanguard in New Portage, Ohio (*History of the Church*, 2:64), now named Barberton, near Akron.

2. Smith's history says he "divided the whole band into companies of twelve, leaving each company to elect its own captain" (ibid.).

3. The official history states that Smith's counselor Frederick G. Williams was appointed "paymaster," confirming that everyone had to forfeit to him any money they had brought with them (ibid.).

4. Levi W. Hancock carved an elegantly decorated flagstaff, procured a square piece of white cloth, and painted an eagle and the word *peace* on it in red (Hancock, Autobiography, 143–44; Launius, *Zion's Camp*, 103).

opportunity for some of the company to try their skill at miracles, and Martin Harris took off his shoes and stockings, to "take up serpents," without being harmed.—He presented his toes to the head of the snake, which made no attempt to bite; upon which Martin proclaimed a victory over serpents; but passing on a few rods farther, another of much larger dimensions was discovered, and on presenting his bare foot to this one also, he received a bite in the ankle, which drew blood. This was imputed to his want of faith and produced much merriment to the company.[5]

A large mound was one day discovered, upon which Gen. Smith ordered an excavation to be made into it; and about one foot from the top of the ground, the bones of a human skeleton were found, which were carefully laid out upon a board, when Smith made a speech, prophesying or declaring that they were the remains of a celebrated General among the Nephites,[6] mentioning his name and the battle in which he was slain, some 1500 years ago. This was undoubtedly done to encourage the troops to deeds of daring, when they should meet the Missourians in battle array.

On arriving at Salt creek, Illinois,[7] they were joined by

---

5. Smith reproved Harris for tempting God, according to the *History of the Church*, 2:95–96; cf. Mark 16:18; Morm. 9:24.

6. To reach Missouri, the militia had to march through Indiana and Illinois. Midway across Illinois in the fourth week of the campaign, Smith declared that the skeleton they found was that of a deceased "white Lamanite … [whose] name was Zelph. He was a warrior and chieftain under the great prophet Onandagus, who was known from the Hill Cumorah, or eastern sea to the Rocky mountains" (*History of the Church*, 2:79–80; cf. Godfrey, "Zelph Story"; Cannon, "Zelph Revisited").

7. There was a Mormon congregation at Salt Creek. The next day more men arrived from settlements north of there (*History of the Church*, 2:87).

Lyman Wight[8] and Hiram Smith, (brother of the prophet,) with a reinforcement of twenty men, which they had picked up on the way. Here the grand army, which being fully completed, encamped for the space of three days.—The whole number was now estimated at 220, *rank and file.* During their stay here, the troops were kept under a constant drill of manual exercise with guns and swords, and their arms put in a state of repair— the Prophet became very expert with a sword, and felt himself equal to his prototype Coriantumr. He had the best sword in the army, (probably a true model of Laban's, if not the identical one itself,) an elegant brace of pistols, which were purchased on a credit of six months, a rifle, and four horses. Wight was appointed second in command, or fighting general, who, to- gether with the prophet, had an *armour bearer* appointed, selected from among the most expert tactitions, whose duty it was to be in constant attendance upon their masters with their arms. The generals then appointed a new captain to each band, organized two companies of rangers, or *sharp shooters,* to act as scouts or flankers, when they should arrive upon the field of carnage. After this they *dubbed* themselves the *"army of Zion,"* and Hiram Smith was chosen to carry the flag, which he kept unfurled during the remainder of the march.[9]

8. Lyman Wight (1796–1858) was originally from upstate New York, served in the War of 1812 when he was sixteen, and became affiliated with the Campbellites in Kirland prior to his conversion to Mormonism in November 1830. Joseph Smith sent him to establish a colony in Texas, where he remained to his death.

9. The militia was actually called the Army of Israel. Howe's other details are more or less correct, the official history reporting that there were 205 sol- diers in the militia and identifying Hyrum as captain of a twenty-man company

The march of the grand army was then resumed for two or three days, when it was agreed to spend half a day in a sham fight. For this purpose four divisions were formed, and took positions, and went to work, agreeably to the most approved forms of Bonaparte, Black Hawk, Coriantumr or Shiz. After coming to close quarters, however, all discipline was lost sight of, and each one adopted a mode agreeable to his taste. Some preferred the real British *push* with the bayonet, some the old Kentucky dodging from tree to tree, while others prefered the Lamanite mode of tomahawking, scalping and ripping open the bowels. The final result was, that several guns and swords were broken, some of the combatants wounded, and each one well pleased with his own exploits.

After crossing the Mississippi, spies on horseback were kept constantly on the look out, several miles in front & rear. The Prophet went in disguise, changing his dress frequently, riding on the different baggage wagons, and, to all appearance, expecting every moment to be his last. Near the close of one day, they approached a prairie, which was 30 miles in extent, without inhabitants. Here an altercation took place between the two generals, which almost amounted to a mutiny. The prophet declared it was not safe to stay there [at the edge of the prairie] over night, as the enemy would probably be upon them. Gen. Wight totally refused to enter the prairie, as they would not be able to find water,[10] or to build a fire to cook their provisions, besides the great fatigue it would cause the troops.

---

of "life guards" protecting General Smith (*History of the Church*, 2:87–88; D&C 105:26, 30, 31).

10. Six weeks into the campaign and 65 miles from their destination, they

Smith said he would show them how to eat raw pork. Hiram said he knew by the spirit that it was dangerous to stay there. The prophet finally exclaimed, "Thus saith the Lord God— March on;" this settled the matter—and they all moved on about fifteen miles, and thinking themselves out of danger, they encamped beside a muddy pool, and went through the *raw pork* operation. Here the controversy was again renewed between the two generals. Smith said "he knew exactly when to pray, when to sing, when to talk, and when to laugh, by the Spirit of God—that God never commanded any one to pray for his enemies." The whole seemed much dissatisfied, and came nigh breaking out into open mutiny.

The Prophet had, besides his other weapons, a large bull dog, which was exceedingly cross during the nights, and frequently attempted to bite persons stirring about. One of the captains, (a High Priest,)[11] one evening, declared to the Prophet that he would shoot the dog, if he ever attempted to bite *him*. Smith replied, "that if he continued in the same spirit, and did not repent, the dog would yet eat the flesh off his bones, and he would not have the power to resist." This was the commencement of a controversy between the Prophet and his High Priest, which was not settled till some time after their return to head-quarters, in Kirtland, when the former underwent a formal trial[12] on divers serious charges, before his Priests,

were reluctant to leave the protection of the Wakenda River, a defensive barrier and water source (*History of the Church*, 2:100–01).

11. Sylvester Smith (no relation) was threatened with being whipped if he harmed the dog, according to Heber C. Kimball (ibid., 2:82–83).

12. The minutes of the trial are in ibid., 2:142–60.

honorably acquitted, and the latter made to acknowledge that he had been possessed of several devils, for many weeks. The dog, however, a few nights after the controversy commenced, was shot through the leg by a sentinel, near the Prophet's tent, and died instantly.

When within twelve miles of Liberty, Clay county, Mo. (the head-quarters of the fanatics in that state,) the "army of Zion" was met by two gentlemen,[13] who had been deputed by the citizens of another county, for the purpose of enquiring into the motive and object of such a hostile and warlike appearance upon their borders. These gentlemen openly warned the military band and their Prophet, to desist from their intended operations, and leave the settlement of their difficulties with the people of Jackson county, in other hands—advised them to be very careful what they did and said, as the citizens of not only Jackson, but some of the adjacent counties, were very much enraged and excited, and were fully determined to resist the first attempt upon them, by an armed force from other States. A few hours after this, the Prophet brought out a revelation,[14] for the use of his troops, which said, in substance, that "they had been tried, even as Abraham was tried, and the offering was accepted by the Lord, and when Abraham received his reward, they would receive theirs." Upon this, the war was declared to be at an end. A call for volunteers, however, was made, to take up their abode in Clay county, when about

13. On June 22, the Clay County sheriff, Cornelius Gillium, visited the camp, apparently accompanied by a deputy (ibid., 2:108).

14. This revelation, which was not included in the 1835 Doctrine and Covenants, is now LDS D&C 105.

150 turned out. The next day they marched to Liberty,[15] and each man received an *honorable* discharge, under the signature of Gen. Wight. The army then scattered in different directions, some making their way back from whence they came, the best way they could, begging their expenses from the inhabitants. The Prophet and his chief men, however, had plenty of money, and travelled as other gentlemen do. Before leaving Liberty, the Cholera broke out among them, and carried off thirteen of their number, viz: John S. Carter, Eber Wilcox, Seth Hitchcock, Erastus Rudd, Algernon S. Gilbert, Alfred Fisk, Edward Ives, Noah Johnson, Jesse B. Lawson, Robert McCord, Eliel Strong, Jessie Smith and Betsey Parish.[16] A new revelation was now had, that the brethren could purchase land and settle in any of the adjacent counties, or "regions round about."[17]

The particulars of this expedition have been related to us by an eye witness, who was one of the *sharp shooters*, and marched the whole distance, full of faith in the assertions of Jo Smith, that "Zion was to be delivered." He came back, well satisfied with Mormonism, and is esteemed a man of truth and veracity, by his acquaintances. And now, had we the pen of a Cervantes, we should be strongly tempted to draw out another volume, as an appendix, from the valorous deeds of our modern Knight of La Mancha, for we do not believe that in all the history of knight errantry, whether true or fabulous,

15. Because the militia was not allowed to enter Liberty, they camped at nearby Rush Creek (*History of the Church*, 2:112).

16. Howe's source, *The Evening and the Morning Star*, July 1834, 176, overlooked one fatality, Warren Ingalls (cf. *History of the Church*, 2:120).

17. D&C 105:28; cf. 115:18.

an excursion by any set of men, so fraught with delusion and nonsense, can be found. And, in fact, it came well nigh loosening the scales from the eyes of most of the dupes to the imposition—and the whole camp came near breaking up, after the return of the Prophet to Kirtland. There was a constant uproar among the brethren, for three or four weeks,[18] which only terminated in a sham trial of the Prophet; wherein, as near as we can learn, he was judge, jury and witness; and, as one of the brethren said, (very imprudently,) a more disgraceful transaction never took place. The Prophet considered it a trying time with himself, and a point on which his future prospects turned. He accordingly put in requisition all his powers of speech and tact at deception, to cover over his transactions, and reclaim his refractory followers. On one occasion he harangued and belabored them for six hours upon a stretch, and finally succeeded in restoring order, with the loss of two or three members. It would seem that the Prophet anticipated trouble, on his return, as he secured a deed of a valuable farm,[19] just before starting, by the contributions of his followers. He also took a deed of the

18. Joseph Smith himself wrote on Aug. 16, 1834, that no sooner had he arrived home in Ohio than "the cry was Tyrant … [for] prophesying lies in the name of the Lord [and] taking consecrated monies" (*History of the Church*, 2:144).

19. On May 3, Smith had bought 1.5 acres from Frederick G. Williams for $178 and two acres from John Johnson for $222 (Hill et al., "Kirtland Economy Revisited," 461). Acting as an agent for the church, he bought 142 acres from Frederick G. Williams for $2,200 (Deeds, Liber 16, 22–23, Geauga County Courthouse, Chardon, Ohio; Hill et al., "Kirtland Economy Revisited," 427, 461; Backman, *Profile of Latter-day Saints in Kirtland, Ohio*, 71–73). Williams said there was actually no exchange of money because everything was consecrated to the Lord (see Williams, "Statement").

ground on which stands a huge stone temple, sixty by eighty feet; and which is now nearly completed. Possessing himself, personally, of this edifice, gave such dissatisfaction, that the deed was finally altered, so as run to him and his successor.[20]

But to return to the Missouri war. On hearing of the approach of the prophet and his troops, the people of Jackson county had a general meeting, organized a military force, and appointed a committee of ten persons to proceed to Liberty, in order to effect a settlement of their controversy with the Mormons. They met the Mormon leaders, in a public meeting, when the following correspondence passed between them; but as the Prophet had not then arrived, nothing could be accomplished.

Propositions of the People of Jackson to the Mormons.[21]

The undersigned committee, being fully authorized by the people of Jackson county, hereby propose to the Mormons, that they will buy all the land that the said Mormons own in the county of Jackson; and also, all the improvements which the said Mormons had on any public lands in said county of Jackson, as they existed before the first disturbances between the people of Jackson and the Mormons, and for such as they have made since. They further propose, that the valuation of said land and improvements shall be ascertained by three disinterested

20. This was more of a rhetorical than strictly factual claim. Smith owned the property only in the sense that he was the church's trustee. The temple property was purchased for $5,000 in April 1833 by two Mormon agents who donated it to the church (Deeds, Liber 17, 359; 18, 480–81, Geauga County Courthouse; Backman, *Profile of Latter-day Saints in Kirtland, Ohio*, 73, 144).

21. The "proposition" was printed in the *Missouri Enquirer*, June 18, 1834, and reprinted, along with the "answer," in *The Evening and the Morning Star*, July 1834, 175 (cf. *History of the Church*, 2:96–99).

arbitrators, to be chosen and agreed to by both parties. They further propose, that should the said parties disagree in the choice of arbitrators, then —— is to choose them. They further propose that twelve of the Mormons shall be permitted to go along with the arbitrators, to show them their land and improvements, while valuing the same, and such other of the Mormons as the arbitrators shall wish to do so, to give them information: and the people of Jackson hereby guarantee their entire safety while doing so. They further propose, that when the arbitrators report the value of the land and improvements, as aforesaid, the people of Jackson will pay the valuation, with *one hundred per cent. thereon*, to the Mormons, within thirty days thereafter. They further propose that the Mormons are not to make any effort ever after to settle, either collectively or individually, within the limits of Jackson county. The Mormons are to enter into bonds to insure the conveyance of their land in Jackson county, according to the above terms, when the payment shall be made; and the committee will enter into a like bond, with such security as may be deemed sufficient, for the payment of the money, according to the above propositions. While the arbitrators are investigating and deciding the matter referred to them, the Mormons are not to attempt to enter Jackson county, or to settle there, except such as are, by the foregoing proposition permitted to go there. They further propose that the people of Jackson will sell all their lands, and improvements on public lands in Jackson county, to the Mormons—the valuation to be obtained in the same manner—the same per cent. in addition to be paid—and the time the money is to be paid is the same as above set forth in our proposition to buy—the Mormons to give good security for the payment of the money, and the undersigned will give good security that the land will be conveyed to the Mormons. They further propose, that all parties are to remain as they are till the payment is made, at which time the people of Jackson will give possession.[22]

Signed:—Samuel C. Owens, Thomas Jeffries, S. Noland, Thos. Hayton, Sen., John Davis, Robt. Rickman, James Campbell, Abr'm McClellan, S. N. Nolan, Richard Fristoe.

Answer.

Gentlemen:—

Your proposition for an adjustment of the difficulties between the citizens of Jackson county, and the Mormons, is before us; and as explained to you in the court house, this day, we are not authorized to say to you that our brethren will submit to your proposals; but we agree to spread general notice, and call a meeting of our people in all, the present week, and lay before you an answer as soon as Saturday or Monday next. We can say for ourselves, and in behalf of our brethren, that peace is what we desire, and what we are disposed to cultivate with all men; and to effect peace, we feel disposed to use all our influence, as far as would be required at our hands, as free born citizens of these United States. And as fears have been expressed that we designed to commence hostilities against the inhabitants of Jackson county, we hereby pledge ourselves to them, and to the hospitable citizens of Clay county, that we

---

22. It is hard to make sense of the proposal, but in general the Missourians said they would purchase the Mormons' property at double its appraised value if the Mormons would promise never again to set foot in the county. The Missourians seem to have been offering their own property as collateral for a bond. Historian Roger Launius commented that through this offer, the people of Jackson County were "admitting they had been wrong in their actions in 1833" and wanted to "make restitution." However, since Mormons saw it as a trick to deprive them of their rights, they would not compromise. They still held out hope that the county would become an exclusive homeland (Launius, "Question of Honor?" p. 13).

will not, and neither have designed, as a people, to commence hostilities against the aforesaid citizens of Jackson county, or any other people.

Our answer shall be handed to Judge Turnham, the Chairman of the meeting, even earlier than the time before stated, if possible.

W. W. Phelps, Wm. E. McLelin, Isaac Morley,
A. S. Gilbert, John Carrill.

N. B. As we are informed that a large number of people are on their way, removing into Jackson county, we agree to use our influence immediately to prevent the said company from entering into Jackson county, until you shall receive an answer to the proposition aforenamed.

About the same time[,] the following correspondence appeared in the Missouri Enquirer, a paper printed at Liberty, Clay Co., Missouri:[23]

Being a citizen of Clay county, and knowing that there is considerable excitement among the people thereof, and also knowing that different reports are arriving almost hourly, and being requested by the Hon. J. F. Ryland to meet the Mormons under arms, and obtain from the leaders thereof the correctness of the various reports in circulation—the true intent and meaning of their present movements, and their views generally regarding the difficulties existing between them and the citizens of Jackson county—I did, in company with

---

23. *Missouri Enquirer,* July 2, 1834. Along with the "Propositions of the Mormons," this letter was reprinted in the *Painesville Telegraph,* Aug. 8, 1834. See also *The Evening and the Morning Star,* July 1834, 176; *History of the Church,* 2:121–22. Cornelius Gillium was the sheriff of Clay County, Missouri.

other gentlemen, call upon the said leaders of the Mormons, at their camp, in Clay county; and now give to the people of Clay county their written statement, containing the substance of what passed between us.

Cornelius Gillium

Propositions of the Mormons.

Being called upon by the above named gentlemen, at our camp, in Clay county, to ascertain from the leaders of our men our intentions, views and designs, in approaching this county in the manner that we have: we, therefore, the more cheerfully comply with their request, because we are called upon by gentlemen of good feelings, who are disposed for peace, and an amicable adjustment of the difficulties existing between us and the people of Jackson county. The reports of our intentions are various, and have gone abroad in a light calculated to arouse the feelings of almost every man. For instance, one report is, that we intend to demolish the printing office in Liberty; another report is, that we intend crossing the Missouri River, on Sunday next, and falling upon women and children, and slaying them; another is, that our men were employed to perform this expedition, being taken from the manufacturing establishments in the East that had closed business; also, that we carried a flag, bearing peace on one side, and war or blood on the other; and various others too numerous to mention. All of which, a plain declaration of our intentions, from under our own hands, will show are not correct. In the first place, it is not our intention to commit hostilities against any man or body of men. It is not our intention to injure any man's person or property, except in defending ourselves. Our flag has been exhibited to the above gentlemen, who will be able to describe it. Our men were not taken from any manufacturing establishment. It is our intention to go back upon our lands in Jackson, by order of the Executive of the State, if possible.[24] We have brought our arms with us for the purpose of self-defence, as it is well known to almost every man of the State that we have every reason to put ourselves in an attitude of defence, considering the abuse we have suffered in Jackson county. We are anxious for a settlement of the difficulties existing between us, upon honorable and constitutional principles. We are willing for twelve disinterested men, six to be chosen by each party, and these men shall say what the possessions of those men [Missourians] are worth who cannot live with us [Mormons] in the county, and they shall have their money in one year; and none of the Mormons shall enter that county to reside until the money is paid. The damages that we have sustained in consequence of being driven away shall also be left to the above twelve men. Or they may all live in the county, if they choose, and we will never molest them if they let us alone, and permit us to enjoy our rights. We wish to live in peace with all men, and equal rights is all we ask. We wish to become permanent citizens of this State, and wish to bear our proportion in the support of the Government, and to be protected by its laws. If the above proposals are complied with, we are willing to give security on our part; and we shall want the same of the people of Jackson county for the performance of this agreement.—We do not wish to settle down in a body, except where we can purchase the lands with money; for to take possession by conquest is entirely foreign to our feelings. The shedding of blood we shall not be guilty of until all honorable means prove insufficient to restore peace.

---

24. This is where "the Mormons balked at th[e] compromise," as Launius noted. "It was a generous offer" from the Missourians, and "the refusal to compromise … led [the Mormons] into repeated difficulties thereafter" (ibid.).

Attest: Joseph Smith, Jr., F. G. Williams, Lyman Wight, Roger Orton, Orson Hyde, John S. Carter, John Lincoln, C. R. Morehead, John Sconce, James H. Long, James Collins, *Clay County, June 21, 1834.*

Messrs. [Robert] Kelley & [William] Davis:[25]

Gentlemen: Having understood that a communication from the Mormons, addressed to the people of Clay county, a copy of which was also forwarded to us, dated 21st inst. has been left with you for publication, we have thought proper to give the said communication a passing notice, especially as it bears the signatures of Jo. Smith, Jr.[,] F. G. Williams, Lyman Wight, Roger Orton, Orson Hyde, and John S. Carter. We are unable to say with precision, who of the Mormons hold land in Jackson county, by any earthly title; but, so far as we can obtain any information at the Register's office at Lexington, so far as the sales of Seminary lands, of the 16th sections of the Township School Lands, inform us, and so far as the Re-corder's Office furnishes any information of lands transferred by deeds recorded, neither of the above gentlemen Mormons own any lands in Jackson County; although, throughout their whole communication, they hold out the idea, that their only wish and desire is to return to their lands in Jackson. From the above, it would seem that if those who signed the commu-nication above alluded to, have titles to any lands in Jackson county, they are titles unknown to the laws of the State, and of a character not known to common conveyances.—Why men, who do not, so far as we can learn, own any lands in Jackson,

25. This letter from Samuel Owens, Jackson County clerk, was written to the editors of the *Missouri Enquirer* and appeared July 2, 1834. It was not reprinted by the Mormons. Howe carried it in the *Painesville Telegraph*, Aug. 8, 1834.

should promulgate to the world, that they have been expelled from them, appears to us inexplicable; unless, indeed, it is done with a view to deceive. Why men, living in the State of Ohio, should there raise an armed force, and march the distance of 6 or 800 miles, under the pretense of taking possession of their lands in Jackson, when, in fact, they have no earthly title to any, that would be to us also inexplicable, had we not the best possible reasons to know and believe their true intent and purpose.—Joseph Smith, jr., whose name is first to [appear in] the paper of which we speak, we confidently believe, does not, neither did he ever, own a foot of land in Jackson county. Said Smith, two years or more ago, was in Jackson county some two or three weeks; since which time, he has not been, or at least known publicly to have been, in Jackson county. F. G. Williams, the second signer, we are informed, on competent authority, has never been a resident of Jackson county. But, if here at all, his stay was short, (our informant was, if not yet, a Mormon.) Lyman Wight had been for some time a resident of this county, but had no title to any land, as we believe, for the facts above stated. Roger Orton is unknown to any of the citizens of this county, so far as we have been able to make inquiry, and is unknown to some of the Mormon faith. Orson Hyde is known, and of famous memory to most of the people of this county, not by personal acquaintance, for, as we are informed, he had been but a short time here; but, by his communications, which appeared in the St. Louis Republican last November,[26] (with what truth we will not here discuss.) John S. Carter is unknown to any person in this county, so far as we can learn.

---

26. Orson Hyde gave a one-sided account of events for the *Daily Missouri Republican*, Nov. 12, 1833, and was countered by Lieutenant Governor Lilburn Boggs in the Dec. 6 issue.

Thus it would seem, that the signers of the above paper, or a majority of them, have no interest whatever in this county, any further than the Mormon church is concerned; and yet, they avow to the citizens of Clay, that their sole object in arming and marching to this county was, and is, to take possession of their lands, when in fact they had no lands to take possession of; that the abuse they [say they] received here last Fall is sufficient to warrant them coming here armed. What abuse, we ask, did the Prophet Jo. Smith, Jr., receive in this county last Fall, and he not in the State? None, indeed, to his person. Again, they say that they never intended to get possession of Zion, (that is Jackson,) by the shedding of blood! But, in Revelation No. 54, given in Kirtland, Ohio, August, 1831, near three years since, which we find in a Book of Revelations, printed by the Mormons, we discover the following in the thirteenth verse, to wit: "Wherefore, the land of Zion shall be obtained but by purchase or by blood,[27] otherwise there is no inheritance for you." Thus it would seem, that either the Revelation is false, or the statement made by Jo. Smith and others to the people of Clay county is false.—And we cannot but conclude, that the statement was got up for the sole purpose of allaying public excitement against them, and without much regard to their real object in coming here. The fact is, that an armed force coming from another State, many, and indeed most of whom have never, as we are informed and believe, been here before, produces the strongest conviction to our minds, that the Mormons do not intend to rely upon the arm of the civil law for protection, and redress of grievances; but that under

---

27. Now LDS D&C 63:29, the revelation was first published in *The Evening and the Morning Star* in Feb. 1833, then in the Book of Commandments, chap. 64.

the pretence of getting back to their lands in Jackson county, a pretence which, applied to nineteen out of twenty of them, is false, they intend to redress of themselves their real as well as imaginary wrongs. We have already offered them two prices for their lands; they will not sell—neither will they buy ours on the same terms. All this pertinacity and infatuation of theirs, show that they are determined, at all hazards, and regardless of all consequences, to shake and convulse not only Jackson but the surrounding counties, to their very centre, and to imbrue the whole upper Missouri in blood and carnage. We will here observe, in conclusion, that our proposition to the Mormons to sell their lands to us on the same terms on which we offer ours to them, must be regarded as a proof of our desire to do them justice, and thus put a final termination to this controversy.

Samuel C. Owens, Chairman of Jackson county
Committee, Independence, (MO.) June 23, 1834.

Copy of a Letter from Daniel Dunklin, Governor of the State of Missouri, to Col. James Thornton, dated

City of Jefferson, June 6, 1834.[28]

Dear Sir: I was pleased at the receipt of your letter, concurred in by Messrs. Ress, Atchison, and Donaphin, on the subject of the Mormon difficulties. I should be gratified, indeed, if the parties could compromise on the terms you suggested, or, indeed, upon any other terms satisfactory to themselves. But I should travel out of the line of my strict duty, as chief executive officer of the government, were I to take upon myself the task of effecting a compromise between the parties. Had I not

---

28. The letter was printed in the *Missouri Enquirer*, June 25, 1834, and *The Evening and the Morning Star*, July 1834, 175–76 (see also *History of the Church*, 2:84–87).

supposed it possible, yes, probable, that I should, as Executive of the State, have to act, I should, before now, have interfered individually, in the way you suggest, or in some other way, in order, if possible, to effect a compromise. Uncommitted as I am, to either party, I shall feel no embarrassment in doing my duty; though it may be done with extreme regret. My duty in the relation in which I now stand to the parties, is plain and straight forward. By an official interposition, I might embarrass my course, and urge a measure for the purpose of effecting a compromise, and if it should fail, and in the end, should I find it my duty to *act* contrary to the *advice* I had given, it might be said, that I either advised wrong, or acted wrong; or that I was partial to one side or the other, in giving advice that I would not, as an officer, follow. A more clear and indisputable right does not exist, than that of the Mormon people, who were expelled from their homes in Jackson county, to return and live on their lands, and if they cannot be persuaded as a matter of *policy*, to give up that right, or to qualify it, my course, as the chief Executive officer of the State, is a plain one. The Constitution of the United States declares,— "That the citizens of each State shall be entitled to all the privileges and immunities of citizens in the several States." Then we cannot interdict any people who have a political franchise, in the United States, from emigrating to this State, nor from choosing *what part* of the State they will settle in providing they do not trespass on the property or rights of others.—Our State Constitution declares that the people's "right to bear arms, *in defense of themselves, and of the State,* cannot be questioned." Then it is their constitutional right to arm themselves. Indeed, our militia law makes it the duty of every man, not exempt by law, between the ages of 18 and 45, to arm himself with a musket, rifle, or some firelock, with a certain quantity of ammunition, &c. And again, our

Constitution says, "that all men have a natural and indefeasible right to worship Almighty God according to the dictates of their own consciences." I am fully persuaded that the eccentricity of the religious opinions and practices of the Mormons, is at the bottom of the outrages committed against them.

They have the right constitutionally guaranteed to them, and it is indefeasible, to believe and *worship Jo Smith*, as a *man*, an *angel*, or even as the *true and living God*, and to call their habitation *Zion*, the *Holy Land,* or even Heaven itself. Indeed, there is nothing so absurd or ridiculous, that they have not a right to adopt as their religion, so that in its exercise, they do not interfere with the right of others.

It is not long since an impostor assumed the character of Jesus Christ, and attempted to minister as such; but I never heard of any combination to deprive him of his rights.

I consider it the duty of every good citizen of Jackson and the adjoining counties, to exert themselves to effect a compromise of these difficulties, and were I assured that I would not have to act in my official capacity in the affair, I would visit the parties in person, and exert myself to the utmost to settle it. My first advice would be to the Mormons to sell out their lands in Jackson county, and to settle somewhere else, where they could live in peace, if they could get a fair price for their lands, and reasonable damages for injuries received. If this failed, I would try the citizens and advise them to rescind their illegal resolves of last summer; and agree to conform to the laws in every particular, in respect to the Mormons. If both these failed, I would then advise the plan you have suggested, for each party to take separate territory and confine their members within their respective limits, with the exception of the right of egress and regress upon the highway. If all these failed, then the simple question of legal right would have to settle it. It is this last that

I am afraid I shall have to conform my action to in the end. And hence the necessity of keeping myself in the best situation to do my duty impartially.

Rumor says that each party are preparing themselves with cannon.—That would be illegal. It is not necessary for self-defence, as guaranteed by the Constitution. And as there are no artillery companies organized in this State, nor field pieces provided by the public, any preparations of that kind will be considered as without right; and in the present state of things, would be understood to be with a criminal intent. I am told that the people of Jackson county expect assistance from the adjoining counties, to oppose the Mormons in taking or keeping possession of their lands. I should regret it extremely, if any should be so imprudent as to do so; it would give a different aspect to the affair.

The citizens of Jackson county have a right to arm themselves and parade for military duty in their own county independent of the commander-in-chief; but if the citizens march there from other counties, with arms, without orders from the commander-in-chief or some one authorized by him, it would produce a very different state of things. Indeed, the Mormons have no right to march to Jackson county in arms, unless by order or permission of the commander-in-chief. Men must not "levy war" in taking possession of their rights, any more than others should in opposing them in taking possession.

As you have manifested a deep interest in a peaceable compromise of this important affair, I presume you will not be unwilling to be placed in a situation, in which, perhaps, you can be more serviceable to these parties. I have therefore taken the liberty of appointing you an Aid to the commander-in-chief, and hope it will be agreeable to you to accept. In this situation you can give your propositions all the influence they would have, were they to emanate from the Executive, without committing yourself or the commander-in-chief in the event of a failure.

I would be glad if you or some other gentleman who joined in your communication, would keep a close correspondence with these parties, and by each mail, write me.

The character of the State has been injured in consequence of this unfortunate affair: and I sincerely hope it may not be disgraced by it in the end.

With high respect, your obedient servant,

Signed: Daniel Dunklin.

Thus ended the far-famed Mormon war, and thus the[29] difficulties stand at the present time. It was set on foot, as they constantly held out, by a command of the Lord, for the sole and express purpose of "redeeming Zion," as the dupes who marched under the orders of the prophet, firmly believed. They entertained not the least doubt that they were to have a *brush* with the people of Jackson county, and some were sorely disappointed and chagrined, when it was first announced that no blood was to be spilt; so much so, that one, at least, manifested a determination not to submit to the decision of the Prophet, and was only pacified by an exhibition of the revelation to his view. After all, Smith had the hardihood and affrontery to declare, after his return, that his sole and only object in marching his troops thither, was to carry money and other supplies to his brethren, who were in destitute circumstances. But the reasons why the expedition was so suddenly terminated, may be readily discovered in the Governor's letter, and the manifestations

---

29. Howe had "thus the the ..."

of the citizens in that part of the country. Smith and his High Priests supposed that they had nothing to do but to make a display of their instruments of destruction, and their *flag*, to restore peace to the country. All the benefit, therefore, which was derived from his long march and expenditure of money, was, for the Prophet to get the information that he had no business there, and that it would be the most prudent course to *"march back again."*

CHAPTER 15.

The following letters were written by Ezra Booth,[1] a Methodist Clergyman, and addressed to a presiding Elder. He was an early convert to Mormonism, and renounced it as soon as he was fully convinced of its nature and design.—He gives a clear and comprehensive view of the whole imposition, in a plain and unvarnished style, and will doubtless carry conviction to every rational mind, that the whole is a base fabrication. They were originally published in the Ohio Star;[2] but their limited circulation has induced us to place them in this work.

LETTER I.

Nelson, Portage Co. Sept. 1831.

Rev. Ira Eddy[3]—

Dear Sir: I received yours of the 2d inst. and heartily thank

---

1. Ezra Booth (1792–1873) became a Methodist minister about 1817. He was living forty-five miles east of Cleveland, Ohio, when he converted to Mormonism in May 1831. A member of the church for only four months, he quickly became disaffected and withdrew his membership.

2. Booth's nine letters were published in the *Ohio Star*, Oct.–Dec. 1831, and reprinted in the *Painesville Telegraph* as each letter appeared. Sidney Rigdon denounced them as a "false representation of the subjects on which they treat," but without giving specifics (*Ohio Star*, Dec. 15, 1831). For more on the contents, see Rowley, "Ezra Booth Letters"; Marquardt, "Ezra Booth on Early Mormonism."

3. Ira Eddy was minister of the Methodist Episcopal Church in Ravenna, Ohio. Prior to his 1831 appointment, he had lived near Booth in Edinburg. According to the census, he was in his thirties.

you for the favor. It revives afresh in my recollection the scenes of past years, upon the remembrance of which, I dwell with a mixture of pleasurable and painful sensations. I arrived at my home on the 1st of the present month, having finished my tour to the west;[4] since which time the scenes and events in the history of my life, for the last few months, have passed in review before my mind.

You are not, it is probable, ignorant of the designs of my most singular and romantic undertaking [in Missouri]: sufficient to say, it was for the purpose of exploring the *promised land*—laying the foundation of the city of Zion,[5] and placing the corner stone of the temple of God. A journey of one thousand miles to the west, has taught me far more abundantly, than I should have probably learned from any other source. It has taught me quite beyond my knowledge, the *imbecility* of human nature, and especially my own weakness. It has unfolded in its proper character, a *delusion* to which I had fallen a victim, and taught me the *humiliating* truth, that I was exerting the powers of both my mind and body, and sacrificing my time and property, to build up a system of delusion, almost unparalleled in the annals of the world.

If God be a God of consistency and wisdom I now know Mormonism to be a delusion; and this knowledge is built upon the testimony of my senses. In proclaiming it, I am aware I proclaim my own misfortune—but in doing it, I remove a burden from my mind, and discharge a duty as *humbling* to myself,

---

4. He and Isaac Morley had been sent on a proselyting mission to Missouri. See pp. 188–89, 276–97.

5. This occurred on August 2, 1831.

as it may be *profitable* to others. You had heard the story of my wanderings, and "was induced to believe that I had been visited with a species of mental derangement," and therefore, you "had given me up, as one among those friends of early association, who in the lapse of time, would be as though they had not existed." You had concluded that the magic charm of delusion and falsehood, had so wrapped its sable mantle around me, as to exclude the light of truth and secure me a devoted slave. But thanks be to God! the spell is dissipated, and the "captive exile hasteneth that he may be loosed, and not die in the pit."

When I embraced Mormonism, I conscientiously believed it to be of God. The impressions of my mind were deep and powerful, and my feelings were excited to a degree to which I had been a stranger. Like a ghost, it haunted me by night and by day, until I was mysteriously hurried, as it were, by a kind of necessity, into the vortex of delusion.—At times I was much elated; but generally, things in prospect were the greatest stimulants to action.

On our arrival in the western part of the State of Missouri, the place of our destination, we discovered that *prophecy* and *vision* had failed, or rather had proved false.—The fact was so notorious, and the evidence so clear, that no one could mistake it—so much so, that Mr. Rigdon himself said, that "Joseph's *vision* was a bad thing."[6] This was glossed over, apparently, to

6. Joseph Smith said that his June 1831 trip to Missouri was preceded by a "heavenly vision" commanding him to make the journey so he could point out to the others where the New Jerusalem would be built (*Messenger and Advocate*, Sept. 1835, 179). Perhaps influenced by a letter from Oliver Cowdery in which the second elder enthused about the prospects for converts in Missouri (*History*

the satisfaction of most persons present; but not fully to my own. It excited a suspicion that some things were not right, and prepared my mind for the investigation of a variety of circumstances, which occurred during my residence there, and indeed, to review the whole subject, from its commencement to that time. My opportunities for a thorough investigation, were far greater than they could have been, had I remained at home; and therefore, I do not regret that I made the journey, though I sincerely regret the cause of it. Since my return, I have had several interviews with Messrs. Smith, Rigdon and Cowdery, and the various shifts and turns, to which they resorted in order to obviate objections and difficulties, produced in my mind additional evidence, that there was nothing else than a deeply laid plan of craft and deception.

The relation in which Smith stands to the church, is that of a Prophet, Seer, Revealer, and Translator; and when he speaks by the Spirit, or says he knows a thing by the communication of the Spirit, it is received as coming directly from the mouth of the Lord. When he says he knows a thing to be so, *thus* it must stand without controversy. A[7] question is agitated between two Elders of the church—whether or not a bucket of water will become *heavier* by putting a living fish in it. Much is said by each of the disputants; when at length, Smith decides it in the negative, by saying—"I know by the spirit, that it will be no heavier." Any person who chooses, may easily ascertain by

---

of the Church, 1:182), Smith foresaw a large congregation awaiting him, but this prophecy proved not to be true (see pp. 280, 289–90).

7. Howe had a typographical error here: "A A question …"

actual experiment, whether the Prophet was influenced in this decision, by a *true or false spirit*.

It is not my design, at this time, to enter into particulars relative to the evidence upon which my renunciation of Mormonism is founded. This evidence is derived from various sources, and is clear and full, and the conviction which it produces, at least on my mind, is irresistible. You are not aware of the nature of this deception, and the spirit that uniformly attends it; nor can you ever know it, unless you yield to its influence, and by experience learn what it is to fall under its power: "from which my earnest prayer is, that you may ever, ever escape."

There probably never was a plan better suited to lead the sinner and the conscientious, when in an unguarded hour they listen to its fatal insinuations. The plan is so ingeniously contrived, having for its aim one principal point, viz: the establishment of a society in Missouri, over which the contrivers of this delusive system, are to possess unlimited and despotic sway. To accomplish this, the Elders of the church, by commandment given in Missouri, and of which I was both an eye and an ear witness, are to go forth to preach Mormonism to *every creature*; and now, said Mr. Rigdon—"The Lord has set us our stint; no matter how soon we perform it—for when this is done, he will make his second appearance."

I do sincerely, and I trust in deep humility, return unfeigned gratitude to the God of infinite mercy, who, in condescension to my weakness, by a peculiar train of providences, brought me to the light, enabled me to see the hidden things of darkness, and delivered me from the snare of the fowler, and from the contagious pestilence which threatened my entire destruction.[8] The scenes of a past few months, are so different from all others in my life, that they are in truth to me "as a dream when one awaketh." Had my fall affected *only myself*, my reflections would be far less painful than they now are. But to know—that whatever influence I may have possessed, has been exerted to draw others into a delusion, from which they may not soon be extricated, is to me a source of sorrow and deep regret. They are at this moment the object of my greatest anxiety and commiseration. I crave their forgiveness, and assure them, that they will ever have an interest in my addresses to the throne of grace. It shall be my endeavor to undo, as far as possible, what I have done in this case, and also to prevent the spread of a delusion, pernicious in its influence, and destructive in its consequences to the body and the soul—to the present and eternal interests of all men.

I am, through restoring mercy and grace, as in former years, though unworthily, yet affectionately yours in Christ,

Ezra Booth.

LETTER 2.

Were there none but myself interested in the exposition of Mormonism, I can assure you my time would be otherwise employed than in writing upon a subject which has heretofore been to me one of deep interest, and at times has occasioned a painful anxiety of mind. I could wish, if possible, to bury it in oblivion;

---

8. Booth's language is biblical: "Surely he shall deliver thee from the snare of the fowler, and from the noisome pestilence" (Ps. 91:3). In the following sentence, "as a dream when one awaketh" comes from Psalm 73.

and to remember it no more forever. But as this is a thing which cannot be accomplished in a moment, for the sake of others, who may be exposed to the delusion, from which, through the mercy of God, I have been recovered, and others who are at present involved in it: and also in compliance with your request, I will, as far as I have ability, unfold a system of darkness, fraught with glaring absurdity, and deceptive as falsehood itself.

This system, to some, carries the face of plausibility, and appears under an imposing form. It claims the Bible for its patron and proffers the restoration of the apostolic church, with all the gifts and graces with which the primitive saints were endowed. It is called *the fullness of the gospel of both Jew and Gentile:* and is the test by which every man's faith is to be tried. Judgments are denounced against the sinners of this generation; or in other words, all who reject the Book of Mormon, are threatened with eternal damnation. Great promises are made to such as embrace it, signs and wonders are to attend them, such as healing the sick, the blind made to see, the lame to walk, &c.; and they are to receive an everlasting inheritance in "the land of Missouri," where the Savior will make his second appearance; at which place the foundation of the temple of God, and the City of Zion, have recently been laid, and are soon to be built. It is also to be a city of Refuge, and a safe asylum when the storms of vengeance shall pour upon the earth, and those who reject the Book of Mormon, shall be swept off as with the besom of destruction. Then shall the riches of the Gentile be consecrated to the Mormonites; they shall have lands and cattle in abundance, and shall possess the gold and silver, and all the treasures of their enemies.

The Mormonite preachers go forth proclaiming repentance and baptism for the remission of sins, and the laying on of hands for the reception of the Holy Ghost. The form of baptism is similar to other orders; only it is prefaced with—"having authority given me of Jesus Christ;"[9] also, the laying on of hands—"In the name of Jesus Christ, receive ye the Holy Ghost." Many of them have been ordained to the High Priesthood, or the order of Melchisedec; and profess to be endowed with the same power as the ancient apostles were. But they have been hitherto unsuccessful in finding the lame, the halt, and the blind, who had faith sufficient to become the subjects of their miracles: and it is now concluded that this work must be postponed until they get to Missouri;[10] for the Lord will not show those signs to this wicked and adulterous generation. In the commandment given to the churches in the State of New York, to remove to the State of Ohio, they were assured that these miracles should be wrought in the State of Ohio;[11] but now they must be deferred until they are settled in Missouri.

As the Mormonite church depends principally upon the commandments, and as most of them are concealed from the world, it will be necessary to make some statement respecting them. These commandments come from Smith, at such times and on such occasions as he feels disposed to speak, and Rigdon or Cowdery to write them. Their exact number I have

---

9. This wording comes from 3 Ne. 11:25 and the Book of Commandments 24:53 (cf. LDS D&C 20:73).

10. Cf. D&C 58:3–7, 64.

11. The revelation promised that in Ohio they would be "endowed with power from on high" (D&C 38:32), but not specifically that they would perform miracles.

never taken pains to ascertain. I have the "27th commandment to Emma my daughter in Zion;"[12] and should presume there are betwixt fifty and a hundred.[13]—They received the addition of five or six while in Missouri;[14] and these are considered a miracle in themselves, sufficient to convince any rational mind. But none but the strong in faith are permitted to witness their origin. I had an opportunity of seeing this wonderful exhibition of the wisdom and power of God, at three different times; and I must say, that it bore striking marks of human weakness and wickedness. They are received in the church as divinely inspired, and the name of the Lord is substituted for that of Smith. They are called "The Commandments of the Lord." They are considered "The mysteries of the Kingdom;" and to divulge them to the world, is the same as casting pearls before swine. When they and the Scriptures are at variance, the Scriptures are wrongly translated; and Smith, though totally ignorant of the original, being a translator or an alterator, can easily harmonize them. Every thing in the church is done by commandment: and yet it is said to be done by the voice of the church. For instance, Smith gets a commandment that he shall be the "head of the church," or that he "shall rule the Conference," or that the Church shall build him an elegant house,

---

12. D&C 25, dictated in July 1830.

13. When Booth left in mid-September 1831, he would have known about some sixty-one revelations that would become numbered sections of the Doctrine and Covenants. Some of those selections would actually be made up of as many as five earlier, shorter revelations (LDS D&C 23, 30, 42), and there were two revelations in circulation that would never be canonized (Cook, *Revelations*, 361), bringing the total he would have known of to about seventy.

14. D&C 57–62.

and give him 1000 dollars. For this the members of the church must vote, or they will be cast off for rebelling against the commandments of the Lord. In addition to the Book of Mormon, and the commandments, there are revelations which are not written.—In this department, though Smith is the principal, yet there are others who profess to receive revelations;[15] but after all, Smith is to decide whether they come from the Lord or the devil. Some have been so unfortunate as to have their revelations palmed upon the latter. These revelations entirely supercede the Bible, and in fact, the Bible is declared too defective to be trusted, in its present form; and it is designed that it shall undergo a thorough alteration, or as they say, translation. This work is now in operation. The Gospel of St. Matthew has already received the purifying touch, and is prepared for the use of the church. It was intended to have kept this work a profound secret,[16] and strict commandments were given for that purpose; and even the salvation of the church was said to depend upon it. The secret is divulged, but the penalty is not as yet inflicted.—Their revelations are said to be an addition to the Bible.—But instead of being an addition, they destroy its use; for every thing which need be known, whether present, past or future, they can learn from Smith, for he has declared to the church, that he "knows all things that will take place

---

15. David Whitmer recalled that "Brother Joseph gave many true prophecies when he was humble before God: but this is no more than many of the other brethren did. Brother Joseph's true prophecies were almost all published, but those of the other brethren were not" (Whitmer, *Address*, 32; cf. D&C 28:8).

16. A revised version of Matthew 24 was released as a broadside "for the benefit of the Saints" (Matthews, *Plainer Translation*, 50; cf. D&C 42:56–57).

from this time to the end of the world." If then, placing the Bible under circumstances which render it entirely useless, is infidelity, Mormonism is infidelity.

Joseph Smith, Jun., Sidney Rigdon, Oliver Cowdery and Martin Harris, may be considered as the principals in this work; and let Martin Harris tell the story, and he is the most conspicuous of the four.—He informed me, that he went to the place where Joseph resided, and Joseph had given it up, on account of the opposition of his wife and others; but he told Joseph, "I have not come down here for nothing, and we will go on with it."[17] Martin Harris is what may be called a great talker, an extravagant boaster; so much so, that he renders himself disagreeable to many of his society. The money he has expended, and the great things he has done, form a considerable topic of his conversation; he understands all prophecies, and knows every thing by the spirit, and he can silence almost any opposer by talking faster, and louder than he [the other person] can: or by telling him, "I know every thing and you know nothing; I am a wise man and you are a fool;" and in this respect he stands a fair sample of many others in the church. Yours affectionately,

E. Booth.

LETTER 3.

Mormonism has in part changed its character, and assumed a different dress, from that under which it made its first

17. Dale Morgan believed this occurred during Harris's first visit to Harmony in February 1828 (Walker, *Dale Morgan on Mormonism*, 280, 387n11). Harris returned two months later to become Smith's scribe.

appearance on the Western Reserve.[18] Many extraordinary circumstances which then existed, have vanished out of sight; and the Mormonites desire, not only to forget them, but wish them blotted out of the memory of others. Those wonders which they wish to have forgotten, stand as the principal foundation of the faith of several hundred of the members of their church.

With the wonders of Mormonism, or some of them, I design to occupy your attention in this letter; and I wish you to observe here, and hereafter remember, that the evidence by which all my statements are supported, is derived from my own experience and observation, or from testimony of persons who still adhere to Mormonism; and I hold myself responsible to any tribunal, whether on earth or in heaven, for the truth of what I write, or at least for an intention to write the truth, and nothing but the truth.

"Being carried away by the spirit," and "I know it to be so by the spirit," are well known phrases, and in common use in the Mormonite church. We will first notice the gift of tongues, exercised by some when carried away in the spirit. These persons were apparently lost to all surrounding circumstances, and wrapt up in the contemplation of things, and in communication with persons not present.—They articulated sounds, which but few present professed to understand; and those few declared them to be the Indian language. A merchant, who had formerly been a member of the Methodist society, observed, he had formerly traded with the Indians, and he knew it to be their dialect. Being myself present on one of these occasions, a

---

18. The Western Reserve was the land claimed at one time by Connecticut, extending west through New York, Pennsylvania, and Ohio.

person proffered his services as my interpreter, and translated these sounds to me which were unintelligible, into the English language. One individual could read any chapter of the Old or New Testament, in several different languages. This was known to be the case by a person who professed to understand those languages. In the midst of this delirium they would, at times, fancy themselves addressing a congregation of their red brethren; mounted on a stump, or the fence, or from some elevated situation, would harangue their assembly until they had convinced or converted them. They would then lead them into the water, and baptize them, and pronounce their sins forgiven. In this exercise, some of them actually went into the water; and in the water, performed the ceremony used in baptizing. These actors assumed the visage of the savage, and so nearly imitated him, not only in language, but in gestures and actions, that it seemed the soul and body were completely metamorphosed into the Indian. No doubt was then entertained but that was an extraordinary work of the Lord, designed to prepare those young men for the Indian mission; and many who are still leaders of the church, could say, "we know by the spirit that it is the work of the Lord." And now they can say, "they know it is the work of the devil." Most of those who were the principal actors, have since apostatized, and the work [of speaking in tongues] is unanimously discarded by the church. The limits which my want of time to write, as well as your want of patience to read compel me to prescribe for myself, will allow me only to touch on some of the most prominent parts of this newly invented, and heterogeneous system.

A new method of obtaining authority to preach the Gospel

was introduced into the church. One declared he had received
a commission, directly from Heaven, written upon parchment.
Another, that it was written upon the palm of his hand, and
upon the lid of his Bible, &c. Three witnesses, and they were
formerly considered persons of veracity, testified that they saw
the parchment, or something like it, when put into the hands
of the candidate. These commissions, when transcribed upon
a piece of paper, were read to the church, and the persons who
had received them, were ordained to the Elder's office, and sent
out into the world to preach. But this also sunk into discredit,
and experienced the fate of the former.

Visions, also, were in high credit, and sounded abroad as
an infallible testimony in favor of Mormonism. The visionary,
at times, imagined he saw the city of New Jerusalem; unlocked
its gate, and entered within the walls; passed through its various apartments, and then returned, locked the gate, and put
the key into his pocket. When this tour was finished, he would
entertain his admiring friends, with a detailed description of
the Heavenly City.

The condition of the ten tribes of Israel since their captivity, unto the present time, has excited considerable anxiety, and
given rise to much speculation among the learned. But after
all the researches which have been made, the place of their
residence has never been satisfactorily ascertained. But these
visionaries have discovered their place of residence to be con-
tiguous to the north pole;[19] separated from the rest of the world
by impassable mountains of ice and snow. In this sequestered

19. D&C 133:26; cf. 2 Esd. 13:39–41.

residence, they enjoy the society of Elijah the Prophet, and John the Revelator,[20] and perhaps the three immortalized Nephites.—By and by, the mountains of ice and snow are to give way, and open a passage for the return of these tribes, to the land of Palestine.

About this time the ministration of angels was supposed to be frequent in the church. The Heavenly visitants made their appearance to certain individuals: they seldom made any communication, but presented themselves as spectacles to be gazed upon, with silent admiration.

Smith is the only one at present, to my knowledge, who pretends to hold converse with the inhabitants of the celestial world. It seems from his statements, that he can have access to them, when and where he pleases. He does not pretend that he sees them with his natural, but with his spiritual eyes; and he says he can see them as well with his eyes shut, as with them open. So also in the translating.—The subject stands before his eyes in print, but it matters not whether his eyes are open or shut; he can see as well one way as the other.

You have probably read the testimony of the three witnesses appended to the Book of Mormon. These witnesses testify that an angel appeared to them, and presented them the golden plates, and the voice of God declared it to be a divine record. To this they frequently testify, in the presence of large

---

20. John Whitmer wrote of how "the spirit of the Lord fell upon Joseph [Smith] in an unusual manner" at a June 1831 conference when Smith "prophecied that John the Revelator was then among the ten tribes of Israel" (Westergren, *From Historian to Dissident*, 69; Davidson et al., *Joseph Smith Papers: Histories*, 2:39).

congregations. When in Missouri, I had an opportunity to examine a commandment given to these witnesses, previous to their seeing the plates.[21] They were informed that they should see and hear those things by faith, and then they should testify to the world, as though they had seen and heard, as I see a man, and hear his voice: but after all, it amounts simply to this—that by faith or imagination, they saw the plates and the angel, and by faith or imagination they heard the voice of the Lord.

Smith describes an angel, as having the appearance of a "tall, slim, well built, handsome man, with a bright pillar upon his head." The Devil once, he says appeared to him in the same form, excepting upon his head he had a "black pillar," and by this mark he was able to distinguish him from the former.

It passes for a current fact in the Mormonite church, that there are immense treasures in the earth, especially in those places in the State of New York from whence many of the Mormonites emigrated last spring: and when they become sufficiently purified, these treasures are to be poured into the lap of their church; to use their own language, they are to be the richest people in the world. These treasures were discovered several years since, by means of the dark glass, the same with which Smith says he translated the most of the Book of Mormon.[22] Several of those persons, together with Smith,

21. The revelation told the witnesses that "it is by your faith that you shall obtain a view" of the ancient record (D&C 17:2–4). The witnesses said the angel placed the record "before *our eyes*," but the entire presentation occurred in vision, as Harris later confirmed when he said he had seen the plates with his "spiritual eyes" (Vogel, "Validity of the Witnesses' Testimonies," 86–90; Gilbert, "Memorandum," 5; Vogel, *Documents*, 2:548).

22. Note that Booth's claim is that he heard this directly from Smith and

who were unsuccessfully engaged in digging and searching for these treasures, now reside in this county, and from themselves I received this information.

Ezra Booth.

LETTER 4.

From the time that Mormonism first made it[s] appearance upon the stage, until the grand tour of the Missouri, an expectation universally pervaded the church, that the time was not far distant, when the deaf, the dumb, the maimed, the blind, &c. would become the subjects of the miraculous power of God, so that every defect in their systems would be entirely removed.

This expectation originated from, and was grounded upon a variety of premises, included in a number of commandments, or verbal revelations from Smith, or, as he is styled "the head of the church." As the 4th of June last was appointed for the sessions of the conference,[23] it was ascertained, that that was the time specified, when the great and mighty work was to be commenced, and such was the confidence of some, that knowledge superceded their faith, and they did not hesitate to declare themselves perfectly assured that the work of miracles would commence at the ensuing conference. With such strong

---

other sources, possibly from Martin Harris, Joseph and Newel Knight, Orrin Porter Rockwell, and Joseph Smith Sr. He will soon name Hiram Page as "one of the 'money diggers'" (p. 305).

23. The conference began on June 3 and must have continued on for several days, the ordinations occurring on the 4th and a revelation being dictated on the 6th (Cannon and Cook, *Far West Record*, 6–9; MacKay et al., *Joseph Smith Papers: Documents*, 1:317–18n412, 324; *History of the Church*, 1:175). Booth is listed in the Far West Record as having been present.

assurances, and with the most elevated expectations, the conference assembled at the time appointed. To give, if possible, energy to expectation, Smith, the day before the conference, professing to be filled with the spirit of prophecy, declared, that "not three days should pass away, before some should see their Savior, face to face."[24] Soon after the session commenced, Smith arose to harangue the conference. He reminded those present of the prophecy, which he said "was given by the spirit yesterday." He wished them not to be overcome with surprise, when that event ushered in. He continued, until by long speaking, himself and some others became much excited. He then laid his hands on the head of Elder Wight, who had participated largely in the warm feeling of his leader, and ordained him to the High Priesthood. He was set apart for the service of the Indians, and was ordained to the gift of tongues, healing the sick, casting out devils, and discerning spirits; and in like manner he ordained several others; and then called upon Wight to take the floor. Wight arose, and presented a pale countenance, a fierce look, with his arms extended, and his hands cramped back, the whole system agitated, and a very unpleasant object to look upon. He exhibited himself as an instance of the great power of God, and called upon those around him, "if you want to see a sign, look at me." He then stepped upon a bench, and declared with a loud voice, he saw the Savior:[25] and thereby, for the time being, rescued Smith's prophecy from merited

---

24. Joseph Smith also predicted that there would be demonic manifestations, saying "the man of Sin should be revealed" (Westergren, *From Historian to Dissident*, 71; Davidson et al., *Joseph Smith Papers: Histories*, 2:40).

25. Lyman Wight "saw the hevans opened, and the Son of man sitting on

contempt.—It, however, procured Wight the authority to ordain the rest. So said the spirit, and so said Smith. The spirit in
Smith selected those to be ordained, and the spirit in Wight
ordained them.[26] But the spirit in Wight proved an erring dic-
tator; so much so, that some of the candidates felt the weight
of hands thrice, before the work was rightly done. Another
Elder, who had been ordained to the same office as Wight,
at the bidding of Smith, stepped upon the floor. Then ensued
a scene, of which you can form no adequate conception; and
which, I would forbear relating, did not the truth require it.
The Elder moved upon the floor, his legs inclining to a bend;
one shoulder elevated above the other, upon which the head
seemed disposed to recline, his arms partly extended; his hands
partly clenched; his mouth partly open, and contracted in the
shape of an italic *O;* his eyes assumed a wild ferocious cast, and
his whole appearance presented a frightful object to the view of
the beholder.—"Speak, Brother Harvey" said Smith. But Harvey intimated by signs, that his power of articulation was in a
state of suspense, and that he was unable to speak. Some conjectured that Harvey was possessed of the devil,[27] but Smith

the right hand of the Father," according to John Whitmer (Westergren, *From Historian to Dissident*, 70; Davidson et al., *Joseph Smith Papers: Histories*, 2:40).

26. According to the official record, the ordinations were reciprocal, Smith ordaining Wight, after which Wight was chosen to ordain eighteen men including Smith. Wight also ordained Ezra Booth (Cannon and Cook, *Far West Record*, 7; MacKay et al., *Joseph Smith Papers: Documents*, 1:326).

27. "The Devil ... bound Harvey Whitlock <and John Murdock> so that [they] could not speak ... but the Lord showed to Joseph the Seer the design of this thing, he commanded the devil in the name of Christ and he departed to our joy and comfort" (Westergren, *From Historian to Dissident*, 71; David-son et al., *Joseph Smith Papers: Histories*, 2:41). Others remembered "strange

said, "the Lord binds in order to set at liberty." After different opinions had been given, and there had been much confusion, Smith learnt by the spirit, that Harvey was under a diabolical influence, and that Satan had bound him; and he commanded the unclean spirit to come out of him.

It now became clearly manifest, that "the man of sin was revealed," for the express purpose that the elders should become acquainted with the devices of Satan; and after that they would possess knowledge sufficient to manage him. This, Smith declared to be a miracle, and his success in this case, encouraged him to work other and different miracles. Taking the hand of one of the Elders in his own, a hand which by accident had been rendered defective, he said, "Brother Murdock, I command you in the name of Jesus Christ to straighten your hand;[28] in the mean while, endeavoring to accomplish the work by using his own hand to open the hand of the other. The effort proved unsuccessful; but he again articulated the same commandment, in a more authoritative and louder tone of voice; and while uttering with his tongue, his hands were at work; but after all the exertion of his power, both natural and supernatural, the deficient hand returned to its former position, where it still remains. But ill success in this case, did not discourage him from undertaking another. One of the Elders, who was decriped [decrepit] in one of his legs, was set upon the floor,

---

manifestations of false spirits, which were immediately rebuked" (Pratt, *Autobiography*, 68), and that an evil spirit "threw one [elder] from his seat to the floor" and "bound another, so that for some time he could not use his limbs nor speak" (Corrill, *Brief History*, 18; Davidson et al., *Joseph Smith Papers· Histories*, 2:145).

28. All other accounts are silent about Smith's attempt to heal John Murdock.

and commanded, in the name of Jeses [Jesus] Christ to walk. He walked a step or two, his faith failed, and he was again compelled to have recourse to his former assistant [crutch], and he has had occasion to use it ever since.

A dead body, which had been retained above ground two or three days, under the expectation that the dead would be raised, was insensible to the voice of those who commanded it to awake into life, and is destined to sleep in the grave till the last trump shall sound, and the power of God easily accomplishes the work, which frustrated the attempts, and bid defiance to the puny efforts of the Mormonite.[29]

Under these discouraging circumstances, the horizon of Mormonism gathered darkness, and a storm seemed to hang impending over the church. The gloom of disappointed expectation, overspread the countenances of many, while they labored to investigate the cause of this failure. To add, if possible, to their mortification, a larger assembly collected on the Sabbath, in order to hear preaching. In the midst of the meeting, the congregation was dismissed by Rigdon, and the people

---

29. Howe inserted a footnote here by means of an asterisk: "That an attempt was made to raise the child, is denied, of course, as every other attempt has been, after the entire failure was obvious to all. The parents of the deceased child, however, state, that they were prevented from procuring medical aid for the child, by the representations of the elders, that it was in no danger—that it would certainly be restored. The father had no other idea but that the child was to be raised; neither did his faith fail him till preparations were made for its interment. He then awoke from his dream of delusion, and dissolved his connexion with the impostors." A similarly unsuccessful attempt to raise Joseph Brackenbury from the dead was made on January 7, 1832 (Prince, *Power from on High*, 18n52). Notice from Howe's footnote that he evidently interviewed the parents of the deceased child to confirm Booth's claim.

sent to their homes. He was directed to do this, he said, by the spirit. But it was generally believed, that he was directed solely by fear; and that he had mistaken the spirit of cowardice, for the spirit of the Lord. Several of the Elders said they "felt the spirit to preach" to the congregation: and Rigdon felt the spirit to send the people home: such was the unity which then prevailed among them.

You will doubtless say, can it be possible that the minds of men, and men who possess the appearance of honesty, can be so strangely infatuated, as still to adhere to a system, after it had occasioned so much agitation, and so much disappointment. One reason which can be assigned for this, is, the adherents are generally inclined to consider the system so perfect, as to admit of no suspicion; and the confusion and disappointment, are attributed to some other cause. Another, and principal reason is, delusion always affects the mind with a species of delirium, and this delirium arises in a degree proportionate to the magnitude of the delusion. These men, upon other subjects, will converse like other men; but when their favorite system is brought into view, its inconsistencies and contradictions are resolved into inexplicable mystery; and this will not only apply to the delusions now under consideration, but in my view, to every delusion, from the highest to the lowest; and it matters not whether it carries the stamp of popularity or its opposite.

Yours affectionately, Ezra Booth.

LETTER 5.

In my last letter I gave you a faint representation of the events which transpired and the circumstances which attended the meeting of the Mormonite Conference. Though many stumbled, yet none irrecoverably fell. Another grand object was presented, and the attention was somewhat diverted from these scenes of disappointment, through which we had recently passed. The tour to the Missouri, revived the sinking expectations, and gave new energy to faith and hope. In that distant region, anticipation was to be realized in full, and the objects of faith and hope, were to become the objects of knowledge and fruition. A commandment was received, and Elders were directed to take their journey for the "promised land." They were commanded to go two by two, with the exception of Rigdon, Smith, Harris, and Partridge; and it was designed that these should find an easier method of transporting themselves, than to travel that distance on foot. They were careful to make suitable provision for themselves, both in money and other articles, that while on their journey, they might carry the appearance of gentlemen filling some important station in life; while many, who were destined to travel on foot, with packs on their backs, were so fired with the ardor of enthusiasm, that they supposed they could travel to Missouri with but little or no money. These carried the appearance, and were justly entitled to the character of beggars, for when the little money they took with them was expended, they subsisted by begging, until they arrived at their journey's end.

Being myself one of the number selected to perform the journey by land, and not being much accustomed to travel on foot, I hesitated for a while; but believing it to be the will of God, I resolved on an unreserved surrender of myself to the work, and on the 15th of June, in company with the one appointed to travel with me, took up my line of march for

Missouri.[30] I do not design to trouble you with a relation of the particulars, but will observe, that after I left the north part of the State of Ohio, I made a speedy and prosperous journey to Missouri. I preached twice in Ohio, thrice in Indiana, once in Illinois, and once in Missouri. We were commanded to preach by the spirit, and my impressions were, that farther to the westward, I should enjoy more of the spirit's influence; and though I travelled one thousand miles to the west, my anticipations in this respect, were never realized. I seldom proclaimed Mormonism with that liberty which I enjoyed in my public exercises, while a member of the Methodist Episcopal Church. I supposed that at some future time, the spirit would endow me to preach with an unusual degree of liberty. That period has never arrived, and I am persuaded it never will, and I now sincerely desire the spirit of truth to direct my pen, while I endeavor to expose the errors and absurdities of the system I then advocated.

When we arrived at the place to which our mission destined us, we perceived to our mortification, that disappointment, instead of being confined to the State of Ohio, had journeyed thither before us. We would gladly have avoided here an interview with this, our old companion [disappointment]; but this was impossible, she met us, and stared us in the face which way soever we turned, nor was it possible to look her out of countenance, or put the blush upon her pallid features, or expel her from our society. Some were for making the best of her they could; but for myself, I resolved that she

---

30. Cf. D&C 52:23. They apparently departed from Kirtland four days before Smith's entourage left.

should be expelled, or at any rate, that her visits should be less frequent, or I would abandon the habitation entirely.

When we commenced our journey for Missouri, we expected an "effectual door" would be opened, to proclaim the new system of faith, in that region; and that those who were ordained to the gift of tongues, would have an opportunity to display their supernatural talent, in communicating to the Indians, in their own dialect.[31] Some who were ordained to this office, absolutely knew that through this medium, they should gain access to the natives; and I will venture to say, I know, that their success will be similar to that of their predecessor, Oliver Cowdery, who stated that he was endowed with the same fore knowledge. But the event has proved his presumption false. For more than two weeks, while I remained there, the disposition of the Elders appeared to be averse to preaching, either to the white or the red people, and indeed adverse circumstances prevented it.

We expected to assemble together in conference according to the commandment, and the Lord would signally display his power, for the confirmation of our faith; but we commenced our journey home before most of the Elders arrived. It is true, a conference was held,[32] but it was considered so unimportant,

---

31. They would continue to periodically display the ecstatic form of unintelligible speech called glossolalia but not the ability to spontaneously and intelligibly speak in a foreign language known as xenoglossia. Missionaries continued to communicate with the Indians through interpreters. See Vogel and Dunn, "Tongue of Angels," 2, 21–23.

32. A conference was held in Kaw township, ten miles west of Independence, on August 4, 1831 (D&C 52, 57; Cannon and Cook, *Far West Record*, 9; Godfrey et al., *Joseph Smith Papers: Documents*, 2:22–24).

that myself and another man were permitted to be absent, for the purpose of procuring the means of conveyance down the river. We expected to find a large church, which Smith said, was revealed to him in a vision, [and] Oliver had raised up there. This large church was found to consist of four females.

We expected to witness the exercise of those miraculous gifts, to which some were ordained while in the State of Ohio. But the same difficulty, the same want of faith among the people, which counteracted them here, prevailed there; consequently no miracles could be wrought. We expected to see the foundation of the City and temple laid; and this we were permitted to see, and it was in fact a curiosity, but not worth going to Missouri to see. The honor of consecrating the land, &c. was conferred on Rigdon.—The commandment reads thus: "let my servant Sidney consecrate and dedicate the land, and the spot for the Temple"—again, "Behold I give unto my servant *Sidney* a commandment, that he shall write a description of the land of Zion, and a statement of the will of God, as it shall be made known to him by the spirit, and a subscription to be presented to the Churches, to obtain money to purchase lands, for the inheritance of the children of God: for behold the Lord willeth that his Disciples, and the children of men, should open their hearts, to purchase the whole region of country, lest they receive none inheritance, save it be by the shedding of blood."[33] The childish exultation of the Mormonite leaders, while they echoed and re-echoed, the Lord has given us this whole region of country; "this whole region of country is ours;" when it was

---

33. D&C 58:57, 50–53.

manifest, agreeable to the commandment, that the gift was only obtained, by purchasing it at a dear rate with money, and that, in order to save themselves the trouble of "the shedding of blood," would, under other circumstances, have been truly diverting. But when viewing it as an instance of a deep laid scheme, and the cunning artifice of crafty impostors, designed to allure the credulous and the unsuspecting, into a state of unqualified vassalage, it presents a melancholy picture of the depravity of the human heart, while destitute of those virtues, inculcated in the Gospel by the blessed Redeemer.

It was conjectured by the inhabitants of Jackson county, that the Mormonites, as a body are wealthy, and many of them entertain fears, that next December, when the list of land is exposed for sale, they will out-bid others, and establish themselves as the most powerful body in the county.—But they may dismiss their fears in this respect; for the Mormonites as a body, are comparatively poor, and destined so to remain, until they pursue a different co[u]rse as it relates to economy and industry, from what they have hitherto pursued. There were ten families, which came by water, landed there the day on which I arrived; and all the land which the Bishop said they had means to purchase, was less than thirty acres to the family; and thirty acres in that country, is little enough for wood and timber land; as fifteen acres upon an average here, are worth thirty there. Neither need they fear that the Mormonites, were they so disposed, will obtain the possession of their lands "by shedding of blood," until the spirit selects more courageous leaders than *Smith* or Rigdon.

Yours affectionately, Ezra Booth.

LETTER 6.

It is well know[n] that the ostensible design of the Mormonites in settling in the western part of Missouri, is to convert the Indians to the faith of Mormonism. In this, the leaders appear to have in view, as a mode, the Jesuits of the 16th century, who established themselves in South America, by gaining an entire ascend[a]ncy over the hearts and consciences of the natives, and thereby became their masters. As Independence is the place of general rendezvous and head quarters of the Mormonites, it may not be amiss to notice it. It is a new town, containing a court-house built of brick, two or three merchant's stores, and 15 or 20 dwelling houses, built mostly of logs hewed on both sides; and is situated on a handsome rise of ground, about three miles south of Missouri river, and about 12 miles east of the dividing line between the United States and the Indian Reserve, and is the county seat of Jackson county. In this place it is designed to establish the Lord's printing press, of which Wm. W. Phelps[34] and O. Cowdery are to have the management; and also, the Lord's store-house, committed in charge to S. Gilbert.[35] By the means of these two grand engines,

---

34. William Wines Phelps (1792–1872) was born in New Jersey. He was in his late thirties when he first encountered the Book of Mormon. Professionally, as editor of the anti-Masonic newspaper in upstate New York, the *Ontario Phoenix*, he was so impressed with the Book of Mormon that he began selling it out of the newspaper office (*Ontario Phoenix*, Dec. 29, 1830). After being imprisoned for debt in April 1831, he decided to submit to baptism and move to Independence, where he edited *The Evening and the Morning Star*, the first Mormon newspaper. He also became a counselor in the Missouri presidency. He left the church for a short time, then became active again and moved to Utah in 1849 (Jenson, *Biographical Encyclopedia*, 3:692–97; Cook, *Revelations*, 87–88).

35. Algernon Sidney Gilbert (1789–1834), Newel Whitney's business

they expect to make the wicked feel the weight of their tremendous power. West of the line lies the territory, selected by the government of the United States, for the future residence of the Indians; to which place, a number of tribes have recently emigrated. The question is frequently asked, do the Indians seem disposed to receive Mormonism; or have any of them as yet embraced it? To which question I have heard some of the leaders reply, "O yes," when the truth is, not an individual had embraced it when I left that place. Nor is there any prospect they will embrace it. It is true, that some of the Indians appear to listen with a degree of attention, while the Mormonite teacher pretends to disclose to them the secrets of their origin, the history of their ancestors, and that the great Spirit designs, in this generation, to restore them to the possession of their lands, now occupied by the whites; and the Indians shall go forth among the white people, "as a lion among the beasts of the forests, and as a young lion among the flocks of sheep, who, if he goeth through, both treadeth down and teareth to pieces, and no man can deliver. Thy hand shall be lifted up against thy adversaries, (the whites) and all their enemies (the whites) shall be cut off."[36] Here you have a fair specimen of the method adopted in the Book of Mormon, and preached by the Mormonite teachers, for the purpose of enlisting the feelings, and ingratiating themselves with the Indians; and should success attend their endeavors, and the minds of the Indians become

partner in Kirtland, was called to operate the church storehouse in Missouri but died of cholera in 1834 when the militia arrived (Zion's Camp) and infected the refugees in Clay County.

36. 3 Ne. 20:16–17.

inflamed with the enthusiastic spirit which Mormonism inspires, they may be inclined to try the experiment, whether "by shedding of blood," [and] they can expel the white inhabitants, or reduce them to a state of servitude; and by this means, regain the possession of the lands occupied by their forefathers.

The laying of the foundation of Zion was attended with considerable parade and an ostentatious display of talents, both by Rigdon and Cowdery. The place being designated as the site where the city was to commence, on the day appointed we repaired to the spot, not only as spectators, but each one to act the part assigned him in the great work of laying the foundation, of the "glorious city of New Jerusalem." Rigdon consecrated the ground, by an address in the first place to the God whom the Mormonites profess to worship; and then making some remarks respecting the extraordinary purpose for which we were assembled, prepared the way for administering the oath of allegiance, to those who were to receive their "everlasting inheritance" in that city. He laid them under the most solemn obligations, to constantly obey all the commandments of Smith. He enjoined it upon them to express a great degree of gratitude for the free donation, and then, as the Lord's Vicegerent, he gratuitously bestowed upon them, that for which they had paid an exorbitant price in money. These preliminaries being ended, a shrub oak, about ten inches in diameter at the butt, the best that could be obtained near at hand, was prostrated, trimmed, and cut off at a suitable length; and twelve men, answering to the twelve Apostles,[37] by means

---

37. Smith said he chose twelve ushers to represent the twelve tribes of Israel (*History of the Church*, 1:196). "Apostle" was not an official title or an

of handspikes, conveyed it to the place. Cowdery craved the privilege of laying the corner stone. He selected a small rough stone, the best he could find, carried it in one hand to the spot, removed the surface of the earth to prepare a place for its reception, and then displayed his oratorical power, in delivering an address, suited to the important occasion. The stone being placed, one end of the shrub oak stick was laid upon it; and there was laid down the first stone and stick, which are to form an essential part of the splendid city of Zion.

The next day the ground for the temple was consecrated,[38] and Smith claimed the honor of laying the corner-stone himself. Should the inhabitants of Independence, feel a desire to visit this place, destined at some future time to become celebrated, they will have only to walk one half of a mile out of the town, to a rise of ground, a short distance south of the road. They will be able to ascertain the spot by the means of a sapling, distinguished from the others by the bark being broken off on the north and on the east side. On the south side of the sapling will be found the letter T, which stands for Temple; and on the east side ZOM! for Zomas; which Smith says is the original word for Zion.[39] Near the foot of the sapling, they will

---

indication that there was an office exclusively reserved for twelve men but a way of referring to the lay Mormon ministry in that day, sometimes as elders and sometimes as apostles.

38. Rigdon dedicated the temple lot in Independence on August 3 (D&C 58:57).

39. When Booth's letter was first published in the *Ohio Star*, the word "Zomar" was used. Smith later used Zomar to define another fanciful term, Adam-ondi-Ahman, which he sketched out as being a garden "filled with fruit trees and precious flowers, made for the healing of man … [a] place of

find a small stone covered over with bushes, which were cut for that purpose. This is the corner stone for the temple. —They can there have the privilege of beholding the mighty work, accomplished by about thirty men, who left their homes, traveled one thousand miles, most of them on foot, and expended more than $1,000 in cash.

Having completed the work, or rather finding but little business for us to accomplish in Missouri, most of us became anxious to return home. And none appeared to be more so than Rigdon and Smith, whose plans for future subsistence were considerably frustrated. They expected to find a country abounding with the necessaries and comforts of life. But the prospect appeared somewhat gloomy, and will probably remain so for some years to come. That they were disappointed, is evident from the change which appeared in their calculations. Before they went to Missouri, their language was "we shall winter in Ohio but one winter more;" and when in Missouri, "it will be many years before we come here,[40] for the Lord has a *great work* for us to do in Ohio," and the great work is, to make a thorough alteration of the Bible, and invent new revelations, and these are to be sent to Missouri, in order to be printed. This coming to save the expense of postage, is parallel

---

happiness—purity, holiness, and rest even Zomar—Zion" (Smith, Egyptian MS #1, 23; thanks to Brent Metcalfe for bringing this to my attention).

40. When Smith returned to Ohio in August, his revelations showed less urgency to gather to Zion. The immigration would now proceed in an orderly way under Smith's direct control, and some members would remain behind until commanded otherwise. Frederick Williams was specifically told to keep his property and "retain a strong hold in the land of Kirtland, for the space of five years" (D&C 63:39, 41; 64:21).

with their other calculations. But no matter for that, it will save
them the difficulties and hardships incident to the settling of
a new country; and also the dangers to which they would be
exposed, in case the Indians should commence hostilities upon
the whites; and moreover, they have an easy method to supply
themselves with cash at any time when occasion requires. The
authority of a commandment will easily untie the purse strings
of those whose consciences are under their control; and they
find it much easier, and better suited to their dispositions, to
write commandments, than to gain a livelihood by the sweat
of the brow; and indeed, Smith has commanded himself not to
labor,[41] and by his mandate, has enjoined it upon the church to
support him. The Bishop, when we were in Missouri, intimated
that he and others were too much inclined to indolence.—He
replied, "I am commanded not to labor."

Yours affectionately, Ezra Booth.

LETTER 7.

The following, with but little variation, is the copy of a letter
to the Bishop of the Mormonite church, who, by commandment, has received his station, and now resides in Missouri. His
business is to superintend the secular concerns of the church. He
holds a deed of the lands,[42] and the members receive a writing
from him, signifying, that they are to possess the land as their
own, so long as they are obedient to Smith's commandments.
The Bishop is, in reality, the Vicegerant of Smith, and those in
coalition with him; and holds his office during their will and

41. D&C 24:1–9; 43:13.
42. Cf. D&C 42:30–34; 51:5.

pleasure. I think him to be an honest man as yet, but there is a point beyond which he cannot go, unless he prostrates his honor in the dust, and prostitutes his conscience to the vilest of purposes. He has frequently staggered and been ready to fall.[43] The conference last year, gave him a tremendous shock, from which with difficulty he recovered. The law of the church enjoins, that no debt with the world shall be contracted. But a thousand acres of land in the town of Thompson could be purchased for one half its value, and he was commanded to secure it; and in order to do it, he was under the necessity to contract a debt to the world. He hesitated, but the command was repeated, "you must secure the land." He was one of the number who was ordained to the gift of discerning spirits;[44] and in a commandment, a pattern was given by which the good spirit might be distinguished from the bad, which rendered the gift of supernatural discernment useless: for the division was to be made from external appearances, and not from any thing discovered internally. He saw the impropriety, and it shook his faith. I am suspicious the time is not far distant, when by commandment, this office will be bestowed upon a more trusty and confidential person; perhaps

---

43. On March 10, 1832, the church heard charges against Partridge for having "insulted the Lord's prophet" and having "assumed authority over" Smith (Cannon and Cook, *Far West Record*, 41). According to Booth's letter to Partridge below, the bishop had expressed some doubt as to whether all the revelations had been divinely inspired (pp. 289–90). That same month, God reprimanded Partridge. He "hath sinned, and Satan seeketh to destroy his soul," the revelation scolded (D&C 64:17). A month later, a clarification was made to be sure Partridge knew the "office of bishop" was "not equal" to that of the presidency (D&C 107:59, 65–69; Vogel, *Religious Seekers*, 112–16).

44. See D&C 46:27.

Smith's brother or father, or some one who has been disciplined in the State of New York. Then it will become his business to make over the whole property, by deed of conveyance, to the person appointed by the commandment to supercede him. The Mormonites will tell you, that business of this nature is done by the voice of the church. It is like this: a sovereign issues his decrees, and then says to his subjects, hold up your right hands, in favor of my decrees being carried into effect. Should any refuse, they are sure to be hung for rebellion.

September 20, 1831.

Mr. Partridge:

Sir—From a sense of duty, I take up my pen, to communicate to you the present impressions of my mind, which originated from facts, which occurred during my stay there, and while returning home. I arrived safely at my home, on the 1st instant, after having passed through a variety of scenes, some of which, I design to disclose to you in this letter. You will probably be surprised, when you learn, that I am no longer a member of the Mormonite church.—The circumstances which led to this are numerous, and of such a character, that I should have been compelled to sacrifice every principle of honesty, or cease to support a system, which I conceive to be grossly inconsistent, and in opposition to the best interests of human society. The first thing that materially affected my mind, so as to weaken my confidence, was the falsehood of Joseph's vision. You know perfectly well, that Joseph had, or said he had, a vision, or revelation, in which it was made known to him by the spirit, that Oliver had raised up a large church in Missouri. This was so confidently believed, previous to our leaving Ohio, that while calculating the number of the church, several hundred were added, supposed to be in Missouri. The great church was found to consist of three or four females. The night we took lodgings in the school house, and the morning which succeeded it, presented circumstances which I had not anticipated. When you intimated to Joseph that the land which he and Oliver had selected, was inferior in point of quality to other lands adjoining, had you seen the same spirit manifested in me, which you saw in him [Smith], would you not have concluded me to be under the influence of violent passions, bordering on madness, rather than the meek and gentle spirit which the Gospel inculcates? When you complained that he had abused you, and observed to him, "I wish you not to tell us any more, that you know these by the spirit when you do not; you told us, that Oliver had raised up a large church here, and there is no such thing;" he replied, "I see it, and it will be so." This appeared to me, to be a shift, better suited to an impostor, than a true Prophet of the Lord. And from that time I resolved to weigh well every circumstance; and I can assure you that no one that has a bearing on the subject, escaped my notice. But the spirit considered your insolence to Joseph too intolerable to be passed over unnoticed. Hence the commandment: "If he repent not of his sins, which is unbelief and blindness of heart, let him take heed lest he fall. Behold his mission is given unto him, and it shall not be given again."[45]—You are to be careful, to submit to all the abuse which Joseph sees fit to pour upon you; and to swallow, passively, all the spurious visions, and false prophecies, that he in his clemency thinks proper to bestow upon you, lest you fall from your Bishoprick, never to regain it. These men under whose influence you act, were entire strangers to you until you embraced this new system of faith. Now, permit me to inquire, have you not frequently observed in Joseph, a want of that

---

45. D&C 58:15–16.

sobriety, prudence and stability, which are some of the most prominent traits in the christian character? Have you not often discovered in him, a spirit of lightness and levity, a temper easily irritated, and an habitual proneness to jesting and joking?[46] Have you not often proven to your satisfaction that he says he knows things to be so by the spirit, when they are not so? You most certainly have. Have you not reason to believe, or at least to suspect, that the revelations which come from him, are something short of infallible, and instead of being the production of divine wisdom, emanate from his own weak mind? Some suppose his weakness, nay, his *wickedness*, can form no reasonable objection to his revelations; and "were he to get another man's wife, and seek to kill her husband, it could be no reason why we should not believe revelations through him, for David did the same."[47] So Sidney asserted, and many others concurred with him in sentiment. The commandment we received to purchase, or make a water craft, directed us to proceed down the river in it as far as St. Louis,[48] and from thence, with the exception of Joseph, and his two scribes, we were to proceed on our journey home two by two. The means of conveyance being procured, we embarked for St. Louis, but unpropitious events rolled on, superceded the commandment, frustrated our plans, and we had

---

46. Smith admitted he possessed "a light, and too often, vain mind, exhibiting a foolish and trifling conversation," as expressed in the *Messenger and Advocate*, Dec. 1834, 40. In his official history, he reiterated that when the angel appeared in 1823, he had been seeking forgiveness for his light-mindedness and levity (Vogel, *Documents*, 1:42, 63, 144; *History of the Church*, 1:9–10).

47. Brigham Young said he had concluded before meeting Joseph Smith that "he may get drunk every day of his life, sleep with his neighbor's wife every night, run horses and gamble, I do not care anything about that [because] … the doctrine he has produced will save you and me" (Nov. 9, 1856, in *Journal of Discourses*, 4:78).

48. D&C 60:5.

separated before we had accomplished one half of the voyage. The cause which produced this disastrous result, was a spirit of animosity and discord, which made its appearance on board, the morning after we left Independence. The conduct of some of the Elders became very displeasing to Oliver, who, in the greatness of his power, uttered this malediction: "as the Lord God liveth, if you do not behave better, some accident will befall you." The manner in which this was handed out, evinced it to be the ebullition of a spirit, similar to that which influenced Joseph in the school-house. No accident, however, befel them, until Joseph, in the afternoon of the third day, assumed the direction of affairs on board that canoe, which, with other matters of difference, together with Oliver's curse, increased the irritation of the crew, who, in time of danger, refused to exert their physical powers, in consequence of which, they ran foul of a sawyer [uprooted tree], and were in danger of upsetting. This was sufficient to flutter the timid spirit of the Prophet and his scribe, who had accompanied him on board of that canoe, and like the sea-tossed mariner, when threatened with a watery grave, they unanimously desired to set their feet once more upon something more firm than a liquid surface; therefore, by the persuasion of Joseph, we landed before sunset, intending to pass the night upon the bank of the river. Preparations were made to spend the night as comfortably as existing circumstances would admit, and then an attempt was made, to effect a reconciliation betwixt the contending parties. The business of settlement commenced, which elicited much conversation, and excited considerable feeling on both sides. Oliver's denunciation was brought into view; his conduct and equipage, were compared to "a fop of a sportsman;" he and Joseph were represented, as highly imperious and quite dictatorial; and Joseph and Sidney were reprimanded for their excessive cowardice. Joseph seemed inclined to arm himself, according to his usual custom, in case of opposition, with the judgment of God, for the purpose of pouring them, like a thunder bolt upon the rebellious Elders; but one or two retorted, "none of your threats:" which completely disarmed him, and he reserved his judgment for a more suitable occasion. Finding myself but little interested in the settlement, believing the principles of discord too deeply rooted to be easily eradicated, I laid myself down upon the ground, and in silence contemplated awhile the events of the evening, as they passed before me. These are the men to whom the Lord has intrusted the mysteries, and the keys of his kingdom; whom he has authorized to bind or loose on earth, and their decision shall be ratified in Heaven. These are the men sent forth, to promulgate a new revelation, and to usher in a new dispensation—at whose presence the "Heavens are to shake, the hills tremble, the mountains quake, and the earth open and swallow up their enemies."—These are the leaders of the church, and the only church on earth the Lord beholds with approbation. Surely, I never witnessed so much confusion and discord, among the Elders of any other church; nevertheless they are all doomed to a perpetual curse, except they receive the doctrines and precepts which Mormonism inculcates, and place themselves under the tuition of men, more ignorant and unholy than themselves. In the midst of meditations like these, I sunk into the arms of sleep, but was awakened at a late hour, to witness and consent to a reconciliation between the parties. The next morning, Joseph manifested an aversion to risk his person any more, upon the rough and angry current of the Missouri, and in fact, upon any other river; and he again had recourse to his usual method, of freeing himself from the embarrassments of a former commandment, by obtaining another in opposition to it. A new commandment was issued, in which a great curse was pronounced against the waters; navigating them, was to be attended with extreme danger; and all the saints in general, were prohibited in journeying upon them, to the promised land. From this circumstance, the Missouri river was named the river of Destruction.[49] It was decreed, that we should proceed on our journey by land, and preach by the way as we passed along. Joseph, Sidney, and Oliver, were to press their way forward with all possible speed, and to preach only in Cincinnati; and there they were to lift up their voices, and proclaim against the whole of that wicked city. The method by which Joseph and Co. designed to proceed home, it was discovered, would be very expensive. "The Lord don't care how much *money* it takes to get us home," said Sidney. Not satisfied with the money they received from you, they used their best endeavors to exact money from others, who had but little compared with what they had; telling them in substance, "you can beg your passage on foot, but as we are to travel in the stage, we must have money." You will find, sir, that the expense of these three men, was one hundred dollars more than three of our company expended, while on our journey home; and for the sake of truth and honesty, let these men never again open their mouths, to insult the common sense of mankind, by contending for equality, and the community of goods in society, until there is a thorough alteration in their method of proceeding. It seems, however, they had drained their pockets, when they arrived at Cincinnati, for there they were under the necessity of pawning their trunk, in order to continue their journey home. Here they violated the commandment, by not preaching; and when an inquiry was made respecting the cause of that neglect, at one time they said, they could get no

---

49. D&C 61. The revelation was accompanied by a vision William W. Phelps had of "the destroyer in his most horrible power, rid[ing] upon the face of the waters" (*History of the Church*, 1:203).

house to preach in; at another time they stated, that they could have had the court-house, had they staid a day or two longer, but the Lord made it known to them, that they should go on; and other similar excuses, involving like contradictions. Thus they turn and twist the commandments to suit their whims, and they violate them when they please with perfect impunity. They can at any time obtain a commandment suited to their desires, and as their desires fluctuate and become reversed, they get a new one to supercede the other, and hence the contradictions which abound in this species of revelation. The next day after, we were cast upon the shore, and had commenced our journey by land, myself and three others went on board of a canoe, and recommenced our voyage down the river. From this time a constant gale of prosperity wafted us forward, and not an event transpired, but what tended to our advancement, until we arrived at our much desired homes. At St. Louis, we took passage in a steam-boat, and came to Wellsville; and from thence in the stage home. We travelled about eight hundred miles farther than the three who took their passage in the stage, and arrived at our homes but a few days later.—It is true, we violated the commandment by not preaching by the way, and so did they by not preaching at Cincinnati. But it seems that none of us considered the commandment worthy of much notice.

In this voyage upon the waters, we demonstrated that the great dangers existed only in imagination, and the commandment to be the offspring of a pusillanimous spirit.—The spirit also revealed to Joseph, that "on the steamboats, plots were already laid for our destruction." This too we proved to be false. While descending the Missouri river, Peter [Whitmer Jr.] and Frederick [Williams], two of my company, divulged a secret respecting Oliver, which placed his conduct on a parallel with Ziba's; for which Ziba was deprived of his Elder and

Apostleship:[50] "Let that which was bestowed upon Ziba be taken from him, and let him stand as a member in the church, and let him labor with his own hands with the brethren." And thus by commandment, poor Ziba, one of the twelve Apostles [who helped dedicate the new Zion],[51] is thrust down; while Oliver the scribe, also an Apostle [elder], who had been guilty of similar conduct, is set on high, to prepare work for the press; and no commandment touches him, only to exalt him higher.—These two persons stated, that had they known previous to their journey to Missouri, what they then knew, they never should have accompanied Oliver thither.

Sidney, since his return has written a description of Zion.[52] But it differs essentially from that which you wrote; so much so, that either yours or his must be false. Knowing him to be constitutionally inclined to exaggerate, and suspecting that this habit would be as likely to preponderate, in his written as in his oral communications, you cautioned him against it. "What I write will be written by the most infallible inspiration of the holy spirit," said he with an air of contempt. You must be careful, sir, or it will again sound in your ears, "if he repent not" for giving a false description of the *land of Zion*, [and]

---

50. D&C 58:60.

51. Again, the reference here is to the twelve elders who were meant to represent twelve tribes of Israel in the dedication ceremony, not a quorum of twelve apostles. The organization of the quorum was still four years distant (see Vogel, *Religious Seekers*, 145–46).

52. Rigdon received a commandment to "write a description of the land of Zion ... as it shall be made known by the Spirit unto him" (D&C 58:50). Rigdon did so but was told his first draft was unacceptable (63:55–56). His second draft was approved (Cook, *Revelations*, 99–101; Davidson et al., *Joseph Smith Papers: Histories*, 2:46–49). The compilers of the *History of the Church*, 1:197–98, substituted a description of Zion by W. W. Phelps (Anderson, "New Data," 494–99).

["]let him take heed lest he fall["] from his office [D&C 58]. This, Sidney said, was one reason why you was not permitted to return to the State of Ohio. The want of time and paper warn me to bring this letter to a close. And now permit me to entreat you, to candidly view the whole matter, from the commencement unto the present time. Look at it with your own eyes, and no longer suffer these strangers to blind your eyes, and daub you over with their untempered mortar. Think how often you have been stumbled by these discordant revelations, false visions, and lying prophecies. Put into practice the resolutions you expressed to me the morning after the collision in the school house, that you would go home, and attend to your own business. Transfer the lands you hold in your hands, to the persons whose money paid for it. Place yourself from under the influence of the men who have deceived you; burst asunder the bands of delusion; fly for your life, fly from the habitations haunted by impostors; and having done this, you most surely will be glad and rejoice, and prove to your own satisfaction, as I have done, the falsity of Joseph's prophetic declaration, "if you turn against us you will enjoy no more satisfaction in the world." E. B.

Some things are intimated in the foregoing letter, which more properly belongs to Cowdery's mission to the Indians; and when I come to notice that mission, those things will probably be more fully exhibited.

It is also indirectly stated, that Rigdon has acquired the habit of exaggeration. The truth of this statement, I presume, will be doubted but by few, who have been long acquainted with him. Most of his communications carry the appearance of high and false coloring; and I am persuaded, that truth by this embellishing touch, often degenerates into fiction. I have heard him several different times, give a representation of the interview between himself, and to use his own phraseology, "the far-famed Alexander Campbell." This man's wonted shrewdness and presence of mind forsook him when in the presence of this gigantic Mormonite; so much so, that "he was quite confused and silly." I will give you a specimen of the language, with which Rigdon said he assailed him: "You have lied, Alexander. Alexander you have lied. If you do not receive the Book of Mormon, you will be damned." With such like arguments he brow-beat his antagonist, until he had silenced and set him down, like the pusillanimous cur, at the feet of his chastising master. "You are a liar, you are a child of the Devil, you are an enemy to all righteousness, and the spirit of the Devil is in you," and the like is dealt out profusely against an obstinate opponent, and especially, one whom they are pleased to *nickname apostate*. I regret the necessity I am under of making such statements, and could wish there had been no occasion for them. But truth compels me to it, and the good of society demands it.—Yours, &c.

Ezra Booth.

LETTER 8.

The origin of the aborigines of this country, and the history before the introduction of eastern literature into the western hemisphere, has afforded a subject for much speculation,[53] and deep research among the learned; and has occasioned

---

53. For a survey of pre-1830 ideas about Native Americans, see Vogel, *Indian Origins.*

considerable curiosity, among various classes of people. But the subject still remains an impenetrable obscurity; and will so remain, unless He who has the power to speak, "let there be light" [speaks], and the light shall break forth out of obscurity. But as this is a subject better calculated to gratify the speculative inquirer, than to purify the heart, by rectifying wrong principles in the mind, or to increase that kind of knowledge intimately connected with, and essential to practical improvements either in civil or religious society, we may reasonably doubt, whether the great Jehovah will soon, if ever, condescend to clear away the darkness, by giving a revelation, merely to gratify the desires of persons, who delight to wander in the region of conjecture and speculation. But he has already done it, cries the Mormonite herald. The Book of Mormon, which I hold in my hand, is a divine revelation, and the very thing we need, to burst the cloud and remove the darkness, which has long surrounded the mysterious and degraded aborigines. We now know that the natives who inhabit the forests of America, are a "branch of the House of Israel" [1 Ne. 15:12]; and by means of this blessed book, they are soon, even in this generation, to be restored to the knowledge, and the true worship of the God of Israel.—Among them is to be built, the "glorious city of the New Jerusalem." In the midst of which is to stand, the splendid and magnificent temple, dedicated to the Most High God, and "Oliver being called and commanded of the Lord God, to go forth among the Lamanites, to proclaim glad tidings of great joy unto them, by presenting unto them, the fullness of the gospel of the only begotten son of God," &c.[54] The grand enterprise of introducing

---

54. The quote is from the so-called Missionaries Covenant below ("We,

this new dispensation, or the *fullness of the Gospel,* among the Indian tribes, who have recently received the appellation of La-manites, was committed in charge to Oliver Cowdery, a young man of high fame among the Mormonites. His credentials, and the credentials of the three others associated with him in the mission, will be found in the following revelations, which I transcribe for your perusal, and also for some further remarks, which I design to offer.

A Revelation unto Oliver, Given September, 1830.[55]

Behold, I say unto you Oliver, that it shall be given thee, that thou shalt be heard by the church in all things whatso-ever thou shalt teach them by the comforter, concerning the revelations and commandments which I have given. But, ver-ily, verily, I say unto you, no one shall be appointed to receive commandments and revelations in the church, excepting my servant Joseph, for he receiveth them even as Moses, and thou shalt be obedient unto the things which I shall give unto him, even as Aaron, to declare faithfully the commandments and revelations, with power and authority unto the church. And if thou art led at any time by the comforter to speak or teach, or at all times by the way of commandment unto the church, thou mayst do it; but shall not write by way of commandment but by wisdom: and thou shalt not command him who is at thy head, and at the head of the church; for I have given him the keys of the mysteries of the revelations which are sealed, until I shall appoint unto him another in his stead—and now behold I

the undersigned …"). Booth drew on other doctrinal sources as well: the Book of Mormon (2 Ne. 30; Hel. 15; 3 Ne. 20, 21) and Doctrine and Covenants (3, 42, 45, 57, 58).

55. D&C 28, dictated on about Sept. 26, 1830.

say unto you, that thou shalt go unto the Lamanites and preach my gospel unto them; and thou shalt have revelations, but write them not by way of commandment.—And now I say unto you, that it is not revealed, and no man knoweth where the city shall be built, but it shall be given hereafter. Behold, I say unto you, that it shall be among the Lamanites. Thou shalt not leave this place until after the conference, and my servant Joseph shall be appointed to rule the conference, by the voice of it; and what he saith unto thee that thou shalt tell. And again, thou shalt take thy brother Hiram [Page] between him and thee alone, and tell him that these things which he hath written from that [seer] stone, are not of me, and that Satan hath deceived him, for these things have not been appointed unto him, neither shall any thing be appointed to any in this church, contrary to the church covenant, for all things must be done in order, and by commandment, by the prayer of faith, and thou shalt settle all these things before thou shalt take thy journey among the Lamanites; and it shall be given from time to time, that thou shalt go, until the time that thou shalt return, what thou shalt do; and thou must open thy mouth at all times, declaring my gospel with the sound of rejoicing.—Amen.

Manchester, October 17, 1830.

I, Oliver, being commanded by the Lord God, to go forth unto the Lamanites, to proclaim glad tidings of great joy unto them, by presenting unto them the fullness of the gospel, of the only begotten son of God; and also, to rear up a pillar as a witness where the temple of God shall be built, in the glorious New Jerusalem; and having certain brothers with me, who are called of God to assist me, whose names are Parley, Peter, and Ziba, do therefore most solemnly covenant with God, that I will walk humbly before him, and do this business, and this glorious work according as he shall direct me by the Holy Ghost; ever praying for mine and their prosperity, and deliver[a]nce from bonds, and from imprisonment, and whatsoever may befal us, with all patience and faith.—Amen.

Oliver Cowdery.

We, the undersigned, being called and commanded of the Lord God, to accompany our brother Oliver Cowdery, to go to the Lamanites, and to assist in the above mentioned glorious work and business. We do, therefore, most solemnly covenant before God, that we will assist him faithfully in this thing, by giving heed unto all his words and advice, which is, or shall be given him by the spirit of truth, ever praying with all prayer and supplication, for our and his prosperity, and our deliverance from bonds, and imprisonments, and whatsoever may come upon us, with all patience and faith.—Amen.[56]

Signed in presence of Joseph Smith, Jun., David Whitmer, P. P. Pratt, Ziba Peterson, Peter Whitmer.

In the preceding revelation, the principal thing which claims your attention, is the mission to the Indians; for with that mission many circumstances are connected, which clearly evince, that it originated from human imbecility, and diabolical depravity.—There are also some other things the meaning of which you will not be likely to apprehend, without some

---

56. On October 17, 1830, before leaving on their mission to Ohio and Missouri, the four elders, Oliver Cowdery, Peter Whitmer Jr., Parley P. Pratt, and Ziba Peterson, signed this covenant vowing to visit the Indians and locate the New Jerusalem site. Booth's transcript was published in the *Ohio Star*, Dec. 8, 1831. It is assumed to be accurate since his related copy of LDS D&C 28 is so precise (Anderson, "Impact of the First Preaching in Ohio," 476–77).

explanation. In this, as well as several of the commandments, it is clearly and explicitly stated, that the right of delivering written commandments, and revelations, belong exclusively to Smith, and no other person can interfere, without being guilty of sacrilege. In this office he is to stand, until another is appointed in his place, and no other person can be appointed in his stead, unless he falls through transgression; and in such a case, he himself is authorized to appoint his successor.[57] But how is he to be detected, should he become guilty of transgression. The commandment makes provision for this. His guilt will become manifest by his inability to utter any more revelations, and should he presume "to get another man's wife," and commit adultery; and "by the shedding of blood, seek to kill her husband,"[58] if he retain the use of his tongue, so as to be able to utter his jargon, he can continue as long as he pleases in the bed of adultery, and wrap himself with garments stained with blood, shed by his own hands, and still retain the spotless innocence of the holiest among mortals; and must be continued in the office of revelator, and head of the church. Some others, and especially Cowdery, have earnestly desired to relieve Smith of some part of his burden. Cowdery's desires for this work were so keen and excessive, as, to use his own language, "it was unto me a burning fire shut up in my bones, and I was weary with forbearing, and I could forbear no longer;"[59] and he did

---

57. Booth refers again to D&C 28:7 and seemingly alludes to 43:4.

58. The scenario is that of David sending Bathsheba's husband, Uriah, into battle, hoping never to see him again (2 Sam. 11). The quote marks were meant to indicate a hypothetical situation, not a real statement.

59. Booth quotes the closing line of a revelation given to Cowdery in

in fact, issue some productions, which he said bore the divine impress; but Smith fixed upon them the stamp of devilish. But it seems, in order to compromise the matter, that Cowdery was permitted to "speak or to teach, at all times, by way of commandment unto the church; but not to write them by way of commandment:"[60] thus Cowdery is authorized to give verbal commandments to the church, by the inspiration of the spirit, which, if he afterwards writes, ceases to be inspiration; therefore, a commandment delivered orally, may be divinely inspired; but the same communicated [on paper], written verbatim, so far loses its former character, that it degenerates into a production of an infernal stamp. Here is a mystery, for aught I know, peculiar to Mormonism; and none but Mormonites, I presume, will attempt to unravel it. But it finds its parallel in the following: Smith asures his followers, that what he speaks by the spirit, and is written, is infallible in operation, but if it is not written, he may sometimes be mistaken.—He tells them that the right to deliver written revelations, belongs exclusively to himself, and no other person shall interfere in the business; and if he transgresses he will graciously condescend to appoint another in his stead, and the only proof produced for the support of such assertions, is barely his word, upon which

---

about June 1829, which itself borrows from Jer. 20:9. A copy of the revelation was presented to the LDS Church by descendants of Simonds Ryder in 1960. It is a three-page document in Cowdery's handwriting, self-described as "a commandment from God," and outlines the "articles of the Church of Christ" in a prototype for the Articles and Covenants of the Church that became D&C 20. The revelation draws heavily on 3 Nephi and D&C 18. See Vogel, *Documents*, 2:409–12.

60. D&C 28:4–5.

they implicitly rely, and become entirely resigned to place their person and property under his control, and even risk the salvation of their souls upon his say-so. Such glaring duplicity on the one hand, and unaccountable credulity on the other, seldom have a parallel in the annals of man.

Never was there a despot more jealous of his prerogative than Smith; and never was a fortress guarded with more vigilance and ardor against every invading foe, than he guards these. Smith apprehended a rival in the department of written inspiration, from another quarter, and hence Cowdery was commissioned to commence an attack and suppress the enemy, before he had acquired sufficient stability and strength so as to become formidable. "Thou shalt take thy brother Hiram, between him and thee alone, and tell him that the things he hath written from that stone, &c." Hiram Page, one of the eight witnesses, and also one of the "money diggers,"[61] found a smooth stone, upon which there appeared to be a writing, which when transcribed upon paper, disappeared from the stone, and another impression appeared in its place. This when copied, vanished as the former had done, and so it continued, alternately appearing and disappearing; in the meanwhile, he continued to write, until he had written over considerable paper. It bore striking marks of a Mormonite revelation, and was received as an authentic document by most of the Mormonites, till Smith, by his superior sagacity, discovered it to be a Satanic fraud.

---

61. There is presently no other evidence of Page's involvement in treasure seeking, although one could conclude from his expertise with a seer stone that he had interests in that direction.

A female professing to be a prophetess, made her appearance in Kirtland, and so ingratiated herself into the esteem and favor of some of the Elders, that they received her, as a person commissioned to act a conspicuous part in Mormonizing the world.[62] Rigdon, and some others, gave her the right hand of fellowship, and literally saluted her with what they called the *kiss* of charity. But Smith, viewing her as an encroachment upon his sacred premises, declared her an impostor [D&C 43], and she returned to the place from whence she came. Her visit, however, made a deep impression on the minds of many, and the barbed arrow which she left in the hearts of some, is not yet eradicated.

Yours affectionately, Ezra Booth.

LETTER 9.

In this letter the mission to the Indians will be brought into view, and with it are connected circumstances and facts, sufficient, one would suppose, to convince every honest and unprejudiced Mormonite, of the fallacy and deception of Mormonism. But a Mormonite of the highest grade is invulnerable by facts the most notorious, and evidence as glaring as the noon-day sun; for they affirm, they know by the spirit that Mormonism is what it pretends to be, and should Smith acknowledge it to be a fabrication, they would not believe him. This forms the highest climax in Mormonism, and but few have attained to it. After Cowdery, and his three associates

---

62. The woman known as Mrs. Louisa Hubble appeared in Kirtland in February 1831 (Davidson et al., *Joseph Smith Papers: Histories*, 2:29; MacKay et al., *Joseph Smith Papers: Documents*, 1:257n95; Westergren, *From Historian to Dissident*, 37–38; LDS D&C 43).

had left the State of New York, while bending their course
to the west, he was directed by the spirit to Kirtland, for the
special purpose of enlisting Rigdon in the Mormonite cause.
I have since learned that the spirit which directed in this enterprise, was no other than Pratt, who had previously become
acquainted with Rigdon and had been proselyted by him into
what is called the Campbellite faith. This new system appears
to have been particularly suited to Rigdon's taste, and calculated to make an impression on his mind. But before he could
fully embrace it, he must "receive a testimony from God." In
order to [do] this he labored as he was directed by his Precep-
tor, almost incessantly and earnestly in praying, till at length
his mind was wrapped up in a vision;[63] and to use his own
language, "to my astonishment I saw the different orders of
professing Christians passing before my eyes, with their hearts,
exposed to view, and they were as corrupt as corruption itself.
That society to which I belonged also passed before my eyes,
and to my astonishment it was as corrupt as the others. Last of
all *that little man*[64] who bro't me the Book of Mormon, passed
before my eyes with his heart open, and it was as pure as an
angel; and this was a testimony from God; that the Book of
Mormon, was a Divine Revelation." Rigdon is one who has
ascended to the summit of Mormonism; and this vision stands

---

63. Concerning his conversion experience, Rigdon said in 1843 that he
was "fully convinced of the truth of the work, by revelation from Jesus Christ,
which was made known to him in a remarkable manner, so that he could ex-
claim 'flesh and blood hath not revealed it unto me, but my father which is in
heaven'" (*Times and Seasons*, Aug. 15, 1843, 290).

64. One early source described Cowdery as "a small, quiet and retiring
man" (*Deseret Evening News,* Mar. 10, 1896, quoting the *Cleveland Plain Dealer*).

as the foundation of his knowledge. He frequently affirms, that these things are not a matter of faith with him, but of absolute knowledge. He has been favored with many remarkable and extraordinary visions, in some of which he saw Kirtland with the surrounding country, consecrated as the promised land, and the churches in the State of New York expected to receive their everlasting inheritance in the State of Ohio, and this expectation was grounded on Rigdon's vision while in the State of New York. These visions are considered by the church as entitled to no credit, and laid aside as mere rubbish.

As it relates to the purity of the heart of "that little man," if a pure and pleasant fountain can send forth corrupt and bitter streams, then may the heart of that man be pure, who enters into a matrimonial contract with a young lady, and obtains the consent of her parents; but as soon as his back is turned upon her, he violates his engagements, and prostitutes his honor by becoming the gallant of another, and resolved in his *heart*, and expresses resolutions to marry her.[65] But as the practice of a man will ever stand as a general criterion by which the principles of the heart are to be tested, we say that the heart of such a man is the reverse of purity.

From Kirtland, Cowdery & Co. were directed by the spirit

---

65. Booth doesn't mean this hypothetically. It is an oblique reference to Cowdery's fraternization with a woman in Ohio at a time Cowdery was still engaged to Elizabeth Ann Whitmer in New York. On May 26, 1832, he was censured by church leaders for "transgression … in the fall of 1830 in the Township of Mayfield Cuyahoga County State of Ohio" (Cannon and Cook, *Far West Record*, 49). There is no other documentation for this, however. He married Elizabeth Ann in December.

to Sandusky,[66] where they contemplated opening their mission,
and proselyting the Indians residing at that place. But neither
Cowdery, nor the spirit which directed him, was able to open
the way to, or make any impression upon their minds. Being
frustrated in this, his first attempt to convert the natives, he
turned his attention and course to the Missouri, and when near
the eastern line of that state, he halted for several days, for the
purpose of obtaining, by inquiry, information respecting the Indians still further west. It appears that he was fearful that his
infallible guide, (the spirit,) was incapable to direct him, while
proceeding further to the west; consequently, he applied to men
more capable of giving instruction than the spirit, by which he
was influenced. When he arrived at the western line of Missouri, he passed into the Indian territory, where he remained
but a short time, before he was notified by the U. S. Agent, that
he must either re-cross the line, or be compelled to take up his
residence in the garrison, forty miles up the Arkansas river. As
there was no other alternative, the former seemed to him the
most expedient; and he never possessed courage sufficient to
pass the line, or visit the residence of the Indians since. Thus
you behold a man, "called and commanded of the Lord God, to
go forth unto the Lamanites," and establish his church among
them; but no sooner is he set down in the field of his mission,

---

66. The missionaries stopped for a few days in Sandusky on the shore
of Lake Erie, west of Cleveland, and were "well received" by the Indians, they
said, whom they presented with "the record of their forefathers." The Indians
"rejoiced" and bid the missionaries Godspeed. They only asked to be updated
on "our success among the tribes further west, who had already removed to the
Indian territory" (Pratt, *Autobiography*, 51).

and surrounded by his anticipated converts, than he is driven by a *comparative nothing*, from the fields, and obliged to relinquish his contemplated harvest.—This is the person commissioned by the Lord to proceed to the western wilds, and as he himself stated, "to the place where the foot of a white man never trod," to rear up a pillar for a witness, where the temple of God shall be built, in the glorious New Jerusalem. But alas! he was arrested by man in his course, and by the breath of man the mighty undertaking was blown into the air, and Cowdery was thrown back among the Gentiles, to wait for the spirit to devise some new plans in the place of those which had been frustrated. But as the city and temple must be built, as every avenue leading to the Indians was closed against the Mormonites, it was thought that they should be built among the Gentiles, which is in direct opposition to the original plan[67]—as foreign from the design of the spirit, expressed in several commandments, as it would have been had the Directors, who were appointed to build the court-house in Ravenna, [Portage County, Ohio,] built it in Trumbull county, foreign from the design of those who intrusted them with the business.

Though their plans had hitherto failed, they were unwilling to abandon the Indian enterprise; and in a commandment it was stated, that Cowdery and others should receive a written recommendation, signed by the Elders, for the purpose of presenting it to the Indian agent, in order to obtain permission to

---

67. The revelations didn't specifically mention a millennial city in Indian Territory, but the Book of Mormon's prediction that Europeans would "assist" Lamanites in building the city seemed to imply as much (3 Ne. 21:23–25; cf. D&C 28:9).

visit the Indians in their settlements.—The recommendation was written according to the commandment, and frequent opportunities occurred in which it might have been presented to the agent, but it never was presented, and of course was useless; he [Cowdery] was censured by some for not presenting it, but I suppose the spirit directed him not to do it.

Another method has been invented, in order to remove obstacles which hitherto had proved insurmountable. "The Lord's store-house," is to be furnished with goods suited to the Indian trade, and persons are to obtain license from the government to dispose of them to the Indians in their own territory; at the same time they are to disseminate the principles of Mormonism among them. From this smuggling method of preaching to the Indians, they anticipate a favorable result. In addition to this, and to co-operate with it, it has been made known by revelation, that it will be pleasing to the Lord, should they form a matrimonial alliance with the natives;[68] and by this means the Elders, who comply with the thing so pleasing to the Lord, and for which the Lord has promised to bless those who do it abundantly, [may] gain a residence in the Indian territory, independent of the agent. It has been made known to one [Martin Harris], who has left his wife in the State of New York, that he is entirely free from his wife, and he is at

---

68. Phelps included a copy of the revelation in an Aug. 12, 1861, letter to Brigham Young (LDS Church History Library; Collier, *Unpublished Revelations*, 57–58) and explained that it was dictated on a Sunday morning on July 17, 1831, near Missouri's western border. The revelation directed the men to "take unto you wives of the Lamanites and Nephites, that their posterity may become white, delightsome and just."

pleasure to take him a wife from among the Lamanites.[69] It was easily perceived that this permission was perfectly suited to his desires. I have frequently heard him state that the Lord had made it known to him, that he is as free from his wife as from any other woman; and the only crime I have ever heard alleged against her is, she is violently opposed to Mormonism. But before this contemplated marriage [with a Lamanite] can be carried into effect, he must return to the State of New York and settle his business, for fear, should he return after that [marriage] affair had taken place, the civil authority would apprehend him as a criminal.

It is with pleasure I close this exposition, having in part accomplished, what I intended when I commenced it. The employment has been an unpleasant one to me, and from the first, I should gladly have avoided it, could I have done it, and maintained a conscience void of offence, towards God and man.—But should an individual by this exposition, be extricated or prevented from falling into the delusion, which has been the subject of consideration, I shall be amply compensated, for the painful task which I have performed.

Yours affectionately, Ezra Booth.

---

69. According to Phelps, Harris was present when the revelation was dictated. "When he first came to Kirtland," remembered S. F. Whitney, Harris was talking about going "to Missouri, and obtain[ing] a Lamanite Indian squaw for a wife to aid … in propagating Mormonism" (qtd. in *Naked Truths about Mormonism*, Jan. 1888, 3).

CHAPTER 16.

We have already given the reader a pretty fair view of this artful imposition, which may be considered all that is requisite to stamp it with infamy, in the estimation of rational minds. The preceding letters alone are amply sufficient to scatter the whole system of deception to the four winds; but we have yet many curious and rare documents in store. A few revelations will be here inserted, as a specimen of the manner in which the Prophet governs and rebukes his dupes. The first will show the means he employed to get over and obviate the contentions among them, on their first visit to Missouri, briefly alluded to by Mr. Booth. In this the cloven foot is very prominent.

Zion, August 3d, 1831.[1]

Hearken, O ye Elders of my Church, and give ear to my word, and learn of me what I will concerning you; for verily I say unto you, blessed is he that keepeth my commandments, whether in life or in death; and he that is faithful in tribulation,

---

1. According to the earliest extant manuscript of the revelation (now D&C 58), Howe's date was off by two days. The manuscript had a header written above the first line that, among other things, identified Independence as Zion: "61 Commandment August 1st 1831[.] A Revelation given to the Elders who were assembeled in on the land of Zion[.] Directions what to do &c &c &c." (Godfrey et al., *Joseph Smith Papers: Documents*, 2:14; neither the 1833 Book of Commandments nor the 1835 D&C had a dateline or header). Differences in wording suggest that Howe copied from an earlier text.

the reward of the same is greater in the Kingdom. Ye cannot behold with your natural eyes, for the present time, the design of your God concerning those things which shall follow after much tribulation, for after much tribulation cometh the blessing. Wherefore, the day cometh that ye shall be rewarded with much glory—the hour is not yet, but is nigh at hand; remember this, which I told you before, that you may lay it to heart, and receive that which shall follow.

Behold, verily I say unto you, for this cause have I sent you—that ye might be obedient, and that your hearts might be prepared to bear testimony of the things which are to come, and also that you might be favored of laying the foundation, and bearing record of the land upon which the Zion of God shall stand, and also that a feast of fat things might be prepared for the poor, yea, a feast of fat things, of wine on the lees well refined, that the earth may know that the mouths of the prophets shall not fail; yea, a supper of the house of the Lord, well prepared; unto which all nations shall be invited: firstly, the rich, and the learned, the wise and the noble; and after that cometh the day of my power—then shall the poor, the lame, and the blind, and the deaf, come in unto the marriage of the lamb, prepared for the great day to come; behold, I the Lord hath spoken it, and that the testimony might go forth from Zion, yea, from the mouth of the city of the heritage of God; yea, for this cause I have sent you hither, and I have selected and chosen my servant [Bishop] Edward [Partridge], and appointed unto him his mission in this land; but if he repent not of his sins, which is unbelief and blindness of heart, let him take heed lest he fall. Behold, his mission is given unto him, and it shall not be given again; and whosoever standeth in that mission is appointed to be a judge in Israel, like as it was in ancient days, to divide the lands of the heritage of God unto his children, and to judge his people by the testimony of the just by the assistance of his counsellors, according to the laws of the kingdom, which were given by the prophets of God; for, verily I say unto you, my laws shall be kept in the land; let no man think that he is ruler, but let God rule, that judgeth according to the council of his own will, or in other words, him that sitteth upon the judgement seat. Let no man break the laws of the land, wherefore, be subject to the powers that be, until he reigns whose right it is to reign and subdue all his enemies under his feet. Behold the laws which ye have recorded from my hand, are the laws of the church—in this light shall ye hold them forth. Behold, here is wisdom, and as I speak concerning my servant Edward, this land is the land of his residence, and those whom he hath appointed for his counsellors, and all the land of the residence of him whom I have appointed to keep my store-house. Wherefore, let them bring their families to this land, as they shall counsel between themselves and me; for, behold it is not meet that I should command in all things, for he that is compelled in all things, is a slothful and not a wise servant; wherefore, he receiveth no reward. Verily I say, men should be anxiously engaged in a good cause, and do many things of their own free will and bring to pass much righteousness, for the power is in them, wherein they are agents unto themselves; and inasmuch as men do good they shall in no wise loose their reward; but he that doeth not any thing until he is commanded, and receiveth a commandment with a doubtful heart, and keepeth it with slothfulness, the same is damned. Who am I that made man, saith the Lord, that will hold him guiltless that obey not my commandments. Who am I, saith the Lord, that have ordained and have not fulfilled. I command, and a man obey[s] not; I revoke, and they receive not the blessing—then they say in their hearts this is not the

work of the Lord, for his promises are not fulfilled; but woe
unto such, for their reward lurketh beneath and not from
above. And now I give unto you further directions concerning
this land; it is wisdom in me that my servant Martin [Harris],
should be an example unto the church, in laying his money
before the bishop of the church; and also, this is the law unto
every man that cometh into this land to receive an inheritance,
and he shall do with his money according as the law directs;
and it is wisdom, also, that there should be lands purchased in
Independence for the place of the store-house, and also for the
house of the printing, and other directions concerning my servant Martin, of the spirit that he may receive his inheritance as
seemeth him good—and let him repent of his sins, for he
seeketh praise of the world; and also let my servant William
[Phelps][2] stand in the office which I have appointed him, and
receive his inheritance in the land; and also he hath need to
repent, for I the Lord am not pleased with him, for he seeketh
to exult, and he is not sufficiently meek. Behold, he that hath
repented of his sins, the same is forgiven, and I the Lord re-
membereth them no more—by this may ye know if a man
repenteth of his sins, behold he will confess them and forsake
them; and now, verily I say concerning the residue of the Elders
of my church, the time has not yet come for many years, for
them to receive their inheritance in this land, except they desire
it through prayer only, as it shall be appointed unto them, for
behold they shall push the people together from the ends of
the earth, wherefore, assemble yourselves together, and he that
is not appointed to stay in the land, let them preach the gospel
in the regions round about; and after that let them return to

2. The current D&C gives the full name of each individual. Originally
they were identified only by first name or by a coded reference.

their homes. Let them preach by the way, and bear testimony of the truth in all places, and call upon the rich, the high, and the low, and the poor, to repent; and let them build up churches, inasmuch as the inhabitants of the earth will repent; and let there be an agent appointed, by the voice of the church. And I give unto my servant Sidney [Rigdon], a commandment, that he shall write a description of Zion, and a statement of the will of God, as it shall be made known by the spirit unto him; and an epistle and a subscription unto all the churches, to obtain moneys to be put into the hands of the Bishop, to purchase lands for an inheritance for the children of God, of himself or of the agent as seemeth him good, or as he shall direct, for behold the Lord willeth that the disciples and the children of men should open their hearts, even to purchase this whole region of country, as soon as time will permit; behold here is wisdom, lest they receive none inheritance, save by the shedding of blood; and again, inasmuch as there is lands obtained, let there be workmen sent forth, of all kinds, unto this land, to labor for the saints of God: let all these things be done in order, and let the privilege of the land be made known from time to time by the Bishop or the agent of the church; and let the work of the gathering be not by haste nor by flight, but let it be done as it shall be counselled by the Elders of the church at the conference—according to the knowledge which they shall receive from time to time; and let my servant Sidney consecrate and dedicate this land, and the spot of the temple, unto the Lord; and let a conference meeting be called. And after that, let my servant Sidney and Joseph return, and also my servant Oliver with them, to accomplish the residue of the work which I have appointed unto them in their own land; and the residue as shall be ruled by the conference. And let no man return from this land, except he bear record by the way of that which he knows and most assuredly believes; let that which has been given to Ziba [Peterson] be taken from him, and let him stand as a member in the church, and labor with his hands with the brethren, until he is sufficiently chastened for all his sins, for he confesseth them not; and he thinketh to hide them. Let the residue of the Elders of this church who are coming to this land, some of whom are exceedingly blessed, also hold a conference upon this land, and let my servant Edward direct the conference which shall be held by them; and let them also return, preaching the Gospel by the way, bearing record of the things which are revealed unto them, for the sound must go forth from this place into all the world, and unto the uttermost ends of the earth, the gospel must be preached unto every creature, with signs following them that believe, and behold the son of man cometh.—Amen.

In many of the special revelations, Martin Harris' money has been the ostensible object with the prophet; he being a willing dupe and an excellent *stool-pigeon,* by which the fiscal department and designs could be accomplished.

The *spiritual eye* of the prophet ever kept in view the finances of his devoted followers, and to filch from their pockets he had only to issue a revelation. In the foregoing manifesto, Martin is called upon, in *propria persona,*[3] to lay his money before the Bishop, merely as an example to all others. In this, the prophet judged correctly; he well knew the manner in which Martin was associated with him, and the case with which, through his agency, others could be deceived.

A small volume of these revelations has been published,

---

3. Meaning by oneself, without legal representation.

but has been carefully and studiously kept from the "aliens from the house of Israel," and only used by the "*strong in faith*;" even those of the dupes who dared to think for themselves, have been denied a copy.[4]

A great variety of commandments are delivered orally, on special occasions. And such is the infatuation of the followers of Smith, that [for] every little domestic transaction which he wishes to control, nothing is necessary but a commandment, and the mandate is obeyed. The control of Smith over his simple devotees, is well exhibited in a revelation which secured to his heirs and assigns, the fee simple of *one hundred and forty-two acres of valuable land,* adjoining their stone temple, in Kirtland; for which the grantor acknowledges the receipt of *two thousand two hundred dollars.* Two other small lots are also deeded to Smith, as president, and his successor in office. (*Query*—will he ever appoint a successor?) Sidney Rigdon also has a deed of two small lots[5] of land, for which $550 purports to be the consideration money. Oliver Cowdery being the next important personage, has a deed of but one small lot.[6]—These lands were no doubt *honestly* acquired, in *their* way of doing business; but we very much doubt whether these large sums of

---

4. Howe misinterpreted what happened in the wake of the July 1833 destruction of the Mormon press in Missouri. The vigilantes threw uncut sheets for the Book of Commandments into the street where Mormons salvaged a handful of the small signatures and privately bound them. Howe was evidently unaware of how scarce copies of the Book of Commandments were even in his day.

5. On April 3, 1834, Rigdon purchased one acre for $100 and another acre for $450 on May 3rd (Backman, *Profile of Latter-day Saints*, 157).

6. Cowdery bought a little less than half an acre for $110 on May 5, 1834 (ibid., 140).

money were obtained in the ordinary way. Thus it is that these self-made prophets and high priests are acquiring possession of real estate in a rich and flourishing country, while their dupes are packed off to the wilds of Missouri, and compelled to "lay their moneys before the bishop," and receive an *"inheritance"* of about 40 acres of land, if they are so fortunate as to have enough to buy it.

Another Revelation.[7]

A word of wisdom for the benefit of the council of high priests assembled in Kirtland, and church; and, also, the saints in Zion: to be sent greeting: not by commandment, or constraint: but by revelation and the word of wisdom: showing forth the order and will of God in the temporal salvation of all saints in the last days. Given for a principle with promise, adapted to the capacity of the weak, and the weakest of all saints, who are or can be called saints.

Behold, verily thus saith the Lord unto you, in consequence of evils and designs which do, and will exist in the hearts of conspiring men in the last days, I have warned you and forewarn you, by giving unto you this word of wisdom by revelation, that inasmuch as any man drinketh wine or strong drink among you, behold it is not good, neither meet in the sight of your Father, only in assembling yourselves together, to offer up your sacraments before him.—And behold, this should be wine, yea, pure wine of the grape of the vine of your own make.

And, again, strong drinks are not for the belly, but for the washing of your bodies.

---

7. This is now LDS D&C 89, known as the Word of Wisdom, received February 27, 1833. For historical context, see Bush, "Word of Wisdom."

And again, tobacco is not for the body, neither for the belly; and is not good for man; but is an herb for bruises, and all sick cattle, to be used with judgment and skill.

And again, hot drinks are not for the body, or belly.

And again, verily I say unto you, all wholesome herbs God hath ordained for the constitution, nature, and use of man. Every herb in the season thereof, and every fruit in the season thereof. All these to be used with prudence and thanksgiving. Yea, flesh also of beasts and of the fowls of the air, I the Lord hath ordained for the use of man, with thanksgiving. Nevertheless, they are to be used sparingly; and it is pleasing unto me, that they should not be used only in time of winter or of cold, or famine. All grain is ordained for the use of man and beasts, to be the staff of life, not only for man, but for the beasts of the field, and the fowls of heaven, and all wild animals that run or creep on the earth: and these hath God made for the use of man only in time of famine, and excess of hunger.

All grain is good for the food of man, as also the fruit of the vine, that which yieldeth fruit, whether in the ground or above the ground. Nevertheless, wheat for man, and corn for the ox, and oats for the horse, and rye for the fowls, and for swine, and for all beasts of the field, and barley for all useful animals, and for mild drinks; as also other grain.

And all saints who remember to keep and do these sayings, walking in obedience to the commandments, shall receive health in their navel and marrow in their bones; and shall find wisdom and great treasures of knowledge, even hidden treasures; and shall run and not be weary, and shall walk and not faint; and I the Lord give unto them a promise, that the destroying angel shall pass by them, as the children of Israel, and not slay them:—Amen.

In the above revelation, we are presented with the will of heaven, not by way of commandment, but by the word of wisdom adapted to the *weakest of all saints.*

If such commands originate in the wisdom of God, let us examine them. The first is, that strong drink is forbid, except as an external application—in this we are inclined measurably to agree with the mandate; but believe there might be reasonable arguments urged in favor of its internal use, under particular circumstances; besides the inspiration of olden time restrained the excessive use and abuse of wine and strong drink, and not its entire abandonment. But like all other modern Mormon inspirations, a little improvement is made to God's former will, as he made it known through his apostles and prophets.

The next command forbids the use of tobacco, but is recommended for all sick cattle as an excellent remedy.—For the first time we are presented with a remedy direct from heaven, but requires human skill to apply it. To this mode of revealing we object, for this reason, that it requires less research to find remedies, than to apply them; therefore, to say that tobacco is a good remedy for sick cattle, and not defining the quantity nor the quality, nor in what sickness, is the summit of folly and ignorance, and none but a religious maniac would give credence to such pretensions.[8]

We are next told that every wholesome herb, God ordained for the use of man!! and we should infer that the writer or

---

8. The most common medicinal application of tobacco for cattle was apparently a tobacco-smoke enema applied with a bellows, which is nicely summarized at "Tobacco Smoke Enema," *Wikipedia: The Free Encyclopedia*, wikipedia.org.

the recording angel had been inducted into the modern use of herbs, by the celebrated Doct. F. G. Williams,[9] who is associated with the prophet and the nominal proprietor of a monthly paper, which is issued from the Mormon kennel, in Kirtland. F. G. Williams is a revised quack, well known in this vicinity, by his herbarium on either side of his horse; but whether he claims protection by right of letters patent from the General Government or by communion with spirits from other worlds, we are not authorized to determine, but should conclude he would be adequate to dictate the above mockery at revelation and rigmarole, in relation to food for cattle, &c.

In conclusion, it is revealed to the "weak saints," that if they live without ardent spirits and tobacco, and use all the herbs which are wholesome, (which they are left to guess at,) and feed each kind of domestic animal their appropriate grain, and not feed corn to horses, they shall have health in their navel and marrow in their bones.—Humph. It is likewise promised them that they shall improve in wisdom, and that their muscular powers shall be strengthened—no little consideration for a weak saint.

---

9. Frederick Granger Williams (1787–1842), originally of Connecticut, practiced medicine in Kirtland during the time of his conversion to Mormonism in November 1830. When *The Evening and the Morning Star* was moved to Kirtland in December 1833, "Williams & Co." was identified as the printer, as it was for the paper's successor, the *Messenger and Advocate*. Williams was a Thomsonian, or "botanic," doctor who advertised "Dr. Samuel Thomson's Vegetable Medicine." For context, see Haller, *People's Doctors*.

CHAPTER 17.

We next present to the reader a few, among the many depositions which have been obtained from the neighborhood of the
Smith family, and the scene where the far famed Gold Bible
had its pretended origin.[1]

The divine authenticity of the Gold Bible or the Book of
Mormon, is established by three special and eight collateral
witnesses, making in the whole eleven, without whom there is
no pretention to testimony; and if their testimony is probable
and consistent with truth, and unimpeached, according to the
common rules of jurisprudence, we are bound to believe them.

Upon the principles of common law, we are prepared to
meet them; and they are offered to us in no other light.—
Under all circumstances, in civil and ecclesiastical tribunals,
witnesses may be impeached, and after a fair hearing, on both
sides, the veracity and credibility may be adjudged.

If the eleven witnesses are considered, from what has already been said, unimpeached, we will offer the depositions
of some of the most respectable citizens of our country, who
solemnly declare upon their oaths that no credit can be given

---

1. This chapter contains twenty-two statements, fifteen from residents
of the Palmyra/Manchester area, collected by Philastus Hurlbut in Nov.–Dec.
1833, and the remainder from residents of Harmony, Pennsylvania, all published in the *Susquehanna Register and Northern Pennsylvanian* in May 1834 at
Howe's instigation.

to any one member of the Smith family. Many witnesses declare that they are in the possession of the means of knowing the Smiths for truth and veracity, and that they are not upon a par with mankind in general.—Then, according to the common rules of weighing testimony, the eleven witnesses stand impeached before the public; and until rebutting testimony can be produced which shall go to invalidate the respectable host which are here offered, we claim that no credit can or ought to be given to the witnesses to the Book of Mormon.

We have not only testimony impeaching the moral characters of the Smith family, but we show by the witnesses, that they told contradictory stories, from time to time, in relation to their finding the plates, and other circumstances attending it, which go clearly to show that none of them had the fear of God before their eyes, but were moved and instigated by the devil.

[TESTIMONY OF PETER INGERSOLL]

Palmyra, Wayne Co. N.Y. Dec. 2d, 1833.

I, Peter Ingersoll,[2] first became acquainted with the family of Joseph Smith, Sen. in the year of our Lord, 1822.—I lived in the neighborhood of said family, until about 1830; during which time the following facts came under my observation.

The general employment of the family, was digging for

---

2. Peter Ingersoll (ca. 1789–1867) was born in the Schenectady area. In the 1830 census for Palmyra, he is listed as Peter Ingerson, along with his wife, Catherine Todd, and nine children. His land bordered that of the Smiths to the north (Lorenzo Saunders interview with E. L. Kelley, Nov. 12, 1884, 6; Vogel, *Documents*, 2.151). Martin Harris remembered that Smith worked for Ingersoll for a time (Harris interview with Joel Tiffany, 168–69; Vogel, *Documents*, 2:309).

money. I had frequent invitations to join the company, but always declined being one of their number. They used various arguments to induce me to accept of their invitations. I was once ploughing near the house of Joseph Smith, Sen. about noon, he requested me to walk with him a short distance from his house, for the purpose of seeing whether a mineral rod[3] would work in my hand, saying at the same time he was confident it would. As my oxen were eating, and being myself at leisure, I accepted the invitation.—When we arrived near the place at which he thought there was money, he cut a small witch hazle bush and gave me direction how to hold it. He then went off some rods, and told me to say to the rod, "work to the money," which I did, in an audible voice. He rebuked me severely for speaking it loud, and said it must be spoken in a whisper. This was rare sport for me. While the old man was standing off some rods, throwing himself into various shapes, I told him the rod did not work. He seemed much surprised at this, and said he thought he saw it move in my hand. It was now time for me to return to my labor. On my return, I picked up a small stone and was carelessly tossing it from one hand to the other. Said he, (looking very earnestly) what are you going to do with that stone? Throw it at the birds, I replied. No, said the old man, it is of great worth; and upon this I gave it to him. Now, says he, if you only knew the value there is back of my

---

3. Joseph Sr.'s brother Jesse wrote to Hyrum Smith on June 17, 1829, that someone in Palmyra had reported about Joseph Sr. that he "has a wand or rod like Jannes & Jambres who withstood Moses in Egypt—that he can tell the distance from India to Ethiopia &c another fool story" (Smith to Smith, June 17, 1829, Letterbook, 2:60; Vogel, *Documents*, 1:553; see Ex. 7:10–12; 2 Tim. 3:8).

house, (and pointing to a place near)—*there,* exclaimed he, is
one chest of gold and another of silver. He then put the stone
which I had given him, into his hat, and stooping forward, he
bowed and made sundry maneuvers, quite similar to those of
a stool pigeon. At length he took down his hat, and being very
much exhausted, said, in a faint voice, "if you knew what I had
seen, you would believe." To see the old man thus try to impose
upon me, I confess, rather had a tendency to excite contempt
than pity. Yet I thought it best to conceal my feelings, prefer-
ring to appear the dupe of my credulity, than to expose myself
to his resentment. His son Alvin then went through with the
same performance, which was equally disgusting.

Another time, the said Joseph, Sen. told me that the best
time for digging money, was, in the heat of summer, when the
heat of the sun caused the chests of money to rise near the top
of the ground. You notice, said he, the large stones on the top
of the ground—we call them rocks, and they truly appear so,
but they are, in fact, most of them chests of money raised by
the heat of the sun.

At another time, he told me that the ancient inhabitants
of this country used camels instead of horses. For proof of this
fact, he stated that in a certain hill on the farm of Mr. Cuyler,
there was a cave containing an immense value of gold and silver, stands of arms, also, a saddle for a camel, hanging on a peg
at one side of the cave. I asked him, of what kind of wood the
peg was. He could not tell, but said it had become similar to
stone or iron.

The old man at last laid a plan which he thought would
accomplish his design. His cows and mine had been gone for

some time, and were not to be found, notwithstanding our diligent search for them. Day after day was spent in fruitless search, until at length he proposed to find them by his art of divination. So he took his stand near the corner of his house, with a small stick in his hand, and made several strange and peculiar motions, and then said he could go directly to the cows. So he started off, and went into the woods about one hundred rods distant and found the lost cows. But on finding out the secret of the mystery, Harrison had found the cows, and drove them to the above named place, and milked them.[4] So that this stratagem turned out rather more to his profit tha[n] it did to my edification.—The old man finding that all his efforts to make me a money digger, had proved abortive, at length ceased his importunities. One circumstance, however, I will mention before leaving him. Some time before young Joseph found, or pretended to find, the gold plates, the old man told me that in Canada, there had been a book found, in a hollow tree,[5] that gave an account of the first settlement of this country before it was discovered by Columbus.

In the month of August, 1827, I was hired by Joseph Smith, Jr. to go to Pennsylvania, to move his wife's household furniture up to Manchester, where his wife then was. When we arrived at Mr. Hale's,[6] in Harmony, Pa. from which place he

4. Ingersoll himself was sued for stealing a cow, then was cleared of the charge (Pierce docketbook under May 26, 1830; Anderson, "Joseph Smith's New York Reputation Reappraised," 298n28).

5. There is no record of this, nor any corroboration for Joseph Sr. having related it.

6. Isaac Hale confirmed that Ingersoll accompanied the Smiths to Pennsylvania, implying that the three young people were friends (see below).

had taken his wife, a scene presented itself, truly affecting. His father-in-law (Mr. Hale) addressed Joseph, in a flood of tears: "You have stolen my daughter and married her.[7] I had much rather have followed her to her grave. You spend your time in digging for money—pretend to see in a stone, and thus try to deceive people." Joseph wept, and acknowledged he could not see in a stone now, nor never could; and that his former pretensions in that respect, were all false.[8] He then promised to give up his old habits of digging for money and looking into stones.[9] Mr. Hale told Joseph, if he would move to Pennsylvania and work for a living, he would assist him in getting into business. Joseph acceded to this proposition. I then returned with Joseph and his wife to Manchester. One circumstance occurred on the road, worthy of notice, and I believe this is the only instance where Jo ever exhibited true yankee wit. On our journey to Pennsylvania, we could not make the exact change at the toll gate near Ithaca. Joseph told the gate tender, that he would "hand" him the toll on his return, as he was coming back in a few days. On our return, Joseph tendered to him 25

---

7. Joseph and Emma married against her father's wishes (see below). Emma said in 1879 that she had not intended to marry Joseph and was persuaded with help from Josiah Stowell (Smith, "Last Testimony," 289; Vogel, *Documents*, 1:540).

8. Alva Hale, Isaac's son, said Smith admitted "that this '*peeping*' was all d—d nonsense. He (Smith) was deceived himself but did not intend to deceive others" (see below).

9. Isaac Hale said in essence the same thing: "Smith stated to me, that he had given up what he called 'glass-looking,' and that he expected to work hard for a living, and was willing to do so" (see below), as did Alva Hale, who remembered Smith saying "that he intended to quit the business, (of peeping) and labor for his livelihood" (see below).

cents, the toll being 12 1/2. He did not recognize Smith, so he accordingly gave him back the 12 1/2 cents. After we had passed the gate, I asked him if he did not agree to pay double gatage on our return? No, said he, I agreed to *"hand"* it to him, and I did, but he handed it back again.

Joseph told me on his return [to Manchester], that he intended to keep the promise which he had made to his father-in-law; but, said he, it will be hard for me, for they [his acquaintances in the Palmyra area] will all oppose, as they want me to look in the stone for them to dig money: and in fact it was as he predicted. They urged him, day after day, to resume his old practice of looking in the stone.—He seemed much perplexed as to the course he should pursue. In this dilemma, he made me his confident and told me what daily transpired in the family of Smiths. One day he came, and greeted me with a joyful countenance.—Upon asking the cause of his unusual happiness, he replied in the following language: "As I was passing, yesterday, across the woods, after a heavy shower of rain, I found, in a hollow, some beautiful white sand, that had been washed up by the water. I took off my frock, and tied up several quarts of it, and then went home. On my entering the house, I found the family at the table eating dinner. They were all anxious to know the contents of my frock. At that moment, I happened to think of what I had heard about a history found in Canada, called the golden Bible; so I very gravely told them it was the golden Bible. To my surprise, they were credulous enough to believe what I said. Accordingly I told them that I had received a commandment to let no one see it, for, says I, no man can see it with the naked eye and live. However, I offered to take out the book and show it to them, but they refuse[d] to see it, and left the room." Now, said Jo, "I have got the damned fools fixed, and will carry out the fun."[10] Notwithstanding, he told me he had no such book, and believed there never was any such book, yet, he told me that he actually went to Willard Chase, to get him to make a chest,[11] in which he might deposit his golden Bible. But, as Chase would not do it, he made a box himself, of clap-boards, and put it into a pillow case, and allowed people only to lift it, and feel of it through the case.

In the fall of 1827 [December], Joseph wanted to go [back] to Pennsylvania. His brother-in-law had come to assist him in moving, but he himself was out of money. He wished to borrow the money of me, and he presented Mr. Hale as security. I told him in case he could obtain assistance from no other source, I would let him have some money. Joseph then went to Palmyra; and, said he, I there met that dam fool, Martin Harris, and told him that I had a command to ask the first *honest man* I met with, for fifty dollars in money, and he would let me have it.[12] I saw at once, said Jo, that it took his notion, for he promptly gave me the fifty.

Joseph thought this sum was sufficient to bear his expenses

---

10. Someone, perhaps Ingersoll, testified in Lyons in March 1829 that Joseph told him the box "contained nothing but sand" (Smith, *Biographical Sketches*, 133–34; Vogel, *Documents*, 1:385), although perhaps evasively to put people off the path.

11. This was confirmed by Willard Chase (see below).

12. Cf. Willard Chase on pp. 345–46 herein and Townsend to Stiles, Dec. 24, 1833, in Tucker, *Origin*, 289. Smith and his mother emphasized that Harris became involved of his own volition: *History of the Church*, 1:19, Smith, *Biographical Sketches*, 113, both in Vogel, *Documents*, 1:69, 349.

to Pennsylvania. So he immediately started off, and since that time I have not been much in his society. While the Smiths were living at Waterloo, William visited my neighborhood, and upon my inquiry how they came on, he replied, "we do better there than here; we were too well known here to do much.

Peter Ingersoll.

State of New York, Wayne County, ss.[13]

I certify, that on this 9th day of December, 1833, personally appeared before me the above named Peter Ingersoll, to me known, and made oath, according to law, to the truth of the above statement. —Th. P. Baldwin, *Judge of Wayne County Court.*[14]

TESTIMONY OF WILLIAM STAFFORD.[15]

Manchester, Ontario Co. N. Y. Dec. 8th, 1833.

I, William Stafford, having been called upon to give a true statement of my knowledge, concerning the character and conduct of the family of Smiths, known to the world as the founders of the Mormon sect, do say, that I first became

---

13. The abbreviation "ss" stands for *scilicet*, Latin for "in particular," meaning here that the testimony was taken in New York but more specifically in Wayne County.

14. For notarized statements certifying affidavits, a dash will replace a line return in the original throughout the chapter.

15. William Stafford (ca. 1786–1863) lived on Stafford Road in Manchester about a mile south of the Smiths. Pomeroy Tucker described him as "a respectable farmer in comfortable worldly circumstances" (Tucker, *Origin*, 24; Vogel, *Documents*, 3:98). Despite his negative appraisal of Joseph Smith, Stafford evidently shared an interest in treasure seeking. His son John said he owned a peep stone (Kelley notebook, Mar. 6, 1881, 13; Vogel, *Documents*, 2:87).

acquainted with Joseph, Sen., and his family in the year 1820. They lived, at that time, in Palmyra, about one mile and a half from my residence. A great part of their time was devoted to digging for money: especially in the night time, when they said the money could be most easily obtained. I have heard them tell marvellous tales, respecting the discoveries they had made in their peculiar occupation of money digging. They would say, for instance, that in such a place, in such a hill, on a certain man's farm, there were deposited keys, barrels and hogsheads[16] of coined silver and gold—bars of gold, golden images, brass kettles filled with gold and silver—gold candlesticks, swords, &c. &c. They would say, also, that nearly all the hills in this part of New York, were thrown up by human hands, and in them were large caves, which Joseph, Jr., could see, by placing a stone of singular appearance in his hat, in such a manner as to exclude all light; at which time they pretended he could see all things within and under the earth,—that he could see within the above mentioned caves, large gold bars and silver plates—that he could also discover the spirits in whose charge these treasures were, clothed in ancient dress. At certain times, these treasures could be obtained very easily; at others, the obtaining of them was difficult. The facility of approaching them, depended in a great measure on the state of the moon.[17] New moon and good Friday, I believe, were regarded as the most favorable times for obtaining these treasures. These tales

---

16. A hogshead was an extremely large cask used for shipping a measured amount of wine or a standard weight of tobacco, among other products.

17. For the supernatural aspects of money digging, see Quinn, *Early Mormonism*, 141–45.

I regarded as visionary. However, being prompted by curiosity, I at length accepted of their invitations, to join them in their nocturnal excursions. I will now relate a few incidents attending these excursions.

Joseph Smith, Sen., came to me one night, and told me, that Joseph Jr. had been looking in his glass, and had seen, not many rods from his house, two or three kegs of gold and silver, some [several] feet under the surface of the earth; and that none others but the elder Joseph and myself could get them. I accordingly consented to go, and early in the evening repaired to the place of deposit. Joseph, Sen. first made a circle, twelve or fourteen feet in diameter.[18] This circle, said he, contains the treasure. He then stuck in the ground a row of witch hazel sticks, around the said circle, for the purpose of keeping off the evil spirits. Within this circle he made another, of about eight or ten feet in diameter. He walked around three times on the periphery of this last circle, muttering to himself something which I could not understand. He next stuck a steel rod in the centre of the circles, and then enjoined profound silence upon us, lest we should arouse the evil spirit who had the charge of these treasures. After we had dug a trench about five feet in depth around the rod, the old man by signs and motions, asked leave of absence, and went to the house to inquire of young Joseph the cause of our disappointment. He

---

18. Stafford describes a well-known magic formula (Quinn, *Early Mormonism*, 26, 68, 70, 117) that was referenced in a backhanded way by Lucy Smith in 1845 when she denied the family spent every moment "drawing Magic circles or sooth saying" to the neglect of "every other obligation" (Smith, History, 1844–45, 40; Vogel, *Documents*, 1:285).

soon returned and said, that Joseph had remained all this time in the house, looking in his stone and watching the motions of the evil spirit—that he saw the spirit come up to the ring and as soon as it beheld the cone which we had formed around the rod, it caused the money to sink. We then went into the house, and the old man observed, that we had made a mistake in the commencement of the operation; if it had not been for that, said he, we should have got the money.

At another time, they devised a scheme, by which they might satiate their hunger, with the mutton of one of my sheep. They had seen in my flock of sheep, a large, fat, black weather. Old Joseph and one of the boys came to me one day, and said that Joseph Jr. had discovered some very remarkable and valuable treasures, which could be procured only in one way. That way, was as follows:—That a black sheep should be taken on to the ground where the treasures were concealed—that after cutting its throat, it should be led around a circle while bleeding.[19] This being done, the wrath of the evil spirit would be appeased: the treasures could then be obtained, and my share of them was to be four fold. To gratify my curiosity, I let them have a large fat sheep. They afterwards informed me, that the sheep was killed pursuant to commandment; but as there was some mistake in the process, it did not have the desired effect. This, I believe, is the only time they ever made money-digging a profitable business. They, however, had around them constantly a worthless gang, whose employment

---

19. Stafford told the sheep story on other occasions as well (Gregg, *Prophet of Palmyra*, 56; Tucker, *Origin*, 24–25; C. R. Stafford, Statement, 3).

it was to dig money nights, and who, day times, had more to do with mutton than money.

When they found that the people of this vicinity would no longer put any faith in their schemes for digging money, they then pretended to find a gold bible, of which, they said, the book of Mormon was only an introduction. This latter book was at length fitted for the press. No means were taken by any individual to suppress its publication: No one apprehended any danger from a book, originating with individuals who had neither influence, honesty or honor. The two Josephs and Hiram, promised to show me the plates, after the book of Mormon was translated. But, afterwards, they pretended to have received an express commandment, forbidding them to show the plates. Respecting the manner of receiving and translating the book of Mormon, their statements were always discordant. The elder Joseph would say that he had seen the plates, and that he knew them to be gold; at other times he would say that they looked like gold; and other times he would say he had not seen the plates at all. I have thus briefly stated a few of the facts, in relation to the conduct and character of this family of Smiths; probably sufficient has been stated without my going into detail.

William Stafford.

State of New York, Wayne County, ss:

I certify, that on this 9th day of December, 1833, personally appeared before me, William Stafford, to me known, and made oath to the truth of the above statement, and signed the same. —Th. P. Baldwin, Judge of Wa[y]ne County Court.

TESTIMONY OF WILLARD CHASE.[20]

Manchester, Ontario Co. N. Y. 1833.

I became acquainted with the Smith family, known as the authors of the Mormon Bible, in the year 1820. At that time, they were engaged in the money digging business, which they followed until the latter part of the season of 1827. In the year 1822, I was engaged in digging a well. I employed Alvin and Joseph Smith to assist me; the latter of whom is now known as the Mormon prophet. After digging about twenty feet below the surface of the earth, we discovered a singularly appearing stone, which excited my curiosity. I brought it to the top of the well, and as we were examining it, Joseph put it into his hat, and then his face into the top of his hat. It has been said by Smith, that *he* brought the stone from the well; but this is false. There was no one in the well but myself. The next morning he came to me, and wished to obtain the stone, alledging that he could see in it; but I told him I did not wish to part with it on account of its being a curiosity, but would lend it. After obtaining the stone, he began to publish abroad what wonders he could discover by looking in it, and made so much disturbance among the credulous part of community, that I ordered the stone to be returned to me again. He had it in his possession about two years.—I believe, some time in 1825, Hiram Smith

---

20. Willard Chase (1798–1871) was a carpentry joiner who married Melissa Saunders, sister of Lorenzo and Benjamin Saunders. In his obituary he was identified as a onetime Methodist minister (*Palmyra Courier,* Mar. 17, 1871). Sometimes his sister Sally would look into a peep stone to see where Willard should dig for treasure, occasionally accompanied by Alvin Smith (W. Kelley notebook, Mar. 6, 1881, 16; Lorenzo Saunders interview with E. L. Kelley, Nov. 12, 1884, 8–9; Vogel, *Documents,* 2:87, 152–54).

(brother of Joseph Smith) came to me, and wished to borrow the same stone, alledging that they wanted to accomplish some business of importance, which could not very well be done without the aid of the stone. I told him it was of no particular worth to me, but merely wished to keep it as a curiosity, and if he would pledge me his word and honor, that I should have it when called for, he might take it; which he did and took the stone. I thought I could rely on his word at this time, as he had made a profession of religion.[21] But in this I was disappointed, for he disregarded both his word and honor.

In the fall of 1826, a friend called upon me and wished to see that stone, about which so much had been said; and I told him if he would go with me to Smith's, (a distance of about half a mile) he might see it. But to my surprize, on going to Smith's, and asking him for the stone, he said, "you cannot have it;" I told him it belonged to me, repeated to him the promise he made me, at the time of obtaining the stone: upon which he faced me with a malignant look and said, "I don't care who in the Devil it belongs to, *you* shall not have it."

In the month of June, 1827, Joseph Smith, Sen., related to me the following story: "That some years ago, a spirit had appeared to Joseph his son, in a vision, and informed him that in a certain place there was a record on plates of gold, and that he was the person that must obtain them, and this he must do in the following manner: On the 22d of September,[22] he must repair to the place where was deposited this manuscript, dressed

---

21. Perhaps Chase means Hyrum's joining the Presbyterian church during the revival of 1824–25 (Marquardt and Walters, *Inventing Mormonism*, 15–41).
22. The fall equinox.

in black clothes, and riding a black horse[23] with a switch tail, and demand the book in a certain name, and after obtaining it, he must go directly away, and neither lay it down nor look behind him. They accordingly fitted out Joseph with a suit of black clothes and borrowed a black horse. He repaired to the place of deposit and demanded the book, which was in a stone box, unsealed, and so near the top of the ground that he could see one end of it, and raising it up, took out the book of gold; but fearing some one might discover where he got it, he laid it down to place back the top stone, as he found it; and turning round, to his surprise there was no book in sight. He again opened the box, and in it saw the book, and attempted to take it out, but was hindered. He saw in the box something like a toad,[24] which soon assumed the appearance of a man, and struck him on the side of his head.— Not being discouraged at trifles, he again stooped down and strove to take the book, when the spirit struck him again, and knocked him three or four rods, and hurt him prodigiously. After recovering from his fright, he enquired why he could not obtain the plates; to which the spirit made reply, because you have not obeyed your orders. He then enquired when he *could* have them, and was answered thus: come one year from this day, and bring with

---

23. This was related by Lorenzo Saunders as well. See his interview with Kelley, Sept. 17, 1884, 11; Vogel, *Documents*, 2:132; Quinn, *Early Mormonism*, 165–66.

24. According to Benjamin Saunders, Smith said "there was something down near the box that looked some like a toad that rose up into a man which forbid him to take the plates." See Saunders interview with Kelley, ca. Sept. 1884, 24; Vogel, *Documents*, 2:137.

you your oldest brother, and you shall have them.[25] This spirit, he said was the spirit of the prophet who wrote this book, and who was sent to Joseph Smith, to make known these things to him. Before the expiration of the year, his oldest brother died; which the old man said was an *accidental providence!*

Joseph went one year from that day, to demand the book, and the spirit enquired for his brother, and he said that he was dead. The spirit then commanded him to come again, in just one year, and bring a man with him. On asking who might be the man, he was answered that he would know him when he saw him.

Joseph believed that one Samuel T. Lawrence[26] was the man alluded to by the spirit, and went with him to a singular looking hill, in Manchester, and shewed him where the treasure was. Lawrence asked him if he had ever discovered any thing with the plates of gold; he said no: he then asked him to look in his stone, to see if there was any thing with them. He looked, and said there was nothing; he told him to look again, and see if there was not a large pair of specks with the plates; he looked and soon saw a pair of spectacles, the same with which Joseph says he translated the Book of Mormon.[27] Lawrence

---

25. The instruction to take Alvin is mentioned by Jonathan Lapham, Joseph Knight, Benjamin Saunders, and Lorenzo Saunders (Vogel, *Documents*, 1:459–60; 4:13; 2:131–32, 159).

26. The naming of Samuel Lawrence as Alvin's substitute was corroborated by Lorenzo Saunders (Saunders interview with W. H. Kelley, Sept. 17, 1884, 10; Vogel, *Documents*, 2:132), whereas other sources mentioned Emma Hale (Henry Harris statement, pp. 353–54 herein; John A. Clark to Dear Brethren, *Episcopal Recorder*, Sept. 5, 1840, 94; Vogel, *Documents*, 2:264).

27. Samuel Lawrence was another local mystic and expert with a seer

told him it would not be prudent to let these plates be seen for about two years, as it would make a great disturbance in the neighborhood. Not long after this, Joseph altered his mind, and said L[awrence] was not the right man, nor had he told him the right place. About this time[28] he went to Harmony in Pennsylvania, and formed an acquaintance with a young lady, by the name of Emma Hale, whom he wished to marry.—In the fall of 1826, he wanted to go to Pennsylvania to be married; but being destitute of means, he now set his wits to work, how he should raise money, and get recommendations, to procure the fair one of his choice. He went to Lawrence with the following story, as related to me by Lawrence himself. That he had discovered in Pennsylvania, on the bank of the Susquehannah River, a very rich mine of silver, and if he would go there with him, he might have a share in the profits; that it was near high water mark and that they could load it into boats and take it down the river to Philadelphia, to market. Lawrence then asked Joseph if he was not deceiving him; no, said he, for I have been there and seen it with my own eyes, and if you do not find it so when we get there, I will bind myself to be your servant for three years. By these grave and fair promises Lawrence was induced to believe something in it, and agreed to go with him. L. soon found that Joseph was out of money, and had to bear his expenses on the way. When they got to Pennsylvania, Joseph wanted L. to recommend him to Miss H., which he

---

stone according to Joseph Knight. The latter said Lawrence went "to the hill and knew the things in the hill and was trying to obtain them" himself (Knight, "Manuscript," 2; Vogel, *Documents*, 4:14–15).

28. About November 1825.

did, [and] although he was asked to do it[,] [he resisted]; but could not well get rid of it as he was in his [Smith's] company. L. then wished to see the silver mine, and he and Joseph went to the river, and made search, but found nothing. Thus, Lawrence had his trouble for his pains, and returned home lighter than he went, while Joseph had got his expenses borne, and a recommendation to his girl.

Joseph's next move[29] was to get married; the girl's parents being opposed to the match: as they happened to be from home, he took advantage of the opportunity, and went off with her and was married.

Now, being still destitute of money, he set his wits at work, how he should get back to Manchester, his place of residence; he hit upon the following plan, which succeeded very well. He went to an honest old Dutchman, by the name of Stowel, and told him that he had discovered on the bank of Black River, in the village of Watertown, Jefferson County, N.Y. a cave,[30] in which he had found a bar of gold, as big as his leg, and about three or four feet long.—That he could not get it out alone, on account of its being fast at one end; and if he would move him to Manchester, N.Y. they would go together, and take a chisel and mallet, and get it, and Stowel should share the prize with him. Stowel moved him.

A short time after their arrival at Manchester, Stowel

---

29. January 18, 1827.

30. Smith probably heard about what the newspapers called a "stupendous cavern" discovered in 1822 near Watertown (Walker, *Dale Morgan*, 369–70n19; *Palmyra Herald, and Canal Advertiser,* June19, 1822; *Niles Weekly Register,* June 22, 1822, 270–71).

reminded Joseph of his promise; but he calmly replied, that he would not go, because his wife was now among strangers, and would be very lonesome if he went away. Mr. Stowel was then obliged to return without any gold, and with less money than he came.

In the fore part of September, (I believe,) 1827, the Prophet requested me to make him a chest, informing me that he designed to move back to Pennsylvania, and expecting soon to get his gold book, he wanted a chest to lock it up, giving me to understand at the same time, that if I would make the chest he would give me a share in the book. I told him my business was such that I could not make it: but if he would bring the book to me, I would lock it up for him. He said that would not do, as he was commanded to keep it two years, without letting it come to the eye of any one but himself. This commandment, however, he did not keep, for in less than two years, twelve men said they had seen it. I told him to get it and convince me of its existence, and I would make him a chest; but he said, that would not do, as he must have a chest to lock the book in, as soon as he took it out of the ground. I saw him a few days after, when he told me that I must make the chest. I told him plainly that I could not, upon which he told me that I could have no share in the book.

A few weeks after this conversation, he came to my house, and related the following story: That on the 22d of September, he arose early in the morning, and took a one horse wagon, of some one that had stayed over night at their house, without leave or license; and, together with his wife, repaired to the hill which contained the book.[31] He left his wife in the wagon,

---

31. The horse and wagon belonged to Joseph Knight, who was visiting

by the road, and went alone to the hill, a distance of thirty or forty rods from the road; he said he then took the book out of the ground and hid it in a tree top, and returned home. He then went to the town of Macedon to work.[32] After about ten days, it having been suggested that some one had got his book, his wife went after him; he hired a horse, and went home in the afternoon, staid long enough to drink one cup of tea, and then went for his book, found it safe, took off his frock, wrapt it round it, put it under his arm and run all the way home, a distance of about two miles. He said he should think it would weigh sixty pounds, and was sure it would weigh forty. On his return home, he said he was attacked by two men in the woods, and knocked them both down and made his escape, arrived safe and secured his treasure.[33]—He then observed that if it had not been for that stone, (which he acknowledged belonged to me,) he would not have obtained the book.[34] A few days afterwards, he told one of my neighbors that he had not got any such book, nor never had such an one; but that he had told the story to deceive the d——d fool, (meaning me,) to get him to make a chest. His neighbors having become disgusted with his foolish stories, he determined to go back to Pennsylvania, to avoid what he called persecution. His wits were now put to the

---

from Colesville (Smith, *Biographical Sketches*, 100; Knight, "Manuscript," 2; Vogel, *Documents*, 1:326, 4:15).

32. Lucy Smith mentioned the trip. Macedon was four miles west of Palmyra (Smith, *Biographical Sketches*, 101–02; Vogel, *Documents*, 1:329–30).

33. For similar accounts, see Vogel, *Documents*, 1:335–38, 524–26.

34. Martin Harris said that Smith used his seer stone to locate the gold plates the first time he went to the hill (Harris interview with Joel Tiffany, 163, 169; Vogel, *Documents*, 2:302, 309; see also 3:53).

task to contrive how he should get money to bear his expenses. He met one day in the streets of Palmyra, a rich man, whose name was Martin Harris, and addressed him thus; "I have a commandment from God to ask the first man I meet in the street to give me fifty dollars, to assist me in doing the work of the Lord by translating the Golden Bible." Martin being naturally a credulous man, hands Joseph the money. In the Spring 1829, Harris went to Pennsylvania,[35] and on his return to Palmyra, reported that the Prophet's wife, in the month of June following would be delivered of a male child that would be able when two years old to translate the Gold Bible.[36] Then, said he, you will see Joseph Smith, Jr. walking through the streets of Palmyra, with a Gold Bible under his arm, and having a gold breast-plate on, and a gold sword hanging by his side.[37] This, however, by the by, proved false.

In April, 1830, I again asked Hiram for the stone which he had borrowed of me; he told me I should not have it, for Joseph made use of it in translating his Bible. I reminded him of his promise, and that he had pledged his honor to return it; but he gave me the lie, saying the stone was not mine nor never was. Harris at the same time flew in a rage, took me by the collar and said I was a liar, and he could prove it by twelve

---

35. It was actually 1828. Harris began serving as scribe on April 12 and returned to Palmyra in mid-June (*History of the Church*, 1:20–21; Vogel, *Documents*, 1:71–72).

36. The baby boy whom Emma Smith bore on June 15, 1828, died the same day (Vogel, *Documents*, 4:418–20).

37. Similar statements were made by residents of Harmony, including Isaac Hale, Sophia Lewis, and Joshua McKune, pp. 371, 375–76, 378.

witnesses. After I had extricated myself from him, Hiram, in a
rage shook his fist at me, and abused me in a most scandalous
manner.[38] Thus I might proceed in describing the character of
these High Priests, by relating one transaction after another,
which would all tend to set them in the same light in which
they were regarded by their neighbors, viz: as a pest to society.
I have regarded Joseph Smith Jr. from the time I first became
acquainted with him until he left this part of the country, as a
man whose word could not be depended upon.—Hiram's character was but very little better. What I have said respecting the
characters of these men, will apply to the whole family. What I
have stated relative to the characters of these individuals, thus
far, is wholly true. After they became thorough Mormons, their
conduct was more disgraceful than before. They did not hesitate
to abuse any man, no matter how fair his character, provided
he did not embrace their creed. Their tongues were continually
employed in spreading scandal and abuse. Although they left
this part of the country without paying their just debts,[39] yet

38. An unsigned note in the newspaper that month read, "Please advise
hyrum smith, and some of his ill-bred associates, not to be quite so imperti-
nent, when *decent* folks denounce the imposition of the 'Gold-Bible[.]' The
anathemas of such ignorant wretches, although not feared, are not quite so
well relished by some people—Apostles should keep cool" (*Palmyra Reflector,*
Apr. 19, 1830; Vogel, *Documents,* 2:230).

39. Other people who said the family left without paying its debts included Joseph Capron, Roswell Nichols, and Jesse Townsend (pp. 360, 364;
Tucker, *Origin,* 290–91; Vogel, *Documents,* 3:23). This is otherwise confirmed
by Joseph Smith's letter to the Colesville Saints, Dec. 2, 1830 (Newel Knight
journal, 206–07; Vogel, *Documents,* 1:22); Joseph Smith to Hyrum Smith, Mar. 3,
1831 (MacKay et al, *Joseph Smith Papers: Documents,* 1:273); two legal cases, *Levi
Daggett vs. Hyrum Smith* and *Lemuel Durfee vs. Joseph Smith and Abraham Fish*

their creditors were glad to have them do so, rather than to
have them stay, disturbing the neighborhood.

Signed, Willard Chase.

On the 11th December, 1833, the said Willard Chase appeared before me, and made oath that the foregoing statement
to which he has subscribed his name, is true, according to his
best recollection and belief. —Fred'k. Smith, *Justice of the Peace
of Wayne County.*

THE TESTIMONY OF PARLEY CHASE.[40]

Manchester, December 2d, 1833.

I was acquainted with the family of Joseph Smith, Sen.,
both before and since they became Mormons, and feel free to
state that not one of the male members of the Smith family
were entitled to any credit, whatsoever. They were lazy, intemperate and worthless men, very much addicted to lying. In
this they freqently boasted of their skill. Digging for money
was their principal employment. In regard to their Gold Bible
speculation, they scarcely ever told two stories alike. The Mormon Bible is said to be a revelation from God, through Joseph
Smith Jr., his Prophet, and this same Joseph Smith Jr. to my
knowledge, bore the reputation among his neighbors of being

(N. Pierce docketbook, 25, 76b; Vogel, *Documents*, 3:487–90); Smith, *Biographical Sketches*, 159–61 (Vogel, *Documents*, 1:428–31); and the W. Kelley notebook,
12 (Vogel, *Documents*, 2:86).

40. Parley Chase (b. 1806), Willard's younger brother, was born in Manchester, New York. When he later corresponded with James Cobb to confirm
an earlier statement about the Smiths, he was living in Michigan (Vogel, *Documents*, 3:135).

a liar. The foregoing statement can be corroborated by all his former neighbors.

Parley Chase.

Palmyra, December 13*th*, 1833.

I certify that I have been personally acquainted with Peter Ingersoll for a number of years, and believe him to be a man of strict integrity, truth and veracity. —Durfey Chase.

Palmyra, December 4*th*, 1833.[41]

I am acquainted with William Stafford and Peter Ingersoll, and believe them to be men of truth and veracity. —J. S. Colt.

Palmyra, December 4*th*, 1833

We the undersigned, are personally acquainted with William Stafford, Willard Chase and Peter Ingersoll, and believe them to be men of truth and veracity. —George Beckwith. Nath'l. H. Beckwith. Thomas Rogers, 2d. Martin W. Wilcox.

THE TESTIMONY OF DAVID STAFFORD.[42]

Manchester, December 5*th*, 1833.

I have been acquainted with the family of Joseph Smith Sen. for several years, and I know him to be a drunkard[43] and

---

41. The date was probably meant to be Dec. 14, in keeping with Durfee Chase's certification of Peter Ingersoll's character, dated Dec. 13.

42. David Stafford is listed as a young man in his thirties in the 1830 Manchester census. He paid taxes for twenty acres on Lot 3 immediately south of the Smiths' farm (Manchester Assessment Records, 1833).

43. In a blessing to his son Hyrum in 1834, Father Smith praised his loyalty even at times when the older man was drunk ("out of the way through wine," Hyrum Smith Papers, LDS Church History Library, cited in Hill, *Quest for Refuge*, 190n5; Vogel, *Documents*, 1:470n11). The charge of intemperance

a liar, and to be much in the habit of gambling.[44] He and his boys were truly a lazy set of fellows, and more particularly Joseph, who, very aptly followed his father's example, and in some respects was worse.[45] When intoxicated he was very quarrelsome. Previous to his going to Pennsylvania to get married, we worked together making a coal-pit. While at work at one time, a dispute arose between us, (he having drinked a little too freely) and some hard words passed between us, and as usual with him at such times, was for fighting. He got the advantage of me in the scuffle, and a gentleman by the name of Ford interfered, when Joseph turned to fighting him. We both entered a complaint against him and he was fined for the breach of the Peace.[46] It is well known, that the general employment of the Smith family was money digging and fortune-telling. They kept around them constantly, a gang of worthless fellows who dug for money nights, and were idle in the day time. It was a mystery to their neighbors how they got their living. I will mention some circumstances and the public may judge for

was repeated by several neighbors (pp. 352, 368; Vogel, *Documents*, 2:127, 156, 163–64, 191, 193, 308).

44. No one else mentioned gambling.

45. On Joseph Smith's early drinking, see pp. 352, 362, 377; Vogel, *Documents*, 2:194, 197; 3:21; Kirtland Council Minute Book, 28–29.

46. In 1843 Joseph remembered that David Stafford's hog had gotten into the Smiths' cornfield and that the Smiths' watchdog had bitten an ear off the hog. Unhappy about this, Stafford and six other young men went and shot the dog, then got into a scrape with Joseph Jr., who "whipped the whole of them—& escaped unhurt," according to Joseph's telling. Joseph added that the whole tale was "recorded in Hurlburt's … Book" (Smith journal, Jan. 1, 1843, in Hedges et al., *Joseph Smith Papers: Journals,* 2:209, redundant punctuation omitted; Vogel, *Documents*, 1:179; cf. Anderson, *Joseph Smith's New York Reputation*, 36–37).

themselves. At different times I have seen them come from the woods early in the morning, bringing meat which looked like mutton. I went into the woods one morning very early, shooting pa[r]tridges and found Joseph Smith Sen. in company with two other men, with hoes, shovels and meat that looked like mutton. On seeing me they run like wild men to get out of sight.—Seeing the old man a few day afterwards, I asked him why he run so the other day in the woods, ah, said he, you know that circumstances alter cases; it will not do to be seen at all time[s].

I can also state, that Oliver Cowdrey proved himself to be a worthless person and not to be trusted or believed when he taught school in this neighborhood. After his going into the ministry, while officiating in performing the ordinance of baptism in a brook, William Smith, (brother of Joseph Smith) seeing a young man writing down what was said on a piece of board, was quite offended and attempted to take it from him, kicked at him and clinched for a scuffle.—Such was the conduct of these pretended Disciples of the Lord.

David Stafford.

On the 12th day of December, 1833, the said David Stafford appeared before me, and made oath that the foregoing statement, by him subscribed, is true. —Fred'k. Smith, *Justice of the Peace of Wayne Co. N. Y.*

THE TESTIMONY OF BARTON STAFFORD.[47]

Manchester, Ontario Co., N. Y. Nov 3d, 1833.

Being called upon to give a statement of the character of

---

47. Barton Stafford was a fish peddler who lived south of the Smiths.

the family of Joseph Smith, Sen. as far as I know, I can state that I became acquainted with them in 1820, and knew them until 1831, when they left this neighborhood.—Joseph Smith, Sen. was a noted drunkard and most of the family followed his example, and Joseph, Jr. especially, who was very much addicted to intemperance. In short, not one of the family had the least claims to respectability. Even since he professed to be inspired of the Lord to translate the Book of Mormon, he one day while at work in my father's field, got quite drunk on a composition of cider, molasses and water.[48] Finding his legs to refuse their office he leaned upon the fence and hung for sometime; at length recovering again, he fell to scuffling with one of the workmen, who tore his shirt nearly off from him. His wife who was at our house on a visit, appeared very much grieved at his conduct, and to protect his back from the rays of the sun, and conceal his nakedness, threw her shawl over his shoulders and in that plight escorted the Prophet home. As an evidence of his piety and devotion, when intoxicated, he frequently made his religion the topic of conversation!!

Barton Stafford.

State of New York, Wayne County, ss:

I certify that on the 9th day of December 1833, personally appeared before me, the above named Barton Stafford, to me known, and solemnly affirmed according to law, to the truth

---

48. Because Stafford failed to clarify whether his information was first-hand or hearsay, Richard L. Anderson questioned its truth (Anderson, "Joseph Smith's New York Reputation," 291); it is at least consistent with other accounts (John Stafford statement, 167; Christopher M. Stafford statement, 1; David Stafford statement, p. 350 herein; Vogel, *Documents*, 2:121, 193–94).

of the above statement and subscribed the same. —Thos. P. Baldwin, *a Judge of Wayne County Court.*

[TESTIMONY OF HENRY HARRIS][49]

I, Henry Harris, do state that I became acquainted with the family of Joseph Smith, Sen. about the year 1820, in the town of Manchester, N. York. They were a family that labored very little—the chief they did, was to dig for money. Joseph Smith, Jr. the pretended Prophet, used to pretend to tell fortunes; he had a stone which he used to put in his hat, by means of which he professed to tell people's fortunes.

Joseph Smith, Jr. Martin Harris and others, used to meet together in private, a while before the gold plates were found, and were familiarly known by the name of the "Gold Bible Company." They were regarded by the community in which they lived, as a lying and indolent set of men and no confidence could be placed in them.

The character of Joseph Smith, Jr. for truth and veracity was such, that I would not believe him under oath. I was once on a jury before a Justice's Court and the Jury could not, and did not, believe his testimony to be true.[50] After he pretended to have found the gold plates, I had a conversation with him, and asked him where he found them and how he come to know where they were. He said he had a revelation from God

49. Henry's statement was notarized in Ohio. He is probably the individual from the 1820 census living twenty miles south of Palmyra (Gorham 1820:228; Nathan Pierce docketbook, Jan. 23, 1830, 33), who moved to Madison, Ohio, in 1830 (1830:194). It is not known if he was related to Martin Harris.

50. That Joseph Smith was called to court as a witness in Manchester cannot be verified.

that told him they were hid in a certain hill and he looked in his stone and saw them in the place of deposit; that an angel appeared, and told him he could not get the plates until he was married, and that when he saw the woman that was to be his wife, he should know her, and she would know him. He then went to Pennsylvania, got his wife, and they both went together and got the gold plates—he said it was revealed to him, that no one must see the plates but himself and wife.[51]

I then asked him what letters were engraved on them, he said italic letters written in an unknown language, and that he had copied some of the words and sent them to Dr. Mitchell and Professor Anthon of New York. By looking on the plates he said he could not understand the words, but it was made known to him that he was the person that must translate them, and on looking through the stone was enabled to translate.

After the Book was published, I frequently bantered him for a copy. He asked fourteen shillings a piece for them; I told him I would not give so much; he told me had had a revelation that they must be sold at that price.[52]

Sometime afterwards I talked with Martin Harris about buying one of the Books and he told me they had had a new revelation, that they might be sold at ten shillings a piece.

[Henry Harris]

State of Ohio, Cuyahoga County, ss:

Personally appeared before me, Henry Harris, and made

---

51. Emma Smith never claimed to have seen the plates, although she accompanied Joseph to the hill to retrieve them.

52. Marks, *Life of David Marks*, 341; Vogel, *Documents*, 5:304.

oath in due form of law, that the foregoing statements subscribed by him are true. —Jonathan Lapham, *Justice of the Peace.*

[TESTIMONY OF ABIGAIL HARRIS][53]

Palmyra, Wayne Co. N. Y. 11*th mo.* 28*th*, 1833.

In the early part of the winter in 1828, I made a visit to
Martin Harris' and was joined in company by Jos. Smith, sen.
and his wife. The Gold Bible business, so called, was the topic
of conversation, to which I paid particular attention, that I
might learn the truth of the whole matter.—They told me that
the report that Joseph, jun. had found golden plates, was true,
and that he was in Harmony, Pa. translating them—that such
plates were in existence, and that Joseph, jun. was to obtain
them, was revealed to him by the spirit of one of the Saints that
was on this continent, previous to its being discovered by Columbus. Old Mrs. Smith observed that she thought he must be
a Quaker, as he was dressed very plain. They said that the plates
he then had in possession were but an introduction to the Gold
Bible—that all of them upon which the bible was written, were
so heavy that it would take four stout men to load them into a
cart—that Joseph had also discovered by looking through his
stone, the vessel in which the gold was melted from which the
plates were made, and also the machine with which they were
rolled; he also discovered in the bottom of the vessel three balls
of gold, each as large as his fist. The old lady said also, that after

---

53. Abigail ("Nabbie") was Lucy Harris's sister-in-law, married to Peter
Harris (1778–1849), a Quaker minister. In November 1825, Peter helped his
sister transfer some of Martin's property into her name (Gunnell, "Martin
Harris," 95).

the book was translated, the plates were to be publicly exhibited—admitance 25 cents.[54] She calculated it would bring in
annually an enormous sum of money—that money would then
be very plenty, and the book would also sell for a great price,
as it was something entirely new—that they had been commanded to obtain all the money they could borrow for present
necessity, and to repay with gold. The remainder was to be kept
in store for the benefit of their family and children. This and
the like conversation detained me until about 11 o'clock. Early
the next morning, the mystery of the Spirit being like myself
(one of the order called Friends) was reveal[ed] by the following circumstance: The old lady took me into another room, and
after closing the door, she said, "have you four or five dollars
in money that you can lend until our business is brought to a
close? the spirit has said you shall receive four fold." I told her
that when I gave, I did it not expecting to receive again—as for
money I had none to lend. I then asked her what her particular
want of money was; to which she replied, "Joseph wants to take
the stage and come home from Pennsylvania to see what we
are all about." To which I replied, he might look in his stone
and save his time and money. The old lady seemed confused,
and left the room, and thus ended the visit.

In the second month following, Martin Harris and his
wife were at my house. In conversation about Mormonites, she
observed, that she wished her husband would quit them, as

---

54. Historian Dale Morgan commented that the way Lucy "exhibited
Joseph's Egyptian mummies and other odds and ends" in Kirtland and Nau-
voo "leaves no room for doubt as to the substantial accuracy of these remarks"
(Walker, *Dale Morgan*, 385n59).

she believed it was all false and a delusion. To which I hea[r]d
Mr. Harris reply: *"What if it is a lie; if you will let me alone I will
make money out of it!*["] I was both an eye and an ear witness of
what has been stated above, which is now fresh in my memory,
and I give it to the world for the good of mankind. I speak the
truth and lie not, God bearing me witness.

Abigail Harris.

[TESTIMONY OF LUCY HARRIS]⁵⁵

Palmyra, Nov. 29, 1833.

Being called upon to give a statement to the world of
what I know respecting the Gold Bible speculation, and also
of the conduct of Martin Harris, my husband, who is a leading
character among the Mormons, I do it free from prejudice,
realizing that I must give an account at the bar of God for
what I say. Martin Harris was once industrious [and] attentive
to his domestic concerns, and thought to be worth about ten
thousand dollars. He is naturally quick in his temper and in his
mad-fits frequently abuses all who may dare to oppose him in
his wishes. However strange it may seem, I have been a great
sufferer by his unreasonable conduct. At different times while
I lived with him, he has whipped, kicked, and turned me out
of the house. About a year previous to the report being raised
that Smith had found gold plates, he became very intimate

---

55. Lucy Harris (1792–1836), probably born in Palmyra, married her first
cousin, Martin. Even so, she was a strong-willed and independent woman who
demanded eighty acres and a house apart from Martin in 1825. She controlled a
portion of the family's finances. She also resented the imposition of Mormonism
and stayed behind when Martin followed the church's migration to Ohio in 1831.

with the Smith family, and said he believed Joseph could see in his stone any thing he wished. After this he apparently became very sanguine in his belief, and frequently said he would have no one in his house that did not believe in Mormonism; and because I would not give credit to the report he made about the gold plates, he became more austere towards me. In one of his fits of rage he struck me with the but end of a whip, which I think had been used for driving oxen, and was about the size of my thumb, and three or four feet long.[56] He beat me on the head four or five times, and the next day turned me out of doors twice, and beat me in a shameful manner.—The next day I went to the town of Marion, and while there my flesh was black and blue in many places. His main complaint against me was, that I was always trying to hinder his making money.

When he found out that I was going to Mr. Putnam's, in Marion, he said he was going too, that they had sent for him to pay them a visit. On arriving at Mr. Putnam's, I asked them if they had sent for Mr. Harris; they replied, they knew nothing about it; he, however, came in the evening. Mrs. Putnam told him never to strike or abuse me any more; he then denied ever striking me; she was however convinced that he lied, as the marks of his beating me were plain to be seen, and remained more than two weeks. Whether the Mormon religion be true or false, I leave the world to judge, for its effects upon Martin Harris have been to make him more cross, turbulent and abusive to me. His whole object was to make money by it. I will

---

56. See also the statement of G. W. Stoddard (p. 365) and the article in the *Palmyra Reflector*, June 22, 1830 (Vogel, *Documents*, 2:234).

give one circumstance in proof of it. One day, while at Peter Harris' house, I told him he had better leave the company of the Smiths, as their religion was false; to which he replied, if you would let me alone, I could make money by it.

It is in vain for the Mormons to deny these facts; for they are all well known to most of his former neighbors. The man has now become rather an object of pity; he has spent most of his property, and lost the confidence of his former friends. If he had labored as hard on his farm as he has to make Mormons, he might now be one of the wealthiest farmers in the country. He now spends his time in travelling through the country spreading the delusion of Mormonism, and has no regard whatever for his family.

With regard to Mr. Harris' being intimate with Mrs. Haggard,[57] as has been reported, it is but justice to myself to state what facts have come within my own observation, to show whether I had any grounds for jealousy or not. Mr. Harris was very intimate with this family, for some time previous to their going to Ohio. They lived a while in a house which he had built for their accommodation, and here he spent the most of his leisure hours; and made her presents of articles from the store and house. He carried these presents in a private manner, and frequently when he went there, he would pretend to be going to some of the neighbors, on an errand, or to be

---

57. Probably the Canadian-born Magdaline Haggart, a woman who was about ten years younger than her blacksmith husband Daniel (Palmyra census, 1830:51; Willoughby, Ohio, census, 1850:169). A March 1830 revelation to Martin Harris warned him "not [to] covet thy neighbor's wife" (D&C 19:25; Levi Lewis statement, pp. 376–77; Vogel, *Documents*, 4:296–97).

going into the fields.—After getting out of sight of the house, he would steer a straight course for [Mrs.] Haggard's house, especially if [Mr.] Haggard was from home. At times when [Mr.] Haggard was from home, he would go there in the manner above described, and stay till twelve or one o'clok at night, and sometimes until day light.

If his intentions were evil, the Lord will judge him accordingly, but if good, he did not mean to let his left hand know what his right hand did. The above statement of facts, I affirm to be true.

Lucy Harris.

[TESTIMONY OF ROSWELL NICHOLS]
Manchester, Ontario County, N. Y. Dec 1st, 1833.

I, Roswell Nichols,[58] first became acquainted with the family of Joseph Smith, Sen. nearly five years ago, and I lived a neighbor to the said family about two years. My acquaintance with the family has enabled me to know something of its character for [deficiency in] good citizenship, probity and veracity—For breach of contracts, for the non-payment of debts and borrowed money, and for duplicity with their neighbors, the family was notorious. Once, since the Gold Bible speculation commenced, the old man was sued; and while the sheriff was at his house, he lied to him and was detected in the falsehood. Before he left the house, he confessed that it

---

58. Roswell and Mary Nichols moved into the Smith house after the Smiths were evicted by Mary's father, Lemuel Durfee, in early 1829. The Smiths retreated to the small adjacent cabin and lived there as neighbors for nearly two years.

was sometimes necessary for him to tell an honest lie, in order to live. At another time, he told me that he had received an express command for me to repent and believe as he did, or I must be damned. I refused to comply, and at the same time told him of the various impositions of his family. He then stated their digging was not for money but it was for the obtaining of a Gold Bible. Thus contradicting what he had told me before: for he had often said, that the hills in our neighborhood were nearly all erected by human hands—that they were all full of gold and silver. And one time, when we were talking on the subject, he [Joseph Sr.] pointed to a small hill on my farm, and said, "in that hill there is a stone which is full of gold and silver. I know it to be so, for I have been to the hole, and God said unto me, *go not in now, but at a future day you shall go in and find the book open, and then you shall have the treasures.*"[59] He said that gold and silver was once as plenty as the stones in the field are now—that the ancients, half of them melted the ore and made the gold and silver, while the other half buried it deeper in the earth, which accounted for these hills. Upon my enquiring who furnished the food for the whole, he flew into a passion, and called me a sinner, and said he, "you must be eternally damned."

I mention these facts, not because of their intrinsic importance, but simply to show the weak mindedness and low character of the man.

Roswell Nichols.

---

59. This is similar to what Brigham Young claimed Oliver Cowdery said (*Journal of Discourses*, 19:38–39).

[TESTIMONY OF JOSHUA STAFFORD]

Manchester, Ontario County, Nov. 15th, 1833.

I, Joshua Stafford,[60] became acquainted with the family of Joseph Smith, Sen. about the year 1819 or 20. They then were laboring people, in low circumstances. A short time after this, they commenced digging for hidden treasures, and soon after they became indolent, and told marvellous stories about ghosts, hob-goblins, caverns, and various other mysterious matters. Joseph once showed me a piece of wood which he said he took from a box of money, and the reason he gave for not obtaining the box, was, that it *moved.*[61] At another time, he, (Joseph, Jr.) at a husking, called on me to become security for a horse, and said he would reward me handsomely, for he had found a box of watches, and they were as large as his fist, and he put one of them to his ear, and he could hear it "tick forty rods."[62] Since he could not dispose of them profitably at Canandaigua or Palmyra, he wished to go east with them. He said if he did not return with the horse, I might take his life. I replied, that he knew I would not do that. Well, said he, I did not suppose you would, yet I would be willing that you should. He was nearly intoxicated at the time of the above conversation.

Joshua Stafford.

---

60. Joshua Stafford (1798–1876), about two miles south of the Smiths, was probably William Stafford's brother. Joshua had his own peep stone and a penchant for digging for "money in his orchard and elsewhere nights," sometimes with Joseph Smith (Butts statement, 2; C. R. Smith statement, 1; Cornelius R. Stafford statement, 3; Vogel, *Documents*, 2:196, 199, 202).

61. Similar stories were told by Brigham Young and Martin Harris (*Journal of Discourses*, 19:37; Jensen, "Testimony," 5; Vogel, *Documents*, 2:376).

62. Cf. the following statement by Joseph Capron, also the *Palmyra Reflector*, July 7, 1830; Vogel, *Documents*, 2:237.

[TESTIMONY OF JOSEPH CAPRON]

Manchester, Ontario County, Nov. 8th, 1833.

I, Joseph Capron,[63] became acquainted with Joseph Smith, Sen. in the year of our Lord, 1827. They have, since then, been really a peculiar people—fond of the foolish and the marvelous—at one time addicted to vice and the grossest immoralities—at another time making the highest pretensions to piety and holy intercourse with Almighty God. The family of Smiths held Joseph Jr. in high estimation on account of some supernatural power, which he was supposed to possess. This power he pretended to have received through the medium of a stone of peculiar quality. The stone was placed in a hat, in such a manner as to exclude all light, except that which emanated from the stone itself. This light of the stone, he pretended, enabled him to see any thing he wished. Accordingly he discovered ghosts, infernal spirits, mountains of gold and silver, and many other invaluable treasures deposited in the earth. He would often tell his neighbors of his wonderful discoveries, and urge them to embark in the money digging business. Luxury and wealth were to be given to all who would adhere to his counsel. A gang was soon assembled. Some of them were influenced by curiosity, others were sanguine in their expectations of immediate gain. I will mention one circumstance, by which the uninitiated may know how the company dug for treasures. The sapient Joseph discovered, north west of my house, a chest of gold watches; but, as they were in the possession of the evil spirit, it required skill and stratagem to obtain

---

63. Joseph Capron was a shoemaker who had lived just south of the Smiths since 1827 (census, 1850:310).

them. Accordingly, orders were given to stick a parcel of large stakes in the ground, several rods around, in a circular form. This was to be done directly over the spot where the treasures were deposited. A messenger was then sent to Palmyra to procure a polished sword: after which, Samuel F. Lawrence, with a drawn sword in his hand, marched around to guard any assault which his Satanic majesty might be disposed to make. Meantime, the rest of the company were busily employed in digging for the watches. They worked as usual till quite exhausted. But, in spite of their brave defender, Lawrence, and their bulwark of stakes, the devil came off victorious, and carried away the watches. I might mention numerous schemes by which this young visionary and impostor had recourse to for the purpose of obtaining a livelihood. He, and indeed the whole of the family of Smiths, were notorious for indolence, foolery and falsehood. Their great object appeared to be, to live without work. While they were digging for money, they were daily harrassed by the demands of creditors, which they never were able to pay. At length, Joseph pretended to find the Gold plates. This scheme, he believed, would relieve the family from all pecuniary embarrassment. His father told me, that when the book was published, they would be enabled, from the profits of the work, to carry into successful operation the money digging business. He gave me no intimation, at that time that the book was to be of a religious character, or that it had any thing to do with revelation.[64] He declared it to be a speculation, and said

---

64. A similar observation was made by Lorenzo Saunders in the Kelley interview of Nov. 12, 1884, 3; Vogel, *Documents*, 2:149.

he, "when it is completed, my family will be placed *on a level* above the generality of mankind"!!

Joseph Capron.

[TESTIMONY OF G. W. STODARD]⁶⁵

Palmyra, Nov. 28*th,* 1833

Having been called upon to state a few facts which are material to the characters of some of the leaders of the Mormon sect, I will do so in a concise and plain manner. I have been acquainted with Martin Harris, about thirty years. As a farmer, he was industrious and enterprising, so much so, that he had, (previous to his going into the Gold Bible speculation) accumulated, in real estate, some eight or ten thousand dollars. Although he possessed wealth, his moral and religious character was such, as not to entitle him to respect among his neighbors. He was fretful, peevish and quarrelsome, not only in the neighborhood, but in his family. He was known to frequently abuse his wife, by whipping her, kicking her out of bed and turning her out of doors &c. Yet he was a public professor of some religion. He was first an orthadox Quaker, then a Universalist, next a Restorationer, then a Baptist, next a Presbyterian, and then a Mormon. By his willingness to become all things unto all men, he has attained a high standing among his Mormon brethren. The Smith family never made any pretentions to respectability.

G. W. Stodard.

---

65. Probably George W. Stoddard, a farmer in Arcadia, ten miles east of Palmyra (census, 1850:277), who in 1823 was disfellowshipped from the First Baptist Church "for profane Swearing" ("Book of Records").

I hereby concur in the above statement. —Richard H. Ford.

[TESTIMONY OF FIFTY-ONE NEIGHBORS]

Palmyra, Dec. 4, 1833.

We, the undersigned,[66] have been acquainted with the Smith family, for a number of years, while they resided near this place, and we have no hesitation in saying, that we consider them destitute of that moral character, which ought to entitle them to the confidence of any community. They were particularly famous for visionary projects, spent much of their time in digging for money which they pretended was hid in the earth; and to this day, large excavations may be seen in the earth, not far from their residence, where they used to spend their time in digging for hidden treasures. Joseph Smith, Senior, and his son Joseph, were in particular, considered entirely destitute of *moral character, and addicted to vicious habits.*[67]

Martin Harris was a man who had acquired a handsome property, and in matters of business his word was considered

---

66. This statement was likely written by Hurlbut and presented to the fifty-one individuals for their consideration, making it potentially less significant than statements written by the witnesses themselves, even though it is not contradicted by the other statements. The signers included leaders of the local Presbyterian Church where Lucy and three of the Smith children attended for four years in the mid-1820s, four members of the Mount Moriah Masonic Lodge where Hyrum was initiated around 1823, four men who had business dealings with the Smiths, and a son of the Smiths' landlord (cf. Hill, Review, 73–74).

67. Three signers of the affidavit, George Beckwith, Henry Jessup, and George Williams, were on a committee of elders that suspended Gain Robinson from the Presbyterian church in 1828 for "immoderate and intemperate use of spiritous liquors to the great injury of his christian character," probably pointing to what lay behind the "vicious habits" euphemism. See the Records of the Session of the Presbyterian Church in Palmyra, 2:1.

good; but on moral and religious subjects, he was perfectly visionary—sometimes advocating one sentiment, and sometimes another. And in reference to all with whom we were acquainted, that have embraced Mormonism from this neighborhood, we are compeled to say, were very visionary, and most of them destitute of moral character, and without influence in this community; and this may account why they were permitted to go on with their impositions undisturbed. It was not supposed that any of them were possessed of sufficient character or influence to make any one believe their book or their sentiments, and we know not of a single individual in this vicinity that puts the least confidence in their pretended revelations.

Geo. N. Williams,	Jas. Jenner,	Josiah Francis,
Clark Robinson,	S. Ackley,	Amos Hollister,
Lemuel Durfee,	Josiah Rice,	G. A. Hathaway,
E. S. Townsend,	Jesse Townsend,	David G. Ely,
Henry P. Alger,	Rich'd. D. Clark,	H. K. Jerome,
C. E. Thayer,	Th. P. Baldwin,	G. Beckwith,
G. W. Anderson,	John Sothington,	Lewis Foster,
H. P. Thayer,	Durfey Chase,	Hiram Payne,
L. Williams,	Wells Anderson,	P. Grandin,
Geo. W. Crosby,	N. H. Beckwith,	L. Hurd,
Levi Thayer,	Philo Durfee,	Joel Thayer,
R. S. Williams,	Giles S. Ely,	E. D. Robinson,
P. Sexton,	R. W. Smith,	Asahel Millard,
M. Butterfield,	Pelatiah West,	A. Ensworth,
S. P. Seymour,	Henry Jessup,	Is[ra]el F. Chilson
D. S. Jackways,	Linus North,	
John Hurlbut,	Thos. Rogers, 2d.	
H. Linnell,	Wm. Parke,	

[TESTIMONY OF ELEVEN NEIGHBORS]

Manchester, Nov. 3d, 1833.

We, the undersigned,[68] being personally acquainted with the family of Joseph Smith, sen. with whom the celebrated Gold Bible, so called, originated, state: that they were not only a lazy, indolent set of men, but also intemperate; and their word was not to be depended upon; and that we are truly glad to dispense with their society.

Pardon Butts, Warden A. Reed, Hiram Smith, Alfred Stafford, James Gee, Abel Chase, A. H. Wentworth, Moses C. Smith, Joseph Fish, Horace N. Barnes, Silvester Worden

[TESTIMONY OF ISAAC HALE][69]

Harmony, Pa. Mar. 20th, 1834.

I first became acquainted with Joseph Smith, Jr. in November, 1825.[70] He was at that time in the employ of a set of men

---

68. Richard L. Anderson thought the signers may have been illiterate and unaware of what had been written (Anderson, "Joseph Smith's New York Reputation," 286), which seems unlikely .

69. Isaac Hale (1763–1839) was Smith's father-in-law. After serving in the Revolutionary War, he married Elizabeth Lewis in 1789 and moved with her from Vermont to Pennsylvania where they had nine children together. Their minister, George Peck, called Isaac a "mighty hunter" and said he took a large quantity of venison to market each year in Philadelphia (Peck, *Life and Times*, 67–68). The statement Hale prepared for Philastus Hurlbut was postmarked Dec. 22, 1833. When Howe asked for confirmation of its contents on Feb. 4, 1834, Hale took less than a month to respond and have it notarized (*Susquehanna Register,* May 1, 1834; see also *Naked Truths about Mormonism,* Jan. 1888, 2; Hine affidavit in Vogel, *Documents,* 4:188).

70. This was when Smith and others boarded at the Hale home while searching for treasure. Isaac signed on as a supporter, "at first a little deluded about the digging, while he boarded the party," as one historian put it (Emily

who were called "money diggers;" and his occupation was that of seeing, or pretending to see by means of a stone placed in his hat, and his hat closed over his face. In this way he pretended to discover minerals and hidden treasure. His appearance at this time, was that of a careless young man—not very well educated, and very saucy and insolent to his father. Smith, and his father, with several other "money-diggers" boarded at my house while they were employed in digging for a mine that they supposed had been opened and worked by the Spaniards, many years since. Young Smith gave the "money-diggers" great encouragement, at first, but when they had arrived in digging, to near the place where he had stated an immense treasure would be found—he said the enchantment was so powerful that he could not see. They then became discouraged, and soon after dispersed. This took place about the 17th of November, 1825; and one of the company gave me his note for $12.68 for his board, which is still unpaid.

After these occurrences, young Smith made several visits at my house, and at length asked my consent to his marrying my daughter Emma.[71] This I refused, and gave my reasons for so doing; some of which were, that he was a stranger, and followed a business that I could not approve; he then left the

Blackman, *History*, 581; Vogel, *Documents*, 4:395), even committing his name to the Articles of Agreement Josiah Stowell drafted in Nov. 1825 ("Interesting Document," 4; Vogel, *Documents*, 4:407–13). Hale changed his mind when Smith began blaming supernatural forces for the enterprise's failure.

71. According to some accounts, Smith returned to Harmony with Samuel Lawrence in the fall of 1826 so Lawrence could recommend his character to Emma's father (Willard Chase statement, pp. 341–43; Saunders interview, Sept. 17, 1884, 9, 11; Vogel, *Documents*, 2:131, 132).

place. Not long after this, he returned, and while I was absent
from home, carried off my daughter, into the state of New York,
where they were married without my approbation or consent.[72]
After they had arrived at Palmyra N.Y., Emma wrote to me
enquiring whether she could take her property, consisting of
clothing, furniture, cows, &c. I replied that her property was
safe, and at her disposal. In a short time they returned, bringing with them a Peter Ingersol, and subsequently came to the
conclusion that they would move out, and reside upon a place
near my residence.[73]

Smith stated to me, that he had given up what he called
"glass-looking," and that he expected to work hard for a living,
and was willing to do so.[74] He also made arrangements with
my son Alva Hale, to go to Palmyra, and move his (Smith's)
furniture &c. to this place. He then returned to Palmyra, and
soon after, Alva, agreeable to the arrangement, went up and
returned with Smith and his family.[75] Soon after this, I was
informed they had brought a wonderful book of Plates down

---

72. Joseph and Emma probably sneaked away on Jan. 17, 1827, the day
before their marriage and a day of the week, Wednesday, when the Methodist
circuit rider held a prayer meeting at the home of Nathaniel Lewis. Emma's
parents were probably in attendance (Newell and Avery, *Mormon Enigma*,
312n3; cf. Hine affidavit; Vogel, *Documents*, 4:184). The clandestine couple was
married by Squire Tarble, a justice of the peace, in South Bainbridge, New York.
Emma was twenty-two and Joseph twenty-one.

73. According to Ingersoll's account, this took place in Aug. 1827 (p. 329
herein). The "place near my residence" was another house on the Hale property.

74. Peter Ingersoll said the same (p. 330).

75. Lucy Smith mentioned that Alva Hale helped (Smith, *Biographical
Sketches*, 112–14; Vogel, *Documents*, 1:348–51). It was in December 1827 (*History of the Church*, 1:19; Vogel, *Documents*, 1:69–70).

with them. I was shown a box in which it is said they were contained, which had to all appearances, been used as a glass box of the common window glass. I was allowed to feel the weight of the box, and they gave me to understand, that the book of plates was then in the box—into which, however, I was not allowed to look.

I inquired of Joseph Smith Jr., who was to be the first who would be allowed to see the Book of Plates? He said it was a young child.[76] After this, I became dissatisfied, and informed him that if there was any thing in my house of that description, which I could not be allowed to see, he must take it away; if he did not, I was determined to see it. After that, the Plates were said to be hid in the woods.

About this time,[77] Martin Harris made his appearance upon the stage; and Smith began to interpret the characters or hieroglyphics which he said were engraven upon the plates, while Harris wrote down the interpretation. It was said, that Harris wrote down one hundred and sixteen pages, and lost them. Soon after this happened, Martin Harris informed me that he must have a *greater witness*,[78] and said that he had talked with Joseph about it—Joseph informed him that he could not, or durst not show him the plates, but that he (Joseph) would go into the woods where the Book of Plates was, and that after he came back, Harris should follow his track in the snow, and

---

76. See the reports by Joshua McKune and Sophia Lewis (pp. 375–76, 378).

77. April 1828 (*History of the Church*, 1:20; Vogel, *Documents*, 1:71).

78. This occurred about March 1829. In his interview with Joel Tiffany, Martin said Joseph offered to show him the plates but that Martin declined, saying he would wait until "the Lord should do it" (Harris interview with Tiffany, 166; Vogel, *Documents*, 2:306).

find the Book, and examine it for himself. Harris informed me afterwards, that he followed Smith's directions, and could not find the Plates, and was still dissatisfied.

The next day after this happened, I went to the house where Joseph Smith Jr., lived, and where he and Harris were engaged in their translation of the Book. Each of them had a written piece of paper which they were comparing, and some of the words were *"my servant seeketh a greater witness, but no greater witness can be given him."*[79] There was also something said about *"three that were to see the thing"*—meaning I supposed, the Book of Plates, and that *"if the three did not go exactly according to the orders, the thing would be taken from them."* I enquired whose words they were, and was informed by Joseph or Emma, (I rather think it was the former) that they were the words of Jesus Christ. I told them, that I considered the whole of it a delusion, and advised them to abandon it. The manner in which he pretended to read and interpret, was the same as when he looked for the money-diggers, with the stone in his hat, and his hat over his face, while the Book of Plates were at the same time hid in the woods!

After this, Martin Harris went away, and Oliver Cowdery came and wrote for Smith, while he [Smith] interpreted as above described.[80] This is the same Oliver Cowdery, whose name may be found in the Book of Mormon. Cowdery continued a scribe for Smith until the Book of Mormon was completed as I supposed and understood.

---

79. Cf. D&C 5.

80. Cowdery arrived with Samuel Smith on Apr. 5, 1829 (*History of the Church*, 1:32–33; Vogel, *Documents*, 1:74).

Joseph Smith Jr. resided near me for some time after this, and I had a good opportunity of becoming acquainted with him, and somewhat acquainted with his associates, and I conscientiously believe from the facts I have detailed, and from many other circumstances, which I do not deem it necessary to relate, that the whole "Book of Mormon" (so called) is a silly fabrication of falsehood and wickedness, got up for speculation, and with a design to dupe the credulous and unwary—and in order that its fabricators may live upon the spoils of those who swallow the deception.

Isaac Hale.

Affirmed to and subscribed before me, March 20th, 1834.
Charles Dimon, *J. Peace.*

State of Pennsylvania, Susquehana County, ss.

We, the subscribers, associate Judges of the Court of Common Pleas, in and for said county, do certify that we have been many years personally acquainted with Isaac Hale, of Harmony township in this county, who has attested the foregoing statement; and that he is a man of excellent moral character, and of undoubted veracity. Witness our hands.

William Thompson. Davis Dimock.

[TESTIMONY OF NATHANIEL C. LEWIS]
March 21*st,* 1834

Elder Lewis[81] also certifies and affirms in relation to Smith as follows:

---

81. Nathaniel Lewis (1769–1860) formed the first Methodist class in Harmony (Blackman, *History*, 484–85), having moved there from Vermont

I have been acquainted with Joseph Smith Jr. for some time: being a relation of his wife, and residing near him, I have had frequent opportunities of conversation with him, and of knowing his opinions and pursuits. From my standing in the Methodist Episcopal Church, I suppose he was careful how he conducted or expressed himself before me. At one time, however, he came to my house, and asked my advice, whether he should proceed to translate the Book of Plates (referred to by Mr. Hale) or not. He said that God had commanded him to translate it, but he was afraid of the people: he remarked, that he was to exhibit the plates to the world, at a certain time, which was then about eighteen months distant. I told him I was not qualified to give advice in such cases. Smith frequently said to me that I should see the plates at the time appointed.[82]

After the time stipulated, had passed away, Smith being at my house was asked why he did not fulfil his promise, show the Golden Plates and prove himself an honest man? He replied that he, himself was deceived, but that I should see them if I were where they were. I reminded him then, that I stated at the time he made the promise, I was fearful "the enchantment would be so powerful" as to remove the plates, when the time came in which they were to be revealed.

These circumstances and many others of a similar tenor, embolden me to say that Joseph Smith Jr. is not a man of truth

---

with his brother-in-law Isaac Hale in 1791. His statement was published in the *Susquehanna Register*, May 1, 1834.

82. Alva Hale claimed Smith made a similar promise to him (p. 376; also pp. 374, 377).

and veracity; and that his general character in this part of the country, is that of an impostor, hypocrite and liar.

Nathaniel C. Lewis.

Affirmed and subscribed, before me, March 20th, 1834.

Charles Dimon, *J. Peace.*

[TESTIMONY OF FIVE OTHERS]

We subjoin the substance of several affidavits, all taken and made before Charles Dimon Esq. by credible individuals, who have resided near to, and been well acquainted with Joseph Smith Jr.—illustrative of his character and conduct, while in this region.[83]

Joshua M'Kune[84] states, that he "was acquainted with Joseph Smith Jr. and Martin Harris, during their residence in Harmony, Pa., and knew them to be artful seducers;"—That they informed him that "Smith had found a sword, breast-plate, and a pair of spectacles, at the time he found the gold plates"—that these were to be ["]shewn to all the world as evidence of the truth of what was contained in those plates," and that "he (M'Kune) and others should see them at a specified time." He also states that "the time for the exhibition of the Plates, &c. has gone by, and he has not seen them." "Joseph Smith, Jr. told him that (Smith's) first-born child was to translate the characters, and hieroglyphics, upon the Plates into our language at

---

83. In these last five statements, Howe summarizes testimony previously published in the *Susquehanna Register*, May 1, 1834, from Joshua and Hezekiah M'Kune, Alva Hale, and Levi and Sophia Lewis.

84. Joshua McKune moved to Pennsylvania with his father in 1810 and married Esther, a daughter of Nathaniel Lewis.

the age of three years; but this child was not permitted to live to verify the prediction." He also states, that "he has been intimately acquainted with Isaac Hale twenty-four years, and has always found him to be a man of truth, and good morals."

Hezekiah M'Kune[85] states, that "in conversation with Joseph Smith Jr., he (Smith) said he was nearly equal to Jesus Christ; that he was a prophet sent by God to bring in the Jews, and that he was the greatest prophet that had ever arisen."

Alva Hale,[86] son of Isaac Hale, states, that Joseph Smith Jr. told him that ["]his (Smith's) gift in seeing with a stone and hat, was a gift from God," but also states "that Smith told him at another time that this *'peeping'* was all d——d nonsense. He (Smith) was deceived himself but did not intend to deceive others;—that he intended to quit the business, (of peeping) and labor for his livelihood." That afterwards, Smith told him, ["]he should see the Plates from which he translated the book of Mormon," and accordingly at the time specified by Smith, he (Hale) "called to see the plates, but Smith did not show them, but appeared angry." He further states, that he knows Joseph Smith Jr. to be an impostor, and a liar, and knows Martin Harris to be a liar likewise.

Levi Lewis[87] states, that he has "been acquainted with Joseph Smith Jr. and Martin Harris, and that he has heard them both say, adultery was no crime. Harris said he did not

85. Hezekiah McKune (1801–84), Joshua's brother, married a daughter of Nathaniel Lewis as well: Elizabeth Lewis.

86. Alva(h) Hale (1795–1882) is known for having helped his sister and brother-in-law move from New York in December 1827.

87. Levi Lewis was a constable, probably a brother of Elizabeth and Esther Lewis.

blame Smith for his (Smith's) attempt to seduce Eliza Winters &c.;"[88]—Mr. Lewis says that he "knows Smith to be a liar;—that he saw him (Smith) intoxicated at three different times while he was composing the Book of Mormon,[89] and also that he has heard Smith when driving oxen, use language of the greatest profanity. Mr. Lewis also testifies that he heard Smith say he (Smith) was as good as Jesus Christ;—that it was as bad to injure him as it was to injure Jesus Christ." "With regard to the plates, Smith said God had deceived him—which was the reason he (Smith) did not show them."

Sophia Lewis,[90] certifies that she "heard a conversation between Joseph Smith, Jr., and the Rev. James B. Roach,[91] in which Smith called Mr. R. a d——d fool. Smith also said in the same conversation that he (Smith) was as good as Jesus

---

88. Elizabeth Winters Squires (b. 1812) was from New York. She moved to Pennsylvania with her mother in 1825 and, after befriending Emma, was often in the Smith home (Stocker, *Centennial History*, 554; Vogel, *Documents*, 4:40–41). She married Elisha Squires in 1837. Interestingly, she neither confirmed nor denied Lewis's statement, even when the claim was made in a newspaper article or when Howe's book was published. She remained equally silent when she was interviewed in 1880 (Mather, "Early Mormons"; Vogel, *Documents*, 4:345–66; cf. Van Wagoner, *Mormon Polygamy*, 4; Newell and Avery, *Mormon Enigma*, 64).

89. In 1834 Martin Harris was alleged to have said Joseph Smith "drank too much liquor when he was translating the Book of Mormon." Smith's history clarified that Harris's complaint had to do with the time period "previous to the translating of the Book" (*History of the Church*, 2:26; "Kirtland Council Minute Book," 28–29). The Methodists were particularly strict about abstaining from alcohol (Melder, *Beginnings*, 49–61).

90. Sophia Lewis (ca. 1799–?), wife of Levi Lewis, lived in Pennsylvania until about 1843 when she and her family moved to Illinois.

91. This is perhaps the James B. Roach listed in the 1820 census of Bridgewater, Pennsylvania, between sixteen and twenty-six years of age (1820:9).

Christ;" and that she "has frequently heard Smith use profane language.["] She states that she heard Smith say "the Book of Plates could not be opened under penalty of death by any other person but his (Smith's) first-born, which was to be a male." She says she "was present at the birth of this child, and that it was still-born and very much deformed."[92]

---

92. This occurred on June 15, 1828 (see Newel and Avery, *Mormon Enigma*, 314n13).

CHAPTER 18.

It is asserted in the Mormon Bible, that the engravings upon the plates, were in the "Reformed Egyptian." In conformity to this, the Mormonite preachers, and others of the sect, have frequently declared that the engravings upon the plates were, by some of our learned men, who had a specimen shown them, pronounced to be "reformed Egyptian hieroglyphics," or "ancient short hand Egyptian."—Among others, Professor Anthon,[1] of New York, was frequently mentioned as giving such an opinion. This act of deception and falsehood is only one among hundreds of others, equally gross, which are resorted to by these impostors, to gain proselytes. It being calculated to have considerable weight, when fully believed, we took the liberty to inform Mr. Anthon of the vile use that was made of his name, in this country; and to request of him a statement of the facts respecting it. The following is his reply:

New York, Feb. 17, 1834.
Dear Sir—I received this morning your favor of the 9th instant, and lose no time in making a reply. The whole story

1. Charles Anthon (1797–1867) was born in New York City. At age fourteen he entered Columbia College, graduating four years later, then studied law. He began practicing in 1819. However, being gifted in Greek and Latin, he became a professor of classical studies in 1820 at Columbia. He wrote a similar letter to the Reverend Thomas Winthrop Coit seven years later (Anthon to Winthrop, April 3, 1841; Vogel, *Documents*, 4:382–86).

about my having pronounced the Mormonite inscription to be "reformed Egyptian hieroglyphics" is *perfectly false*. Some years ago, a plain, and apparently simple-hearted farmer, called upon me with a note from Dr. Mitchell[2] of our city, now deceased, requesting me to decypher, if possible, a paper, which the farmer would hand me, and which Dr. M. confessed he had been unable to understand. Upon examining the paper in question, I soon came to the conclusion that it was all a trick, perhaps a *hoax*. When I asked the person, who brought it, how he obtained the writing, he gave me, as far as I can now recollect, the following account: A "gold book," consisting of a number of plates of gold, fastened together in the shape of a book by wires of the same metal, had been dug up in the northern part of the state of New York, and along with the book an enormous pair of *"gold spectacles"*! These spectacles were so large, that, if a person attempted to look through them, his two eyes would have to be turned towards *one* of the glasses merely, the spectacles in question being altogether too large for the breadth of the human face. Whoever examined the plates through the spectacles, was enabled not only to *read* them, but fully to *understand* their meaning. All this knowledge, however, was confined at that time to a young man, who had the trunk containing the book and spectacles in his sole possession. This young man was placed behind a curtain,[3] in the garret of a farm house, and, being thus concealed from view, put on

---

2. Samuel L. Mitchell (1764–1831) was born on Long Island. He became a professor of chemistry and natural history at New York College of Physicians and Surgeons in 1808, a professor of botany and pharmaceuticals in 1820, and vice president of Rutgers Medical School in 1826. He was nevertheless well-known for his interest in philology.

3. Harris told the same detail to John A. Clark, *Episcopal Recorder*, Sept. 5, 1840, 94. See Vogel, *Documents*, 2:268.

the spectacles occasionally, or rather, looked through one of the glasses, decyphered the characters in the book, and, having committed some of them to paper, handed copies from behind the curtain, to those who stood on the outside. Not a word, however, was said about the plates having been decyphered "by the gift of God." Every thing, in this way, was effected by the large pair of spectacles. The farmer added, that he had been requested to contribute a sum of money towards the publication of the "golden book," the contents of which would, as he had been assured, produce an entire change in the world and save it from ruin. So urgent had been these solicitations, that he intended selling his farm and handing over the amount received to those who wished to publish the plates. As a last precautionary step, however, he had resolved to come to New York, and obtain the opinion of the learned about the meaning of the paper which he brought with him, and which had been given him as a part of the contents of the book, although no translation had been furnished at the time by the young man with the spectacles.[4] On hearing this odd story, I changed my opinion about the paper, and, instead of viewing it any longer as a hoax upon the learned, I began to regard it as part of a scheme to cheat the farmer of his money, and I communicated my suspicions to him, warning him to beware of rogues. He requested an opinion from me in writing, which of course I declined giving,[5] and he then took his leave carrying the paper

4. This conflicts with Smith's claim that he had translated some of the characters and that Anthon wrote a statement "certifying to the people of Palmyra that they were true characters and that the translation was also correct" (*History of the Church*, 1:20; Vogel, *Documents*, 1:70).

5. Anthon's letter to the Reverend Coit stated that he had no hesitation writing down what he thought of the ruse (Anthon to Coit, April 3, 1841, 231; Vogel, *Documents*, 4:384).

with him. This paper was in fact a singular scrawl. It consisted of all kinds of crooked characters disposed in columns, and had evidently been prepared by some person who had before him at the time a book containing various alphabets. Greek and Hebrew letters, crosses and flourishes, Roman letters inverted or placed sideways, were arranged in perpendicular columns, and the whole ended in a rude delineation of a circle divided into various compartments, decked with various strange marks, and evidently copied after the Mexican Calender given by Humboldt,[6] but copied in such a way as not to betray the source whence it was derived.[7] I am thus particular as to the contents of the paper, inasmuch as I have frequently conversed with my friends on the subject, since the Mormonite excitement began, and well remember that the paper contained any thing else but *"Egyptian Hieroglyphics."* Some time after, the same farmer paid me a second visit.[8] He brought with him the golden book in print, and offered it to me for sale. I declined purchasing. He

---

6. See Humboldt, *Concerning the Institutions & Monuments of the Ancient Inhabitants of America*, plates 23, 49. A more likely model for the circle would have been a magic talisman similar to the ones painted on a parchment the Smith family owned (Quinn, *Early Mormonism*, fig. 50).

7. The Community of Christ Library-Archives in Independence, Missouri, has the small piece of paper David Whitmer said was "the identical specimen which was sent to Prof. Anthon ... by Martin Harris" (*St. Louis Republican*, July 16, 1884, 7). However, the symbols are arranged horizontally rather than vertically or in circles, so there is some question as to whether it is the same scrap of paper. Conceivably Smith created more than one sample of the script. According to Orsamus Turner, an "informant" who had seen the "manuscript title page" said it contained "concentric circles, between above and below which were characters" similar to hieroglyphics (Turner, *History*, 215; Vogel, *Documents*, 3:52).

8. The date and circumstances of Harris's second visit to Anthon are unknown.

then asked permission to leave the book with me for examination. I declined receiving it, although his manner was strangely urgent. I adverted once more to the roguery which had been in my opinion practised upon him, and asked him what had become of the gold plates. He informed me that they were in a trunk with the large pair of spectacles. I advised him to go to a magistrate and have the trunk examined. He said the "curse of God" would come upon him should he do this. On my pressing him, however, to pursue the course which I had recommended, he told me that he would open the trunk, if I would take the "curse of God" upon myself. I replied that I would do so with the greatest willingness, and would incur every risk of that nature, provided I could only extricate him from the grasp of rogues. He then left me.

I have thus given you a full statement of all that I know respecting the origin of Mormonism, and must beg you, as a personal favor, to publish this letter immediately, should you find my name mentioned again by these wretched fanatics. Yours respectfully,

Chas. Anthon.

E. D. Howe, Esq. Painesville, Ohio.

That the impostors made the declarations respecting Professor Anthon, they will undoubtedly deny, as this is their uniform practice, after being fully convinced of any act which militates against them; but in this case it will be in vain. The following letter from Wm. W. Phelps, a very important personage among them,[9] (who was for a time denominated the Lord's printer) in answer to some enquiries touching the origin

---

9. At the time he wrote the letter, Phelps was still five months away from Mormon baptism.

of Mormonism, will show what was taught him while a pupil under Smith and Rigdon, and that the story about Mr. Anthon's declarations, was one upon which they placed great reliance. We give the letter in full, for the purpose of further comments:

Canandaigua, Jan. 15, 1831.

Dear Sir—Yours of the 11th, is before me, but to give you a satisfactory answer, is out of my power. To be sure, I am acquainted with a number of the persons concerned in the publication, called the *"Book of Mormon."*—Joseph Smith is a person of very limited abilities in common learning—but his knowledge of *divine things,* since the appearance of his book, has astonished many. Mr. Harris, whose name is in the book, is a wealthy farmer, but of small literary acquirements; he is honest, and sincerely declares upon his soul's salvation that the book is true, and was interpreted by Joseph Smith, through a pair of silver spectacles, found with the plates. The places where they dug for the plates, in Manchester, are to be seen. When the plates were said to have been found, a copy of one or two lines of the characters, were taken by Mr. Harris to Utica, Albany and New York; at New York,[10] they were shown to Dr. Mitchell, and he referred to professor Anthon who translated and declared them to be the ancient shorthand Egyptian. So much is true. The family of Smiths is poor, and generally ignorant in common learning.

I have read the book, and many others have, but we have nothing by which we can positively detect it as an imposition, nor have we any thing more than what I have stated and the

---

10. John H. Gilbert mentioned Harris visiting Lt. Governor Luther Bradish in Albany (Gilbert, "Memorandum," 4; Vogel, *Documents,* 2:546–47), but Phelps is alone in naming Utica as a stop on Harris's trip.

book itself, to show its genuineness. We doubt—supposing, if it is false, it will fall, and if of God, God will sustain it.

I had ten hours discourse with a man from your state, named Sidney Rigdon, a convert to its doctrines, and he declared it was true, and he knew it by the power of the Holy Ghost, which was again given to man in preparation for the millennium: he appeared to be a man of talents, and sincere in his profession. Should any new light be shed on the subject, I will apprise you. Respectfully,

W. W. Phelps.

E. D. Howe, Esq.

The author of the above letter is, perhaps, deserving of a little more notice. Before the rise of Mormonism, he was an avowed infidel; having remarkable propensity for fame and eminence, he was supercilious, haughty and egotistical. His great ambition was to embark in some speculation where he could shine pre-eminent. He took an active part for several years in the political contests of New York,[11] and made no little display as an editor of a partizan newspaper, and after being foiled in his desires to become a candidate for Lt. Governor of that state, his attention was suddenly diverted by the prospects which were held out to him in the Gold Bible speculation. In this he was sure of becoming a great man, and made the dupes believe he was master of fourteen different languages,[12] of which they frequently boasted. But he soon found that the prophet would suffer no growing rivalships, whose sagacity [Smith's] he had

---

11. As an anti-Mason, Phelps was opposed to any Freemason holding public office.

12. Phelps liked to sprinkle his editorials with phrases from various languages, mostly simple aphorisms.

not well calculated, until he was met by a revelation, which informed him that he could rise no higher than a printer: "Let my servant William stand in the office which I have appointed him, and receive his inheritance in the land, and also he hath need to repent, for I the Lord [Jo] am not pleased with him, for he seeketh to *exult.*" It will be noticed by the foregoing letter, that he had already made up his mind to embrace Mormonism, but still wished to conceal his intentions. It was not till about six months after that he had made definite arrangements to join them; by first fully understanding what his business was to be. After being created an Elder and Lord's printer, he repaired to Missouri with the squad that first went out, and on his return called on us to "acknowledge his gratitude," as he expressed it, for first directing his attention to Mormonism, saying that he knew nothing about it, till the receipt of our letter—that he then commenced an investigation of the subject, "and found it to be true"! stating that he had made great sacrifices, and abandoned a business worth $2500 a year. We mention these things to show the hypocrisy of the man.

His letter it will be seen is dated the 15th Jan. in answer to ours of the 11th, only *four* days intervening. During these four days, then, our letter must have traveled over 300 miles, he talked with Rigdon *ten* hours, examined the holes where Smith had dug for money, and obtained all the other information which he communicates. Besides it is a well known fact that, notwithstanding his large income, he had been thrown into jail[13] on a small debt, and offered to sell out his printing

---

13. Phelps later wrote that he was "thrown into prison at Lyons, N.Y. by a couple of Presbyterian traders, for a small debt, for the purpose, as I was informed,

establishment for *one hundred and fifty dollars*. For his *honesty*, however, the prophet has left him to till the soil in Missouri, while the business of printing has been transferred to Kirtland, Ohio, and placed under the direction of O. Cowdery.

REMARKABLE EVENTS—THE CUT.[14]

The reader will already have observed, that a great variety of contradictory stories were related by the Smith family, before they had any fixed plan of operation, respecting the finding of the plates, from which their book was translated. One is, that after the plates were taken from their hiding place by Jo, he again laid them down, looked into the hole, where he saw a *toad*,[15] which immediately transformed itself into a spirit, and gave him a tremendous blow. Another is, that after he had got the plates, a spirit assaulted him with the intention of getting them from his possession, and actually jerked them out of his hands—Jo, nothing daunted, in return seized them again, and started to run, when his Satanic Majesty, (or the spirit) applied his foot to the prophet's seat of honor, which raised him three or four feet from the ground.[16] This being the opening scene of

---

of 'keeping me from joining the Mormons'" (*Messenger and Advocate*, April 1835, 97). In a letter from jail on Apr. 30, 1831, Phelps blamed his arrest on "members of the [Presbyterian] church and *pretended* anti-masons" who "obtained a judgment against me, on a balance of their account." His letter was published in the *Geneva Gazette*, May 11, and *Wayne Sentinel* two days later.

14. The reference here is to the two-panel woodcut used as the frontispiece in Howe's book. This section of chapter 18 is an extended caption to the illustration.

15. See p. 340; Vogel, *Documents*, 2:67.

16. Philastus Hurlbut's attorney for the 1833–34 court case, James A. Briggs, remembered that Smith testified to being "kicked by the Devil when

Mormonism, we have represented the wonderful event in our frontispiece. That the prophet has related a story of this kind, to some of his "weak saints," we have no manner of doubt.

Here, then, is the finding of the plates, containing a new revelation from Heaven; and the *modus operandi* may seem to the Mormon, truly wonderful, and in character with that Being who upholds and sustains the Universe; but to the rational mind it can excite no other emotion than contempt for his species.

One scene in the drama of disposing of the plates, we have also placed upon the same cut—being two of the most important events in the history of Mormonism. The latter story was related by *Lemon Copley*,[17] (who had been an elder of the society, and was at the time for aught that appeared [to the contrary]) under oath, before two magistrates, of Painesville Township, on a trial where the prophet had sworn the peace against one of his seceding brethren.[18]

Mr. Copley testified, that after the Mormon brethren

---

he uncovered the plates and stooped down to get them" (*International Review*, Sept. 1881; Vogel, *Documents*, 1:206).

17. Leman Copley (1781–1862) was born in Connecticut. He joined a Shaker community near Cleveland about 1820, which prepared him to preach to other Shakers in 1831 after he became a Mormon (D&C 49). Despite his proselyting zeal as a Mormon, he was disfellowshipped before the year was out, restored to fellowship in late 1832, and ejected again for testifying against Joseph Smith in court. He was readmitted in 1836. Smith's history explains for April 1 that Copley "confessed that he bore a false testimony against me [Smith] in that suit, but verily thought, at the time, that he was right, but on calling to mind all the circumstances connected with the things that happened at that time, he was convinced that he was wrong, and humbly confessed it, and asked my forgiveness, which was readily granted" (*History of the Church*, 2:433; Jessee et al., *Joseph Smith Papers: Journals*, 1:216).

18. Joseph Smith feared that Philastus Hurlbut, a former adherent,

arrived here from the Susquehannah, one of them, by the name of Joseph Knight,[19] related to him a story as having been related to him by Joseph Smith, Jun. which excited some curiosity in his mind, [and] he determined to ask Joseph more particularly about it, on the first opportunity. Not long after it was confirmed to him by Joseph himself, who again related it in the following manner: "After he had finished translating the Book of Mormon, he again buried up the plates in the side of a mountain, by command of the Lord;[20] some time after this, he was going through a piece of woods, on a by-path, when he discovered an old man dressed in ordinary gray apparel, sitting upon a log, having in his hand or near by, a small box. On approaching him, he asked him what he had in his box. To which the old man replied, that he had a monkey, and for five coppers

---

"would beat or kill him," in response to which the court asked Hurlbut for $200 in bail (*Ohio v. Dr. P. Hurlbut*).

19. Joseph Knight Sr. (1772–1847) was born in Massachusetts. In 1809 he moved to Bainbridge, about a hundred miles west of Albany, then to neighboring Colesville in 1811. At Colesville he acquired a farm and gristmill on the Susquehanna River. Undoubtedly he became acquainted with Joseph Smith through one of Bainbridge's prominent citizens, Josiah Stowell, who hired Smith to dig for buried treasure. In the fall of 1826, Smith was hired by Knight as a mill worker and occasional treasure seer. Following Smith's elopement with Emma Hale, Knight conveyed them to Manchester, New York; he was visiting the family again in September 1827 when Smith is said to have extracted the plates from the hill. Knight was baptized in late June 1830 in Colesville and died in Iowa during the trek west.

20. William Smith said his brother was directed to bury the plates "in the same manner" he had found them (*Congregational Observer*, July 3, 1841, 1; Vogel, *Documents*, 1:479). Peter Bauder was told Smith took them into the woods near Fayette and gave them back to the angel (Bauder, *Kingdom and Gospel*, 37; Vogel, *Documents*, 1:17).

he might see it. Joseph answered, that he would not give a cent to see a monkey, for he had seen a hundred of them. He then asked the old man where he was going, who said he was going to *Charzee.* Joseph then passed on, and not recollecting any such place in that part of the country, began to ponder over the strange interview, and finally asked the Lord the meaning of it. The Lord told him that the man he saw was Moroni, with the plates, and if he had given him the five coppers, he might have got his plates again."

Here we have a story related by our modern prophet, to his followers, for no other purpose, as we conceive, but to make his pretensions more "marvelous in their eyes." A celebrated Mormon prophet, of ancient times, and one of modern date, have an interview in the woods, and hold a conversation about a monkey; one prophet of the Lord relating a falsehood to another!!!

CHAPTER 19.

We proposed in the commencement of this work, to give to the world all the light, of which we were in possession, as to the real and original author or authors of the Book of Mormon. That there has been, from the beginning of the imposture, a more talented knave behind the curtain, is evident to our mind, at least;[1] but whether he will ever be clearly, fully and positively *unvailed* and brought into open day-light, may of course be doubted. For no person of common prudence and understanding, it may well be presumed, would ever undertake such a speculation upon human credulity, without closing and well securing every door and avenue to a discovery, step by step, as he proceeded. Hence, our investigations upon the subject have necessarily been more limited than was desirable. At the same time, we think that facts and data have been elicited, sufficient at least to raise a strong presumption that the leading features of the "Gold Bible" were first conceived and concocted by one Solomon Spalding,[2] while a resident of Conneaut, Ashtabula county, Ohio. It is admitted by our soundest jurists, that a train of circumstances may often lead the mind to a more satisfactory

---

1. Notice the unexpected, veiled compliment to the Book of Mormon. It reflects the incorrect assumption of many in Smith's day that he was illiterate and therefore incapable of writing the Book of Mormon.

2. See addendum 1, "Solomon Spalding as Plagiarized Author," at the end of this chapter.

and unerring conclusion, than positive testimony, unsupported by circumstancial evidence—for the plain reason, that the one species of testimony is more prone to falsehood than the other. But we proceed with our testimony.

The first witness is Mr. *John Spalding*, a brother of Solomon, now a resident of Crawford county, Pa. who says:

> Solomon Spalding was born in Ashford, Conn. in 1761, and in early life contracted a taste for literary pursuits. After he left [elementary] school, he entered Plainfield Academy, where he made great proficiency in study, and excelled most of his class-mates. He next commenced the study of Law, in Windham county, in which he made little progress, having in the mean time turned his attention to religious subjects. He soon after entered Dartmouth College, with the intention of qualifying himself for the ministry, where he obtained the [master's] degree of A. M. and was afterwards regularly ordained. After preaching three or four years, he gave it up, removed to Cherry Valley, N. Y, and commenced the mercantile business in company with his brother Josiah.—In a few years he failed in business, and in the year 1809 removed to Conneaut, in Ohio. The year following, I removed to Ohio, and found him engaged in building a forge. I made him a visit in about three years after; and found that he had failed, and considerably involved in debt. He then told me had he been writing a book, which he intended to have printed, the avails of which he thought would enable him to pay all his debts. The book was entitled the "Manuscript Found," of which he read to me many passages.—It was an historical romance of the first settlers of America, endeavoring to show that the American Indians are the descendants of the Jews, or the lost tribes. It

gave a detailed account of their journey from Jerusalem,[3] by land and sea, till they arrived in America, under the command of Nephi and Lehi.[4] They afterwards had quarrels and contentions, and separated into two distinct nations, one of which he denominated Nephites and the other Lamanites.[5] Cruel and bloody wars ensued, in which great multitudes were slain. They buried their dead in large heaps, which caused the mounds so common in this country. Their arts, sciences and civilization were brought into view, in order to account for all the curious antiquities, found in various parts of North and South America. I have recently read the Book of Mormon, and to my great surprize I find nearly the same historical matter, names, &c.

---

3. This claim is repeated by three others in this chapter, sometimes as shorthand for the theory that Indians were descended from the lost tribes of Israel, an idea that was popular in Joseph Smith's day and that many people read into the Book of Mormon. The theory was derived from 2 Esdras 13:40–41, where ten tribes "go forth into a further country, where never mankind dwelt." Modern readers assumed the uninhabited country was America, but neither the Book of Mormon nor the Spalding manuscript made that claim. Spalding offered no explanation for Indian origins, saying only that they were discovered by Roman sailors. Hurlbut's witnesses were apparently influenced by the popular misconception about the Book of Mormon's contents.

4. Several of Spalding's friends and relatives claimed he invented these Book of Mormon names, but they are not in his manuscript. He has other invented names in his novel; that his neighbors only remembered the ones they had recently read in the Book of Mormon suggests their twenty-year-old memories were contaminated by the recent engagement with the Mormon scripture and by their discussions with one another.

5. Both the Oberlin document and the Book of Mormon describe wars between a light-skinned race and the Indians, drawing perhaps on the prevailing assumption that the burial mounds in the Great Lakes area were constructed by an extinct race, the so-called Mound Builders. That was the assumption of Ethan Smith's 1825 *View of the Hebrews; or the Tribes of Israel in America* (see discussion in Vogel, *Indian Origins*, 35–69).

as they were in my brother's writings. I well remember that he wrote in the old style, and commenced about every sentence with "and it came to pass,"[6] or "now it came to pass," the same as in the Book of Mormon, and according to the best of my recollection and belief, it is the same as my brother Solomon wrote, with the exception of the religious matter.—By what means it has fallen into the hands of Joseph Smith, Jr. I am unable to determine.

John Spalding.

Martha Spalding, the wife of John Spalding, says:—

I was personally acquainted with Solomon Spalding, about twenty years ago. I was at his house a short time before he left Conneaut; he was then writing a historical novel founded upon the first settlers of America. He represented them as an enlightened and warlike people. He had for many years contended that the aborigines of America were the descendants of some of the lost tribes of Israel, and this idea he carried out in the book in question.—The lapse of time which has intervened, prevents my recollecting but few of the leading incidents of his writings; but the names of Nephi and Lehi are yet fresh in my memory,[7] as being the principal heroes of his tale. They were officers of the company which first came off from Jerusalem. He gave a particular account of their journey by land and sea,

---

6. The phrase does not appear in the Oberlin manuscript, but it occurs over 300 times in the Old Testament.

7. Lester E. Bush concluded that we might charitably assume a similarity between Moonrod/Moroni, Mammoon/Mormon, Lamesa (wooly mammoth)/Laman, and Hamelick/Amelickiah, but most names (Bombal, Chianga, Hamboon, Lobasko, Ulipoon) are not remotely connected to those from the Book of Mormon (Bush, "Spalding Theory Then and Now," 42–43).

till they arrived in America, after which, disputes arose between the chiefs, which caused them to separate into different
lands, one [group] of which was called Lamanites and the other
Nephites. Between these were recounted tremendous battles,
which frequently covered the ground with the slain; and their
being buried in large heaps was the cause of the numerous
mounds in the country.—Some of these people he represented
as being very large.[8] I have read the Book of Mormon, which
has brought fresh to my recollection the writings of Solomon
Spalding; and I have no manner of doubt that the historical
part of it, is the same that I read and heard read, more than
20 years ago. The old, obsolete style, and the phrases of "and it
came to pass," &c. are the same.

Martha Spalding.

We would here remark by the way, that it would appear
that Sol. Spalding, like many other authors, was somewhat vain
of his writing, and was constantly showing and reading them
to his neighbors. In this way most of his intimate acquaintances became conversant at that time with his writings and
designs. We might therefore introduce a great number of witnesses all testifying to the same general facts; but we have not
taken the trouble to procure the statements of but few, all of
whom are the most respectable men, and highly esteemed for
their moral worth, and their characters for truth and veracity,

---

8. The claim that the Mound Builders were near giants was common (see
Vogel, *Indian Origins*, 18, 139). Their assumed connection to mammoths may
be why they became enlarged in folk tales, "taller on average than" Europeans,
according to Spalding. The Book of Mormon implies that the Jaredites were
also large and that some individuals among the Nephites were tall enough to
merit comment (Mosiah 8:10; 1 Ne. 2:16; Mormon 2:1).

are unimpeachable. In fact, the word of any one of them, would have more weight in any respectable community, than the whole family of Smiths and Whitmers, who have told about hearing the voice of an angel.

Conneaut, Ashtabula Co. O[hio]. September, 1833.

I left the state of New York, late in the year 1810, and arrived at this place, about the 1st of Jan. following. Soon after my arrival, I formed a co-partnership with Solomon Spalding, for the purpose of re-building a forge which he had commenced a year or two before. He very frequently read to me from a manuscript which he was writing, which he entitled the "Manuscript Found," and which he represented as being found in this town. I spent many hours in hearing him read said writings, and became well acquainted with its contents. He wished me to assist him in getting his production printed, alleging that a book of that kind would meet with a rapid sale. I designed doing so, but the forge not meeting our anticipations, we failed in business, when I declined having any thing to do with the publication of the book. This book represented the American Indians as the descendants of the lost tribes, gave an account of their leaving Jerusalem, their contentions and wars, which were many and great. One time, when he was reading to me the tragic account of Laban, I pointed out to him what I considered an inconsistency, which he promised to correct; but by referring to the Book of Mormon, I find to my surprise that it stands there just as he read it to me then.[9]— Some months ago I borrowed the Golden Bible, put it into my pocket, carried

___

9. The reference to the story of Laban is suspicious since it was rewritten for the Book of Mormon after Martin Harris lost the 116-page transcript. The replacement changed the narrative from third-person to first-person and the emphasis from historical/political to religious.

it home, and thought no more of it.—About a week after, my wife found the book in my coat pocket, as it hung up, and commenced reading it aloud as I lay upon the bed. She had not read 20 minutes till I was astonished to find the same passages in it that Spalding had read to me more than twenty years before, from his "Manuscript Found." Since that, I have more fully examined the said Golden Bible, and have no hesitation in saying that the historical part of it is principally, if not wholly taken from the "Manuscript Found." I well recollect telling Mr. Spalding, that the so frequent use of the words "And it came to pass," "Now it came to pass," rendered it ridiculous. Spalding left here in 1812, and I furnished him the means to carry him to Pittsburgh, where he said he would get the book printed, and pay me. But I never heard any more from him or his writings, till I saw them in the Book of Mormon.

Henry Lake.

Springfield, Pa. September, 1833.

In the year 1811, I was in the employ of Henry Lake and Solomon Spalding, at Conneaut, engaged in rebuilding a forge. While there, I boarded and lodged in the family of said Spalding, for several months. I was soon introduced to the manuscript of Spalding, and perused them as often as I had leisure. He had written two or three books or pamphlets on different subjects;[10] but that which more particularly drew my attention, was one which he called the "Manuscript Found." From this he would frequently read some humorous passages[11] to the company present. It purported to be the history of the first settlement of America, before discovered by Columbus.

---

10. Spalding is also thought to have written "Romance of the Celes[tials]: Or the Florentine Heroes and the Three Female Knights of the Chasm."

11. There is nothing intentionally humorous in the Book of Mormon.

He brought them off from Jerusalem, under their leaders; detailing their travels by land and water, their manners, customs, laws, wars, &c. He said that he designed it as a historical novel, and that in after years it would be believed by many people as much as the history of England. He soon after failed in business, and told me he should retire from the din of his creditors, finish his book and have it published, which would enable him to pay his debts and support his family. He soon after removed to Pittsburgh, as I understood.

I have recently examined the Book of Mormon, and find in it the writings of Solomon Spalding, from beginning to end, but mixed up with scripture and other religious matter, which I did not meet with in the "Manuscript Found." Many of the passages in the Mormon Book are verbatim from Spalding, and others in part. The names of Nephi, Lehi, Moroni, and in fact all the principal names, are bro't fresh to my recollection, by the Gold Bible. When Spalding divested his history of its fabulous names, by a verbal explanation, he landed his people near the Straits of Darien, which I am very confident he called *Zarahemla*, they were marched about that country for a length of time, in which wars and great blood shed ensued, he brought them across North America in a north east direction.[12]

John N. Miller.

Conneaut, August, 1833.

I first became acquainted with Solomon Spalding in 1808 or 9, when he commenced building a forge on Conneaut creek. When at his house, one day, he showed and read to me a history

---

12. Neither Spalding's Romans nor the Book of Mormon Lehites land near the Darien Gap (Panama). Lehi lands south of Zarahemla, considerably south of the "narrow neck of land." Spalding's tale lacks a northeastern migration.

he was writing, of the lost tribes of Israel, purporting that they were the first settlers of America, and that the Indians were their decendants. Upon this subject we had frequent conversations. He traced their journey from Jerusalem to America, as it is given in the Book of Mormon, excepting the religious matter. The historical part of the Book of Mormon, I know to be the same as I read and heard read from the writings of Spalding, more than twenty years ago; the names more especially are the same without any alteration. He told me his object was to account for all the fortifications, &c. to be found in this country, and said that in time it would be fully believed by all, except learned men and historians. I once anticipated reading his writings in print, but little expected to see them in a new Bible. Spalding had many other manuscripts, which I expect to see when Smith translates his other plate. In conclusion, I will observe, that the names of, and most of the historical part of the Book of Mormon, were as familiar to me before I read it, as most modern history. If it is not Spalding's writing, it is the same as he wrote; and if Smith was inspired, I think it was by the same spirit that Spalding was, which he confessed to be the love of money.

Aaron Wright.

Conneaut, August, 1833.

When Solomon Spalding first came to this place, he purchased a tract of land, surveyed it out and commenced selling it. While engaged in this business, he boarded at my house, in all nearly six months. All his leisure hours were occupied in writing a historical novel, founded upon the first settlers of this country. He said he intended to trace their journey from Jerusalem, by land and sea, till their arrival in America, give an account of their arts, sciences, civilization, wars and contentions. In this way, he would give a satisfactory account of all of the old mounds, so common to this country. During the time he was at my house, I read and heard read one hundred pages or more. Nephi and Lehi were by him represented as leading characters, when they first started for America. Their main object was to escape the judgments which they supposed were coming upon the old world. But no religious matter was introduced, as I now recollect. Just before he left this place, Spalding sent for me to call on him, which I did.— He then said, that although he was in my debt, he intended to leave the country, and hoped I would not prevent him, for, says he, you know I have been writing the history of the first settlement of America, and I intend to go to Pittsburgh, and there live a retired life, till I have completed the work, and when it is printed, it will bring me a fine sum of money, which will enable me to return and pay off all my debts—the book, you know will sell, as every one is anxious to learn something upon that subject. This was the last I heard of Spalding or his book, until the Book of Mormon came into the neighborhood. When I heard the historical part of it related, I at once said it was the writings of old Solomon Spalding. Soon after, I obtained the book, and on reading it, found much of it the same as Spalding had written, more than twenty years before.

Oliver Smith.

Conneaut, August, 1833.

I first became acquainted with Solomon Spalding, in Dec. 1810. After that time I frequently saw him at his house, and also at my house. I once in conversation with him expressed a surprise at not having any account of the inhabitants once in this country, who erected the old forts, mounds, &c. He then told me that he was writing a history of that race of people; and afterwards frequently showed me his writings, which I read. I have lately read the Book of Mormon, and believe it to be the same as Spalding wrote, except the religious part. He told me that he intended to get his writings published in Pittsburgh, and he thought that in one century from that time, it would be believed as much as any other history.

Nahum Howard.

Artemas Cunningham, of Perry, Geauga county, states as follows:

In the month of October, 1811, I went from the township of Madison to Conneaut, for the purpose of securing a debt due me from Solomon Spalding. I tarried with him nearly two days, for the purpose of accomplishing my object, which I was finally unable to do. I found him destitute of the means of paying his debts. His only hope of ever paying his debts, appeared to be upon the sale of a book, which he had been writing. He endeavored to convince me from the nature and character of the work, that it would meet with a ready sale. Before showing me his manuscripts, he went into a verbal relation of its outlines, saying that it was a fabulous or romantic history of the first settlement of this country, and as it purported to have been a record found buried in the earth, or in a cave, he had adopted the ancient or scripture style of writing.[13] He

---

13. The language of the Oberlin manuscript is not Elizabethan. As for the hill where Spalding finds a chamber containing a stone box with scrolls concealed by a flat stone with engravings on it, the story sounds like an 1820 account of an explorer to the same hill who found the burial place for a race of people who were ironically "of small stature" (Atwater, "Description," 124). Irish traveler Thomas Ashe discovered a stone vault containing an unusually large skeleton and engraved brass rings near Marietta, Ohio,

then presented his manuscripts, when we sat down and spent a
good share of the night, in reading them, and conversing upon
them. I well remember the name of Nephi, which appeared
to be the principal hero of the story. The frequent repetition
of the phrase, "I Nephi,"[14] I recollect as distinctly as though it
was but yesterday, although the general features of the story
have passed from my memory, through the lapse of 22 years.
He attempted to account for the numerous antiquities which
are found upon this continent, and remarked that, after this
generation had passed away, his account of the first inhabitants
of America would be considered as authentic as any other history. The Mormon Bible I have partially examined, and am
fully of the opinion that Solomon Spalding had written its
outlines before he left Conneaut.

[Artemas Cunningham]

Statements of the same import, might be multiplied to
an indefinite length; but we deem it unnecessary. We are here
willing to rest the question, in the hands of any intelligent
jury, with a certainty that their verdict would be, that Solomon Spalding first wrote the leading incidents of the Book of
Mormon, instead of its being found by the Smith family, while
digging for gold, and its contents afterwards made known by
the Supreme Being.

But our enquiries did not terminate here. Our next object
was to ascertain, if possible, the disposition Spalding made of

---

with an entrance at the top of the mound, concealed by a large stone (Ashe,
Travels, 1:308–18).

14. This claim is highly unlikely in light of Smith's replacement of the
dictation Harris lost with Nephi's first-person narrative.

his manuscripts. For this purpose, a messenger [Hurlbut] was despatched to look up the widow of Spalding, who was found residing in Massachusetts.[15] From her we learned that Spalding resided in Pittsburgh, about two years, when he removed to the township of Amity, Washington Co. Pa. where he lived about two years, and died in 1816. His widow then removed to Onondaga county, N. Y., married again, and lived in Otsego county, and subsequently removed to Massachusetts. She states that Spalding had a great variety of manuscripts, and recollects that one was entitled the "Manuscript Found," but of its contents she has now no distinct knowledge.[16] While they lived in Pittsburgh, she thinks it was once taken to the printing office of *Patterson & Lambdin*;[17] but whether it was ever brought back to the house again, she is quite uncertain: if it was, however, it was then with his other writings, in a trunk which she had left in Otsego county, N.Y.[18] This is all the information that could be obtained from her, except that Mr. Spalding, while living, entertained a strong antipathy to the Masonic Institution, which may account for its being so frequently mentioned

---

15. Matilda Spalding Davison was then living in Massachusetts.

16. In 1839, Matilda Spalding remembered her husband having written "in the most ancient style, and as the Old Testament is the most ancient book in the world, he imitated its style as nearly as possible" (*Boston Recorder,* Apr. 1839, cited in Roberts, *Defense,* 2:144). In an interview conducted that same year, she added that she thought a "few names are alike" (*Times and Seasons,* Jan. 1840, 47). As memories normally fade, we need to be skeptical of recollections that improve over time.

17. Robert Patterson and J. Harrison Lambdin became business partners in 1818, two years after Spalding's death (Roberts, *Defense,* 2:37–38).

18. The trunk was in the possession of Matilda's cousin Jerome Clark in Hartwick, New York.

in the Book of Mormon. The fact also, that Spalding, in the latter part of his life, inclined to infidelity, is established by a letter in his hand-writing, now in our possession.[19]

The trunk referred to by the widow, was subsequently examined, and found to contain only a single M.S. [manuscript] book, in Spalding's hand-writing, containing about one quire of paper [25 sheets]. This is a romance, purporting to have been translated from the Latin, found on 24 rolls of parchment in a cave, on the banks of Conneaut Creek, but written in modern style, and giving a fabulous account of a ship's being driven upon the American coast, while proceeding from Rome to Britain, a short time previous to the Christian era, this country then being inhabited by the Indians. This old M.S. has been shown to several of the foregoing witnesses, who recognise it as Spalding's, he having told them that he had altered his first plan of writing, by going farther back with dates, and writing in the old scripture style, in order that it might appear more ancient. They say that it bears no resemblance to the "*Manuscript Found.*"

Here, then, our enquiries after facts partially cease, on this subject. We have fully shown that the Book of Mormon is the joint production of Solomon Spalding and some other designing knave, or if it is what it purports to be, the Lord God has graciously condescended, in revealing to Smith his will, through spectacles, to place before him and appropriate

---

19. Howe means to insinuate religious disbelief rather than marital disloyalty (see *American Dictionary of the English Language*, 1828). However, if Spalding was an infidel, one would not expect him to write in support of a biblical origin of Native Americans. The Oberlin manuscript, with its tale of pagan Romans in America, is more in line with what one would expect of an unbeliever.

to his own use, the writings and names of men which had been invented by a person long before in the grave. Having established the fact, therefore, that most of the names and leading incidents contained in the Mormon bible, originated with Solomon Spalding, it is not very material, as we conceive, to show the way and manner by which they fell into the hands of the Smith family. To do this, however, we have made some enquiries.

It was inferred at once that some light might be shed upon this subject, and the mystery revealed, by applying to Patterson & Lambdin, in Pittsburgh. But here again death had interposed a barrier. That establishment was dissolved and broken up many years since, and Lambdin died about eight years ago. Mr. Patterson says he has no recollection of any such manuscript being brought there for publication, neither would he have been likely to have seen it, as the business of printing was conducted wholly by Lambdin at that time. He says, however, that many M.S. books and pamphlets were brought to the office about that time, which remained upon their shelves for years, without being printed or even examined. Now, as Spalding's book can no where be found, or any thing heard of it after being carried to this establishment, there is the strongest presumption that it remained there in seclusion, till about the year 1823 or '24, at which time *Sidney Rigdon* located himself in that city.[20] We have been credibly informed that he was

---

20. Rigdon began as pastor of the First Baptist Church of Pittsburgh on January 28, 1822, and was dismissed for doctrinal differences on Oct. 11 the following year. He remained in the area, working as a tanner, until his move to Bainbridge, Ohio, in Dec. 1825 (see Van Wagoner, *Sidney Rigdon*, 28, 34, 39).

on terms of intimacy with Lambdin, being seen frequently in his shop. Rigdon resided in Pittsburgh about three years, and during the whole of that time, as he has since frequently asserted, abandoned preaching and all other employment, for the purpose of *studying the bible*. He left there and came into the county where he now resides, about the time Lambdin died, and commenced preaching some new points of doctrine, which were afterwards found to be inculcated in the Mormon Bible.[21] He resided in this vicinity about four years previous to the appearance of the book, during which time he made several long visits to Pittsburgh, and perhaps to the Susquehannah, where Smith was then digging for money, or pretending to be translating plates.[22] It may be observed also, that about the time Rigdon left Pittsburgh, the Smith family began to tell about finding a book that would contain a history of the first inhabitants of America, and that two years elapsed before they finally got possession of it.[23]

---

21. Rigdon's beliefs were not unique. Many in Europe and America in the nineteenth century were seeking a radical reformation to restore the simplicity of original Christianity, not only in ecclesiastical organization and form of worship but also in the enjoyment of miracles and spiritual gifts (see Vogel, *Religious Seekers*, 41).

22. See addendum 2, "Alleged Smith-Rigdon Connection," following this chapter.

23. This, of course, is incorrect. Rigdon left Pittsburgh in 1825–26. Lucy Smith reported that Joseph began talking about the plates in 1823 before Alvin's death and that his recitals included discussions about "the ancient inhabitants of this continent" (Smith, *Biographical Sketches*, 85; Vogel, *Documents*, 1:296). Willard Chase remembered Samuel Lawrence saying that he and Smith visited the hill in 1825 and saw the plates through their seer stones (see pp. 341–42 herein; Vogel, *Documents*, 2:68).

We are, then, irresistibly led to this conclusion:—that Lambdin, after having failed in business, had recourse to the old manuscripts then in his possession, in order to *raise the wind*, by a book speculation, and placed the "Manuscript Found," of Spalding, in the hands of Rigdon, to be embellished, altered, and added to, as he might think expedient; and three years' study of the bible we should deem little time enough to garble it, as it is transferred to the Mormon book. The former dying, left the latter the sole proprietor, who was obliged to resort to his wits, and in a mir[a]culous way to bring it before the world; for in no other manner could such a book be published without great sacrifice. And where could a more suitable character be found than Jo Smith, whose necromantic fame and arts of deception, had already extended to a considerable distance? That Lambdin was a person every way qualified and fitted for such an enterprise, we have the testimony of his partner in business, and others of his acquaintance. Add to all these circumstances, the facts, that Rigdon had prepared the minds in a great measure, of nearly a hundred of those who had attended his ministration to be in readiness to embrace the first mysterious *ism* that should be presented—the appearance of Cowdery at his residence as soon as the Book was printed—his sudden conversion, after many pretentions to disbelieve it—his immediately repairing to the residence of Smith, 300 miles distant, where he was forthwith appointed an elder, high priest, and a scribe to the prophet—the pretended vision that his residence in Ohio was the "promised land,"—the immediate removal of the whole Smith family thither, where they were soon raised from a state

of poverty to comparative affluence. We therefore, must hold
out Sidney Rigdon to the world as being the original "author
and proprietor" of the whole Mormon conspiracy, until further
light is elicited upon the lost writings of Solomon Spalding.

F I N I S.

ADDENDA

1. Solomon Spalding as Plagiarized Author

When Solomon Spalding (1761–1816) was twenty-four, he
graduated from Dartmouth, plagued by theological doubts. He
entered the ministry, but soon resigned. Ten years later he married Matilda Sabin and went into business with his brother,
Josiah Spalding, in New York, sixty miles west of Albany. In
1809 he moved to New Salem, Ohio (later renamed Conneaut), and began writing a story about the ancient builders of
burial mounds found in the region. The manuscript is housed
in the library of Oberlin College (for a transcription, see Jackson, *Manuscript Found*).

Failing in business and health, he moved to the Pittsburgh
area and continued writing (for more, see Whittier and Stathis,
"Enigma of Solomon Spaulding"). The theory that the Book
of Mormon was plagiarized from a Spalding manuscript has
fallen into disrepute with most investigators, but it is occasionally revived on the theory that the Oberlin manuscript may
not be the one from which the Book of Mormon was taken
(see Bush, "Spalding Theory Then and Now"; Roper, "Mythical

'Manuscript Found'"). There are at least four good reasons why this is not the case.

First, the eyewitnesses said there was not a manuscript present during the Book of Mormon dictation. Joseph Smith pronounced the text for the entire book while gazing at a seer stone which he placed in the bottom of his hat. Second, Smith's reaction to the loss of the first 116 pages of dictation in 1828, and his inability to reproduce the lost material, indicated that the wording was free-formed. Third, the fact that Smith ultimately had to produce a replacement text for the missing 116 pages, involving a change in emphasis and narrative voice, casts doubt on the witnesses who thought they recognized direct borrowings. Fourth, as Mormon leader Brigham H. Roberts observed, if the Book of Mormon had been authored by Spalding and edited by Rigdon, a noted grammarian, "it would not have been so full of petty errors in grammar and the faulty use of words as is found in the first edition of the Book of Mormon" (Roberts, "Origin of the Book of Mormon," Mar. 1909, 181–82).

The individuals who knew Spalding said they remembered that characters in his story named Lehi and Nephi spoke in biblical language. In saying so, his friends and relatives may have demonstrated what psychologists call false memory syndrome, wherein without knowing it, someone suggests details that become incorporated into one's own recollection (see, e.g., Loftus, "Memory Malleability"; Loftus and Pickrell, "Formation of False Memories"; Zaragoza and Mitchell, "Repeated Exposure to Suggestion"; Bolles, *Remembering and Forgetting*). It is likely in this instance that their memories became tainted by reading the Book of Mormon and discussing it with each other. Additionally, as an untrained interviewer, Hurlbut may have asked leading questions and unintentionally influenced the content of the responses. That is not to say that he or the individuals he interviewed lacked sincerity. Far from it, the interviewees were trying to remember what they had heard over twenty years previously, their minds no doubt playing some tricks on them.

2. Alleged Smith-Rigdon Connection

When journalist Pomeroy Tucker tried to establish a pre-1830 link between Joseph Smith and Sidney Rigdon, he reported in 1867 that people remembered having seen a "mysterious stranger" at the Smith residence in the "summer of 1827." In retrospect, he thought it could have been none other than Rigdon (Tucker, *Origin*, 28; Vogel, *Documents*, 3:100). Whatever else might be said, the Smiths were visited in 1827 by unfamiliar callers including Alvah Beaman, Joseph Knight, and Josiah Stowell.

When Palmyra resident John H. Gilbert took up the investigation of Mormon origins in 1879 for James T. Cobb of Salt Lake City, he traced the rumor of Rigdon's alleged 1827 visit to Palmyra to Tucker, but "where Tucker got his information, I am unable to say," he wrote (Gilbert to Cobb, Feb. 10, 1879, 2; Vogel, *Documents*, 2:523). Eventually he was able to find someone willing to swear they had been informed by the Smith family that the stranger was Rigdon (Abel D. Chase, Affidavit, May 2, 1879, in Wymetal, *Joseph Smith*, 230; Vogel, *Documents*, 3:137), and before the year was out he had in hand a letter from Lorenzo Saunders confirming the same (Wymetal, *Joseph Smith*, 231; Vogel, *Documents*, 2:529).

Gilbert told two representatives of the Reorganized LDS Church, Edmund and William Kelley, that "at first [Saunders] said he did not remember of ever seeing Rigdon until after 1830 sometime; but after studying it over a while, he said it seemed to him that one time he was over to Smiths, and that there was a stranger he never saw before, and that they said it was Rigdon" (Kelley, "Hill Cumorah," 166; Vogel, *Documents*, 2:110). In order to accept this recovery of lost memory as valid, one would have to overlook the fact that in 1867 Saunders helped prepare Tucker's book for publication (Saunders interview with Kelley, Sept. 17, 1884, 14; Vogel, *Documents*, 2:134) and that Tucker had previously said no one could positively identify the stranger, that the Smiths "withheld all explanation of his identity" and that "no intimation of the name or purpose of this personage" was communicated to even "the Smith's nearest neighbors" (Tucker, *Origin*, 46, 28; Vogel, *Documents*, 2:134; 3:111, 100). In this context, Saunders himself told the Kelleys during an 1879 stay in Palmyra that he and his brother had struggled to remember events and dates from fifty years ago until finally they were confident they had seen Rigdon, a "well dressed man," in mid-March 1827, probably on the 10th or 15th (Saunders interview with Kelley, Sept. 17, 1884, 3–4; Nov. 12, 1884, 7; Vogel, *Documents*, 2:128–29, 151).

Saunders thought he remembered one of the Smiths indentifying Rigdon, but he could not remember which member of the family had imparted that information to him, at one time naming Samuel and another time Hyrum (ibid.). In all probability, these memories were based on a blending of visits from the well-to-do Josiah Stowell or Joseph Knight in 1827 and Rigdon's subsequent visit to the area in 1830, as well as the desire to be of help to the interviewer. Regardless, they are not credible enough to base a theory of Book of Mormon authorship on.

Eber D. Howe, co-founder of the *Cleveland Herald* and *Painesville Telegraph,* became interested in Mormonism when his wife and sister converted to the faith in the early 1830s. *Courtesy Lake County Historical Society*

An ardent abolitionist, E. D. Howe allowed his home (left) near Painesville, Ohio, to serve as an Underground Railroad station in conveying fugitive slaves to Canada. *Courtesy Ohio Historical Society*

MORMONISM UNVAILED:

OR,

A FAITHFUL ACCOUNT OF THAT SINGULAR IMPOSITION AND

DELUSION,

FROM ITS RISE TO THE PRESENT TIME.

WITH SKETCHES OF THE CHARACTERS OF ITS

PROPAGATORS,

AND A FULL DETAIL OF THE MANNER IN WHICH THE FAMOUS

GOLDEN BIBLE

WAS BROUGHT BEFORE THE WORLD.

TO WHICH ARE ADDED,

INQUIRIES INTO THE PROBABILITY THAT THE HISTORICAL PART

OF THE SAID BIBLE WAS WRITTEN BY ONE

SOLOMON SPALDING,

MORE THAN TWENTY YEARS AGO, AND BY HIM INTENDED TO HAVE

BEEN PUBLISHED AS A ROMANCE.

. . . .

BY E. D. HOWE.

. . . .

PAINESVILLE:
PRINTED AND PUBLISHED BY THE AUTHOR.

1834.

Howe's original title page for the 1834 printing of *Mormonism Unvailed. Courtesy Hugh McKell of Bear Hollow Books*

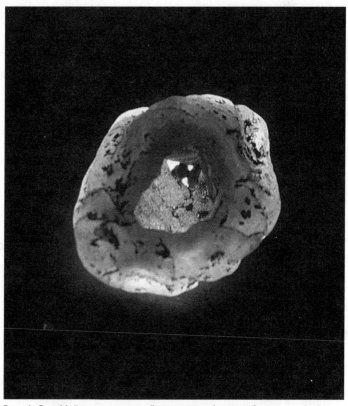

Joseph Smith's "green seer stone" was gray with green deposits and a large hole in the center and three smaller holes on the other side. It was preserved by Philo Dibble, who is known for having created the death masks of Joseph and Hyrum Smith. *Courtesy Rick Grunder, antiquarian bookseller*

Self-proclaimed prophetess Joanna Southcott, portrayed here in *Devonshire Characters and Strange Events* by Sabine Baring-Gould. The author reported that Southcott supported herself by selling "passports to heaven."

Oliver Cowdery, the church's assistant president, said *Mormonism Unvailed* was written, not by Howe, but by the devil. This portrait is thought by LDS educator Patrick A. Bishop and *BYU Studies* to be of Cowdery. *Courtesy Library of Congress*

William W. Phelps was editor of the *Ontario Phoenix* in Canandaigua, fifteen miles south of Palmyra, at the time of his conversion. He soon became editor of *The Evening and the Morning Star.*

Martin Harris forsook everything for Mormonism—family, fortune, standing in the community, and peace of mind. *Courtesy Utah State Historical Society*

The E. B. Grandin building in Palmyra where the first edition of the Book of Mormon was printed. The presses were on the third floor and the book bindery on the second. *Courtesy Utah State Historical Society*

The Smith home in Harmony, Pennsylvania, at the edge of the Hale family property, where most of the Book of Mormon was dictated. *Courtesy Utah State Historical Society*

BIBLIOGRAPHY

Allen, James B., and Leonard J. Arrington. "Mormon Origins in New York: An Introductory Analysis." *Brigham Young University Studies* 9 (Spring 1969): 241–74.

Anderson, Richard Lloyd. "The Impact of the First Preaching in Ohio." *Brigham Young University Studies* 11 (Summer 1971): 474–96.

———. *Investigating the Book of Mormon Witnesses*. Salt Lake City: Deseret Book, 1981.

———. "Joseph Smith's New York Reputation Reappraised." *Brigham Young University Studies* 10 (Spring 1970): 283–314.

———. "The Mature Joseph Smith and Treasure Searching." *Brigham Young University Studies* 24 (Fall 1984): 489–560.

———. "New Data for Revising the Missouri 'Documentary History.'" *Brigham Young University Studies* 14 (Summer 1974): 488–501.

———. Review of *Joseph Smith's New York Reputation Reexamined* by Rodger I. Anderson, *Review of Books on the Book of Mormon* 3 (1991): 59–62.

Anderson, Rodger I. *Joseph Smith's New York Reputation Reexamined*. Salt Lake City: Signature Books, 1990.

Anthon, Charles. Letter to Thomas Winthrop Coit, Apr. 3, 1841. *Church Record*, Apr. 17, 1841, 231–32.

Arrington, Leonard J. "Early Mormon Communitarianism: The Law of Consecration and Stewardship." *Western Humanities Review* 7 (Autumn 1953): 341–69.

———. "James Gordon Bennett's 1831 Report on 'The Mormonites.'" *Brigham Young University Studies* 10 (Spring 1970):
353–64.

Ashe, Thomas. *Travels in America, Performed in 1806, for the Purpose
of Exploring the Rivers Alleghany, Monongahela, Ohio, and
Mississippi, and Ascertaining the Produce and Condition of Their
Banks and Vicinity*. 3 vols. London: Richard Phillips, 1808.

Atwater, Caleb. "Description of the Antiquities Discovered in the
State of Ohio and Other Western States." *Archaeologia Amer-
icana: Transactions and Collections of the American Antiquarian
Society* 1 (1820): 105–267.

Backman, Milton V., Jr. *A Profile of Latter-day Saints of Kirtland,
Ohio, and Members of Zion's Camp, 1830–1839: Vital Statistics
and Sources.* Provo, UT: Brigham Young University, 1983.

Bauder, Peter. *The Kingdom and Gospel of Jesus Christ: Contrasted
with That of Anti-Christ. A Brief Review of Some of the Most
Interesting Circumstances, Which Have Transpired Since the
Institution of the Gospel of Christ, from the Days of the Apostles*.
Canajoharie, NY: By the author, 1834.

Bennett, James Gordon. Diary, Aug. 12–18, 1831. Rare Books and
Manuscripts Division, New York Public Library, New York
City.

———. "Mormon Religion—Clerical Ambition—Western New
York—The Mormonites Gone to Ohio." Part II. *Morning Courier and Enquirer,* Sept. 1, 1831.

Bitton, Davis. *Guide to Mormon Diaries and Autobiographies*. Provo,
UT: Brigham Young University Press, 1977.

Blackman, Emily. *History of Susquehanna County, Pennsylvania*.
Philadelphia: Claxton, Remsen, and Haffelfinger, 1873.

Bolles, Edmund Blair. *Remembering and Forgetting: Inquiries into the Nature of Memory*. New York: Walker and Company, 1988.

"Book of Records for the First Baptist Church in Palmyra," 1813–28. Baptist Historical Society, Rochester.

Brodie, Fawn M. *No Man Knows My History: The Life of Joseph Smith*. 2nd ed. New York: Alfred A. Knopf, 1976.

Brothers, Richard. *A Revealed Knowledge of the Prophecies and Times*. London: George Riebau, 1794.

Bunyan, John. *The Pilgrim's Progress: From This World to That Which Is to Come*. 2 vols. London: Nathaniel Ponder, 1678/1684. Digital transcript, 2008, Project Gutenberg, www.gutenberg.org.

Bush, Lester E., Jr. "The Spalding Theory Then and Now." *Dialogue: A Journal of Mormon Thought* 10 (Autumn 1977): 40–69.

———. "The Word of Wisdom in Early Nineteenth-Century Perspective." In *The Word of God: Essays on Mormon Scripture,* ed. Dan Vogel. Salt Lake City: Signature Books, 1990, 161–85.

Butts, Isaac. Statement to Arthur Deming, ca. Mar. 1885. *Naked Truths about Mormonism* newsletter, Jan. 1888, 2.

Campbell, Alexander. "The Mormonites." *Millennial Harbinger*, Feb. 1831, 85–100.

Cannon, Donald Q. "Zelph Revisited." In *Regional Studies in Latter-day Saint Church History: Illinois*, ed. H. Dean Garrett. Provo, UT: BYU Department of Church History and Doctrine, 1995, 99–111.

Cannon, Donald Q., and Lyndon W. Cook. *Far West Record: Minutes of the Church of Jesus Christ of Latter-day Saints, 1830–1844.* Salt Lake City: Deseret Book, 1983.

Carter, John S. Diary, 1831–33. MS 1440, LDS Church History Library, Salt Lake City, online at churchhistorycatalog.lds.org/.

Chandler, Albert. Letter to William Linn, Dec. 22, 1898. In *The Story of the Mormons* by William Linn. New York: Macmillan, 1902, 48–49.

Chardon Spectator and Geauga Gazette (OH), Mar., June 1831; Jan., Apr. 1834.

Clark, John A. "Gleanings by the Way." *Episcopal Recorder*, Oct. 10, 1840, 114.

———. Letter to Dear Brethren, Aug. 24, 1840. *Episcopal Recorder* (Philadelphia), Sept. 5, 1840, 94.

———. Letter to Dear Brethren, Aug. 31, 1840, *Episcopal Recorder* (Philadelphia), Sept. 12, 1840, 98–99.

Clarke, Adam. *The Holy Bible ... with a Commentary and Critical Notes*. 7 vols. New York, 1810.

Cleveland Herald, Nov. 1830.

Collier, Fred C. Comp. *Unpublished Revelations of the Prophets and Presidents of the Church of Jesus Christ of Latter-day Saints*. Salt Lake City: Collier's Publishing, 1979.

"Conference Minutes." *Times and Seasons*, May 1, 1844, 522–24.

Congregational Observer (Hartford), July 1841.

Cook, Lyndon W. *David Whitmer Interviews: A Restoration Witness*. Orem, UT: Grandin Book, 1991.

———. *Joseph Smith and the Law of Consecration*. Provo, UT: Grandin Book, 1985.

———. *The Revelations of the Prophet Joseph Smith: A Historical and Biographical Commentary of the Doctrine and Covenants*. Provo, UT: Seventy's Mission Book Store, 1981.

Corrill, John. *Brief History of the Church of Christ of Latter Day Saints*. St. Louis: By the author, 1839.

Cowdery, Oliver. Letter to W. W. Phelps, Oct. 1835. *Messenger and Advocate*, Oct. 1835, 195–202.

Crawford, Charles. *The Christian: A Poem, in Four Books*. Philadelphia: By the author, 1783.

Daily Missouri Republican (St. Louis), Nov., Dec. 1833.

Davidson, Karen Lynn, David J. Whittaker, Mark Ashurst-McGee, Richard L. Jensen, eds. *The Joseph Smith Papers: Histories, Volume 1: Joseph Smith Histories, 1832–1844*. Salt Lake City: Church Historian's Press, 2012.

Davidson, Karen Lynn, Richard L. Jensen, David J. Whittaker, eds. *The Joseph Smith Papers: Histories, Volume 2: Assigned Histories, 1831–1847*. Salt Lake City: Church Historian's Press, 2012.

Deseret Evening News (Salt Lake City), Aug. 1878; Mar. 1896.

Dickinson, Ellen E. *New Light on Mormonism*. New York: Funk & Wagnalls, 1885.

Divett, Robert T. "Medicine and the Mormons: A Historical Perspective." *Dialogue: A Journal of Mormon Thought* 12 (Fall 1979): 16–25.

Doctrine and Covenants Student Manual. Salt Lake City: LDS Church, 2001. Online at 2015 Lesson Manuals: Institute for Religion 324, 325, www.lds.org/manual.

"A Document Discovered." *Utah Christian Advocate*, Jan. 1886, 1.

Dowen, John C. Affidavit, Jan. 2, 1885. Arthur B. Deming Collection, Chicago Historical Society, Chicago.

Eaton, Ann Ruth. *The Origin of Mormonism*. New York: Woman's Executive Committee of Home Missions, 1881.

Elders' Journal (Ohio/Missouri), Nov. 1837.

Enders, Donald L. "The Joseph Smith Sr. Family: Farmers of the Genesee." In *Joseph Smith: The Prophet, the Man*, eds. Susan

Easton Black and Charles D. Tate Jr. Provo, UT: BYU Religious Studies Center, 1993, 213–25.

Evening and the Morning Star (Independence, MO), July 1832; Feb., Dec. 1833; Jan., Mar., May, July 1834.

Firmage, Edwin B., and R. Collin Mangrum. *Zion in the Courts: A Legal History of the Church of Jesus Christ of Latter-day Saints, 1830–1900.* Urbana: University of Illinois Press, 1988.

Flake, Chad J., comp. *A Mormon Bibliography, 1830–1930: Books, Pamphlets, Periodicals, and Broadsides Relating to the First Century of Mormonism.* Salt Lake City: University of Utah Press, 1992.

Fluhman, J. Spencer. *"A Peculiar People": Anti-Mormonism and the Making of Religion in Nineteenth-Century America.* Chapel Hill: University of North Carolina Press, 2012.

Geneva Gazette (New York), May 1831.

Gilbert, John H. Letter to James T. Cobb, Feb. 10, 1879. Theodore A. Schroeder Papers, Rare Books and Manuscripts Division, New York Public Library, New York City.

———. "Memorandum, made by John H. Gilbert Esq, Sept. 8th, 1892, Palmyra, N.Y.," Palmyra King's Daughters Free Library, Palmyra, NY.

Godfrey, Kenneth A. "The Zelph Story." *Brigham Young University Studies* 29 (Spring 1989): 31–56.

Godfrey, Matthew C., Mark Ashurst-McGee, Grant Underwood, Robert J. Woodford, William G. Hartley, eds. *The Joseph Smith Papers: Documents, Volume 2: July 1831–Jan. 1833.* Salt Lake City: Church Historian's Press, 2013.

Gregg, Thomas. *The Prophet of Palmyra.* New York: John B. Alden, 1890.

Grua, David W. "Joseph Smith and the 1834 D. P. Hurlbut Case." *BYU Studies* 41, no. 1 (2005): 33–54.

———. "Winning against Hurlbut's Assault in 1834." In *Sustaining the Law: Joseph Smith's Legal Encounters*, eds. Gordon A. Madsen, Jeffrey N. Walker, and John W. Welch. Provo, UT: BYU Studies, 2014, 141–54.

Guernsey Times (Cambridge, OH), Apr. 1831.

Gunnell, Wayne C. "Martin Harris: Witness and Benefactor to the Book of Mormon." Master's thesis, Brigham Young University, Provo, UT, 1955.

Hale, Isaac. Agreement with Joseph Smith, Apr. 6, 1829, Joseph Smith Collection, 1827–1844, LDS Church History Library, Salt Lake City.

Hale, Jonathan H. Reminiscence and Journal, 1837–1840. MS 1704, LDS Church History Library, Salt Lake City, online at churchhistorycatalog.lds.org/.

Haller, John S., Jr. *The People's Doctors: Samuel Thomson and the American Botanical Movement, 1790–1860*. Carbondale: Southern Illinois University Press, 2000.

Hancock, Levi W. Autobiography, ca. 1854. MS 8174, LDS Church History Library, Salt Lake City, online at churchhistorycatalog.lds.org/.

Harding, Stephen S. Letter to Thomas Gregg, Feb. 1882. In Thomas Gregg, *The Prophet of Palmyra*. New York: John B. Alden, 1890, 34–56.

Harris, Martin. Interview with Joel Tiffany, 1859. "Mormonism." *Tiffany's Monthly*, Aug. 1859, 163–70.

———. Testimony dictated to Edward Stevenson, Sept. 4, 1870. Edward Stevenson Collection: Papers, MS 4806, LDS Church

History Library, Salt Lake City, currently restricted from public access.

Hayden, Amos. *Early History of the Disciples on the Western Reserve.* Cincinnati: Chase and Hall, 1875.

Hill, Marvin S. "Joseph Smith the Man: Some Reflections on a Subject of Controversy." *BYU Studies* 21, no. 1 (Spring 1981): 175–86.

———. *Quest for Refuge: The Mormon Flight from American Pluralism.* Salt Lake City: Signature Books, 1989.

———. Review of *Joseph Smith's New York Reputation Reexamined* by Rodger I. Anderson. In *Brigham Young University Studies* 30 (Fall 1990): 70–74.

Hill, Marvin S., C. Keith Rooker, Larry T. Wimmer. "The Kirtland Economy Revisited: A Market Critique of Sectarian Economics." *Brigham Young University Studies* 17 (Summer 1977): 391–472.

Hine, William R. Affidavit, ca. Mar. 1885. *Naked Truths about Mormonism* newsletter, Jan. 1888, 2.

History of the Church of Jesus Christ of Latter-day Saints (by Joseph Smith et al.), ed. B. H. Roberts. 7 vols. 2nd ed. rev. Salt Lake City: Deseret Book, 1948.

The Holy Bible. Cooperstown, NY: H. and E. Phinney, 1828. Copy used for Joseph Smith's Bible revision in Community of Christ Library-Archives, Independence, MO.

Howe, E. D. Affidavit, Apr. 8, 1885. Arthur B. Deming Collection, Chicago Historical Society, Chicago.

———. *Mormonism Unvailed.* Painesville, OH: By the author, 1834. Digital scan, 2010, Internet Archive, University of Pittsburgh Library System, archive.org/details/mormonismunvaile00howe.

Hubble, Martin J. Account, Nov. 13, 1886. CO121 Hubble Family Papers, Manuscript Collections, State Historical Society of Missouri, Columbia.

Hullinger, Robert N. *Joseph Smith's Response to Skepticism*. Salt Lake City: Signature Books, 1992.

Humboldt, Alexander von. *Concerning the Institutions & Monuments of the Ancient Inhabitants of America, with Descriptions & Views of Some of the Most Striking Scenes in the Cordilleras!* Trans. Helen Maria Williams. London: Longman, 1814.

Huntington, Oliver B. Diary, 1835–1900. Typescript, 2 vols. Special Collections, Harold B. Lee Library, Brigham Young University, Provo, UT.

Hyde, Orson. Journal, Feb. 1–Dec. 22, 1832. MS 1386, LDS Church History Library, Salt Lake city, online at churchhistorycatalog.lds.org/.

Hyde, William. "The Birth of Mormonism." *Deseret Evening News*, Nov. 10, 1888, 2.

"An Interesting Document. Articles of Agreement Between Joe Smith, the Father of Mormonism and Other Persons in 1825." *Salt Lake Daily Tribune*, Apr. 23, 1880, 4.

International Review (New York City), Sept. 1881.

Jackson, Kent P., ed. *Manuscript Found: The Complete Original "Spaulding Manuscript."* Provo, UT: BYU Religious Studies Center, 1996.

James, Rhett. *The Man Who Knew: The Early Years. A Play About Martin Harris, 1824–1830*. Cache Valley, UT: Martin Harris Pageant Committee, 1983.

Jensen, Ole A. "Testimony of Martin Harris (One of the Witnesses of the Book of Mormon)," ca. 1918. Photocopy, Utah State Historical Society, Salt Lake City.

Jensen, Robin Scott, Robert J. Woodford, Steven C. Harper, eds. *The Joseph Smith Papers: Revelations and Translations, Volume 1: Manuscript Revelation Books*, facsimile edition. Salt Lake City: Church Historian's Press, 2009.

Jenson, Andrew. *Latter-day Saint Biographical Encyclopedia.* 4 vols. 1901–36; Salt Lake City: Western Epics, 1971.

Jessee, Dean C., ed. *The Personal Writings of Joseph Smith.* 2nd rev. ed. Salt Lake City: Deseret Book, 2002.

Jessee, Dean C., Mark Ashurst-McGee, Richard L. Jensen, eds. *The Joseph Smith Papers: Journals, Volume 1: 1832–1839.* Salt Lake City: Church Historian's Press, 2008.

Joseph Smith Collection, 1827–1844. MS 155, LDS Church History Library, Salt Lake City, online at churchhistorycatalog. lds.org/.

Journal of Discourses of the Church of Jesus Christ of Latter-day Saints. 26 vols. London and Liverpool: Latter-day Saints Book Depot, 1854–86.

Kelley, William H. "The Hill Cumorah and the Book of Mormon." *Saints' Herald*, June 1, 1881, 161–68.

———. Notebook no. 5, Mar. 6, 1881. William H. Kelley Papers, Community of Christ Library-Archives, Independence, MO.

Kirkham, Francis W. *A New Witness for Christ in America: The Book of Mormon.* 2 vols. Independence, MO: Zion's Printing and Publishing, 1951.

Kirtland Council Minute Book, Dec. 1832–Nov. 1837. MS 3432, LDS Church History Library, currently restricted to public access; see online at Minute Books 1–2, Administrative Records, josephsmithpapers.org.

Knight, Joseph, Sr. "Manuscript of the Early History of Joseph Smith Finding the Plates," ca. 1835–1847, MS 22148, Knight Family History, LDS Church History Library, Salt Lake City.

Lake County Historical Society Quarterly (Painesville, OH), Aug. 1972.

Lancaster, James E. "The Translation of the Book of Mormon." In *The Word of God: Essays on Mormon Scripture*, ed. Dan Vogel. Salt Lake City: Signature Books, 1990, 97–112.

Lapham, Fayette. "Interview with the Father of Joseph Smith, the Mormon Prophet, Forty Years Ago. His Account of the Finding of the Sacred Plates," *Historical Magazine and Notes and Queries Concerning the Antiquities, History, and Biography of America* (New York), May 1870, 305–09.

Launius, Roger D. "A Question of Honor? A. W. Doniphan and the Mormon Expulsion from Jackson County." *Nauvoo Journal* 10 (Fall 1998): 3–17.

———. *Zion's Camp: Expedition to Missouri, 1834.* Independence, MO: Herald Publishing House, 1984.

Laws of the State of New-York, Revised and Passed at Thirty-Sixth Session of the Legislature. 2 vols. Albany: Henry C. Southwick, 1813.

Lewis, Joseph. "Review of Mormonism. Rejoinder to Elder Cadwell." *Amboy Journal* (Illinois), June 11, 1879, 1.

Loftus, Elizabeth F. "Memory Malleability: Constructivist and Fuzzy-Trace Explanations." *Learning and Individual Differences* 7 (1995): 133–37.

Loftus, Elizabeth F., and Jacqueline E. Pickrell. "The Formation of False Memories." *Psychiatric Annals* 25 (Dec. 1995): 720–25.

Lyons Gazette (Lyons, NY), Aug. 1854.

MacKay, Michael Hubbard, Gerrit J. Dirkmaat, Grant Underwood, Robert J. Woodford, William G. Hartley, eds. *The Joseph Smith Papers: Documents, Volume 1: July 1828–June 1831*. Salt Lake City: Church Historian's Press, 2013.

Madsen, Gordon A., Jeffrey N. Walker, John W. Welch, eds. *Sustaining the Law: Joseph Smith's Legal Encounters*. Provo, UT: BYU Studies, 2014.

Manchester Assessment Records, Ontario County Records Center and Archives, Canandaigua, NY.

Marks, David. *The Life of David Marks*. Limerick, MI: Morning Star, 1831.

Marquardt, H. Michael. "Ezra Booth on Early Mormonism: A Look at His 1831 Letters." *John Whitmer Historical Association Journal* 28 (2008): 65–87.

Marquardt, H. Michael, and Wesley P. Walters. *Inventing Mormonism: Tradition and the Historical Record*. Salt Lake City: Signature Books, 1994.

Marshall, Charles. "The Original Prophet: By a Visitor to Salt Lake City." *Fraser's Magazine* (London), Feb. 1873, 225–35.

Mather, Frederick G. "The Early Mormons: Joe Smith Operates at Susquehanna." *Binghamton Republican* (New York), July 29, 1880.

Matthews, Robert J. *"A Plainer Translation": Joseph Smith's Translation of the Bible*. Provo, UT: Brigham Young University Press, 1975.

Mayhew, Henry. *History of the Mormons*. Auburn, NY: Derby and Miller, 1853.

McMaster, John Bach. *A History of the People of the United States*. 8 vols. New York: D. Appleton, 1914.

Melder, Keith. *Beginnings of Sisterhood: The American Women's Rights Movement, 1800–1850*. New York: Schocken Books, 1977.

Messenger and Advocate (Kirtland, OH), Dec. 1834; Apr., Sept., Oct., Dec. 1835; Mar.–May 1836.

Missouri Enquirer (Liberty, MO), July 1834.

Missouri Intelligencer and Boon's Lick Advertiser (Columbia, MO), Aug. 1833.

Morning Courier and New York Enquirer (New York City), Sept. 1831.

Morton, Sunny McClellan. "The Forgotten Daughter: Julia Smith Murdock." *Mormon Historical Studies* 3, no. 2 (Fall 2002): 35–60.

Moss, Jasper J. Letter to James T. Cobb, Dec. 17, 1878. Theodore Schroeder Papers, 1845–1901, Wisconsin Historical Society, Madison, WI.

Mulder, William, and A. Russell Mortensen, eds. *Among the Mormons: Historic Accounts by Contemporary Observers*. Lincoln: University of Nebraska Press, 1958.

New York Telescope (New York City), Mar. 1825.

Newell, Linda King, and Valeen Tippetts Avery. *Mormon Enigma: Emma Hale Smith*. Garden City, NY: Doubleday, 1984.

Niles Weekly Register (Baltimore), June 1822.

Norman, Keith D. "How Long, O Lord? The Delay of the Parousia in Mormonism." *Sunstone*, Jan.–Apr. 1983, 49–58.

Ohio v. Dr. P. Hurlbut, Mar. 31, 1834. Geauga County Courthouse, Chardon, OH.

Ohio Star (Ravenna), Dec. 1830; Oct.–Dec. 1831; Jan. 1832.

Ontario Phoenix (Canandaigua, NY), Dec. 1830.

Page, John E. *The Spaulding Story Concerning the Origin of the Book of Mormon.* Pittsburgh: n. p., 1843.

Painesville Telegraph (OH), Nov. 1830; Jan.–Apr., Sept. 1831; Jan. 1832; Jan., Aug. 1834.

Palmyra Courier (NY), Mar. 1871, May 1872.

Palmyra Herald and Canal Advertiser (NY), June 1822.

Palmyra Reflector (NY), Sept. 1829; Apr., June, July 1830; Jan.–Mar., June, July 1831.

Peck, George. *The Life and Times of Rev. George Peck, D.D., Written by Himself.* New York: Nelson and Phillips, 1874.

Peterson, Daniel C. Review of Mormonism by Kurt Van Gorden, *FARMS Review of Books,* 8, no. 1 (1996): 95–103.

Phelps, William W. "Free People of Color," *The Evening and the Morning Star,* July 1833, 109.

Pierce, Nathan. Docketbook, 1827–1830. Manchester Township Office, Clifton Springs, NY.

Pilkington, William. Affidavit, Apr. 3, 1934. "The Dying Testimony of Martin Harris, as given to William Pilkington by Martin Harris Himself in Clarkston, Cache County, Utah." MS 27368, LDS Church History Library, Salt Lake City.

Pittsburgh Telegraph (PA), Aug. 1876.

Pratt, Henry. Letter to Addison Pratt, May 20, 1838. MS 3729 (photocopy), LDS Church History Library, Salt Lake City.

Pratt, Orson. *A[n] Interesting Account of Several Remarkable Visions and of the Late Discovery of Ancient American Records.* Edinburgh: Ballantyne and Hughes, 1840.

Pratt, Parley P. *Autobiography of Parley P. Pratt,* ed. Parley P. Pratt Jr. Salt Lake City: Deseret Book, 1976.

Prince, Gregory A. *Power from on High: The Development of Mormon Priesthood.* Salt Lake City: Signature Books, 1995.

Prince, Walter F. "Psychological Tests for the Authorship of the Book of Mormon." *American Journal of Psychology* 28 (July 1917): 373–89.

Quinn, D. Michael. *Early Mormonism and the Magic World View.* 2d. ed., rev. and enl. Salt Lake City: Signature Books, 1998.

———. *The Mormon Hierarchy: Origins of Power.* Salt Lake City: Signature Books, 1994.

"Records of the Session of the Presbyterian Church in Palmyra." Western Presbyterian Church, Palmyra, NY. Microfilm copy, Harold B. Lee Library, Brigham Young University, Provo, UT.

Redmount, Carol. "Bitter Lives: Israel in and out of Egypt." In *The Oxford History of the Biblical World,* ed. Michael D. Coogan. New York and Oxford: Oxford University Press, 1998.

Reed, John S. Letter to Brigham Young, Dec. 6, 1861. CR 12341, Incoming Correspondence, 1839–77, Brigham Young Collection. LDS Church History Library, Salt Lake City, online at churchhistorycatalog.lds.org/.

Reynolds, George. *The Myth of the Manuscript Found, or The Absurdities of the Spaulding Story.* Salt Lake City: Juvenile Instructor Office, 1883.

Richmond, Velma Bourgeois. *The Legend of Guy of Warwick.* New York and London: Garland, 1996.

Roberts, B. H. *Defense of the Faith and the Saints.* 2 vols. Salt Lake City: Deseret News, 1907.

———. *New Witnesses for God.* 3 vols. Salt Lake City: Deseret News, 1909.

———. "The Origin of the Book of Mormon." *American Historical Magazine* (New York City), Mar. 1909, 168–96.

Rochester Advertiser and Telegraph (NY), Aug. 1829.

Rochester Daily Democrat (NY), June 1841.

Roper, Matthew. "The Mythical 'Manuscript Found.'" Review of *Who Really Wrote the Book of Mormon? The Spalding Enigma* by Wayne L. Cowdrey, Howard Davis, Hugh O'Neal, Arthur Vanick. *FARMS Review* 17, no. 2 (2005): 7–140.

Rowley, Dennis. "The Ezra Booth Letters." *Dialogue: A Journal of Mormon Thought* 16, no. 3 (Autumn 1983): 133–37.

Saunders, Benjamin. Interviewed by William H. Kelley, ca. Sept. 1884. "Miscellany," Community of Christ Library-Archives, Independence, MO.

Saunders, Lorenzo. Interview with William H. Kelley, Sept. 17, 1884. E. L. Kelley Papers, Community of Christ Library-Archives, Independence, MO.

———. Interview with E. L. Kelley, Nov. 12, 1884. E. L. Kelley Papers. Community of Christ Library-Archives, Independence, MO.

———. Letter to Thomas Gregg, Jan. 28, 1885. In Charles A. Shook, *The True Origin of the Book of Mormon*. Cincinnati: Standard Publishing, 1914, 134–35.

Scott, Thomas. *The Holy Bible ... with Original Notes*, 3 vols. Philadelphia: William W. Woodward, 1816–18.

Shook, Charles A. *Cumorah Revisited; or, "The Book of Mormon" and the Claims of the Mormons Reexamined from the Viewpoint of American Archaeology and Ethnology.* Cincinnati: Standard Publishing, 1910.

Shorter Oxford English Dictionary: On Historical Principles, ed. Lesley Brown. 2 vols. 5th ed. Oxford: Oxford University Press, 2002.

Shumway, Eric B. "Polynesians." In *Encyclopedia of Mormonism*, ed. Daniel H. Ludlow, 4 vols. New York: Macmillan Publishing, 1992.

Smith, Caroline Rockwell. Statement to Arthur B. Deming, Mar. 25, 1885. *Naked Truths about Mormonism* newsletter, Apr. 1888, 1.

Smith, Ethan. *View of the Hebrews; or the Tribes of Israel in America*. 2nd ed. Poultney, VT: Smith and Shute, 1825.

Smith, Jesse. Letter to Hyrum Smith, June 17, 1829. Joseph Smith Letterbook (1837–43) 2:59–61, Joseph Smith Collection, 1827–1844, LDS Church History Library, online at josephsmithpapers.org.

Smith, Joseph, Jr. "Answers to Questions." *Elders' Journal* (Ohio/Missouri), July 1838, 43.

———. Deed of sale on land in Harmony, PA, June 28, 1833. Liber 9, p. 290, deed books, Susquehanna County Courthouse, Montrose, PA.

———. Egyptian Manuscript 1. Kirtland Egyptian Papers, 1835–36, MS 1295. LDS Church History Library, online at churchhistorycatalog.lds.org/.

———. History, 1832. In Joseph Smith Letterbook 1: 1–[6], Joseph Smith Collection, 1827–1844. LDS Church History Library, Salt Lake City, online at josephsmithpapers.org.

———. Journal, 1842–1843. MS 155, Joseph Smith Collection, 1827–1844. LDS Church History Library, Salt Lake City, online at churchhistorycatalog.lds.org/.

———. Letter to Colesville Saints, Dec. 2, 1830. In Newel Knight journal, ca. 1846, 206–07, in private possession.

———. Letter to Martin Harris, Feb. 22, 1831. Letters Sent, 1831–39, MS 155/b0002/f0003, Joseph Smith Collection,

1827–1844, LDS Church History Library, online at churchhistorycatalog.lds.org/.

Smith, Joseph, Jr./Sr. Agreement with Martin Harris, Jan. 16, 1830. Simon Gratz Autograph Collection, 1517–1925, Historical Society of Pennsylvania, Philadelphia; also online "Interim Content," josephsmithpapers.org.

Smith, Joseph III. "Last Testimony of Sister Emma." *Saints' Herald*, Oct. 1, 1879, 289–90.

Smith, Lucy. *Biographical Sketches of Joseph Smith the Prophet, and His Progenitors for Many Generations.* Liverpool: Samuel W. Richards, 1853.

———. History, 1844–1845. LDS Church History Library, Salt Lake City, online at josephsmithpapers.org.

Smith, N. Lee. "Herbal Remedies: God's Medicine?" *Dialogue: A Journal of Mormon Thought* 12 (Fall 1979): 37–60.

Smith, William. "Notes Written on 'Chamber's Life of Joseph Smith,'" ca. 1875. MS 2807, LDS Church History Library, Salt Lake City.

Spalding, Solomon. *The "Manuscript Story" of Reverend Solomon Spalding; or "Manuscript Found."* Lamoni, IA: Reorganized Church of Jesus Christ of Latter Day Saints, 1885. Digital scan, 2009, Internet Archive, Harold B. Lee Library, Brigham Young University, online at archive.org/details/manuscriptfoundo00spau.

———. "Romance of the Cele[stials]: Or the Florentine Heroes and the Three Female Knights of the Chasm." Library of Congress, Washington, DC.

Spear, Philetus B. "Joseph Smith and Mormonism … Some Incidents Related About Smith By Professor Philetus B. Spear,

D.D., a Man Born in Palmyra in 1811." *Marion Enterprise* (Newark, NY), Sept. 28, 1923, 1.

St. Louis Republican (MO), July 1884.

Stafford, Christopher M. Statement to Arthur B. Deming, Mar. 23, 1885. *Naked Truths about Mormonism* newsletter, Apr. 1888, 1.

Stafford, Cornelius R. Statement to Arthur B. Deming, Mar. [23], 1885. *Naked Truths about Mormonism* newsletter, Apr. 1888, 3.

Stevenson, Edward. Journals, 1852–96. MS 4806, Edward Stevenson Collection, LDS Church History Library, Salt Lake City.

———. *Reminiscences of Joseph, the Prophet and the Coming Forth of the Book of Mormon*. Salt Lake City: By the author, 1893.

———. "The Three Witnesses to the Book of Mormon," part 3. *Millennial Star*, June 21, 1886, 389–91.

Stocker, Rhamanthus M. *Centennial History of Susquehanna County, Pennsylvania*. Philadelphia: Rufus T. Peck, 1887.

Susquehanna County Archives. Deed books, 1829, liber 9. Susquehanna County Courthouse, Montrose, PA.

Susquehanna Register and Northern Pennsylvanian (Montrose, PA), May 1834.

Taylor, John. "The Church of England," unsigned editorial. *Times and Seasons*, Feb. 15, 1845, 810–11.

Thayer, Douglas. *Nephites at War: Alma 20–Helaman 4*. Reader's Book of Mormon series, eds. Robert A. Rees and Eugene England. 7 vols. Salt Lake City: Signature Books, 2008.

Tiffany's Monthly (New York City), Aug. 1859.

Times and Seasons (Nauvoo, IL), Jan. 1840; Apr. 1842; May, Aug. 1843; May 1844.

Townsend, Jesse. Letter to Phineas Stiles, Dec. 24, 1833. In Pomeroy Tucker, *Origin, Rise, and Progress of Mormonism*. New York: D. Appleton, 1867, 288–91.

Tucker, Pomeroy. *Origin, Rise, and Progress of Mormonism*. New York: D. Appleton, 1867.

Turner, O[rsamus]. *History of the Pioneer Settlement of Phelps and Gorham's Purchase.* Rochester: William Alling, 1851.

Tuttle, Daniel S. "Mormons." In *A Religious Encyclopaedia*, ed. Philip Schaff, vol. 2. New York: Funk and Wagnalls, 1883.

Underwood, Grant. "The Earliest Reference Guides to the Book of Mormon: Windows into the Past." *Journal of Mormon History* 12 (1985): 69–89.

Utica Directory. NY: William Williams, 1817; rpt. 1920, Utica Typesetting Company.

Van Wagoner, Richard. *Mormon Polygamy: A History.* Salt Lake City: Signature Books, 1986.

———. *Sidney Rigdon: A Portrait of Religious Excess*. Salt Lake City: Signature Books, 1994.

Van Wagoner, Richard, and Steven Walker. "Joseph Smith: The Gift of Seeing." *Dialogue: A Journal of Mormon Thought* 15 (Summer 1982): 48–68.

Vogel, Dan. "Anti-Universalist Rhetoric in the Book of Mormon." In *New Approaches to the Book of Mormon: Explorations in Critical Methodology*, ed. Brent Lee Metcalfe. Salt Lake City: Signature Books, 1993, 21–52.

———. "The Earliest Mormon Concept of God." In *Line upon Line: Essays on Mormon Doctrine*, ed. Gary James Bergera. Salt Lake City: Signature Books, 1989, 17–33.

———, ed. *Early Mormon Documents,* 5 vols. Salt Lake City: Signature Books, 1996–2003.

———. *Indian Origins and the Book of Mormon: Religious Solutions from Columbus to Joseph Smith*. Salt Lake City: Signature Books, 1986.

———. "The Locations of Joseph Smith's Early Treasure Quests." *Dialogue: A Journal of Mormon Thought* 27 (Fall 1994): 197–213.

———. "Mormonism's 'Anti-Masonick Bible.'" *John Whitmer Historical Journal* 9 (1989): 17–30.

———. *Religious Seekers and the Advent of Mormonism*. Salt Lake City: Signature Books, 1988.

———. "The Validity of the Witnesses' Testimonies." In *American Apocrypha: Essays on the Book of Mormon*, eds. Dan Vogel and Brent Lee Metcalfe. Salt Lake City: Signature Books, 2002, 79–121.

Vogel, Dan, and Scott C. Dunn. "'The Tongue of Angels': Glossolalia among Mormonism's Founders." *Journal of Mormon History* 19 (Fall 1993): 1–34.

Walker, John Phillip, ed. *Dale Morgan on Early Mormonism: Correspondence and a New History*. Salt Lake City: Signature Books, 1986.

Walker, Ronald W. "Martin Harris: Mormonism's Early Convert." *Dialogue: A Journal of Mormon Thought* 19 (Winter 1986): 29–43.

Walker, Sylvia. Statement to Arthur B. Deming, Mar. 20, 1885. *Naked Truths about Mormonism* newsletter, Apr. 1888, 1.

Walters, Wesley P. "The Use of the Old Testament in the Book of Mormon." Master's thesis, Covenant Theological Seminary, St. Louis, Apr. 1981.

Wayne Sentinel (Palmyra, NY), May 1831; Dec. 1833.

Webster, Noah. *An American Dictionary of the English Language*. New York: S. Converse, 1828.

————. *Compendious Dictionary of the English Language.* Hartford: Hudson & Goodwin, 1806.

Westergren, Bruce N., ed. *From Historian to Dissident: The Book of John Whitmer.* Salt Lake City: Signature Books, 1995.

Western Courier (Ravenna, OH), May, Sept. 1831.

White, Joseph W. "The Influence of Sidney Rigdon upon the Theology of Mormonism." Master's thesis, University of Southern California, 1947.

Whitmer, David. *An Address to All Believers in Christ.* Richmond, MO: By the author, 1887.

Whittier, Charles H., and Stephen W. Stathis. "The Enigma of Solomon Spalding." *Dialogue: A Journal of Mormon Thought* 10 (Autumn 1977): 70–73.

Willers, Diedrich. Letter to Reverend Brethren, June 18, 1830. Collection 6050, Christ Church (German Reformed) of Bearytown Records, 1813–1941, Carl A. Kroch Library, Cornell University, Ithaca, NY.

Williams, Frederick G. "Statement of facts relative to Joseph Smith and myself." MS 782, Frederick G. Williams Papers, 1834–1842, LDS Church History Library, Salt Lake City.

Williams, George Huntston. *The Radical Reformation*, 3rd ed. Kirksville, MO: Truman State University Press, 2000.

Winchester, Benjamin. *The Origin of the Spaulding Story, Concerning the Manuscript Found; With a Short Biography of Dr. P. Hulbert [sic], the Originator of the Same.* Philadelphia: Brown, Bicking & Guilbert, 1840.

Wright, David P. "'In Plain Terms That We May Understand': Joseph Smith's Transformation of Hebrews in Alma 12–13." In *New Approaches to the Book of Mormon: Explorations in*

Critical Methodology, ed. Brent Lee Metcalfe. Salt Lake City: Signature Books, 1993, 165–230.

———. "Isaiah in the Book of Mormon: Or Joseph Smith in Isaiah." In *American Apocrypha: Essays on the Book of Mormon*, eds. Dan Vogel and Brent Lee Metcalfe. Salt Lake City: Signature Books, 2002, 157–234.

Wymetal, Wilhelm Ritter von. *Joseph Smith the Prophet, His Family and His Friends*. Salt Lake City: Tribune Printing and Publishing, 1886.

Young, Brigham. "History of Brigham Young." *Millennial Star*, July 11, 1863, 439.

Zaragoza, M. S., and K. J. Mitchell. "Repeated Exposure to Suggestion and the Creation of False Memories." *Psychological Science* 7 (Sept. 1996): 294–300.

INDEX

Abinadi (Book of Mormon), 101–02, 104

abolition, *see* slavery

Abraham (biblical), 51, 137, 215, 218, 236, 347–48n39

Adam (biblical), 137, 139, 158

Albany (NY), 389n19, 408; Howe born near, vii; Martin Harris visits, 384; missionaries sent to, 171n9; Shakers settle in, 10–11n6

Alma (Book of Mormon), 91–92n7, 104–06, 109, 111–13, 117n9, 123; prophesies destruction of Nephites, 121; sons of, 119, 121, 124

Amaleki (Book of Mormon), 94, 95, 134

Ammon (Book of Mormon), cuts off men's arms, 91n7, 100, 118–19, 123; taken prisoner, 117–18, 122

Anabaptists, 10nn4–5, 69, 104

angels, 56–57n12, 87, 98, 106, 200, 354, 389, 396; appearances to Book of Mormon witnesses, 20–22, 24n37, 25, 30–32, 142, 146; appearances to church members, 154–55,

157n15, 269; appearances to Joseph Smith, 17n9, 35, 270, 291n46, 353–54; "destroying angels," 171–72n9, 207, 321; guardians of plates, 27, 120–21, 389n20; "recording angels" (Howe's term), 134, 138–39, 322–23

Anthon, Charles, 354, 379, 381–82; letter of, 379–84; letter to, xxii, xxiii, 36n5

anti-Mormons, vii–viii, xiv, 42n23; anti-Mormon committee (Missouri), 206–12, 239–41

apostasy, xi–xii, 9–10, 52, 105, 267, 298

apostles, ancient American, 83, 132–34, 154, 160, 164, 177, 198, 347; apostleship, 296; Book of Mormon apostles named, 133; gift of tongues, 203; modern, 164n27, 199n4, 284–85, 295–96; Paul of Tarsus, 82, 106, 175; persecuted, 213; "should keep cool," 147n38; twelve biblical, 57, 171

Arianism, 55n10, 69; versus deism, 115n7, 169; versus paganism, 2, 143, 404n19; versus

447

ABOUT THE AUTHOR

Eber Dudley Howe (1798–1885) was born in Clifton Park, New York. A newspaperman, he launched the *Telegraph* in Painesville, Ohio, in 1822. An abolitionist, he offered his home for runaway slaves as part of the Underground Railroad. In 1878 he published his memoir, *Autobiography and Recollections of a Pioneer Printer*.

Dan Vogel is editor of the five-volume series, *Early Mormon Documents*; editor of two anthologies, *American Apocrypha: Essays on the Book of Mormon* (with Brent Lee Metcalfe) and *The Word of God: Essays on Mormon Scripture;* and is the author of *Indian Origins and the Book of Mormon: Religious Solutions from Columbus to Joseph Smith*, *Religious Seekers and the Advent of Mormonism*, and *Joseph Smith: The Making of a Prophet*. He is the recipient of Best Book awards from the John Whitmer Historical Association and the Mormon History Association.